Mobilizing for Democracy

Mobilizing for Democracy

Comparing 1989 and 2011

Donatella della Porta

OXFORD
UNIVERSITY PRESS

OXFORD
UNIVERSITY PRESS

Great Clarendon Street, Oxford, OX2 6DP,
United Kingdom

Oxford University Press is a department of the University of Oxford.
It furthers the University's objective of excellence in research, scholarship,
and education by publishing worldwide. Oxford is a registered trade mark of
Oxford University Press in the UK and in certain other countries

Published in the United States of America by Oxford University Press
198 Madison Avenue, New York, NY 10016, United States of America

British Library Cataloguing in Publication Data
Data available

Library of Congress Control Number: 2013954181

ISBN 978–0–19–968932–3

Printed and bound in Great Britain by
CPI Group (UK) Ltd, Croydon, CR0 4YY

For Herbert

Acknowledgements

This book, as many, starts from (some) challenges and (many) opportunities. I encountered the first challenge in the very limited attention that social movement studies had paid to democratization processes, strongly paralleled by the very limited attention democratization studies had paid to social movements. This puzzled me all the more, as in my life history there have been at least two moments of intense participation in struggles for democracy. First, I come from a country, Italy, in which the collective memory of the popular resistance to fascism and Nazism had a foundational value in the development of the Republic's identity. While I was not present in 1945, the myth of resistance became part of my personal memory. Second, I happened to be in Berlin in 1989, at the Wall that separated the West and the East, a few hours after it started to fall. Throughout this eventful moment, citizens mobilized in various forms of protest with high degrees of emotional intensity. Shortly after I started my research, the Arab Spring emerged as yet another testimony to the role of people—and social movements—in history.

If the gap in the social science literature was certainly a challenge, further challenges emerged in the attempt to fill it. First, there were theoretical challenges related to the richness in social movement studies of a toolkit of concepts and theories, built however on so-called advanced democracies. Second, from the empirical point of view, working on geopolitical areas I had little frequented in the past was also a clear challenge.

A series of conjunctural and structural opportunities pushed me to face the challenges of entering a largely unknown terrain. First, at the European University Institute (EUI) I had the enormous luck to work with PhD students and post-doctoral fellows, as well as colleagues, who stimulated me to overcome the limited, mainly west-European, borders of my empirical research. Second, a generous Advanced Scholars' Grant from the European Research Council (GA 2691) has given me enough resources to engage in the ambitious project of bridging, so to speak, social movement studies and democratization studies, through research on democratization from below. I am grateful to ERC for this opportunity, while, of course, they are not responsible for the ideas developed in the text.

Acknowledgements

The research project on Mobilizing for Democracy, on whose second part this volume reports, benefited greatly from the collaboration and contributions of young scholars at EUI, especially in the form of the Working Papers on most of the cases I address in my analysis. I'm grateful to Kivanc Atak, Luisa Chiodi, Teije Donker, Grzegogz Piotrowski, Emin Poljarevic, Daniel Ritter, Federico Rossi, and Jana Warkotsch, for the passion and care they put into this work.

Important stimulus in improving my analysis also came during presentations of preliminary results during conferences and lectures, among others at the Viadrina University in Frankfurt am Oder, at Central European University in Budapest, at the Economic Consortium for Political Research (ECPR) joint sessions in Mainz, at the Consortium for European Studies general conference in Amsterdam, at the ECPR general conference in Bordeaux, as well as on frequent occasions at the Centre on Social Movement Studies (Cosmos) that I direct at the Political and Social Science department at EUI.

For extremely helpful comments on a previous version of this manuscript I am particularly grateful to Sidney Tarrow, Robert Fishman, and Tiago Fernandes, as well as Béla Greskovits and the members of his reading group on social movements at Central European University: Karena Avedissian, Dénes Csurgó, Elisabetta Ferrari, Lela Rekhviashvili, Imre Gergely Szabó, Lili Török, and Caitlin Wyndham. At EUI, when I called for advice and suggestions, my colleagues Laszlo Bruszt and Philippe Schmitter have been there to help.

Sarah Tarrow, my editor in chief, has helped me more than ever to communicate my thoughts.

Contents

List of Figures

List of Tables

Abbreviations

AGEG	Anti-Globalisation Egyptian Group
ANC	Anti-Nuclear Campaign Hungary
ATTAC	Comité pour l'Annulation de la Dette du Tiers-Monde—Committee for the Abolition of Third World Debt Association pour la Taxation des Transactions financière et l'Aide aux Citoyens' (Association for the Taxation of financial Transactions and Aid to Citizens)
ATTAC-CADTM	Comité pour l'Annulation de la Dette du Tiers-Monde—Committee for the Abolition of Third World Debt Association pour la Taxation des Transactions financière et l'Aide aux Citoyens' (Association for the Taxation of financial Transactions and Aid to Citizens)
BSPSH	Union of the Independent Trade Unions of Albania
CF	Civic Forum
COMECON	the Council for Mutual Economic Assistance
CPG	Phosphate Company of Gafsa
CPY	Communist Party of Yugoslavia
CSCE	Conference for Security and Cooperation in Europe
CTUWS	Center for Trade Union and Workers Services
DA	Initiative for a Democratic Awakening
DDR	German Democratic Republic
DN	Democracy Now
DP	Democratic Party
DTK	Democratic Society Congress
ECPR	Economic Consortium for Political Research
EHOR	Egyptian organization for human rights
EKA	Opposition Round Table (Ellenzéki Kerekasztal)
END	European Nuclear Disarmament
EPCSI	Egyptian Popular Committee in Solidarity with the Intifada
EUI	European University Institute

FDJ	Free German Youth (Freie Deutsche Jugend)
FIDESZ	Young Democrats (Hungary)
FJF	Independent Lawyers' Forum (Független Jogasz Forum)
FLN	National Liberation Front
FRG	Federal Republic of Germany
FSA	Free Syrian Army
GDR	German Democratic Republic
GJM	Global Justice Movement
HDF	Hungarian Democratic Forum (Magyar Demokrata Fórum)
HuT	Liberation party (Hizb al-Tahrir)
IFM	Initiative Frieden und Menschenrechte (Initiative for Peace and Human Rights)
IGL	Initiative Group for Life
ISP	Independent Smallholders' Party
KAN	Club of Non-Party Engagés
KDP	Kurdish Democratic Party
KOR	Workers' Defense Committee (Komitet Obrony Robotników)
KPD	Communist Party of Germany
KPN	Confederation of Independent Poland (Konfederacja Polski Niepodległej)
LCCs	Local Coordination Committees
LCCS	Local Coordinating Committees of Syria
LFL	Lithuanian Freedom League
LIFG	Libyan Islamic Fighting Group
LNIM	Latvian National Independence Movement
LTDH	Tunisian league of Human Rights (Ligue Tunisienne de Droits de l'Homme)
MB	Muslim Brotherhood
MDF	Hungarian Democratic Forum (Magyar Demokrata Fórum)
MENA	Middle East and North Africa
MKS	Inter-Factory Strike Committees (Międzyzakładowy Komitet Strajkowy)
MOST	The Bridge (civic initiative)
NC	National Coalition for Syrian Revolutionary and Opposition Forces, or National Coalition
NEM	New Economic Mechanism
NF	New Forum (Neues Forum)
NPA	New People's Army
NPD	National Democratic Party
NSC	National Security Council
NSF	National Salvation Front

NTC	National Transitional Council
NZS	Niezależne Zrzeszenie Studentów
OAS	Organization of American States
ORT	Opposition Round Table (Ellenzéki Kerekasztal)
PDS	Party of Democratic Socialism
PDsh	Democratic Party of Albania (Partia Demokratike e Shqipërisë)
PKK	Partîya Karkerén Kurdîstan (Kurdish workers' party)
PLA	Albanian Party of Labour
PPU	Plastic People of the Universe
PREs	Politically Relevant Elites
RCD	Constitutional Democratic Rally (Rassemblement Constitutionnel Démocratique)
RCP	Romanian Communist Party
RPP	Republican People's Party
RSA	Movement for an Alternative Society (Ruch Społeczeństwa Alternatywnego)
SB	Security Service (Służba Bezpieczeństwa)
SED	Socialist Unity Party of Germany (Sozialistische Einheitspartei Deutschlands)
SFB	Sender Freies Berlin
SFRY	Socialist Federal Republic of Yugoslavia
SMO	social movement organization
SNC	Syrian National Council
SPD	Social Democratic Party
STUHA	student organisation (Czechoslovakia)
SSM	official students union (Czechoslovakia)
SZDSZ	Alliance for Free Democrats (Szabad Demokraták Szövetsége)
UGTT	Tunisian General Labour Union (Union Générale Tunisienne du Travail)
UL	United Link
VONS	Committee for the Defense of the Unjustly Persecuted (Výbor na Obranu Nespravedlivě Stihaných)
WiP	Freedom and Peace (Wolność i Pokój)

1

Democratization and Social Movements

Introduction

Most scholars of democratization have either ignored movements altogether or regarded them with suspicion as dangers to democracy, while most students of social movements have focused on fully mature democratic systems and ignored the transition cycles that place the question of democratization on the agenda and work it through to either democratic consolidation or defeat (Tarrow 1995, 221–2).

Strangely enough, while the pictures used to illustrate the most recent wave of protests for democracy in North Africa represent mass protest, as Sidney Tarrow stated some time ago, research on social movements and on democratization have rarely interacted. In this volume, I aim at filling this gap by looking at episodes of democratization through the lens of social movement studies. Without assuming that democratization is always produced from below, I will however single out different paths of democratization by looking at the ways in which the masses interacted with the elites, and protest with bargaining. My focus will be on one of these paths: eventful democratization, that is cases in which authoritarian regimes break down following—often short but intense—waves of protest. Recognizing the particular power of some transformative events (Sewell 1996), I will however locate them within the broader mobilization processes, including the multitude of less visible, but still important protests that surround them. In this, using Sidney Tarrow's concepts, I will try to combine attention to eventful history and the one on event history with detailed descriptions of some 'great protest events' but also consideration for the cascades of small protest events that accompany, precede and follow them (Tarrow 1996, 586). Following recent research on social movements, I will look at the relations between structure and agency within these transformative moments. Cognitive, affective and relational mechanisms will be singled out as transforming the contexts in which dissidents act.

While in eventful democratization protests develop from the interaction between growing resources of contestation and closed opportunities, social movements are not irrelevant players in the other two paths. First of all, when opportunities open up because of misalignment in the elites, participated pacts might ensue from the encounter of reformers in institutions and moderates among social movement organizations. Protest, although rarely used, is nevertheless important here as a resource to threaten or use on the negotiating table.

If in participated pacts a strong (or strengthening) civil society meets emerging opportunities, more troubled democratization paths ensue when very repressive regimes thwart the development of any autonomous associational form. In these cases violence often escalates from the interaction of suddenly mobilized opposition and brutal regime repression. Especially when there are divisions in and defections from security apparatuses, skills and resources for military action contribute to coups d' état and civil war dynamics.

In all three paths, mobilization of resources, framing processes, and appropriation of opportunities will develop into action, in different combinations. The comparison of different cases within two waves of protests for democracy, in Central Eastern Europe in 1989 and in the Middle East and North Africa in 2011, will allow me to describe and theorize about causal mechanisms and conditions as they emerge in the three mentioned paths.

In this analysis, democratization struggles will be seen as processes whose outcomes are influenced by the interaction of different players, some of whom pursue democracy as a goal, some oppose it, while others initially remain neutral. For most of them, positions towards democracy tend however to change during the action, as frames on democratization are bridged with socio-economic and/or ethno-nationalist frames.

In this introduction, I will first look at the literature on transition as well as on social movement studies in search of some key contributions that could help us understand processes of democratization from below. Then I will present my research design and the structure of this volume.

Social Science Literature on Transition and Social Movements: Bridging Gaps

The social science literature on democratization is large, but fragmented. Not only has 'first' democratization (in its slow form) attracted the attention of major scholars, but each new wave of (rapid) regime shift has produced related waves of research and thinking. Case studies and within-area comparisons have thus flourished, bringing not only rich empirical evidence, but also new concepts and interpretative frameworks.

However, the very spread and depth of democratization studies have also contributed to fragmentation in the field. First, political and social sciences have focused on the West and the North of the globe, where core disciplines such as comparative politics and political sociology have flourished, while the various waves of democratization have been addressed mainly by area studies. With all their value in attempting to go beyond ethnocentric visions of politics and society, however, area studies are pillarized around homogeneous geographical areas, each with their own focuses and biases. The very efforts involved in learning the histories and the languages of these areas have encouraged high levels of specialization (e.g. Dutton 2005; Burawoy 2005). With few, valuable exceptions, new waves of democratization in different geopolitical areas were in fact addressed by different (area) specialists, who stressed different aspects: for example, political parties and elite pacts in Southern Europe, military power in Latin America, civil society in Eastern Europe, electoral processes in the 'orange revolutions', religion in North Africa and the Middle East.

There is also another reason for fragmentation. Democratization can be (and has been) related to various processes: slow or fast, violent or non-violent, radical or moderate, nationally chosen or internationally imposed. This has been reflected in the fact that democratization processes have been addressed under that label, but also under others—for example, revolutions or non-violence or civil society—with, unfortunately, little communication between different subfields or between those subfields and social movement studies. While the literature on revolutions originally concentrated on violent processes and deep social transformation, it has now expanded (perhaps with good reason) to include non-violent regime changes, although remaining quite isolated from studies on democratization or social movements. Similarly, research on non-violence has developed, especially on some waves of democratization, but with limited interactions with studies carried out, often on the same empirical realities, under different labels. The focus of non-violence literature on Gandhi or anarchist theorists—which never occupied centre stage in cognate research fields—as well as its orientation towards activists and its rootedness in peace studies have contributed to the lack of dialogue with other related fields (Schock 2005). Since the wave of democratization in the late 1980s in Eastern Europe, attention has focused on the role of civil society, defined as 'a solidarity sphere in which a certain kind of universalizing community comes gradually to be defined and to some degrees enforced' (Alexander 1998, 7). While often looking at the same empirical reality, studies on social movements and studies on Non-Governmental Organizations (NGOs) developed within political sociology and international relations respectively, with different theoretical focuses and, again, few reciprocal contacts.

As McAdam, Tarrow, and Tilly (2001) rightly observed, if conceptual distinctions are indeed useful to avoid theoretical confusion, a more intense dialogue among different streams of literature could help in identifying similar dynamics, as well as differences in structural conditions. As I will argue in what follows, it would be especially important to bridge social movement studies and democratization studies, which have remained, until now, worlds apart.

Even though social movement organizations (SMOs) are increasingly recognized, in political as well as scientific debates, as important actors in democratic processes, their performance during the different steps of the democratization process has rarely been addressed in a systematic and comparative way. On the one hand, in fact, social movements have been far from prominent in research on democratization, which has mainly focused on either socio-economic preconditions or elite behaviour. As Nancy Bermeo (1997) aptly synthesized, in general the literature on democratization 'accords much less attention to popular organizations than to political elites. Thus, the role of popular organizations in the transition process remains a subject of some confusion. Many of the major theoretical works on democratization suggest that popular mobilization is important for regime change, but even this very simple proposition is not universally shared.' On the other hand, social movement scholars, until recently, have paid little attention to democratization processes, mostly concentrating their interest on democratic countries (especially on the West European and North American experiences), where conditions for mobilization are more favourable.

Democratization Studies

Research on democratization developed initially with a structuralist approach. Within *modernization* theory, Martin S. Lipset's (1959) pioneering work associated the potential for the emergence of a democratic regime with economic development. Although powerful in explaining the survival of established democracies, modernization theory tended however to ignore the role of social actors and movements in crafting democracy, leaving the timing of democratization processes unexplained. Democratization has also been linked to elite strategies oriented to state building or political competition (Rokkan 1970, 3). When scholars within this approach did examine the role of organized and mobilized actors in society, they tended—as did Samuel Huntington (1965, 1991)—to consider mobilization, particularly of the working class, as a risk more than an asset.

Results on the relations between democracy and capitalism are ambivalent. Various streams of literature have paid particular attention to the role of capitalism in the development of democracy. In particular, but not only in the traditional Marxist approaches, democracy has often been presented as the typical political form of capitalism. As Dietrich Rueschemeyer, Evelyn Huber Stephens, and John D. Stephens (1992, 1) summarized, 'in this view capitalism and democracy go hand in hand because democracy, while proclaiming the rule of the many, in fact protects the interests of capital owners.... The unrestrained operation of the market for capital and labour constitutes the material base of democracy.' Even though capitalism might prosper without democracy, 'virtually all full-fledged democracies we know are associated with capitalist political economics' (Rueschemeyer et al. 1992, 2).

Even though scholars have often stressed the link between democracy and capitalism, different trends of research on social structures and democratization have offered different conclusions. Quantitative research, based on large-N comparisons, consistently presented a positive correlation between economic development and democracy; small-N comparisons have instead limited this relationship to specific—and even rare—historical conditions. Lipset (1959, 1980) stated early on that the economically better off a country, the higher the chances that it is a democracy (1980, 31). Education, along with related values of tolerance and moderation as well as the development of a middle class, are considered main causal mechanisms. Linking democracy to modernization theory, Cutright (1963) explained the dominance of democracy in modern countries, citing their complex structure, which made democracy effective in dealing with increasingly differentiated societies. Cutright and Wiley (1969) confirmed the role of literacy as a relevant measure of social development, also observing the stabilizing effect of high provisions in social security: by satisfying the needs of the population, democracies increase support for the status quo.

Some comparative historical investigations (O'Donnell 1973) pointed instead at the capitalist interest in authoritarian regimes, especially in dependent countries. According to Ken Bollen (1979), the development of capitalism favoured the development of democracy only for earlier economic development (and first democratization), while latecomers (especially at the periphery) were more likely to be ruled by autocrats. Barrington Moore (1966) influentially singled out various paths to economic development, with a fascist path dominated by powerful landowners and a bourgeoisie that needed protectionist support by the state. In his work, O'Donnell (1973) stressed an 'elective affinity' between bureaucratic authoritarianism and capitalist development, while even democracies offer to different classes asymmetrical chances to articulate their interests, privileging some over others. In fact, Offe and Wiesenthal (1980) have noted the paradox that democratization represents primarily an increase in political equality, but with tensions between democracy and inequalities, as 'democracy may soften but it certainly does not eliminate the differences of power, wealth and status in class-divided societies' (Offe and Wiesenthal 1980, 43).

These debates are also reflected in discussions on the role of some social classes as main carriers of democratization processes (see also above). Barrington Moore Jr (1966), R. Bendix (1964), and T. H. Marshall (1992) all recognized the impact of class struggles in early democratization. While the focus has usually been on the middle class as promoters of democratization, more recently Rueschemeyer, Stephens, and Stephens have pointed to the role of the working class in the last two waves of democratization in Southern Europe, South America, and the Caribbean. According to them (1992, 6), 'one would have to examine the structure of class coalitions as well as the relative power of different classes to understand how the balance of class power would affect the possibilities for democracy.' The assumption is that 'Those who have the most to gain from democracy will be its most reliable promoters and defenders' (Rueschemeyer et al. 1992, 57; see also Collier and Collier 2002).

While for some scholars democracy can fit various social structures, these three authors emphasized a mutual reinforcement between democracy and capitalism: 'capitalist development is associated with democracy because it transforms the class structure, strengthening the working and the middle-class and weakening the landed upper class. It was neither the capitalist market nor capitalists as the new dominant force, but rather the contradictions of capitalism that advanced the cause of democracy' (Rueschemeyer et al. 1992, 7). In contrast to Barrington Moore's approach, they stated in fact that 'The working class was the most consistent democratic force' (Rueschemeyer et al. 1992, 8). Noting that 'It is ironic that not only liberal historians but also the orthodox Marxist accounts of the rise of democracy see the bourgeoisie as *the* protagonist of democracy', they assert instead that 'it was the subordinated classes that fought for democracy' (Rueschemeyer et al. 1992, 46). In their view, 'the chances of democracy then must be seen as fundamentally shaped by the balance of class power' (Rueschemeyer et al. 1992, 47). The middle class usually played an ambivalent role, pressing for its own inclusion, but only occasionally (when weak) allying with the working class in order to extend democracy to them as well. The peasantry and rural workers took different positions, according to their capacity for autonomous organization and the influence of dominant classes upon them (Rueschemeyer et al. 1992).[1]

Even if the urban and rural middle classes might play an important role, the working class has been considered here as the most coherent pro-democratic actor (e.g. Theborn 1995). 'The primary economic interest of the bourgeoisie

---

[1] In particular, small independent family farmers tended to be more pro-democratic than were peasants from large land holdings.

as a class lies in the development and guarantee of the institutional infrastructure of capitalist development—in the institutions of property and contract,
in the predictability of judicial decisions, in the functioning of markets for
capital, goods and services, and labor, and in the protection against unwel-
come state intervention' (Rueschemeyer et al. 1992, 61). A dependent development restricts the differentiation of the capitalist class as well as reducing
the margins of negotiation with exploited classes.

Whatever the chosen class, a structuralist bias in the traditional vision of
democratization is criticized by the *transitologist* approach, which stresses
instead the dynamic characteristic of the process, while focusing on elite
strategies and behaviour (O'Donnell and Schmitter 1986; Higley and
Gunther 1992). This trend of research has the advantage of refocusing attention towards agency. As Terry Lynn Karl (1990, 1) summarized, 'the manner
in which theorists of comparative politics have sought to understand democracy in developing countries has changed as the once-dominant search for
prerequisites of democracy has given way to a more process-oriented emphasis on contingent choice. Having undergone this evolution, theorists should
now develop an interactive approach that seeks explicitly to relate structural
constraints to the shaping of contingent choice.' The inconsistent results of
the structuralist approaches pushed scholars away from the search for general
theory aimed at discovering identical conditions for the presence or absence
of democratic regimes,[2] and towards the analysis of 'a variety of actors with
different followings, preferences, calculations, resources, and time horizons'
(Karl 1990, 5–6).

Indeed, literature from the transitology perspective tends to downplay the
impact of structural conditions, which had received much attention in the
past, instead stressing the role of leadership. For O'Donnell and Schmitter,
transitions from authoritarian rule are illustrations of 'underdetermined
social change, of large-scale transformations which occur when there are
insufficient structural or behavioral parameters to guide and predict the outcome' (1986, 363). In fact, their influential collection of research on the transition from authoritarian rule emphasizes its 'structural indeterminacy'.

In these underdetermined processes, in times of uncertainty, the predispositions of elites are seen as determining whether democratization occurs
at all. They are linked not so much to their material interests as to a sort
of concern for their future reputation. In this narrative, 'Individual heroics
may in fact be key: the "catalyst" for the process of democratization comes,

---

[2] In particular, research on Latin America pointed at the need for revision, indicating that 'there
may be no single precondition that is sufficient to produce such an outcome. The search for causes
rooted in economic, social, cultural/psychological, or international factors has not yielded a general law of democratization, nor is it likely to do so in the near future despite the proliferation of
new cases' (Karl 1990).

not from a debt crisis or rampant inflation or some major crisis of industrialization, but from gestures by exemplary individuals who begin testing the boundaries of behavior' (Bermeo 1990, 361). This stream of research has also been said to be extremely stato-centric, with a privileged role accorded to institutional actors. Class also tends to stay out of the picture, as strategies are analysed in game theoretical terms as interactions of incumbents and challengers, soft-liners and hard-liners.

Non-elite and non-institutional actors are considered as marginal. As Ruth Collier (1999, 5) summarized, transitologists emphasize 'elite strategic choices, downplaying or ignoring the role of labour in democratization'. If social movements might be effective in promoting the transition process, the 'resurrection of civil society' is seen as a short disruptive moment in which movements, unions, churches, and society in general push for the initial liberalization of a non-democratic regime into a transition towards democracy. In their seminal work, in fact, O'Donnell and Schmitter (1986, 53–4) observe that: 'In some cases and at particular moments of the transition, many of these diverse layers of society may come together to form what we choose to call the popular upsurge. Trade unions, grass-roots movements, religious groups, intellectuals, artists, clergymen, defenders of human rights, and professional associations all support each other's efforts toward democratization and coalesce into a greater whole which identifies itself as "the people."' Even if these are moments of intense expectations, 'regardless of its intensity and of the background from which it emerges, this popular upsurge is always ephemeral' (O'Donnell and Schmitter 1986, 55–6).

While mass mobilization is recognized as important in expanding the limits of mere liberalization, defined by some increase in civil and political rights, and partial democratization, contentious action is seen more as a symptom than a cause. Moreover, masses are presented as vulnerable to elite co-optation or manipulation, often focusing on very instrumentally defined purposes (see Przeworski 1991, 57; for a critique, Baker 1999). The analytic framework 'focuses squarely on the strategic choices of elites, and popular action is considered relevant primarily for its indirect effects on intra-elite bargaining in situations in which a transition is already underway' (Ulfelder 2005, 313). Mass mobilization is thus conceived of as a short phase, while the analysis addresses 'the process by which soft-line incumbents and moderate opposition party leaders reach some implicit or explicit agreement on a transition from an authoritarian regime. To a substantial extent this is a model of democratization in which collective actors, mass mobilization and protest are largely exogenous' (Collier 1999, 6).

As in this wave of reflection the *reforma pactada/ruptura pactada* in Spain was considered (explicitly or implicitly) as the model for successful democratization, the ephemeral life of civil society tended to be perceived as not only inevitable—given the re-channelling of participation through the political parties and the electoral system—but also desirable, in order to avoid frightening authoritarian soft-liners into abandoning the negotiation process with pro-democracy moderates. Moderation was therefore seen as a positive evolution, as the attitudes and goals of the various actors change along the process. This point was neatly made by Huntington, who stated:

> If democratization did not produce the dangers they feared, people who had been liberal reformers or even standpatters might come to accept democracy. Similarly, participation in the processes of democratization could lead members of extremist opposition groups to moderate their revolutionary propensities and accept the constraints and opportunities democracy offered. The relative power of the groups shaped the nature of the democratization process and often changed during that process. If standpatters dominated the government and extremists the opposition, democratization was impossible, as, for example, where a right-wing personal dictator determined to hang on to power confronted an opposition dominated by Marxist-Leninists (Huntington 1991, 589).

A somewhat more positive view of intervention from below developed with research on the wave of democratization in Eastern Europe. Influentially, Linz and Stepan (1996) suggested that 'A robust civil society, with the capacity to generate political alternatives and to monitor government and state, can help transitions get started, help resist reversals, help push transitions to their completion, help consolidate, and help deepen democracy. At all stages of the democratization process, therefore, a lively and independent civil society is invaluable' (1996, 9). This theoretical attention notwithstanding, their empirical research still focused on the elites.

So, even though the dynamic, agency-focused approach of transitology allowed for some interest in the role played by social movements especially in the phase of liberalization (Pagnucco 1995), it did not bring much attention to them.

Democratization in Social Movement Studies

In contrast, the field of social movement studies has stressed the relevance of contention. Rarely focusing on social movements in democratization phases, such research has flourished in (and on) established democracies (for a review, see Rossi and della Porta 2009). Even in established democracies, the relationship between movements and democracy has been mainly looked at in terms of institutional opportunities for protest, rather than the attitudes on and practices of democracy by activists and their organizations (della Porta 2009a, 2009b; della Porta and Rucht 2013). As critics have observed, even the rare

9

research concerned with the issue 'stops short of a systematic inquiry into the political principles of popular organizations and strategic choice, and so fails to pursue the connections between popular politics and processes of institutional change within political regimes' (Foweraker 1995, 218).

If a systematic analysis of processes of transition from below is lacking, however, there has been some potential for the development of research on social movements and democratization. On the one hand, the emergence of the global justice movement encouraged some social movement scholars to pay more attention to issues of democracy, as well as to social movements in the global South (e.g. della Porta 2009a; della Porta and Rucht 2013). At the theoretical level, recognizing the structuralist bias of the political process approach, a more dynamic vision of protest has been promoted, with a focus on the social mechanisms that intervene between macro-causes and macro-effects (McAdam et al. 2001).[3] Recently, some scholars within this approach proposed the reformulation of the transitology perspective, taking into account the role played by contentious politics (McAdam et al. 2001; Schock 2005; Tilly 2004). Like transitologists, they have stressed agency as well as the importance of looking at democratization as dynamic processes. On the other hand, some pioneering research has aimed at applying social movement studies to research on authoritarian regimes, from the Middle East (Wiktorowicz 2004; Hafez 2003; Gunning 2009) to Asia (Boudreau 2004) and the former Soviet Union (Beissinger 2002). Moreover, however dominant, the 'elitist' approach has not gone unchallenged in studies of democratization.

First of all, some normative reflections have pointed at the democratizing capacity of civil society, theoretically located between the state and the market, with diminishing confidence in the role played by political parties as carriers of the democratization process. The very conceptualization of a global civil society emphasizes the democratizing input coming 'from below' (Kaldor 2003; Keane 2003). In some of these interpretations, civil society is conceptualized as almost synonymous with social movements (Cohen and Arato 1992; Kaldor 2003). Within this frame, several programmes of civil

---

[3] A similar evolution was identified in the related field of revolutions. Foran (2005) distinguished different generations in research on revolutions. The first generation tended to present a natural history of revolution, which starts when intellectuals cease to support the regime and continues with regime changes (reform and crisis), conflicts within the opposition between radical and moderates, who usually eventually prevail. A second generation stressed instead root causes such as dysfunctions, which bring about relative deprivation; structural causes are also emphasized by a third generation, which focuses on socio-economic as well as international conditions. Against the structuralist dominance, a fourth generation searches for agency, as organizational resources, emotions, and culture. So, Foran (2005, 18) singled out five necessary conditions for a successful revolution: '1) dependent development; 2) a repressive, exclusionary, personalist state; 3) the elaboration of effective and powerful political cultures of resistance; and a revolutionary crisis consisting of 4) an economic downturn; 5) world-systemic opening (a let-up of external controls)'. These various conditions and mechanisms have been seen as supporting each other.

society promotion have been initiated, sponsored by international governmental organizations as well as individual states.

An empirical linkage between social movements and democratization processes has been established as well. Among others, Charles Tilly has observed 'a broad correspondence between democratization and social movements'. On the one hand, many of the processes that cause democratization also promote social movements, and 'democratization as such further encourages people to form social movements' (Tilly 2004, 131). On the other, 'under some conditions and in a more limited way, social movements themselves promote democratization' (Tilly 2004, 131).

Historical research has pointed at the pivotal role (some) social movements played in the struggle for expanding social rights. The labour movement was particularly active in calling for the right of association, as well as the right to form unions, and for increasing political participation (Sewell 1996; della Porta 2011). Even when 'only a very small number of well-to-do English men (no women, no poor) could actually vote, parliamentary elections became occasions to air different viewpoints' (Markoff 1996, 47). Claims framed by movements in the name of rights, citizenship, and their political practices played a crucial function in creating citizenry (Foweraker and Landman 1997; Eckstein and Wickham-Crowley 2003), as 'the struggle for rights has more than a merely rhetorical impact. The insistence on the rights of free speech and assembly is a precondition of the kind of collective (and democratic) decision-making which educates citizens' (Foweraker 1995, 98).

Movements on behalf of excluded groups often cooperated and learned from each other. Many activists in the movement for women's rights before the American Civil War had experience in the abolitionist movement, for example, just as the 'British antislavery movement was a major source of many forms of activism in that country' (Markoff 1996, 57). There were also alliances between women's and labour movements for suffrage and welfare (Markoff 1996, 84; also della Porta, Valiente, and Kousis forthcoming). The labour movement developed specific public spheres in which a taste for freedom was nurtured as a necessary complement to calls for social justice (della Porta 2013a, 2005a). Also later on, case studies as well as comparative analyses have shown the crucial role played by mobilized actors in the emergence of democracy, and in its preservation or expansion (della Porta 2007, 2009a, 2009b).

In addition, case studies on recent transitions have demonstrated the importance of social movements in the struggle for democracy, and in its preservation or expansion (see Rossi and della Porta 2009 for a review). As Ulfelder (2005, 313) synthesized, 'Various subsequent studies of democratic transitions have afforded collective actors a more prominent role, allowing for the possibility that mass mobilization has a substantial impact on the transition process and is sometimes the catalyst that sets a transition in motion.' Not even in the Spanish case can transition be considered a purely elite-controlled bargaining process, as massive strike waves, terrorist attacks by nationalist movements, and an ascending cycle of protest characterized the transition (see, among others, Foweraker 1989; Maravall 1978; 1982; McAdam et al. 2001, 171–86; Reinares 1987; Sánchez-Cuenca and Aguilar 2009; Tarrow 1995).[4]

Much research has indicated that protests (especially strikes) often constitute precipitating events that trigger *liberalization*, spreading the perception among authoritarian elites that they need to open some spaces of freedom in order to avoid an imminent or potential civil war or violent takeover of power by democratic and/or revolutionary actors (e.g. Bermeo 1997; Wood 2000). Already research on first democratization had noted the importance of liberalization, as the granting of opposition rights, and the gradual extension of these rights, as a main path to democracy (Dahl 1971). Also in other cases, liberalization, in turn, opened up some (although limited) opportunities for social movements to develop. Trade unions and urban movements often exploited those openings, pushing for social rights but also political reform (Slater 1985; Collier 1999; Silver 2003; Schneider 1992; 1995; Hipsher 1998a), sometimes in alliance with transnational actors (e.g. in Latin America, as well as in Eastern Europe; Keck and Sikkink 1998; Glenn 2003).

During the *transition*, old movements and new social movements have been noted as participants in large coalitions asking for democratic rights and social justice (Jelin 1987; Tarrow 1995). The mobilization of a pro-democracy coalition of trade unions, churches, and social movements has often been pivotal in supporting the movement towards democracy when faced with contending counter-movements opposing liberalization. Protests can then be used by modernizing elites to push for free elections (Casper and Taylor 1996, 9–10; Glenn 2003, 104).

Social movements are then important in the *consolidation* phase, which opens up with the first free elections, the end of the period of uncertainty, and/or the implementation of a minimum quality of substantive democracy (Linz and Stepan 1996; O'Donnell 1993, 1994). In some cases, this phase is accompanied by a demobilization of civil society organizations as energies are channelled into party politics; in others, however, democracy fuels social movements. The presence of a tradition of mobilization and of political allies can in fact help maintain a high level of protest, as with the shantytown dwellers' protests in Chile (Hipsher 1998b; Schneider 1992; 1995), the peasants' and labour movements in Brazil (Branford and Rocha 2002;

---

[4] This would in fact be better defined as a destabilization/extrication process (Collier 1999, 126–32) or as 'a cycle of protest intertwined with elite transaction' (McAdam et al. 2001, 186).

Burdick 2004), or the environmental movements in Eastern Europe (Flam 2001). Movements then call for extending rights to those who are excluded by 'low intensity democracies' and target authoritarian legacies (Eckstein 2001; Yashar 2005; della Porta 2013a). Also later in the consolidation phase, movements' alternative practices and values have often helped in sustaining and expanding democracy (Santos 2005; della Porta 2009a). Keeping elites under continuous popular pressure after transition can be important for a successful consolidation (Karatnycky and Ackerman 2005).

When looking at the impact of social movements on democracy, however, the empirical evidence is mixed. First, as mentioned, their relevance in democratization processes is discussed within a 'populist approach' emphasizing participation from below—with social movements as important actors in the creation of democratic public spheres—but denied by an 'elitist approach' considering democratization as mainly a top-down process (Tilly 2004). Moreover, empirical research has noted the potential but also the limitations of development from below, both during and after democratization processes (della Porta 2005b). Research on the global South, but also on transnational institutions, has addressed the inconsistent qualifications of civil society organizations and social movements in terms of their autonomy from the political system, their civility as inclusive conceptions of citizenship, their plurality as the capacity of representation of different groups in the population, as well as their legitimacy and internal accountability. In contemporary social movements, participatory and deliberative practices have indeed attracted some interest, but they have also been difficult to implement, as activists are the first to admit (della Porta 2009a, 2009b). Considered as particularly relevant for the successful implementation of a democratic process, to which they can contribute important resources of knowledge and commitment, civil society organizations are often quite critical participants and/or observers of the institutional policies that aim at implementing these goals.

Indeed, social movements contribute to democratization only under certain conditions. Collective mobilization has frequently produced destabilization of authoritarian regimes, but it has also led to an intensification of repression or the collapse of weak democratic regimes, particularly when social movements do not keep to democratic conceptions. Labour, student, and ethnic movements brought about a crisis in the Franco regime in Spain in the 1960s and 1970s, but the workers' and peasants' protests and the fascist counter-movements contributed to the failure of the process of democratization in Italy in the 1920s (Tarrow 1995). Beyond a social movement's propensity to support democracy, democratization processes might follow different paths, being more or less influenced by the mobilization of social movements. Some democratization processes are protest-driven, others moved by pacts. And social movements might be strong in mobilizing, but also opt for bargaining instead.

As the relationship between social movements and democratization is not simple, a systematic cross-national comparison is needed to single out the conditions and mechanisms through which democratization is moved from below. A similar question has been addressed by Ruth Collier who, comparing Latin American with European experiences, asked 'whether a group of workers became part of the democratization process as a self conscious collectivity and played an active role that affected the democratic outcome' (1999, 15). In this volume, I intend to broaden this question in time and space, as well as with reference to types of social movements other than labour. Bridging the useful insights arising from existing research on democratization processes with those developed within social movement studies, I will focus on participation from below in episodes of democratization.

Democratization from Below: The Research Questions

Building on the most recent developments in social movement studies as well as democratization studies, I will pay particular attention to the causal mechanisms that intervene between macro-causes and macro-effects, in order to understand the way in which social movements exercise, or do not exercise, agency within a certain structure.

My research aims at understanding what I define as democratization from below, looking at the protest waves that accompanied democratic reforms. With Beissinger, I define protest events as 'contentious and potentially subversive practices that challenge normalized practices, modes of causation, or systems of authority' (2002, 14). Protest events might indeed change structures, as they are, in Hannah Arendt's words, 'occurrences that interrupt routine processes and routine procedures' (1970, 7).

Of course, events are also rooted in structures (see Figure 1.1). Giddens (1979) speaks of an intrinsic relation between structures and actions, as agency is inherent in the development of structure and structure influences, to a certain extent, action. Also according to Beissinger, pre-existing structural conditions are embedded in the orderliness of institutions as 'institutions constrain and otherwise positively define the ways in which agents pursue their interests through their power to instil regularity and predictability in social affairs and to preclude alternative ways of acting' (2002, 13). It is therefore important to consider the influence of structures, including political opportunities, as well as the capacity for agency in participation from below in the different stages of democratization processes (della Porta and Diani 2006; Rossi and della Porta 2009).

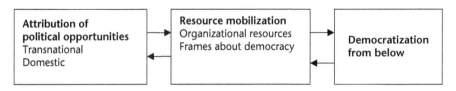

Figure 1.1 The theoretical model

What to Explain: Democratization from Below

A very first and general way to look at *democratization from below* would sim-ply aim at balancing the mentioned empirical focus on elites with more attention to what non-elites (in particular, social movements) have done. As Collier and Mahoney stressed, 'The dominant paradigm has built upon the founding essay by O'Donnell and Schmitter, which emphasizes the role of leadership and elite interaction. While that essay suggests that "the great-est challenge to the transitional regime is likely to come from the collective action of the working class", it also emphasizes the ephemeral nature of the "popular upsurge" and the subsequent "decline of the people"' (1997, 285). Addressing democratization from below would first of all help in redressing that bias.

My research design, however, goes beyond this empirical enrichment by aiming at explaining different paths of democratization from below, with particular attention given to eventful democratization, that is, protest-driven episodes of democratization. Following Ruth Collier (1999), we might dis-tinguish different meanings of the term 'from below' as linked to: a) the power of certain actors, distinguishing insiders from outsiders; b) the social background of those actors, distinguishing, in particular, between upper and lower classes; c) the arenas in which the conflicts take place, distinguishing institutional arenas from protest arenas.

Additionally, we can easily assume that the balance of participation by out-siders and contention in empirical cases varies. Focusing attention on the mobilization of labour, Ruth Collier (1999) has indeed inductively distin-guished different paths. Assuming that each empirical case involves a com-bination of different aspects, and leaving aside for the moment the social background of those who mobilize, I started by building a typology that crosses the dimensions of insiders versus outsiders and moderation versus contestation. The first dimension defines the degree of participation of civil society and the second its forms.

The ensuing types are reported in Table 1.1. Differently from *pacted transi-tion*, where citizens are not mobilized, in *participatory pacts* social movements are strong enough to push for democratization; in *disruptive coups d'état*, elites

Table 1.1 A typology of episodes of mobilization for democracy

	Elite driven	Mass driven
Moderation	[pacted transition]	Participatory pact
Contestation	Disruptive coup d'état	Eventful democratization

manipulate mass protest in order to win over conservative groups in participatory pacts; and in *eventful democratization* it is protest by outsiders that moves the episodes of democratization.

Explaining Democratization from Below

The research presented in this volume focuses on paths of democratization from below, with particular attention given to eventful democratization. As democratic transitions display a wide variety of trajectories and outcomes, 'the role of social movements within them is conditioned by the specific rhythm of the "protest cycle", the shape of the political opportunity structure, and the contingency of strategic choice' (Foweraker 1995, 90, n. 2).

Breaking with essentialist, deterministic, and structuralist understandings, the project follows Beissinger's (2002) stress on temporality, contextualization, and agency. I consider agency as inherent in the development of structure, and structure as influencing action, at least to a certain extent. As Beissinger observed in his illuminating analysis of the breakdown of the Soviet empire, 'nationalism needs to be understood not only as a cause of action, but also as the product of action. This recursive quality of human action—the fact that action can function as both cause and effect—and the significance of this for the study of nationalism are the central theoretical issues' (Beissinger 2002, 11). A causal analysis, artificially distinguishing dependent and independent variables, risks obscuring this continuous relationship. In Beissinger's words, 'the idea that identities could be defined in the context of agency or that nationalism is both a structured and a structuring phenomenon has not received sufficient attention' (2002, 9).[5]

In parallel, when looking at social movements more in general, we should understand them as both structured and structuring phenomena. They are, that is, both constrained in their action by the context in which they move, but also able, through their action, to change relations among and between

[5] As he notes, even constructivist approaches have not sufficiently 'investigated the ways in which the action itself may be constitutive of nationhood' (Beissinger 2002, 11), for example by looking at how nationalism suddenly crystallizes rather than developing gradually (Brubaker 1996).

actors. As Sewell (1990) has shown in his brilliant analysis of the Bastille take-over, this does not happen only in the long term, but also in the (very) short, *événementiel* one, as events are relational processes in which various actors make choices that are, at least in part, linked to others' expected reactions.

In my study I want in fact to stress the effects of protest on the social move-ment itself, by focusing on what, inspired by the historical sociologist William H. Sewell (1996), I have called 'eventful protest' (della Porta 2008). Sewell defines events as a 'relatively rare subclass of happenings that *significantly transform structure*', and an eventful conception of temporality as 'one that takes into account the transformation of structures by events' (Sewell 1996, emphasis added). I suggest that, especially during cycles of protest, some con-tingent intense events tend to affect the given context by fuelling mecha-nisms of social change: organizational networks develop; frames are bridged; personal links foster reciprocal trust. In this sense, some protest events con-stitute processes during which collective experiences develop through the interactions of different individual and collective actors, taking part with dif-ferent roles and aims. The event has a transformative effect as it alters the conditions for action 'largely by constituting and empowering new groups of actors or by re-empowering existing groups in new ways' (Sewell 1996, 271). Predictability and structural determinacy are indeed challenged as these protest events set in motion social processes that 'are inherently contingent, discontinuous and open ended' (Sewell 1996, 272).

This bridging of structure and action can be observed through a focus on protest events during episodes of democratization. While the social science literature on first democratization paid attention to long-lasting processes of increase (and sometimes, decrease) in democratic rights, literature on tran-sitology has looked at relatively short moments. Rather than analysing the long-term effects of these moments as foundational (or not) for democracy, I will reconstruct protests during episodes of democratization, their origins, characteristics, and short-term effects. Without assessing the long-term con-sequences of these episodes to see if they bring about sustained changes, I define them on the basis of their short-term effects in moving a step forward in the direction of democracy.

When looking at eventful democratization, I shall indeed focus on short periods of intense protest, looking at the relational, affective, and cognitive mechanisms that take place within them. As we will see, the historical con-text of the selected cases varies, as do the characteristics of the selected organ-izations. Rather than searching for invariant determinants, I want to identify some common dynamics that are present in the evolution of various cases of democratization. For this purpose, I use the concept of causal mechanisms.

In recent years, the language of mechanisms has become fashionable in the social sciences, signalling dissatisfaction with correlational analysis

(Mahoney 2003). Distinguishing as many as nine ways to define a mechanism, Gerring (2007) proposed a minimal common denominator in the search for the means through which a cause produces an effect. Thus, he singled out the core meaning of mechanism in 'the pathway or process by which an effect is produced or a purpose is accomplished' (Gerring 2007, 178).[6] In one understanding, the concept of causal mechanism has then been used to refer either to (historical) paths, with a search for events, which are observable and context dependent, or to micro-level explanations, with a search for variables at the individual level in the quest for universal, law-like causal explanations. In macro-analyses, causal mechanisms have been linked to systematic process tracing (Hall 2003) through a causal reconstruction that aims at explaining a given social phenomenon, be it an event or a structure, by singling out the process through which it is generated (Mayntz 2003). Mechanisms refer, therefore, to intermediary steps between conditions and outcomes. In micro-level explanations, instead, the theoretical focus is on individual agency. According to Hedstrom and Bearman (2009, 4), 'Analytical sociology explains by detailing mechanisms through which social facts are brought about, and these mechanisms invariably refer to individuals' actions and the relations that link actors to one another.'[7]

In my own understanding, mechanisms are categories of action that filter structural conditions and produce effects (see della Porta 2013b). Following Tilly (2001), I conceptualize mechanisms as relatively abstract patterns of action that can travel from one episode to the next, explaining how a cause creates a consequence in a given context. I would not restrict capacity of action to individuals, however, instead including collective actors. I will in fact consider mechanisms as a concatenation of generative events linking macro causes (such as contextual transformation) to aggregated effects (for example, cycles of protest) through individual and/or organizational agents. In this way, I believe that the search for mechanisms helps in combining attention to structure and to agency.

Looking at mechanisms, my approach is *relational*, as it locates eventful democratization in the interactions of various institutional and

---

[6] Mahoney (2003) instead considered mechanisms as 'unobserved entities, processes or structures through which an independent variable exerts an effect on a dependent variable' (Mahoney 2003, 1). They generate outcomes, but do not themselves require explanation as they are 'hypothetical ultimate causes' that explain 'why a causal variable exerts an effect on a given outcome variable' (Mahoney 2003, 1–2). Identifying mechanisms with general approaches, he distinguishes three main mechanisms: rational choice (micro-level); structural functionalism (macro-level); and power of collective actors (meso-level).

[7] Mechanisms should allow us to build general causal explanations: 'A mechanism is a precise, abstract and action-based explanation which shows how the occurring of triggering events regularly generates the type of outcome to be explained' (Hedstrom and Bearman 2009, 6).

non-institutional actors; *constructivist*, as it takes into account not only the external opportunities and constraints, but also the social construction of their experiential reality by the various actors participating in social and political conflicts; and *emergent*, as it recognizes that democratization from below involves the capacity of events to change structures (della Porta 2013b). Cognitive and affective processes intervene in the mobilization, contributing to define the situation as well as forging solidarities and identities. Considering the constraining power of the context in which episodes of mobilization take place, I shall address both endogenous, social movement properties and exogenous, environmental ones.

First, I shall look at democratization events as transformative, insofar as they alter the cultural meanings or signification of political and social categories and fundamentally shape people's collective loyalties and actions (Sewell 1990). They are settings in which one sees better the structural influences, but also 'the spectacle-like quality of the event makes it an important site of cultural transactions at which national identities are potentially formed' (Beissinger 2007, 22). The contention intrinsic to the event is strongly constitutive of identities (Beissinger 2007, 23). As Jeffrey Alexander noted, 'Social dramas, unlike theatrical ones, are open-ended and contingent. They can be staged, but nobody is certain whether the actors will arrive, who they will be, how events will unfold, which side will win a confrontation, and what the drama's effects on the audience will be' (2011, 36).

Even recognizing this transformative capacity of events, however, I expect the relevance of opposition from below during democratization processes to be influenced by some characteristics of the social movements that mobilize. Social movements are here defined as (1) informal networks of individuals and organizations, based on (2) shared beliefs and solidarity, which mobilize about (3) conflictual issues, through (4) the frequent use of various forms of protest (della Porta and Diani 2006, ch. 1). Even as social movement studies tend to consider democracy as a precondition for their development, various actors (sometimes defined as civil society) have targeted the legitimacy and the (national and international) support for authoritarian regimes (on the Latin American cases, see Jelin 1987; Corradi et al. 1992; Escobar and Álvarez 1992). Among the social movement organizations that have played a pro-democratic role are church-related actors (see Lowden 1996 on Chile; Burdick 1992; Levine and Mainwaring 2001 on Brazil; della Porta and Mattina 1986 on Spain; Glenn 2003; Osa 2003b on Poland); human rights networks, sometimes in transnational alliances (Brysk 1993; Brito 1997; Sikkink 1996; Keck and Sikkink 1998, ch. 3; Wright 2007); cultural groups (Glenn 2003 on Czechoslovakia); as well as, very often, the labour movement, sometimes in alliance with new social movements. Human rights' movements campaign to delegitimize authoritarian regimes in international forums such as the

United Nations, and in clandestine or open resistance to the authoritarian regime at the national level.

Following social movement studies, we can assume that three sets of characteristics of these networks can affect their role in democratization processes: their frames on democratic issues, organizational structures, and action repertoires (on these concepts, see della Porta and Diani 2006).

Frames are schemata of interpretation that enable individuals to locate, perceive, identify, and label occurrences within their life space as well as in the world at large (Snow et al. 1986, 464). Social movement framings about democracy and democratization vary. For example, past research indicated that the labour movement was often divided in its positions about representative democracy. Even if it tended to support the various stages of (initial) democratization, cross-national differences were relevant (Marks, Mbaye, and Kim 2009). More generally, social movements propose alternative conceptions of democracy, often mixing participatory and deliberative models. Beyond support for democracy in general, specific conceptions of democracy vary. On the whole, social movements tend to consider a representative conception of democracy as, at least, insufficient, focusing instead on democracy as a *process* that is variously defined as participatory, direct, open and deliberative. Traditionally, social movements have emphasized the *participatory* conception of democracy, stressing the importance of increasing direct forms of participation. In this line, social movement organizations have been said to assert that direct democracy is closer to the interests of the people than is liberal democracy, which is based on the delegation of power to representatives who can be controlled only at the moment of election and who have full authority to take decisions between one election and another (Kitschelt 1990). Moreover, following visions of *deliberative* democracy, recent movements have stressed the importance of building public spaces where consensual decision-making develops. Conceptions of democracy are also embedded in visions of the enemy and the self, in diagnostic and prognostic assumptions, in which a civil society is often pitted against tyranny. Different (more or less inclusive) appeals to the nation might be mobilized as well. The moderation versus radicalization of claims for autonomy/independence has been mentioned as favouring rather than jeopardizing the transition to democracy (among others, Oberschall 2000; Glenn 2003; Reinares 1987).

As already proved by previous research on social movements in democracies (della Porta 2009a, 2009b, 2013a), I expect that, in democratization processes as well, conceptions of democracy interact with other *organizational characteristics* of social movements. Since an organization is also a 'context for political conversation' (Eliasoph 1998), frames interact with organizational structures as well as the repertoire of contentious action. Indeed, organizational forms have been analysed in relation to the cultural meaning that activists give to them (see Breines 1989; Clemens 1993; Polletta 2002). Various pieces of research on social movements have confirmed that informal, decentralized groups tend to espouse more participatory and consensus-oriented conceptions of democracy (della Porta 2009a, 2009b; della Porta, Andretta, Mosca, and Reiter 2006).[8] Social networks of various types have emerged as fundamental, especially for some paths of mobilization under authoritarian regimes (Osa and Corduneanu-Huci 2003). The resilience of these resistance networks under the impact of repression can lead to splits within the ruling authoritarian elites (Schock 2005).

Conceptions of democracy have also been linked to *repertoires of action*. Previous research has in fact indicated that an emphasis on protest brings about a 'logic of membership' that favours participatory democratic models (della Porta 2009a). In addition, social movement organizations and activists that embrace non-violent practices tend to emphasize consensual internal decision-making. In reverse, the use of violent forms of action tends to reduce both participation and deliberation (della Porta 1995). As mentioned, research on non-violence has developed as a research field, pointing at the growing spread and success of (almost oxymoronical) peaceful revolutions. The extent to which non-violence is tenable in the presence of high levels of repression is, however, an open question.

In this process, major *transnational* influences are at stake. The conceptions of democracy expressed by local social movement organizations and the Western conceptions promoted by transnational actors may develop into cross-fertilization, but may also hamper efforts at developing an autonomous civil society (e.g. Challand 2008; Wada 2006; Dorronsoro 2005; Lelandais 2008). Based on previous research (Keck and Sikkink 1998; Chiodi 2007b), I expect all of these aspects to have an indirect or direct impact on mobilization from below in democratization processes. I also expect to find relevant cross-national phenomena of diffusion of ideas, often based on active strategies of promotion (e.g. Beissinger 2007; Chessa 2004; Henderson 2002).

Moving from endogenous to exogenous contextual constraints, I also expect *social and political opportunities*, especially as they are perceived by civil society actors, to influence the role they play in democratization processes. As mentioned, structuralist approaches have investigated external conditions that might explain paths of democratization. Democratization studies have looked at economic development and class structure, while social movement studies have focused attention on political dimensions, defined with reference to stable characteristics such as the functional and territorial distribution of power, political culture, and cleavage structure, as well as more

---

[8] Research in non-EU countries has in fact found a tension between rich NGOs, often funded by international actors, and grassroots local groups (e.g. Chandhoke 2003).

dynamic features such as the positions of potential allies and opponents. The basic assumption of the political process approach in social movement studies is that the more opportunities a political system offers to social movements, the more moderate, single issue and open-structured those movements will be. Drawing on this previous research, I expect political as well as social opportunities to influence mobilization levels (Kriesi 1991; Tarrow 1989; Kriesi et al. 1995), strategies (Eisinger 1973; Kitschelt 1986), ideologies/framing and behaviour (della Porta and Rucht 1995; Kriesi et al. 1995), and the organizational structures of social movements (Rucht 1996; Kriesi 1996). This, however, does not happen automatically, without the agency power of mobilization itself, as opportunities must be perceived and 'appropriated' by the collective actors (McAdam, Tilly, and Tarrow 2001).

In looking at political opportunities, the research on democratization has mainly addressed the *characteristics of the authoritarian regime.* Linz and Stepan (1996) hypothesized that the type of non-democratic regime influences the potential for the emergence of movements, protests, strikes, and underground resistance networks that precede liberalization and accompany democratization. Regimes have usually been divided into totalitarian, authoritarian, and sultanistic types (e.g. Linz and Stepan 1996), and each of them is expected to have a different impact on civil society, especially through different levels and styles of repression. Different *transition paths* can also offer different opportunities to social movements. Linz and Stepan (1996, ch. 2) singled out the specific challenges of multiple simultaneous transitions, where regime changes are accompanied by changes in the economic system and/or the nation-state arrangement. It is in fact important not only whether the previous regime was authoritarian or totalitarian, but also whether it was capitalist or communist (Stark and Bruszt 1998). Especially in the case of a triple transition, the problem of nation-state building is reflected in the emergence of nationalist movements mobilizing in the name of contending visions of what the *demos* of the future democracy should be (Beissinger 2002).

International actors also intervene as (often powerful) allies or opponents. Shifts in the constellation of states supporting versus opposing the dictators play an important role in opening or closing windows of opportunity for the opposition. Also influential are the evolving international regimes that define the global normative context for action by states and parties engaged in violent conflicts as well as the development of transnational epistemic communities that link states and civil society organizations against human rights violations.

Research Design

My research aims at building theory through understanding the dynamics of episodes of mobilization for democracy. In order to do this, I will—as mentioned—bridge insights from two fields of the social sciences (social movement studies and transition studies), building upon empirical evidence collected on a (relatively large) number of cases.

I address mobilizations for democracy, mixing most similar and most different research designs (della Porta and Keating 2008). Intra-area comparisons allow for a finer understanding about how specific contextual conditions operate. However, cross-area comparisons are particularly suited to assessing the robustness of findings. As much research on each wave of mobilization for democracy in a particular geographical region has been framed within specific area studies traditions, it has inherited their special sensitivity towards some theories and interpretations but also tended to overlook others. While contextual conditions across waves tend to vary, we might expect instead that some common mechanisms might be at play. Combining infra-area with cross-area comparisons will therefore allow exploiting the strengths of both comparative strategies.

Within this cross-area perspective, I will compare the major episodes of democratization in Eastern Europe in 1989 and in the so-called MENA region (Middle East and North Africa) in 2011. While on the East European cases a relevant amount of research allowed for more in-depth interpretation, the MENA region has been chosen not only for its diversity in comparison with the other wave, but also for its actual relevance. To a certain extent, one could say that one can draw from the Eastern European cases some well-founded analytic frames, whose validity for the MENA region can be preliminarily assessed.

Within each area, my case selection was based on the following assumptions. First, my main focus is on eventful protests that leads to episodes of democratization. The German Democratic Republic (GDR) and Czechoslovakia are positive cases of eventful democratization in Eastern Europe; Tunisia and Egypt in the MENA region. These are the cases I will analyse in more depth in order to understand the specific mechanisms of eventful democratization.

When moving from agency to contextual constraints, however, I will also introduce cases that followed different paths—thus avoiding selecting on the dependent variable. In order to do this, I will consider all other countries in Central Eastern Europe, the Baltic, and the Balkans during the 'velvet revolutions' of 1989 as well as all MENA countries where relevant mobilizations for democracy developed around 2011.

In this sense, rather than sampling a few cases based on theoretical assumptions, I aim at covering all critical cases in two specific waves, in different historical moments, geopolitical conditions, and with different regime types and socio-economic structures. In particular, I will consider, together with GDR and Czechoslovakia, also Poland, Hungary, Romania, and Albania for

Eastern Europe; and, together with Tunisia and Egypt, also Libya and Syria for the MENA region. I will also introduce some references to the Baltic States, former Yugoslavia, Yemen, Morocco, and Turkey. More specifically, GDR and Czechoslovakia as well as Egypt and Tunisia will be analysed, as mentioned, as cases of eventful democratization. Hungary and Poland will be considered instead as cases of (more or less) participated pacts and contrasted with Morocco, Yemen, and Turkey. Romania and Albania, as well as Libya and Syria, will be discussed under the label of participated coup d'état. Finally, the Baltic and the Balkan areas will be compared as examples of evolution of democratization processes when other, nationalist social movements dominate the scene.

Even though the main aim is theory building, this volume reports much empirical evidence. I have in general relied on historical comparative analysis. Empirical evidence is derived in part from analysis of existing studies (especially on Central Eastern Europe) and in part from fieldwork (mainly on the MENA region). On all cases, I relied upon research reports I have commissioned from country experts endowed with relevant linguistic knowledge, as well as my own secondary analysis of existing research and conversations with experts. All reports were written by social movement scholars using a common analytic scheme to investigate episodes of mobilization for democracy. To case reports, I have added the collection of systematic evidence on protest events, derived from various media sources.

This brings me to the issue of the potential outdating of the empirical results, in a situation in constant change. While it is true that our knowledge of the recent upheaval in the MENA region is, as I mention above, shallower than the one we now have on the 1989 'revolutions', I will focus attention not so much on the outcomes, which are still open, but rather on the characteristics (frames, organizational structures, forms of action) and dynamics of the past episodes of mobilization. As we do not know where these countries are going in terms of democratization, I focus on the insurgent moments rather than their long-term outcomes. Even if it is still uncertain to which extent (some of) the Arab Spring protests will bring about democratic consolidation, we can already study them as episodes of mobilization for democracy.

This Volume

Given my background in social movement studies, I see the original contribution of this volume in a systematic discussion of the heuristic capacity of concepts and hypotheses developed in that field to illuminate the dynamics of episodes of mobilization from below, but also of their limitations when applied to non-democracies. While much of the social science literature that has looked at democratization from below has done it either from within transition studies or referring to the traditionalist, more structuralist approach to social movements, I strive instead to propose a more dynamic approach, looking at the constructive and relational nature of episodes of mobilization for democracy.

In this analysis, and resonant with recent changes in the social sciences, I will aim at combining focuses on agency with the acknowledgment of contextual constraints on it. In order to do this, I will first look at the eventfulness of some episodes of democratization, singling out relational, cognitive, and affective mechanisms within them. An in-depth comparison of GDR, Czechoslovakia, Tunisia, and Egypt will be developed here in order to find robust mechanisms, common to all cases. While social movement studies have long considered the opening of political opportunities as a precondition for mobilization and transition studies mainly focused upon elites, I will point at the relevance of protest events as producers of opportunities (see Chapter 2).

Embedding eventful democratization in its broader environment, I will look at social movements' resource mobilization (Chapter 3) and collective framing (Chapter 4). While social movement studies consider organizational resources as fundamental for mobilization, and transition studies talks of short moments of popular (spontaneous) mobilization, I will specify when and how civil society organizations did contribute to protest, but also when they did not, highlighting the (potential and actual) tensions between civil society organizations and insurgents. While social movement studies developed upon cross-national comparison, I will follow some recent innovations in transition studies that allow for incorporating concepts of wave and diffusion in the analysis of domestic and international opportunities. The concept of civil society will be discussed here.

Repression and facilitation will emerge as central aspects in the mobilization processes. Rather than considering them, however, simply as costs and benefits, I will look at the interaction of various actors within the protests at large (Chapter 5). While social movement studies have tended to overlook capitalist developments, focusing on political opportunities, and transition studies has addressed the type of authoritarian regimes, I will then look at appropriation of opportunities by considering (also) the economic bases of political regimes (Chapter 6).

In order to assess the peculiarity of eventful democratization, I will then analyse cases in which (more or less) strong civil societies have opted for bargaining rather than mobilization (such as Hungary and Poland), looking also at the troubled history of democracy in Morocco and Turkey (Chapter 7) as well as at cases in which strong repression thwarted civil society developments (such as Romania and Albania, but also Libya and Syria) (Chapter 8). Finally, I shall discuss cases in which nationalism was used in mobilization against democratization rather than for it (Chapter 9). In all chapters, as well as in the conclusion (Chapter 10), reference to other cases will be introduced in order to discuss the external validity of my findings.

2

Eventful Democratization: When Protest Changes Relations

Introduction

On 25 January 2011, four meeting points were set in four areas of Cairo, including working-class neighbourhoods such as Shubra and Imbab. Before moving towards the city centres, the marchers travelled through narrow residential streets, gathering participants on their way. The choice was a strategic one: 'The physical passage of marchers across different areas of Cairo provided the movement with an opportunity for agitating among the shaabi, many of whom resented the regime for the economic hardships they were suffering. Taking to the streets was the only way for the movement to break the double barrier of the digital divide and the censorship of the state-owned news media. In order to maximise the movement's visibility on the streets and the possibility of contact with the local population, activists resorted to the tactic of "feeder marches"' (Gerbaudo 2012, 84).

This tactic was explained in a leaflet published online before the event that asked the reader to: '1) Assemble with your friends and neighbours in residential streets away from where security forces are. 2) Shout slogans in the name of Egypt and the people's freedom (positive slogans). 3) Encourage other residents to join (again with positive language). 4) Go out into the major streets in very large numbers in order to form the biggest possible assembly. 5) Head towards important government buildings while shouting positive slogans, to take them over' (Gerbaudo 2012, 65). *In order to get people involved, an activist recalled, 'We always made sure we were going through small streets, where there are residential areas, not the big streets, where there are no residential buildings...because that way you encourage people to come down and see the stuff'. The marches thus became 'a bus and everybody was riding it.... The bigger the march became, the more people get confidence and want to join it'* (Gerbaudo 2012, 65).

The choice proved successful. As an activist remembered,

On the 25th I went to Mustafa Mahmud square in Giza. We were about 700 people, very few, in fact. Yes we were so stupid all of them Facebook activists, and like that, only coming there from the Internet. We moved there and it was about 11am in the morning.... We met and we went to Tahrir by foot.... When we reached the square we were 50,000 people. Yes many people came. They don't know anything. But when they hear what we are saying and when they saw us they joined us. They came from everywhere: from the shops, from the streets, from their homes, from everywhere (Gerbaudo 2012, 65).

Marches thus created physical occasions to join, then carrying participants to their destination. As a protestor put it, 'You're taken to Tahrir by the demonstration itself as the head of the march guides it there' (el-Chazli 2012). In a rich reconstruction of the 25 January demonstration, el-Ghobashy (2011) noted how planning and contingency interacted:

Envision a sizable Kifaya demonstration walking down a tiny, picturesque lane in the inter-confessional neighborhood of Shubra, calling on residents watching them from the balconies to come down and join. Actor 'Amr Wakid is there, demonstrators are waving Egyptian flags and veteran sloganeer Kamal Khalil is providing the soundtrack with his unique sing-song rhymes. By the time this group surged toward the announced rally point of Shubra Circle, they had collected 1,000 bodies and police officers had started to chase them. Khalil was arrested, and the other legendary sloganeer and seasoned unionist Kamal Abu Eita just barely escaped. 'That's when I realized that Abu Eita runs much faster than me!' said thirty-something activist Ahmad 'Urabi of Abu Eita, who is nearly 60. By that point at 2:30 pm, the Shubra people received calls and text messages that crowds were filling streets in the working-class neighborhoods of Boulaq, Imbaba and Bab al-Khalq, and that Arab League Street in middle-class Muhandisin was overflowing with people marching toward Tahrir Square downtown. So they individually hopped into taxis and headed for the square. Meanwhile, outside the High Court building near Tahrir, middle-aged opposition parliamentarians and tweedy professors were scuffling with riot police. Lawyers from the bar association nearby had broken through the cordon and were approaching, as was a third roving group passing by the Judges' Club around the corner and chanting over and over again, 'Hurriyya! Hurriyya!' (Freedom! Freedom!). The police were disoriented by the convergence of the three formations. State security officers negotiated with parliamentarians, trying to convince them to persuade the crowds that they could chant as much as they liked but had to remain stationary on the High Court steps. But there was another logic at work. The bodies gleefully broke through the cordons and rushed toward Gala' Street and from there to 'Abd al-Mun'im Riyad Square abutting the Egyptian museum, a stone's throw from Tahrir.

The day of 25 January 2011 was thick with consequences for the Egyptian democratization process, which emerged from the interactions of various actors, influenced by their strategic choices but also from the (in part unexpected, and certainly not determined) outcomes of them. As in this example, protest campaigns linked to episodes of democratization often appear as sudden and unexpected. Tocqueville's statement about the French revolution applies well to democratization from below: 'never was any such event, stemming from factors so far back in the past, so inevitable yet so completely unforeseen' (1955, 1).

Surprise clearly applied to 1989. Giuseppe Di Palma noted that 'before the demise of communism made the front pages around the world, few if any of the revisionist students of communism were betting on it' (1991, 52). Even in 1984, an expert in democratization such as Samuel Huntington still considered as nil the possibility of a regime change in Eastern Europe. Not only were Western scholars stunned, but the sudden change surprised East European dissidents as well: for instance, as late as the end of 1988, Czech dissident Vaclav Havel had expected the opposition to remain 'for the time being merely the seed of something that will bear fruit in the dim and distant future'. According to an opinion poll conducted a few months after the transition, only five per cent answered affirmatively to the question 'A year ago did you expect such a peaceful revolution?' (cit. in Kuran 1991, 10–11).[1]

Surprise was also widely mentioned with regard to the Arab Spring, as 'the vast majority of academic specialists on the Arab world were as surprised as everyone else by the upheavals that toppled two Arab leaders last winter and now threaten several others' (Gause III 2011, 81). In the public opinion, as well, incredulity for the rebellion followed on expectations of immobility, as—'the cosy images of turistic Tunisian beaches tended to hide the Tunisia of rage' (Khader 2012). As the Egyptian one, in addition, 'The Tunisian revolution has clearly constituted a real political surprise inside as well as outside the country. No specialist, observer or politician, Tunisian or non Tunisian, really predicted this revolution, either for Tunisia or for any other country of the region' (Ayeb 2011, 467).

Paradoxically, however, surprise at extraordinary events is often accompanied by interpretations that stress their unavoidability. As Kuran noted, 'While the collapse of the post-World War II political order of Eastern Europe stunned the world, in retrospect it appears as the inevitable consequence of a multitude of factors. In each of the six countries the leadership was generally despised, lofty economic promises remained unfulfilled, and freedoms taken for granted elsewhere existed only on paper'. The question to address is therefore, 'if the revolution was indeed inevitable, why was it not foreseen? Why did people overlook signs that are clearly visible after the fact?' (Kuran 1991, 12–13). In order to explain this paradox, Kuran cites the individual's tendency to select information consistent with a dominant interpretative

---

[1] To cite another example, in China, 'the 1989 student demonstrations came about suddenly. Students turned from seeming apathy, games of mah-jongg, and study to concerted protest with startling speed' (Calhoun 1994, 155).

model, so that what does not fit the dominant view is temporarily removed when the regimes are still stable, and then acquires visibility when regimes fail. Besides this cognitive trap, however, there is also the inherently undetermined nature of these processes, which are indeed unpredictable as they develop in action.

What is important, then, is that events suddenly start to fuel themselves, as action produces action. Protest events tend to cluster in time, as 'events and the contention over identity which they represent are not distributed randomly over time and space. Their appearance is structured both temporally and spatially' (Beissinger 2002, 16). In fact, protests come in chains, series, waves, cycles, and tides, 'forming a punctuated history of heightened challenges and relative stability' (Beissinger 2002, 16).

Explanations for this clustering have been offered at the micro, individual level, looking in particular, within game theoretical perspectives, at the demonstrative effects of protest. As Kitschelt summarized, 'In game-theoretic language, people begin to redefine the payoff matrix of participation in collective action from that of a prisoner's dilemma in which individual participation is costly and counter-productive to that of a coordination or even an assurance game in which individuals' incentives to contribute and collective benefits reinforce each other in a virtuous circle' (Kitschelt 1993a, 416).

Within this type of approach, Kuran (1991) has interestingly suggested that—as 'mass discontent does not necessarily generate a popular uprising against the political status quo'—in order to explain conditions 'under which individuals will display antagonism toward the regime under which they live', one must consider the distinction between public and private preferences. In Kuran's account, each individual has personal views on the government that do not necessarily overlap with his or her position in public.

While private preferences are considered as fixed, the decision to express them in public is influenced by a calculation of the risks involved in that choice (1991, 17). So, when the dissidents in Eastern Europe were few, they enjoyed private but not public support, as people who shared their preferences did not want to risk expressing them and even resented the courage of the dissidents. As Havel noted, open defiance was then considered 'as an abnormality, as arrogance, as an attack on themselves, as a form of dropping out of society' (cit. in Kuran 1991, 30). The effect was widespread ignorance about how prevalent anti-regime positions were, as people who opposed the regime in private but not in public:

> ...could sense the repressed discontent of their conformist relatives and close friends; they could observe the hardships in the lives of their fellow citizens; and they could intuit that past uprisings would not have occurred in the absence of substantial discontent. Still, they lacked reliable, current information on how many

of their fellow citizens favored a change in regime. The government-controlled press exploited this ignorance by stressing the 'unity of socialist society' and its 'solidarity in supporting the Party'. Insofar as such propaganda led potential revolutionaries to underestimate the prevalence of discontent, it weakened their incentives to join the minuscule opposition (Kuran 1991, 30).

In this approach, protest is expected to spread when particular conditions make less risky the public expression of oppositional preferences that have been held in private. The payoff for publically expressing dissent increases with the size (S) of the dissenting masses, which reduces the cost of expressing the private preferences as others do so. Those who have critical private preferences, which they had refrained from publicizing because of the potential costs of challenging the regime, in fact see a decline in those costs as protest becomes massive. In Kuran's analysis, 'The larger S, the smaller the individual dissenter's chances of being persecuted for his identification with the opposition and the fewer hostile supporters of the government he has to face'. In fact, as even those who are privately sympathetic to the opposition out of conformity do participate in the repression of those who publicly oppose the regime, 'a rise in S leaves fewer people seeking to penalize members of the public opposition'. When, on the other hand, people do have the possibility of expressing in public what they feel in private, they will be pushed to do so, in order to avoid the 'psychological cost of preference falsification' as 'the suppression of one's wants entails a loss of personal autonomy, a sacrifice of personal integrity. It thus generates lasting discomfort, the more so the greater the lie' (Kuran 1991, 17–18, *passim*).

Thus, a sort of revolutionary bandwagon derives from the contemporary fall in thresholds and rise in public opposition. As public opposition increases, it becomes easier to convince those with private preferences against the government to mobilize, but also to change the preference of others.

The focus on the individual level is justified by the methodological individualism to which these scholars subscribe—the assumption, that is, that 'after all, a mass uprising results from multitudes of individual choices to participate in a movement for change; there is no actor named "the crowd" or "the opposition"' (Kuran 1991, 16). Going beyond the individual level, the analysis of eventful democratization I want to articulate in this chapter points at the power of action itself in creating and recreating environmental opportunities and organizational resources that influence the strategic interactions of various actors. If events fuel each other, it is because they are linked 'in the narrative of the struggles that accompany them, in the altered expectations that they generate about subsequent possibilities to contest; in the changes that they evoke in the behaviour of those forces that uphold a given order, and in the transformed landscape of meaning that events at times fashion' (Beissinger 2002, 17). If structural conditions are not (or do not seem) ripe, they might still mature during protest campaigns. That is, protest campaigns are eventful, as they produce new relations and resources that favour mobilization, rather than being a simple product of external and internal conditions.

In this analysis, I stress the emergent nature of protest. Notwithstanding the relevance of protest events for social movements, they have been mainly studied as aggregated collective action (for example, in protest cycles). In social movement studies, in fact, protest has mainly been considered as a 'dependent variable' and explained on the basis of political opportunities and organizational resources.

In my conception of eventful democratization (see also Chapter 1), looking at waves of protest for democracy, I share the focus on the internal dynamics and transformative capacity of protest, looking however at a broader range of events than those included under the label of transformative protest. My assumption is that protest events have cognitive, affective, and relational impacts on the very actors that carry them out. Some forms of action or specific campaigns have a particularly high degree of eventfulness. Through these events, participants experiment with new tactics, send signals about the possibility of collective action (Morris 2000), create feelings of solidarity, and consolidate organizational networks, while sometimes public outrage at repression develops (Hess and Martin 2006). In what follows, I shall look at the capacity of protest to develop in eventful democratization through some specific cognitive, affective, and relational mechanisms.

From the cognitive point of view, I will stress mechanisms of growth in discursive generality and politicization as they develop in action. By *growth in discursive generality* I mean the cognitive expansion of protest claims, from more specific to more general concerns, as a way to bridge different constituencies. For instance, Foweraker and Landman (1997, 13) have observed the way in which claims develop in action, as in protest campaigns, which start with specific claims and then move towards the call for a broader set of rights. In fact, rights have high symbolic power. Not only are they conquered through struggles, but the discourse on rights is effective in bonding collective demands. In the long history of social movements in Latin America, 'participants learn their right lessons through the rigor of organization and the debates over strategy, so learning the language of rights' in action (Foweraker and Landman 1997, 33). There, liberalization processes have usually been prompted by mobilization on various rights: social movements have, indeed, been catalysts for change.[2] Similarly, protests against the construction of big

---

[2] In Brazil, Chile, Mexico, and Spain, transitions were started by labour, with a shift from material and economic claims to claims for political and civil rights: 'The gradual liberalization of citizenship rights over time in Brazil was accompanied by an increase in social movement activity.

infrastructures often start from circumscribed concerns with the defence of the local environment, but then expand their discourses from Nimby ('not in my back yard') to Nope ('not on planet earth'), while ecological claims are bridged with claims of justice (della Porta and Piazza 2008).

Together with the growth in generality, there is a mechanism of *politicization of the protest discourse*, as the target of action is singled out in the government and the regime. While waves of protest might start with specific complaints against economic decline or diffuse corruption, protest gains momentum especially when a cognitive link is made between these grievances and government actions. In social movement studies, this attribution of political responsibility has often been noted as a characteristic of very different types of protest, from labour strikes to ethnic riots.

Cognitive mechanisms are paralleled by emotional ones, such as moral shocks, but also feelings of collective empowerment. Scholars of social movements have compiled lists of emotions relevant for research, in recognition that 'Social movements are awash in emotions. Anger, fear, envy, guilt, pity, shame, awe, passion, and other feelings play a part either in the formation of social movements, in their relations with their targets...and in the life of potential recruits and members' (Kemper 2001, 58). *Moral shocks* are emotionally intense reactions of indignation against an action perceived as ethically unbearable, and thus alter ways of thinking (Gould 2004). Research on protest in authoritarian regimes has in fact stressed how episodes of brutal repression might increase rather than quell opposition, as they are perceived as outrageous by the population (see also Chapter 5). They do facilitate mobilization in authoritarian regimes through the transformation of fear into rage.

As negative emotions must be balanced by positive ones in order to fuel collective action, moral shocks must be accompanied by a *feeling of collective empowerment*, as a set of positive emotions that produce an enhanced sense of agency through identity building and solidarity ties. While the breakdown approach to social movements tended to consider emotions as negative and social movement activists as carriers of those negative emotions (for example, frustration, aggression, and so on), recent research has pointed out the relevance of additional emotions—negative, but also positive (such as joy, pride, pleasure, and love)—for understanding social movement dynamics. Emotional liberation has been considered as important in explaining the development of protest, especially in risky forms of activism (Flam 2005).

Citizenship rights in Chile remained relatively static until the 1988 plebiscite, even if the struggle for those rights began in the late 1970s. The increasing divergence between rights-in-principle and rights-inactive in Mexico was punctuated by peaks of labour and other social movement activity. Despite growing social mobilization in Spain in the 1960s, citizenship rights were denied until the beginning of the democratic transition, and the massive upsurge in mobilization that accompanied it' (Foweraker and Landman 1997, 165).

Reciprocal emotions (positive ones such as love and loyalty) have especially important effects on movement dynamics.

Cognitive and affective mechanisms fuel relational ones, which take shape during eventful democratization. In various ways, coordination reduces the cost of participation as mobilization spreads: this emerges, in fact, in *networked* and *aggregated* forms. In his analysis of recent anti-austerity protests, Jeff Juris has distinguished these two forms of coordination, noting that 'whereas the use of listservs and websites in the movements for global justice during the late 1990s and 2000s helped to generate and diffuse distributed networking logics, in the #Occupy movements social media have contributed to powerful logics of aggregation' (2012, 260–1). While the logic of networking aims at connecting diverse collective actors, the logic of aggregation involves the assembling of diverse individuals in physical spaces. This distinction applies also to eventful democratization, where the two forms of coordination interact. As Osa (2003a) noted, in Poland, waves of protest for democracy proceeded by bridging various groups, so that coordination was, at the same time, a precondition and an effect of mobilization. Eventually, it is the very definition of a collective actor which is at stake (see also Chapter 3).

In what follows, I shall identify the ways in which these mechanisms developed in action in the four analysed cases of eventful democratization: the GDR and Czechoslovakia in Eastern Europe, and Tunisia and Egypt in the MENA region.

Eventful Democratization in 1989

Notwithstanding the fact that the most visible civil society organization, Solidarity, belongs to the history of Poland, the two Eastern European cases in which protests had the most relevance in the breakdown of authoritarian regimes were the GDR and Czechoslovakia. While in Poland a strong opposition negotiated transition (see Chapter 7), it is in the GDR and in Czechoslovakia that a path of democratization by rupture developed. This section is devoted to the crucial days of the transition in these two countries.

Eventful Democratization in the GDR

After a slow start, the protest for democracy began to intensify in the GDR in the autumn of 1989. As Charles Maier noted, 'Protest builds upon itself and its success—or even conflict—in the street. Contestation of power in public places, violent or non-violent, really matters. If repressive regimes cannot control public space, they are shown to possess neither efficacy nor legitimacy. If day after day protesters claim the streets with impunity, no regime can survive intact' (2011, 274).

In the previous couple of years, notwithstanding growing *Verdrossenheit* (dissatisfaction), protest had spread very slowly. While oppositional marches may have become more frequent in 1987, they remained limited to only a few hundred activists. Throughout, however, the repertoire of contention grew: while actions during the previous years mainly consisted of seminars in private apartments or readings in churches (Fehr 1995), after 1987 debates and documents were accompanied by protest actions such as vigils for those who had been arrested. In particular, the *Friedensgebete* (peace prayers) that had started in 1981 with the peace movement were transformed by the mobilization of an opposition for democracy and of migrant applicants. In 1988, the repression of 'exiters' (those who applied for visas to emigrate) brought about a wave of solidarization (Neubert 1997, 785). Small demonstrations started to take place after each peace prayer, often repressed through high fines and occasional arrests. In March, in Berlin, there were also protests against the arrest of Havel in Czechoslovakia.

Protest intensified in 1989, when the crises in Hungary (in January non-communists were legalized) and Poland (in February, roundtable talks started) acted as catalysts for mobilization in neighbouring countries. In January 1989, a protest wave started as local groups, united in the Demokratische Initiative, promoted a demonstration for democracy in Leipzig on the occasion of the commemoration of the assassinations of Rosa Luxemburg and Karl Liebknecht, who had stated that 'Freedom means always the freedom of those who disagree'. As many as 800 participated (Neubert 1997, 43). A few months later, an appeal to boycott local elections in May was signed by forty-eight members of the opposition; some groups organized a monitoring of electoral results, while others leafleted before, during, and after the elections, the monitoring of which indicated widespread fraud, prompting discontent. Protests ranged from public statements by individual priests (the church as an institution had spoken against protest) to a demonstration with 1,000 participants in Leipzig, with leaflets signed as 'concerned electors' or 'committed citizens'. Protests were also organized to denounce the quelling of the democratization movement in China, with brutally repressed demonstrations in front of the Chinese embassy on 22 June, and services for the victims. Alternative church-days were organized for the 450th anniversary of the reformation jubilee (Neubert 1997, 817).

It was in the autumn of 1989, however, that protests skyrocketed in number and size, as the Stasi (secret police) warned of an increasing interest among the population in what was happening in the other Eastern European countries. Between August 1989 and April 1990, as many as 2,600 public demonstrations, 300 rallies, 200 strikes, and a dozen factory occupations took place, the largest demonstration involving up to one million people, with about five million participating in protest (Dale 2005, 181). As many as twenty-three demonstrations took place in Leipzig between September 1989 and March 1990. There, participants in the *Montagsdemos* (demonstrations taking place every Monday) increased from 5,000 (on 25 September), to 20,000 (2 October), to 70,000 (9 October), 120,000 (16 October), 250,000 (23 and 30 October), 450,000 (6 November), and about 200,000 (on 13, 20, 27 November and 4, 11, 18 December) (Pollack 2009). In the first week of October, demonstrations (with up to 20,000 participants) spread to Dresden, Halle, Magdeburg, and other cities.

The autumn uprising started on 4 September in Leipzig, during the international autumn fair, as more than a thousand protestors attended a Monday service and then marched to the city centre. About a hundred were arrested, spurring other protests for their release. On 11 September, the opening of the Hungarian border prompted strong emotions among the population, including anger, but also anticipation, even a 'fantastic mood', while hopes about the removal of Premier Honecker and Stasi Chef Mielke increased. On that day and every succeeding Monday, thousands of citizens marched in Leipzig, with increasing participation.

The following week in Leipzig, the police encircled St Nicholas square as a peace service was taking place. As 'a thousand prayer service participants exited and joined another thousand demonstrators outside the church, security officers ordered them to immediately disperse. As the crowd hesitated, the police aggressively arrested a hundred people. In response, churches throughout East Germany held vigils to pray for the release of the prisoners' (Nepstad 2011, 46). During the next week, on 25 September, 'Pastor Wonneberger took to the pulpit. In front of an audience of thousands, he drew on prophetic inspiration to preach stirringly: "He who practices violence, who threatens violence and employs it, will himself be the victim of that violence"' (Pfaff 2006, 103–4). On this occasion, as 4,000 people took to the street after the service, only a few arrests were made (Nepstad 2011, 46). As Ritter (2012a) summarized, 'the lack of repression was crucial as it likely helped reduce the fears of both protesters and onlookers of participating in future events. Furthermore, some scholars have suggested that the fact that even in the tense context of September 1989 the Peace Prayers weren't either decisively broken up or prohibited contributed to the institutionalization of the protests: the people of Leipzig not only knew when the protests would take place, but had also become familiar with the nonviolent methods used'. The number of protestors at the *Montagsdemo* further increased, with up to 10,000 attending the Peace Prayer on 2 October (coincidentally Gandhi's 120th birthday) in front of St Nicolas church.

On 3 October, protests in Dresden against the closing of the border with Czechoslovakia included some violence, such as the storming of an Intershop (a store reserved for clients who could pay in Western currencies) and blocks at the railway station as a sealed train from Prague, bringing Germans who had asked for the right to migrate from the GDR, passed by. About 18,000 marched, singing the *Internationale*, and occasionally fighting against the police. On the next day, a non-violent march, with demonstrators carrying candles, resisted police repression. As the police deployed batons and water cannon, repression backfired, and Hans Modrow, the mayor, had to accept talks with a delegation.

A turning point took place on 7 October, as the regime celebrated in Berlin the fortieth anniversary of the foundation of the GDR, with dignitaries from eighty countries assisting in the official parade. With the media focused on the event, the demonstrators exploited the chance to have their voices heard: 10,000 demonstrated in the capital city chanting 'Gorbi! Gorbi!' (Naimark 1992, 89; Nepstad 2011, 46). While the demonstration was broken up by police (16,000 policemen were deployed, and 1,000 demonstrators arrested), it seemed that 'the people were no longer intimidated and on October 8 demonstrations took place in Dresden, Leipzig, Berlin, Potsdam, and many other towns and cities' (Naimark 1992, 90). According to the Ministry of Interior, 17,000 attended protests between 6 and 8 October, with the presence of young people especially high in Berlin.

A further important step, on 9 October, was a march in Leipzig, this time without police intervention, notwithstanding previous rumours of plans for brutal repression—the hospitals had allegedly stocked up on blood, while the Stasi reported divisions among party members about how to react (Maier 1997). After Premier Honecker had announced that he was prepared to call for a state of emergency and 8–10,000 troops had encircled St Nicholas church in Leipzig, protest organizers called for non-violence, as 'violence produces violence. Violence cannot solve any problem. Violence is inhuman. Violence cannot be a sign of a new, better society…abstain from violence' (Nepstad 2011, 47). As between 50 and 100,000 gathered at St Nicholas church, their lack of violence discouraged military intervention (Dale 2005, 155; Naimark 1992, 92; Saxonberg 2001, 311).

The Leipzig demonstration of 9 October has been considered as the 'crucial moment when the Socialist Unity Party (SED) lost control of East Germany. Convinced now that they were free to vent their frustrations in public, crowds began gathering regularly in towns throughout East Germany' (Stokes 1993, 140). In fact, on the following Monday as many as 150,000 people participated in the Peace Prayer; the week after, following Honecker's resignation on 18 October, 200,000 demonstrated.

On 4 November, up to one million gathered at Alexander Platz in Berlin, while there were already talks of a roundtable between opponents and regime leaders. As the cabinet resigned on 8 November, the politburo followed suit

(Reich 1990). On 9 November, in Leipzig, 70,000 (out of 700,000 inhabitants) peacefully marched on the city Ring. On that very day, the Wall that separated East Berlin from West Berlin came down, as GDR authorities decided to allow their citizens to freely exit the country. Later in the month, roundtables were organized, while exiled artists came back to the GDR. However, the paradox was, the crisis in the opposition since December.

The regime's reactions were, all along, inconsistent. Repression was tried and tested, but then abandoned, as apparently the police had shown little capacity (and probably also propensity) to attack masses of peaceful demonstrators (Nepstad 2011). The lack of Soviet support for a repressive solution certainly discouraged SED leaders from taking responsibility for a bloodbath, which would have been useless in stopping the revolt. Therefore, as the crowd remained non-violent, the security forces did too (Maier 1997, 156; Nepstad 2011, 48; Pfaff 2006, 169–71; Saxonberg 2001, 313–14; Stokes 1993, 140). The regime's weak control of the means of coercion as well as the police's lack of training and experience to deal with demonstrations (Jobard 2006) goes some way to explain the lack of repression of the mass protests during the first week of November. Non-violent protest indeed catalysed existing discontent in the military—the Stasi warned against the use of the military, as rank-and-file troops were considered unreliable and the party-mobilized militia leaders had declared themselves unable or unwilling to intervene against the demonstrators. Many members of both militia started in fact to identify with the slogan *Wir sind das Volk* (We are the people). As one militia man declared, 'many honest comrades actually thought this was the mob. Then we saw they were entirely normal people shouting *Wir sind das Volk*...and we belong to them too' (Nepstad 2011, 48).

In the evolution of the events, cognitive shifts were at play, including growth in generality and politicization.[3] The opposition had grown since September, with open calls for democracy, more economic freedom, free elections, an independent judiciary, free movement, and de-ideologization. In the autumn, after the repression of demonstrations on 11 and 18 September, there were warnings about agents provocateurs sent by the regime, while the protest claims became increasingly politicized. At the beginning of November, 'opposition also spread from the streets to the workplace, where small waves of strikes occurred. The people's demands became stronger and clearer: an end to SED dominance, genuinely free elections, and unrestricted travel rights' (Nepstad 2011, 51).

Protests were also strengthened by the cognitive bridging of various issues. Oppositional activities addressed human rights, protection of the

---

[3] Carol Mueller (1999), through protest event analysis, found clear evidence of what she called claims radicalization: a move, that is, from specific claims to anti-regime ones.

environment, conditions in the Third World, and conscientious objection. Not only did groups on peace, human rights, and women's rights become increasingly coordinated in their resistance to state repression, but there were also—although with some tensions—connections made with issues of migration and democratization. In fact, 'In the autumn of 1989 there were two major movements in East Germany, each of which involved hundreds of thousands of citizens. One consisted of individuals heading for the "exit." The other involved collectively expressed "voice"' (Dale 2005, 156). Mobilization from below came from the encounter of exit and voice, as exiters helped both insurgent (spontaneous) and loyalist (organized) protests.

In fact, the number of those applying for visas to emigrate exploded in the second half of the 1980s. In 1986, about half a million—mainly young and well educated—had asked for legal emigration in the face of economic decline and the rejection of the path of liberalization by the regime. If, in the market, exit is traditionally considered as easier than voice, this was not the case when it implied leaving a country as in the GDR. Already applying for an exit visa had in fact a high cost: expulsion from the party, dismissal from one's job, and prohibition from pursuing a professional career or occupying a public office, as well as the remittance of all assets to the state.

After those who had applied for visas found help and space to organize in the church, their action became increasingly politicized. Their voices became more audible in June 1989 (120,000 exit applications were pending by then), when the Stasi reported on the formation of a movement of 'would-be exiters'.[4] So the regime started to suspect that, 'would-be exiters joined dissent protests in the hopes of being classified as seditious by the state, which, they reasoned, would lead to a swifter exit via political expulsion' (Pfaff 2006, 101). While, especially in Berlin, there were tensions with intellectuals, who viewed exiting as renouncing the struggle in the country—in fact, the demonstrations in early 1988 did not include slogans on migration—the exit movement nevertheless became politicized, as the would-be migrants started to attend demonstrations as well as staging their own events in 1988.[5]

The exiters' protest was especially notable in Leipzig, supported by sympathetic pastors and made visible thanks to the biannual East-West trade fairs. An exit-voice coalition developed, then, facilitated by similar grievances and

---

[4] In 1984, there were 35,000 exiters, 25,000 in 1985. Many of them were from the opposition, but according to the Stasi, about a thousand SED members per year asked for a visa and about 25,000 were active in the resistance (Neubert 1997, 501).

[5] While the regime facilitated travel in an attempt to ease tensions, in September 1989, Hungary opened its borders. Over 80 per cent of those who fled that summer were below 40, and 90 per cent of them declared they were motivated by the search for freedom. Thus, blocked exit stimulated voice.

socio-demographic characteristics.[6] From the Leipzig district, which had eight per cent of the GDR population, came twenty per cent of visa applicants. Half of the protestors arrested after the *Montagsdemos* (Monday demonstration) on 22 May had applied to emigrate: 'In subsequent interrogations some revealed that they were less interested in the struggle for democracy than they were in getting out of the GDR' (Pfaff 2006, 101). In 1989, during the international spring fair, there were demonstrations with participants who carried a black beret with white ribbons symbolizing the number of years since they had applied for a visa. The encounter of the two groups was noticeable when demonstrators started to carry banners 'for an open country with free people' (Pfaff 2006, 102).

The interaction of exit and voice intensified during the events. Two days after the 4,000 exiters in the FRG (Federal Republic of Germany) embassy in Prague were allowed to leave on 1 October, and the GDR government announced that that those who left did not have to renounce citizenship. In the same month, 50,000 East Germans crossed the Hungarian border with Austria, and another 50,000 left via Czechoslovakia over the next five days.

Emotionally very intense, protests were accompanied by a chain of moral shocks and feelings of empowerment. Fear of repression was widespread. As a protestor recalled, 'we all reckoned with a high probability of bloodshed on October 9' (Opp, Voss, and Gern, 138). Another (about 7 October) noted, 'we went scared stiff to the demonstration on Monday. I went in an old coat and wore different glasses' (Opp, Voss, and Gern 1995, 142). As members of oppositional groups called for non-violence, however, this fear turned into rage, and repression had radicalizing effects: 'I became a participant to the extent that I became so furious' (Opp, Voss, and Gern 1995, 147). Also, fear declined week by week—especially when migrating to the West became an alternative to prison.

Feelings of solidarity developed during the struggle (Neubert 1997, 870), as moments of repression produced waves of indignation. In the words of a future participant, 'I was indignant, because I had never thought that a workers' and peasants' state would go after workers the way it happened on October 7 and 8' (Saxonberg 2001, 312). Influenced by the peace movement, the repertoire of action—including hunger strikes, human chains, peace services, vigils, candles, and chants (we shall overcome) (Neubert 1997, 869)—helped to overcome fear. As a participant observed, 'Courage is not the opposite of fear. It has rather to do what is necessary to do, even when legs are trembling' (Neubert 1997, 869).

---

[6] Exiters were in fact 60 per cent men; 80 per cent were less than 40 years old; and more than 40 per cent were skilled workers (Pfaff 2006). Civic movement supporters were 60 per cent men and 80 per cent less than 40 years old, even though migrants were mainly skilled workers, and the militants educated white collar and professional strata (Pfaff 2006).

With the development of the protests spread in fact a sense of empower-ment, along with protest norms that gave a positive value to participation. According to a survey, many protestors thought that: one should engage in protest if dissatisfied with governmental policies; one can make a difference; and politics is not only a matter for elected politicians (Opp, Voss, and Gern 1995, 88). In parallel, norms against the use of violence also gained ground, perceived as inefficacious (by 94 per cent of interviewees) because of expected state sanctions and social incentives for non-violence (Opp, Voss, and Gern 1995, 93).

Coordination also increased with action. According to the secret police, in August there were about 2,500 opponents in about 160 groups (Pfaff 2006, 113). Although initially there was limited communication between the Berliner opposition and the rest of the country, in September, solidari-zation against repression occurred. During the protests, new organizations emerged, playing an important role in coordination: among them, New Forum (NF), Demokratie Jetz, and Demokratisce Aufbruch. On 9 September, NF was founded and presented itself as a political platform for people of vary-ing backgrounds who wanted to participate in a process of reform (Neubert 1997, 83). Protest propelled the organizational process: for instance, 'New Forum organized itself as a protest movement only after the first large pro-tests in many cities' (Pfaff 2006, 221). As mobilizations continued, 200,000 signed the NF manifesto.

Together with organized coordination, a less organized form of coordination developed, as some places and spaces became available for the convergence of demonstrators and critical citizens. In Leipzig, a compact urban structure facilitated the protest. Notwithstanding the destruction during the war, the remaining enclosed city centre favoured the development of subcultural and informal structures (Neubert 1997, 783). As a protestor observed: 'there was no head of the revolution, the head was the Nicholas Church and the body was the city center' (Neubert 1997, 132). This geography of protest interacted with pre-existing networks: Leipzig was in fact, since 1946, a city of resistance and oppositional activities, with an independent Left and influential critical members of the Protestant Church. A similar capacity for aggregation was seen in neighbourhoods such as Prenzlauer Berg in Berlin. Spaces of conver-gence interacted with social incentives in facilitating mobilization. According to a survey, sixty-six per cent of those who mobilized had friends who were in favour of protest. As a protestor recalled, he decided to participate as 'A friend of mine said to me, "what will you do when your children ask in 10 years why you didn't do anything?"' (Opp, Voss, and Gern 1995, 82).

Aggregation and coordination brought about an extension of the number of protestors. While the intellectuals of the opposition had started the pro-tests, they were now joined by different social groups. There were tensions, as workers thought intellectuals were locked up in their ivory tower, and intellectuals apparently feared the workers. According to some commentators, at least initially, an opposition mainly consisting of authors, artists, scientists, and priests held the biased view that workers had little interest in democracy and freedom, being rather materialistic. NF's refusal of the workers' offer to organize a general strike testified to their fear of masses that could get out of control, and a focus instead on negotiation, which ended in the acceptance of an offer of dialogue and a roundtable in December as the citizens' movement radicalized. The workers, on their side, reciprocated these stereotypes, seeing intellectuals as privileged.

Still, through action, cross-class contacts intensified. In the factories, support for NF grew, and Stasi reports warned that 'the influence of "New Forum" is rising steeply amongst sections of the working class' (Dale 2005, 180). Workers did participate in the struggle for democracy, bringing specific claims: they asked for independent unions, contesting managerial control and attempting to increase workers' influence. Not only did they join in the demonstrations (often with groups of colleagues, walking together), but they also discussed politics in the factories. While in the uprisings of 1953 they were involved as workers, in 1989 they were more involved as citizens, given a downturn in industrial conflict.

Needing economic help from Bonn, on 1 December the new premier Modrow abolished the first article of the constitution which mandated the leading role of the SED, started a reorganization of the Stasi, and launched a roundtable. Demonstrations for democratization continued, however: 200 were reported by the ministry of internal affairs between 14 and 28 January, with NF still supporting participatory democracy and grassroots politics.

Eventful Democratization in Czechoslovakia

In Czechoslovakia, the collapse of the regime following mass protest has been characterized as an example of democratization from below, as 'in contrast to Poland where the regime agreed to negotiations with Solidarity that led to partially free elections, a national general strike in Czechoslovakia provoked the subsequent resignation of the Central Committee and agreement for a new government'. The general strike has in fact been defined as 'a turning point that demonstrated the loss of confidence in the old regime and popular support for new civic movements' (Glenn 2003, 11).

After a long period of repression, potential for change also emerged here with the new course in the Soviet Union and crises of the regimes in Poland and Hungary. And also here, after a slow start, protest spiralled quickly. Mobilization began in January 1989, after Vaclav Havel, a leader of the opposition, was imprisoned. On 15 January 1989, about 5,000 activists celebrated the twentieth anniversary of Jan Palach's self-immolation in protest against the invasion by the Soviet army in 1968 and in the name of Czechoslovakian independence (Urban 1990, 114). The protestors pointed at 'the differences between the pretensions of the government, which on this day was signing a new accord on human rights at the Vienna meeting of the Conference on Security and Cooperation in Europe (CSCE), and the realities of its repression' (Stokes 1993, 154). As they tried to lay flowers on the place where Palach had killed himself, the police charged them, arresting about one hundred people, including future president Havel. Further demonstrations were organized in the following five days, with up to 5,000 demonstrators, again ending in police charges and arrests (Stokes 1993; Urban 1990). These did not stop the protest, however, as about 20,000 signed a petition supporting freedom of assembly and free media.

Solidarization fuelled the mobilization, but also a bridging of different themes, with growth in generality and politicization of the protestors' discourse. On 29 June, a petition (signed then by 11,500 people, which eventually grew to 30,000) demanded 'the release of political prisoners, the ending of persecution of independent initiatives, the freeing of the media and all cultural activity, respect for religious rights, the public presentation of all projects on the environment, and free discussion of the events of the 1950s, the Prague Spring and Warsaw pact invasion, and the period of normalization' (Skilling 1991, 20; see also Stokes 1993, 155).

Mobilization intensified during the summer. On 21 August (one day after the announcement of the establishment of a Solidarity-led government in Poland), 3,000 people protested in Wenceslas Square on the twenty-first anniversary of the Warsaw Pact invasion; 400 of them were arrested. After protests developed in the GDR, on 28 October another demonstration was called to celebrate the founding, in 1918, of the Republic of Czechoslovakia. As many as 10,000 people participated (Humphrey 1990).

Social bridging and organization building—that is, coordination by both aggregation and networking—were visible during the action. Students played an important role in starting the protests. At Charles University, over 400 students had signed a petition against the expulsion of four of their colleagues after the aforementioned demonstration in honour of Jan Palach, creating a student forum. There were also petitions on university issues, for example against mandatory courses on scientific Marxism. In the summer, they started an independent student organization with the aim of self-government, the core of which was constituted by a group of friends.

Networking intensified also as student activists, who had gone to observe the Monday marches in Leipzig (Williams 2011, 114), used the lessons they had learned there in the organization of a demonstration during an official celebration. If the Prague Spring of 1968 had culminated on Independence Day (28 October), in 1989 the occasion for protest was the anniversary of the

Nazis' assassination of a Czech student in 1939, which had led to the proclamation of 17 November as Students' Day. With city permission, established
youth unions and semi-official student unions participated in the event.
After the officially authorized student ceremony in honour of the Czech student, about 50,000 participants continued toward the city centre. Riot police
charged them brutally as, apparently, they 'were almost certainly operating
under orders to overreact, though it remains unclear just who so instructed
them, and why' (Judt 1992, 98).

Outrage increased with the rumour that a demonstrator had been killed.
At a meeting at the Drama Academy, the students then called for a national
students' strike, forming a coordination committee. They also called for
meetings, every day at 4 p.m., in front of the statue of the patron Vaclav in
Wenceslas Square in Prague, as well as for a nationwide general strike on 27
November. On 18 November, 400 actors assembled from all over the country
and voted to go on strike. So, 'within days, small groups of students were
knocking on the doors of factories and visiting villages to bring the message
of freedom' (Judt 1992, 156); they were accompanied by famous actors.

As the repression of the student demonstration produced a wave of solidarization, new movement organizations emerged to coordinate the protest: the Civic
Forum in the Czech Republic, and Public Against Violence in Slovakia. There
was also a process of less-organized coordination, through the mobilization of
various networks. Theatres were particularly important here. As it was observed,

> Lacking prior history or organizational resources, the new movements had to cre-
> ate a national network within days to organize the strike as a demonstration of
> their popular support. Like Solidarity's alliance with the Catholic Church, Civic
> Forum and Public Against Violence sought to transform pre-existing cultural net-
> works outside the political sphere, in this case the network of theatres which had
> gone on strike in support of the students after the repression of the demonstra-
> tion. While this may seem curious, theatres in Czechoslovakia, like the Catholic
> Church in Poland, could draw on the association with the birth of the nation
> (Judt 1992, 12).

Striking theatres became not only important networks for the protest, but
also spaces where critical citizens could converge and organize. Given the
important role of theatre for the nation, and the presence of the densest
theatre networks in Europe, theatres on strike functioned as free spaces and
networks for social movements. Actors on strike travelled with students to
factories and to the countryside, while theatres hosted public discussions
within their performances:

> Each evening at Semafor started with the broadcast of the television news,
> analysed and supplemented by uncensored information about current events.

Afterwards, prominent members would read the proclamations of the students and the theater community and later of Civic Forum. The evenings continued with the presentation of, or telephone calls to guests, including students who had participated in the November 17 demonstration, legal experts, economic experts from Forecasting institute, and cultural figures (Glenn 2001, 155).

Members of the audience were then asked to speak about their own personal experiences, while the actors on stage moderated the debates: 'Many of these evenings had a curious quality to them, a cross between a political rally, a therapy session and a cabaret' (Glenn 2001, 155).

Theatres functioned, then, as spaces of aggregation. As protest intensified, after 18 November there was 'the transformation of the theaters into local branches of the movement' (Glenn 2001, 143). On that day, in fact,

> much of the Czech theater community gathered at the Realistic Theater in Prague, where one of the demonstrators from the theater academy read the students' proclamation calling for a general strike on November 27. The same afternoon, the coordinating committee of Prague students was formed, composed of two representatives of each faculty....That evening, members of the theater community at the Realistic Theater prepared a proclamation declaring themselves to be on strike and in support of the student demands, including the general strike (Glenn 2001, 132–3).

In a similar way, during and after the Prague Spring, the theatres had functioned as public spheres where politics were openly discussed, as 'theatrical language that enabled them to express opinions in a manner difficult for the state to control' (Glenn 2001, 148).

The theatre network also played an important coordinating function; in particular, the Theater Institute in Prague collected information and documentation, while branches of the Civic Forum were established in fourteen theatres in Prague and eighteen other cities, including all six regional capitals. Theatres 'founded in factories, research institutes, or schools,...they did not represent one group of society but rather, like their parent body, a forum in which members of all groups of society met regularly' (Glenn 2001, 147). As Glenn observed, 'This provided an important network of communication throughout the country, located in places that would be familiar to all citizens (who might not, for example, know where the university or a particular factory room would be) and would be heated (which was important, since it was, after all, November). In the packed theaters at night, people from all parts of society came to listen or to present information about the situation and to discuss the course of events' (Glenn 2001, 154).

As the protest thus expanded beyond the students, a civil society grew with the events: 'If an independent society had been slow in forming in Czechoslovakia in comparison with Poland and Hungary, it almost caught up in the ten days following the November 17th events' (Stokes 1993, 156). On 19 November, future president Havel and a group of his friends from the civil rights organization Charter 77 decided to establish a Civic Forum (CF), as a coalition of civil society groups, and expressed support for the students' call. CF had a small crisis group for tactical decisions, a media monitoring group, and a liaison group which met at the Magic Lantern theatre. A very decentralized organization allowed for rapid diffusion of the strikes and mass demonstrations. CF was in fact loosely coordinated, as its local branches worked independently from each other to organize debates, strikes, and demonstrations.

In turn, these public spheres facilitated the development of cognitive mechanisms, such as growth in generality and politicization. As Glenn noted, despite the fall of the authoritarian regimes in neighbouring countries, initially protestors 'did not call for fundamental changes in the system, but almost a reformist spirit calling for the redress of human rights abuses' (Glenn 2001, 146). While CF had raised at its foundation moderate requests for the resignation of those responsible for the student repression (but also of the Prague Spring in 1968), the students, more radical, asked for the removal of the constitutional clause concerning the leading role of the communist party. Demands escalated further as students and intellectuals looked for workers' support, actors and actresses went to the factories to mobilize, and declarations were translated into foreign languages.

During the November mobilization, the discourse became more openly politicized, with calls for a new government emerging at the daily demonstrations. On 21 November, the prime minister met with spokespersons from student, artistic, and civic circles in search of a political rather than a military solution. On 24 November, Havel and Dubček spoke from a balcony, while a spirit of carnival spread on the streets. Politicization quickly produced the breakdown of the regime. Division within the party and misunderstanding of the strength of the opposition added up to the success of a two-hour general strike called on 27 November—which involved three quarters of the population.

Opposition groups and elites in disarray reacted, in fact, on a day-by-day basis, without much of a strategy. As the call for mobilization of a people's militia failed, mass demonstrations multiplied: among others, 200,000 rallied on Prague's Wenceslas Square on 20 November, growing to half a million on both 25 and 26 November (Humphrey 1990). This produced a sense of empowerment, reducing fear. The 30 November represented in fact a new turning point. As students marched, wearing nationalist signs, participants resorted to humour in order to diffuse tensions in encounters with the police. While slogans were addressed to party leaders ('Thank you, now leave'), this time the police did not intervene.

From the moral shock at the repression of the first protests to the feeling of empowerment produced by collective action, mobilization also spread quickly through the raising of powerful emotions. The Velvet Revolution, Ivan Havel recalled, 'was not regular politics. It was a very revolutionary situation, where the decisions were more or less made in a very often nondemocratic way. Somebody had an idea and immediately realized it without discussing it with the others. And then sometimes we spent hours and hours with the discussion of some issues' (Long 1996, 31). Another activist, Eda Krieova, described her involvement in CF as 'so natural. First of all, [the authorities] oppressed you. They didn't let you publish...I think life is something so precious that you are not allowed to let it be limited' (Long 1996, 69). Then, she recalled the intensity of the feelings of empowerment felt at the demonstrations: 'I was on National Street on the seventeen of November, because both of my daughters went there and I was so frightened I went also. But I lost them, of course, in this mess. And then a couple of days after I learned that Havel had founded Civic Forum, I called him and told him "I am at your disposal." And he said "will you come immediately?" and I came in half an hour' (Long 1996, 70). Excitement is thus recalled as bringing about an enhanced feeling of empowerment. As a participant remembered, 'it was a wonderful time in our lives. It was like a miracle. And we were full of euphoria and full of optimism. And we were thinking you can move the world. It was beautiful. I'm very happy I was there' (Long 1996, 71). Similarly, former dissident Dana Nemcova recalled the 'Initial euphoria, the enthusiasm of the whole society, the goodwill—is something that lasts a certain limited time period. Then things have to go back into their track, and that's another story' (Long 1996, 87).

Calls for a new government then provoked the 'unexpectedly swift resignation of the communist prime minister and Central Committee, and resulted in the formation of a new government led by the civic movements in which representatives of the old regime continued to hold positions of power, such as that of the prime minister. The key to the ability of the new movements to form a new government in a matter of weeks was the successful mobilization for the general strike that established their authority to speak for the "nation"' (Long 1996, 11–12). On 9 December, Premier Husak resigned, after agreeing to all protestors' requests (Urban 1990). The next day, twenty-three days after the first demonstration, a new government, with a non-communist majority, entered into office.

In sum, in the two Central and Eastern Europe (CEE) cases of eventful democratization, the mobilization for democracy had effects on the actors that mobilized. Starting from more focused concerns (such as the right to leave the country), the protests then grew in generality and became increasingly politicized, ending up with the call for the breakdown of the old regime. During spirals of protest and repression, moral shocks fuelled empowerment, as the mobilization capacity of the movement grew exponentially. Following the needs of the mobilization, organizations were created to coordinate protest, while specific places developed a strong capacity for aggregation of informal networks.

Eventful Democratization in The Arab Spring

During the Arab Spring, mobilization also developed through 'a heterogeneity of forms of action: general strikes, disruptive marches, political funerals, meetings and riots, but also guerrilla action. This heterogeneity is linked to the forms of politicization of the actors, on their preexisting networks, on the places in which they invest, the time they chose to mobilize' (Bannani-Chraibi and Fillieule 2012, 788). Collective action moved from below—little institutionalized and 'in any case, in dissonance with the oppositional political class and the direction of the unions' (Allal 2012, 827).

Eventful Democratization in Tunisia

The Tunisian Jasmine Revolution is clearly a case of eventful democratization. On 17 December, protests started in the peripheral region of Sidi Bouzid. The catalyst for mobilization was the suicide of Mohammad Bouazizi, who had set himself on fire in front of the regional office of the government. As Joseph Pugliese (2013, 7) noted,

> Bouazizi's incendiary act of revolt in the public street of Sidi Bouzid is tinder to the other citizens ground down by the violent practices of the Tunisian state. His sister, Leila Bouazizi, contextualizes his act of self-immolation within larger relations of state power and violence: 'What kind of repression do you imagine it takes for a young man to do this? A man who has to feed his family by buying goods on credit when they fine him . . . and take his goods. . . . In Sidi Bouzid, those with no connections and no money for bribes are humiliated and insulted and not allowed to live'.

Bouazizi's public suicide was interpreted as produced by a society in which some members were 'not allowed to live'. So, 'His self-immolation inflames a citizenry that is ready to revolt: "The fear had begun to melt away and we were a volcano that was going to explode," says Attia Athmouni, a union leader and official of the opposition Progressive Democratic Party in Sidi Bouzid. "And when Bouazizi burnt himself, we were ready" '(Pugliese 2013, 7).

While there had been other examples (for example, in March and August) of young people immolating themselves in front of government buildings, the new victim had relatives in the progressive party and in unions. A group of activists, supported by friends and relatives of the victim, promoted a sit-in in front of the regional government headquarters. An activist thus recalled those moments: 'So on Friday 17 December we gathered in front of the regional government building: hundreds of unionists and activists. We made a sit-in in front of the government building and stopped traffic, until 8 at night.... together with the unemployed; and friends of Bouazizi—all throwing oranges and other fruit at the regional government building' (Donker 2012b). While the police intervened to repress, young people responded in kind, as a new occurrence was noted: 'demonstrations organised at night to harass the security forces' (Ayeb 2011).

Self-immolation as a form of protest spread. On 22 January, another young person killed himself in Sidi, leaving a note that read: 'no more misery, no more unemployment'. This fuelled other protests, which became stronger after, on 24 January, two demonstrators were killed by police fire in Menzel Bouzaienne, a small town of 5,000 inhabitants. Social claims were central to the mobilization. In fact, 'the Tunisian revolution was started not by the middle class or in the northern urban centres, but by marginalised social groups (the southern mining region workers and the unemployed, particularly graduates) from southern regions, which themselves are suffering from economic, social, and political marginalisation. We had to wait till the beginning of January 2011 to see the middle class intervening actively in the revolutionary process' (Ayeb 2011, 468).

On 26 January, the mobilization grew in Kasserine and other cities. On 27 January 1,000 people demonstrated in Tunis, followed the next day by marches of lawyers, who remained in the street also later on (a national demonstration was held on 31 January). Immolations continued; from 3 January, the day schools reopened, and the day after, when Bouazizi died, protest fuelled protest, and repression fuelled repression.

Between 8 and 12 January, fifty demonstrators were killed by police, and half a dozen citizens killed themselves in protest. The massacres in Tala and Kasserine reinforced 'national solidarity and the radicalization of the movement—the slogans of which have become overtly political and directed against the government and the regime' (Habib 2011, 474). In these days, 'the movement propagation is made towards two directions: from the centre of the country to the south (Kebili, Tozeur, Douz, Ben Guerdane, Mednine) and to the north (Beja, Jendouba, Kef) and in the small towns which are peripheral to the coastal metropolis (Jebeniana near the city of Sfax)' (Habib 2011). On 10, 'January demonstrations reach the city of greater Tunis through neighbourhoods such as Ettadhamoun, Intilaka and Ibn Khaldoun, where most of the inhabitants, generally of modest means, come from poor or marginalised regions' (Habib 2011, 474). Between 11 and 14 January, violent fights—with several victims—broke out in Tunis. On 14 January 2011, a huge crowd gathered on Bourguiba Avenue, the main thoroughfare in Tunis, until the news arrived that Ben Ali had left the country.

Three days later, there were renewed protests against the new government led by Ben Ali's former prime minister. On 23 January, thousands of people occupied Tunis' Kasbah Square until the police intervention on 27 January, then returning on 20 February and remaining until 4 March, when the demands for a new government and free elections were met.

During these events, mechanisms developed that were similar to those in the GDR and Czechoslovakia. After the self-immolation, the activists aimed at a growth in generality and politicization of the protest discourse. Unionists (among them relatives of the victim) took the heavily wounded Mohammad to the hospital and formed a local committee, listing concrete proposals and calling on authorities to address the local economic problems. The national anthem was sung at the funeral. Fights with police developed on the following days. Critical of what they saw as bureaucratic, young people threw Molotov cocktails and sang slogans: 'work is a right, you band of thieves' (Hmed 2012, 810). Videos were uploaded on Facebook by students who, just back for winter holidays, participated en masse in the upheavals.

As protest spread to other towns and neighbouring regions like Kairouan, Sfax, and Ben Guerdane—with participation jumping from a few hundred to a few thousand—demands became more general in scope and increasingly politicized, bridging calls for social justice with those for political reforms. Local unions and oppositional parties mobilized from the very beginning. Throughout the protest, activists from opposition parties, student movements, and unions coordinated their efforts at the periphery. Inclusive umbrella social movement organizations helped to sustain the mobilization, organizing meetings and issuing press releases and explanatory documents.

Emotions became more and more intense during these days. As at the beginning of January, the movement reached Kasserine, where lawyers and unionists demonstrated together, with heavy repression leading to broadened protests as moral shock fed mobilization. The Lawyers' National Council then became a leading force in the protest. On 8 January, four people were killed there with bullets in the back. This was the first time the police had shot to kill since the 1984 riots, and the number of protestors killed reached fifty by 12 January (Beinin and Vairel 2011b).

A week after it began, protest reached Tunis, with a few hundred union members, student activists, and representatives of the opposition converging in front of the UGTT (Tunisian General Labour Union) building in the capital to show solidarity with those who had mobilized throughout the week, denouncing heavy police repression and calling for better economic development and political reforms (but not the end of the regime). Posters read '*al-huriya, karama, wataniya*' (Freedom, dignity and nationalism), and '*as-sharal Istihqaq*' (Work is a Right) (Donker 2012b). However, it was not until 8 January that mobilization also developed in the capital city, after, over the two preceding days, the police killed about twenty people (Allal and Geisser 2011). Politicization increased, calling for the fall of the regime—this caused 'shock waves through the country as the city was deemed "liberated" and providing encouragement for protests throughout the country' (Donker 2012b).

On 4 January, the national leaders of the union UGTT declared their support for the protest, even calling for a national strike on 14 January, with previous general strikes in particular regions. Overnight between 10 and 11 January, massive protests erupted in the city centre; protestors clashed with the police and continued to do so, with increasing brutality, in the following days. On the day of the national strike, tens of thousands marched peacefully to the Ministry of Interior. As a demonstrator recalled, empowerment developed out of moral shock:

> ...there were huge crowds gathered here, at the Avenue Bourghiba, in front of the Ministry of Interior. And there were lines of police between the ministry and the protesters. People were pushing with increasing strength. [. ..] Apparently the story had gone around that there was a standoff at the Ministry of Interior. Some youngsters came on mopeds, drove through the crowds and straight into the police. This is when the clashes started. I was standing here [hundred meters from the ministry] and saw it happening: they were just aiming and shooting straight into the protesters. This is when you realize you can die at any moment. The strange thing is, at a day like that, you just don't care (cit. in Donker 2012b).

In the evening, as President Ben Ali left the country,

> street battles erupted and regular police, army and security forces loyal to Ben Ali were fighting each other. Dozens of civilians were shot randomly by snipers loyal to the security forces of Ben Ali. It took until the beginning of February for the situation to stabilize and basic security to return with almost 3000 members of the political police being arrested by the army. Despite these arrests, violent clashes continued in the periphery (particularly al-Kef, Gafsa and Qabla) throughout February between police and youngsters aiming to destroy and arson police stations (Donker 2012b).

Repression did not stop the protest, which was instead fuelled by feelings of injustice. As tens of thousands of demonstrators continued to ask for the dissolution of the former ruling party, for the end of the interim government, and for democracy, on 28 January 2011 Premier Mohamad Ghannouchi removed the ministers of the ruling party, while the unions promised their support for the new government. As Teije Donker (2012b) summarized,

> After the exit of Ben Ali a mobilization wave rolled over the country. This wave was highly fragmented: all kinds of specific groups mobilized around (material) grievances: the police wanted increases in their pay, journalists demanded improved media, people protested around the country in front of regional state offices to claim their right to work, (wildcat) strikes demanded higher wages for factory workers, etc. They would continue well into the consolidation phase, after the elections of 23 October 2011.... The UGTT itself was in disarray for much of this period, rendering any kind of effective management over its local branch organizations limited.

Some formal and informal mechanisms of coordination developed, with the intensification of the protest. In mid-February, protests continued to push for a new government, free elections, punishment of those responsible for the police killings, and inclusion of civil society in the reform process. As the oppositional parties and human rights organizations joined the protest, on 20 February an encampment was set up at Kasbah Square, functioning as a point of aggregation where protestors converged from all over the country. On 25 February there were half a million of them, asking for a new government. The next day, the police charged as protestors tried to enter the Ministry of Interior; five people were killed in violent clashes which continued well into the night. On the next morning, however, Mohammad Ghanoushi resigned and a new government was formed.

After Ben Ali left, a slogan read, 'Nothing will be as before' (Allal 2012). The encampment was slowly disbanded, but protest remerged from time to time—for instance as, in mid-July, a social movement of young people and human rights activists camped again in Kasbah Square calling for more civil society inclusion (especially, of young people) in the transition process, farther-reaching reforms, and the punishment of those involved in the repression of the protest over the previous months.

Eventful Democratization in Egypt

The successful example of Tunisia inspired protests for democracy in Egypt. Since 2007, dissidents organized counter police day—this also happened, with unexpected success, on 25 January 2011. Spontaneous demonstrations followed over the next two days, with confrontations with the police. On 28 January, a Friday of Rage was called for, with various demonstrations starting from mosques and churches. While the police attacked the protestors with teargas, the protestors attacked police headquarters as well as the headquarters of the regime party, the NDP (National Democratic Party) (el-Chazli and Hassabo 2013, 203). From then on, the camps in Tahrir Square attracted more and more people, while social media allowed intense participation also at a distance as mobile phones were used to take pictures, to be then uploaded on the web (Howard and Hussain 2013, 29). A shift in the balance of power between the regime and its critics was produced then by 'four continuous days of street fighting, January 25–28, that pitted the people against police all over the country' (el-Ghobashy 2011). From 1 February various Million Marches were called for.

The mainstream narrative links the beginning of the successful, mainly peaceful revolution to the demonstration against torture and police brutality called for by the Facebook group 'We Are All Khaled Said' on 25 January, the National Police Day. The call was immediately supported by members of various youth groups such as the April 6 Youth Movement, the Coalition to Support el-Baradei, the youth wing of the Democratic Front party, and the Justice and Freedom movement. When it emerged on 29 December, the proposal of a mass demonstration on 25 January initially had little resonance; but it spread quickly beginning on 14 January, the day Ben Ali left Tunisia. In Warkotsch's reconstruction,

> On the day itself, what was expected to be a larger than usual demonstration, but nonetheless a singular event, for the first time managed to gather huge masses oftentimes spontaneously from the neighborhoods, which they passed through. In between the 25th and the 28th, protests erupted in a number of Egyptian cities, which turned fiercely violent in the case of Suez, where battles with the police ensued for days to avenge the death of protesters (Warkotsch 2012, 3–4).

In fact, the protest called for 25 January 2011 found broad resonance in a politically charged atmosphere (partly because of the Alexandria church bombing on 1 January and subsequent fights between police and Coptic protestors), while 'unwittingly, the regime itself provided the calendar date for the "day of rage," having designated 25 January a bank holiday to mark Police Day. The holiday freed up citizens for assembly, practically inviting them to convert the official celebration into a popular harangue against police rule'. In action, the social and political basis for the protest broadened, as various collective actors, from workers from Mahalla to Sinai and from civil servants to supporters of national football teams joined in (Warkotsch 2012).

This broadening was not predicted by either the organizers or the police. In el-Ghobashy's (2011) words, 'The January 25 protest started as a midsize demonstration and ended as a massive uprising against autocratic rule. But no one leaving their house that morning knew that they were stepping into the largest policing failure of Mubarak's tenure. The uprising was forged in the heat of street fighting, unanticipated both by its hopeful strategists and its watchful adversaries.' As an organizer of el-Baradei's campaign told him,

'We went out to protest that day and expected to be arrested in the first ten minutes, just like usual', and police confirmed that they expected a 'normal situation' (el-Ghobashy 2011).

It was in fact the very success of the protest on 25 January that produced an acceleration in the mobilization, involving actors that had not participated on that day—including oppositional parties as well as the Muslim Brotherhood joined in (el-Ghobashy 2011). Over the next days, protest grew stronger and stronger, as

> ...a majestic scene unfolded all over Egypt. Grand processions of thousands upon thousands of people in every province made their way to the abodes of the oppressive forces that controlled their lives. Beckoning those watching from their windows, they chanted, 'Our people, our people, come and join us!' When the crowds reached town and city centers, they encircled police stations, provincial government buildings and NDP headquarters, the triad of institutions emblematic of the regime. The syncopated chorus that had travelled from Sidi Bouzid to Tunis now shook the Egyptian earth: 'The people...want...to overthrow the regime!' (el-Ghobashy 2011).

Marches often started from mosques, after common prayers, growing on their way towards symbols of power.

The brutality shocked the citizens, but it enraged them more than scaring them. In Charles Kurzman's words, what happened was a 'sudden prominence of bravery—the ineffably but potentially influential desire to engage in risky protest' (2012, 377). Activists appeal to demonstration pointed in fact at the need to 'be brave,' and bravery became a mobilizing disposition. As repression during this exceptional time resonated with the everyday experience of harassment, the police were finally 'rendered inefficient by the dynamism and stamina of exceptionally diverse crowds, each with their own know-how in the art of interfacing with gendarmes' (el-Ghobashy 2011). As a demonstrator explained, 'I went out to buy some hashish and then, my friend, I saw that the demonstrations were really there. I couldn't believe it'. He then went to call his cousin, saying 'this time is true'. After being tear-gassed for the first time in his life, 'he went back to Tahrir on the next day, the 28th, still with his cousin' (el-Chazli 2012, 857).

The police use of tear gas, rubber bullets, and even live ammunition (as well as stones, when other weapons were no longer available) produced moral shocks. In just four days, 365 citizens and thirty-two police officers died and ninety-nine police stations as well as 3,000 vehicles were attacked, while government offices and symbols of the regime were stormed. Repression involved more than brutal charges. By 27 January, the police officials had devised

> ...a comprehensive scheme to cut off physical and virtual means of linkage. They ordered a shutdown of Internet and cellular phone service for the next day; cell

phones were especially important for demonstrators to spread news of protest diffusion in real time, and to share spot instructions or eleventh-hour location changes. Cairo was sealed off from the provinces and put under lockdown. All of the arteries and bridges leading into Tahrir Square from east and west were closed to traffic—even to pedestrians. Additional Metro stops were closed, not just the two nearest the square. And mosques were carefully primed in advance. The 'Umar Makram mosque in Tahrir was ordered shuttered. Friday preachers all over the country were instructed to deliver sermons denouncing assembly and disobedience of the ruler. At the Giza mosque where Mohamed ElBaradei was set to attend prayer before joining the protests, the preacher of 20 years was replaced with a government pick. For their part, the youth groups and opposition forces coordinating the protest added new locations and reacquainted themselves with landlines to cope with the cellular shutdown (el-Ghobashy 2011).

Empowerment built upon the protestors' acquired skills to bypass repression. As el-Ghobashy (2011) recalls in a careful day-by-day reconstruction of the events, on 25 January new technologies had already been used to organize the protest, circumventing repressive moves:

> Zero hour, as announced by protest organizers, was to be 2 pm. The stated plan was to demonstrate in front of the Interior Ministry and then disband at 5 pm. Security forces therefore sealed off all the vital downtown streets leading to and from the Ministry, allowing pedestrians to pass only after checking ID cards. But it was a ruse. On the morning of January 25, organizers used cell phones and landlines to disseminate the real locations of the protests and the actual start time: noon.

As an organizer explained, 'The protest locations announced on Facebook and to the press were the major landmarks. The idea was to start marching down small side streets and pick up people along the way, so that by the time demonstrators reached the announced locations, they would be large crowds that security couldn't corral' (el-Ghobashy 2011). Later on, the shutdown of the internet was overcome by the use of several other means of communication, such as satellite broadcast of tweets, radio to people, leaflets, while Anonymous (hackers) threatened to punish media corporations that cooperated with dictators (Dunn 2011). An analysis of the origin of YouTube videos indicates a large capacity for citizens' journalism to spread critical knowledge.[7]

Repressive attempts proved increasingly unsuccessful as the spread of mobilization fuelled the feeling of empowerment. So, 'on the 28th of January, in

---

[7] Especially at the beginning of the protest, protestors' videos were more significant in terms of quantity and number of views than professional ones were (Nanabhay and Farmanfarmaian 2011, 585). This was particularly true on days such as 2 February, the battle of Tahrir. In addition, the most widespread videos are those which are less elaborated, simply letting the pictures speak (Nanabhay and Farmanfarmaian 2011).

Cairo alone, hundreds of thousands of protesters marched on the streets, chanting the by now well known slogan that united their demands, from economic to political—"the people want the overthrow of the regime"' (Dunn 2011). Here as well, the events mobilized various social and political groups that had grown in opposition to the dictatorship for many years.

As with the encampment in Tunis, the one in Tahrir Square—set up on 25 January by about 50,000 protestors, growing to 250,000 by 31 January and one million by 1 February, and continuing until 11 February 2011, when President Mubarak stepped down—assumed an aggregative function, becoming all the more relevant as the regime blocked internet communication. In the Egyptian history of contention, Tahrir had a symbolic role: it had been the location for sit-ins by students in 1972, it was the site of the bread intifada in 1977, and it was occupied for two days during the protests against the war on Iraq in 2003, as well as being the arrival point for many demonstrations. This symbolic value was strengthened during the protest. On 28 January, when the day of rage was particularly violent, the square developed into a free space (el-Chazli 2012). Tahrir Square became a magnet as, in the words of an activist, 'people simply knew they needed to go to Tahrir'. So, as Gerbaudo noted, 'The square rather than the internet became the main coordination platform of the revolutionary movement'. Reacting to the communication shutdown, people established a permanent sit-in in Tahrir, effectively building a centre for aggregation and public debate. As an activist recalled: 'when they shut down the internet they brought back the people together in a way they never even imagined' (Gerbaudo 2012, 69). Face to face relations then substituted for 'virtual ones'.

At Tahrir—defined as the largest open air exhibition (Findlay 2012)—intense feelings developed. On the 28th, the intensification of emotions brought an acceleration of history, with a cognitive shift from a language of demonstration to a language of revolution (el-Chazli 2012). In a participant's words, 'I'm so very happy, so very happy. Look how beautiful' (el-Chazli 2012, 860). Another recalled, 'It was one of the most profound moments of my life. The sight of the square filled with tens of thousands heralded the long-awaited dawn. As we entered the square, the crowds installed there cheered the coming of a new battalion, greeting us with joy. I wept' (cit. in el-Ghobashy 2011). Tahrir has been described as 'the square that sings, dances, cries and hopes' (Guibal and Tangi 2011, 39), as 'Tahir vibre, Tahir exulte' (Guibal and Tangi 2011, 40).

Cognitive mechanisms of frame bridging were important to broaden the mobilization capacity of protestors. During the demonstrations, slogans such as 'bread, freedom, and dignity', as well as 'the people want the removal of the regime', were shouted along the way, and bystanders were called to join in. With the creation of a protest camp, Tahrir Square became the heart of the mobilization, 'participants ranging from Cairo's poor to middle and upper class people, across the political spectrum, as well as across religious divides' (Warkotsch 2012).

Emotional reactions were accompanied by cognitive processes, as 'Tahrir was not all fun and festivity. The space was also infused with serious politics: fierce battles were waged against government thugs trying to break in, fiery speeches were delivered denouncing the regime, and animated discussions about Egypt's political future resounded in the night air' (Shokr 2012, 43). Interactions developed in the many Tahrir squares that were built all over Egypt. There were political speeches, but also an atmosphere of permanent parties ('like a night of Ramadan'). There was talk of the old Egypt (before the 15th), and obsessive, if ironic references to the revolution (revolutionary eating, revolutionary hunger, revolutionary joints). There were podiums for speakers, and an island in the square with tents. Thousands of posters showed much use of humour. An activist reminded us that, while there, 'We had no idea that the world was following us, we had no idea of what the media was saying, what the TV was saying, what Al-Jazeera was reporting, what the people in the streets were doing...we were living in another dimension' (Gerbaudo 2012, 69). The heterogeneity of the participants there was mentioned with pride—'people of different backgrounds, of different classes, just sitting together talking' (Gerbaudo 2012, 69).

Carried by intense emotions and cognitive transformation, protest spread from Cairo into the periphery, through formal and informal communication networks. Large demonstrations took place, with different degrees and forms of repression outside the capital city as well. During the protest, Tahrir became a model in other regions, where the police were most hostile and corrupt, and people tired of harassment. During the days of the upheaval, the activists formed citizens' committees, as self-help groups, rather than political organizations, but in conflict with corrupt local institutions. A member of one such committee thus described his reaction to the Tahrir revolution: 'I cannot describe my joy...we were waiting for something to happen but ever expected that it would be a revolution of this sort. It surprised us as much as it surprised the world. And it was not just what happened in Tahrir square: in every village and in every hamlet of every village was another square like Tahrir' (cit. in Abu-Lughod 2012, 25).

Cognitive processes of politicization and growth in generality thus developed out of the mobilization itself, as:

> When protesters arrived at Tahrir on January 29, they did not come with the intention of creating a radical utopia....In many ways, Tahrir had come to represent the overall decline of public space—people could barely congregate or mingle, let alone protest—under Mubarak's thirty-year rule. The commune that Tahrir was to become was wholly improvised through the lived experience of

sharing the area and protecting it from the regime encroachment. As the revolution unfolded, Tahrir was elevated from a rally site to a model for an alternative society (Shokr 2012, 42).

In a society characterized by gated communities for the rich and slums for the masses of poor, the clean-up but also the painting of murals represented a reappropriation of public space, especially after thirty years of emergency law had prevented gatherings (Winegard 2012).

Coordination built up gradually. It was after the killing of Khaled that Ghonim, a young liberal and devoted Muslim, began a blog. His model in planning the campaign was a multi-step 'sales tunnel': 'The first phase was to convince people to join the page and read its posts. The second was to convince them to start interacting with the content by "liking" and "commenting" on it. The third was to get them to participate in the page's online campaign and to contribute to its content themselves. The fourth and final phase would occur when people decided to take the activism onto the streets. This was my ultimate aspiration' (Ghonim 2012, 67–8, cit. in Gerbaudo 2012, 56). Bloggers thus came to network, meeting face-to-face in demonstrations, and also established a reputation for trustworthiness as well as linkages with mass media (some of them were also journalists) (De Angelis 2011).[8] To coordinate the 25 January protest, a Revolutionary Youth Coalition gathered activists from 6 April, the revolutionary socialists, el-Baradei's National Association for Change, and some young dissidents from the Muslim Brotherhood. In fact, as an activist noted, the march

was much more organised than people in the West think. There were several meeting places and phone numbers and mobile numbers for the lawyers. The 6th of April group played a particularly important role in coordinating events on the ground. They set up a 'war-room' in an office nearby Tahrir square from which they would coordinate activists in the different marches. Moreover, in anticipation of the 25th, they organised a series of rehearsal demonstrations in popular neighborhoods to experiment with different tactics and test the reaction of the people on the streets. Activists also tried to convince established opposition groups to join them. While the Muslim Brotherhood and all other opposition parties initially turned down the invitation, key figures in the ultras pledged their support (Gerbaudo 2012, 61).

---

[8] A survey of 1,200 Tahrir participants (with a mean age of 28.5) interviewed in February 2011 indicated that 80 per cent had internet access at home and 52 per cent through their phones. In addition, 35 per cent had previous involvement in politics—8 per cent in unions, 6 per cent in parties, 11 per cent in charities, 9 per cent in SMOs. Of those interviewed, 82 per cent used phones and 52 per cent used a Facebook account to communicate about the protest. Half of them had heard about Tahrir from face-to-face communication, 28 per cent from Facebook, 13 per cent by phone, and only 3 per cent from television. Participation on the first day was predicted by internet access at home and using Facebook, Twitter, blogs, and printed media. About 48 per cent had disseminated visuals, 25 per cent on Facebook (Tufekci and Wilson 2012).

While the internet was important, mobilization increased only when the opposition decided to move beyond virtual protest. So, activists expressed the need to do something, which would allow them to get out of their own circle. Action in the streets included 'silent stands'—a sort of flash mob, with people convening in the city centre and standing in silence in some public areas.

Intense emotions, often recalled in the very names given to protests ('day of rage', for instance), played an important role from the very beginning. The blog devoted to Khaled was particularly effective in catalysing strong feelings. Written in the first person, as if Khaled were speaking himself, it built on his figure as a martyr, while videos on police abuse and torture targeted the police as a common enemy. In the words of an activist, 'Ours was first and foremost a hate for police. . . . The police represented everything that was wrong with Egyptian society'. In fact, as Gerbaudo observed, 'Different categories of people had different reasons for harbouring this anger. Football "ultras"—fans of popular clubs like Zamalek and el-Ahly—hated the police because of the frequent clashes after matches. Microbus drivers hated them for being constantly targeted with arbitrary road fines, with which officers were topping up their miserable salaries. Young people resented them because of random searches and harassment' (2012, 59).

Emotionally, protest appeals needed to overcome despair ('I had lost all trust in this country', said an activist) as well as anti-political sentiments ('Myself, politics. . . no thanks. . . those habits, full of police around, and then, end. That told me nothing', said another [el-Chazli 2012, 857]). The mobilization of personal networks in the liberated spaces was very important in this regard—an activist thus recalled the beginning of his commitment: 'I didn't really want to go, in general I'm not interested by such things. But on the 26th, there are people that I like, from the neighborhood, who had come back from Tahrir, with torn clothes and black eyes. Just kids. I was a bit of a model for them in the neighborhood. So I felt ashamed' (el-Chazli 2012, 857).

During the mobilization, messages targeted in particular the fear that had kept people away from demonstrations on other occasions, through statements like 'I'm not a coward, I demonstrate'. Activist Asmaa Mafhouz, in her famous YouTube video, even played on a macho stereotype to invite participants to the protest:

> If you think yourself a man, come with me on 25 January. Whoever says women shouldn't go to protests because they will get beaten, let him have some honor and manhood and come with me on 25 January. Whoever says it is not worth it because there will only be a handful of people, I want to tell him, 'You are the reason behind this, and you are a traitor, just like the president or any security cop who beats us in the streets'(Gerbaudo 2012, 63).

In action and through action, organizational coordination also brought about a social broadening of the protests, which implied the bridging of calls

59

for democracy and calls for social justice. It was in fact during the eighteen days of the revolutionary situation that young people shifted from apathy to politicization (el-Chazli 2012). Besides the need to go into the streets, young middle class activists also felt a need to link with the working class. In his Facebook account, Ghonim warned that 'reaching working class Egyptians is not going to happen through the Internet and Facebook', calling on people to 'get out' and 'spread out to streets, factories, mosques, and churches', and 'especially in poor areas.... We all should move to the streets now and lessen the usage of Facebook' in order 'to reach the other 60 million people who don't have [access to the] Internet'. His feelings were shared by many other young people. In an activist's account, 'The people of the Internet and the Facebook activists, they went to speak with the normal people who are without Internet'. Ahmed Sabry recounts how 'before the 25th we were leafleting, and distributing flyers and talking to people. Myself I went to have a haircut and I convinced everyone in the barber shop that we are going on the 25th' (Gerbaudo 2012). As noted in the incipit, the importance of the broadening of the social basis as well as the empowering power of action itself is reflected in the choice of some specific protest forms.

New technologies supported exchanges of information, in what Bennet and Segerberg (2013) call connective action. The role of new media was particularly relevant before and during the Egyptian uprising. It enabled 'cyberactivism, which was a major trigger for street activism; encouraging civic engagement, through aiding the mobilization and organization of protests and other forms of political expression; and promoting a new form of citizen journalism, which provides a platform for ordinary citizens to express themselves and document their own versions of reality' (Khamis and Vaughn 2011). Different new media were used in different ways. Facebook allowed for the spreading of information from (virtual) friend to (virtual) friend, as it is a social network enabling the sending of messages to thousands of people, 'with the added benefit that those receiving the messages were already interested and trusted the source' (Idle and Nunns 2011, 20). 'We Are All Khaled Said', founded by Google executive Wael Ghonim and named, as mentioned, after a young activist killed by the police, already had a Facebook page with over 350,000 members before 14 January 2011. The National Coalition for Change used Facebook, Twitter, and YouTube to send text messages, such as 'Look what is happening in Tunisia'. Ghonim invited 'We Are All Khaled Said' Facebook members to protest on 25 January; within three days more than 50,000 people responded that they would attend. Within Facebook, the pages of April 6 Youth Movement and Kolona Khaled Said, as well as those of high-profile individuals (such as Mohamed el-Baradei, Aida Seif-al-Dawla, or Hossam el-Hamalawy), were not only meeting points particularly instrumental in mobilizing youth, but also contributed to the circulation of many SMSs, e-mails, Tweets, and Facebook posts (Aouragh and Alexander 2011, 1348). In a virtuous circle, as the use of social media increased during the mobilization: 'Facebook became something one had to have. Egypt gained more than 600,000 new Facebook users between January and February 2011 alone. On the day the Internet switched back on (February 2), 100,000 users joined this social networking space and it became the most accessed website in the country (followed by YouTube and Google), and aljazeera. net saw an incredible increase in page views and search attempts' (Aouragh and Alexander 2011, 1348).

The blogging service Twitter (with 175 million registered users in 2010) allowed participants to post their comments and 'tweet' about specific subjects, including hashtags (such as #Jan25 for Egypt or #sidibouzid for Tunisia) that permitted users to launch as well as to follow protest events. In the very first week of the protest, as many as 1.5 million Egypt-related tweets were counted (Aouragh and Alexander 2011), in many cases allowing for contact between activists and foreign journalists (Lotan et al. 2011). The #Jan25 hashtag produced up to twenty-five tweets per minute during the day of the protest (Lotan et al. 2011).

Digitally encoded video, audio, or text were uploaded on the internet, aggregated by topic and by type. YouTube allowed, for instance, the uploading of user-created content, including self-made videos. Particularly influential was the mentioned call to action from a YouTube video posted by activist Asmaa Mahfouz that stated, 'If you stay home, you deserve all that's being done to you, and you will be guilty before your nation and your people. Go down to the street, send SMSes, post it on the 'Net, make people aware' (Wall and el-Zahed 2011).

Materials produced by activists were also collected and made public. An activist recalled:

> We built a media camp in Tahrir Square. It was two tents, and we were around five or six technical friends with their laptops, memory-readers, hard disks. We had all physical means with us and we hung a sign in Arabic and English on the tent itself saying, 'Focal point to gather videos and pictures from people in the street'. And we received a huge amount of videos and pictures and then we go back online and keep posting them online. In the first few hours, I gathered 75 gigabytes of pictures and videos from people in the streets' (Aouragh and Alexander 2011).

Social media were also used to reduce the risks of repression (for example through tools such as Hotspot Shield and Tor, which protect the anonymity of the user), as well as spreading information about how to improve security and calling for attention when in danger (Eltantawy and Wiest 2011, 1215). Creative responses were given to the regime's ban on internet and mobile phone access (from 28 January 2011 and for about five days): by tweeting the websites of proxy servers; setting up FTP (file transfer protocol) accounts to transmit videos to international media; 'using landlines to connect to internet services in neighboring countries by calling international numbers with older dial-up modems'; even resorting 'to using Morse code, fax machines, and ham radio to get the word out about events on the ground'. The website of the group We Rebuild transcribed transmissions from Egyptian amateur radio stations; resources for circumventing the blackout were published; there was the smuggling of 'satellite phones and satellite modems into Egypt, which did not depend on Egypt's infrastructure to function' (Khamis and Vaughn 2011). Blogs gave advice about how to use dial-up on mobile phones and laptops, also suggesting that users connect to the internet service provider Noor, which was left operational as it was used by the Egyptian stock exchange and Western companies. To facilitate communication by protestors, some of its subscribers even removed their passwords for wi-fi access. When the Al Jazeera television channel in Cairo was shot, people started watching the station via Hotbird and Arabsat. Citizens also continued to tweet by calling friends abroad and asking them to tweet their messages or using the 'speak to tweet' tool provided by some engineers from Twitter, Google, and SayNow, which transformed voice transmissions into Twitter messages (Eltantawy and Wiest 2011). With some irony, one blog stated: 'great news, blackout not affecting morale in Cairo, veteran activists from 60s and 70s giving advice on how to do things predigital #Jan25' (Jamal 2012).

As repression increased the politicization of the protest, the regime oscillated between the carrot and the stick: traditional repression was mixed with concessions, such as, on 29 January, the dismissal of the Nazif government—one of the main targets of the protest—and the appointment of his former security chief, Omar Suleiman, as first vice president of Egypt. While the police withdrew from the streets, the military appeared in and outside Cairo. On 1 February, Mubarak promised liberal constitutional amendments and committed not to run in the upcoming presidential elections, instead guiding a peaceful transition process in the six months until the elections took place. In this way, 'while the numbers protesting in Cairo and other cities at points approached millions of Egyptians (some say about 12 million were involved overall), the President managed to garner the support of not a few. Events on the following day would, however, shift the balance again back in favour of the protests, when the by now famous "battle of the camel" saw the largely peaceful anti-regime protests in Tahrir attacked by pro-Mubarak supporters on horses and camels armed with knives, sticks, and clubs' (Warkotsch 2012).

On 5 February, the president's son and supposed successor, Gamal Mubarak, resigned, together with the leadership of the ruling National Democratic Party. The subsequent release from prison (after twelve days of detention) of activist Wael Ghonim, from the group 'We are all Khaled Said', increased popular sympathy for the protestors. Especially on 7 and 8 February, the largest crowds since the beginning of the revolution converged in Tahrir Square. It was the call for a general strike on the following day that strengthened the protestors and gave a final blow to the regime. In fact, many observers suggested that the workers' involvement in the protest, by paralysing the economy, actually pushed the military to de-align itself from the regime (Warkotsch 2012).

It was, in fact, after new mass demonstrations on 11 February that Mubarak did finally step down. Protests actually continued well after that date, focusing on social issues and against corruption, and various commissions of inquiry were established.[9]

In sum, in the two Arab cases of eventful democratization, the protest catalysed existing streams of collective action (from labour mobilization to human rights), bringing about cognitive mechanisms of growth in generality and politicization. In both countries, the occupied public spaces, such as the Kasbah in Tunisia and Tahrir Square in Egypt, constituted public spheres in which aggregation happened. At the same time, coordinating committees developed, accompanying the different steps of the protest. Moments of extraordinary politics, the protests were fuelled by and, at the same time, fuelled moral shocks and a sense of empowerment.

Eventful Democratization: A Summary

Eventful democratization appears as sudden and unexpected, not only to observers or dictators, but also often to the very activists who mobilize against the authoritarian regimes. This difficulty in prediction is linked to agency and contingency: intense protest events are indeed under-determined moments as structural constraints are, if not overcome, at least weakened by the very capacity of mobilization to quickly transform relations. As Kurzman suggested in his analysis of the Iranian revolution, estimations of participation cannot be known in advance as 'they shift drastically from moment to moment on the basis of amorphous rumours, heightened emotions, and conflicting senses of duty' (Kurzman 2004, 170).

Although under different external conditions, similar causal mechanisms were at work in the days of eventful democratization in the four cases I have analysed. As mentioned, previous literature has stressed changes in individual preferences, or better, in the propensity to express them in public. In

---

[9] The NGO Awlad al-Ard collected information on nearly a thousand protest events between January and July 2011, half of them occurring in February.

Table 2.1 Mechanisms in eventful democratization

Cognitive	Emotional	Relational
Growth in generalization	Moral shock	Networking
Politicization	Empowerment	Aggregating

Kuran's account, the East European regimes were more vulnerable than they seemed, as 'Millions were prepared to stand up in defiance if ever they sensed that this was sufficiently safe. The people's solidarity with their leaders would then have been exposed as illusory, stripping the veneer of legitimacy from the communist monopoly on power'. The development of the events then also shifted the preferences of those who supported the regime in private, but with increasing doubts. In a similar analysis, Karl Opp and his collaborators suggested that political events themselves changed the structure of individual incentives due to increasing dissatisfaction and perceived political influence, plus social incentives. So, 'an increase in protest may therefore have caused many individuals who hadn't protested before to view action as a "must"' (Opp, Voss, and Gern 1995, 195).

Following the social movement literature, I have instead looked at causal mechanisms at the collective level (see Table 2.1). From the point of view of relational mechanisms, coordination (more structured but also less so) occurred in action, linked to the daily needs of the mobilization itself. In action, cognitive mechanisms developed also: there was, here as well, a growth in generality of the claims and a politicization of the discourse. Emotional mechanisms were also at work, intensifying positive ties of solidarity among protestors, and transforming fear into rage.

Similar mechanisms developed in other intense moments of protest for democracy. In 1989, in China, not only did protest bring about organizational coordination, as in the creation of a coordinating body of autonomous student unions, but the occupation of the square provided a space where people could autonomously converge, without the need for specific calls. So, according to Craig Calhoun's insightful analysis,

> When students seized Tiananmen, they seized a powerful, multivocal symbol. The Square spoke at once of the government, which used it to display its power, and of the people, who gathered there to acclaim official leaders. It linked the Imperial Palace to revolutionary monuments; it represented the center of China. But by their action the students transformed the meaning of the square: its popular side became dominant....For a time, the students also made Tiananmen Square into a genuine place of public discussion (Calhoun 1994, 196).

Indeed, these reflections point at the role of agency as the necessary complement of structures. If protests in eventful temporality change the structure of relations, this does not mean that contextual characteristics are not important in influencing the timing and fate of the mobilization for democracy. As Craig Calhoun observed in his analysis of the 1989 protests in China, 'Underlying conditions make a movement possible, but they do not make the movement happen...movements are products of human action...the action in social movements consists also of choices made in the heat of struggle, decisions made on the run' (1994, 19).

In sum, while protest is a resource that some groups utilize to put pressure upon decision-makers, it should not be viewed in purely instrumental terms (see for this Taylor and van Dyke 2004). During the course of a protest, both time and money are invested in risky activities, yet often resources of solidarity can be created (or re-created). Many forms of protest 'have profound effects on the group spirit of their participants', since 'in the end there is nothing as productive of solidarity as the experience of merging group purposes with the activities of everyday life' (Rochon 1998, 115), as protest promotes a sense of collective identity, which is a condition for collective action (Pizzorno 1993). For workers, strikes and occupations represent not only instruments for collective pressure, but also arenas in which a sense of community is formed (Fantasia 1988); this is also true of student occupations of schools and universities (Ortoleva 1988) or in squatted youth centres. The same can be said of the marches in 1989 and the camps in 2011.

In 1989, as during the Arab Spring, what has been called a relational process of subversion developed, made up of various sequences of multi-sector mobilization and political fluidity (Bennani-Chraibi and Fillieule 2012). Some differences are nevertheless worth noting. The events took more dramatic turns in the second than in the first wave. Even though in all the cases the prevalence of non-violent forms of protest has often been mentioned, in the Arab Spring—as the crude indicator of the number of demonstrators' deaths dramatically testifies—there was a more significant escalation. At the same time, the transition to democracy was faster and less disputed after the 1989 wave than after the 2011 one.

In the following chapters, I shall provide some explanations for both similarities and differences. As we will see, even if resources need to be mobilized and opportunities appropriated, their presence and perception cannot be underestimated. In fact, an in-depth look at the eventful moments of democratization also allows us to see, as through a magnifying lens, the ways in which temporalities other than the eventful one also play a role in the development and outcome of episodes of democratization from below.

3

Mobilizing Resources for Democracy

Introduction

First accounts of revolutions—and even of waves of protest—are often influenced by the so-called 'immaculate conception syndrome' (Rupp and Taylor 1987): they seem to come from nowhere, and develop suddenly and 'spontaneously'. However, research has also found that, rather than coming from the Virgin Mary, new movements buildupon previous movements, which help in structuring the mobilization.

The issue of an organized versus a spontaneous process was indeed central in the (political and scientific) debate on 1989 in the GDR. Research such as that of Opp, Voss, and Gern (1989) downplayed the role of civil society organizations, emphasizing instead the rationality of individual exiters. Other scholars countered that those who stress the individual mechanisms of changing preferences 'may overestimate the spontaneity of the protest of October 9 by overlooking the role of the dissidents in providing elementary means of coordination' (Pfaff 2006, 126). Moreover, as Pfaff noted, 'the evidence suggests that ordinary citizens did not join the mass demonstration in a disorderly fashion. It appears that informal groups provided vehicles for mobilization. A citizen's willingness to protest may be based less on formal organizational ties than on the support of family, friends and acquaintances' (Pfaff 2006, 129).

The capacity of the civil society organizations to lead the protest varied, however, in time and space. In the GDR, dissident groups and protest seemed to move together in only one specific moment of the transition period: the one that started in October and ended with the fallof the Wall on 9 November 1989. After that date, the main civil rights organizations lost ground. If, on 25 September, demonstrators carried 'we stay here' banners and on 9 October they stated 'we are the people', on 9 November the slogan of the mass protests shifted to 'Wir sind ein Volk' (We are one people), indicating support for reunification, a position that the dissidents tended to oppose (Jessen 2009).

This emerges clearly if we look at the evolution of the most influential of the social movement organizations during the transition: the NF. The great increase in mass participation in the autumn of 1989 was unexpected for NF which, after its foundation in September 1989, planned its first meeting for December. Even though the NF was initially weak in mobilization capacity, particularly in Leipzig, during the Montagsdemos in October its popularity reached a peak. About ten thousand mobilized at NF's first political rally in Leipzig on 18 November.

By then, demands were already radicalizing among protestors. Protestors were mostly not members of oppositional groups, and they shared less and less NF's hopes for reform socialism and their call for collaboration with party reformers. In fact, NF was accused of looking for alliances with elites rather than with the people, showing a fear of acting in the streets. As an activist admitted later, 'When the time was ripe, we didn't act, but simply stood by and waited to see how things would develop. And they developed too quickly' (Jessen 2009, 223). In November, the increasing size of demonstrations had in fact produced fear among police but also among NF. NF's control of the protests tended in fact to decline, as its leadership supported dialogue with the regime and reform, while protestors were starting to ask for reunification with the FRG. Even when, on 5 December, NF led the occupation of the political police (Stasi) office, thus partially restoring its image, its action seemed coordinated with the authorities in order to avoid riots. Even after the formation of political platforms, such as NF, the opposition seemed 'slow to envisage a radical and sharp historical turn' (Dale 2005, 149). Its weakness was in part linked to isolation, in part to its orientation to civic initiatives rather than mass protest. As a former dissident noted, 'Their style was a "communicative" one, gearing to thinking and acting in terms of group consensus. It was in a sense appropriate. But then again it was later to hinder the opposition from making its mark...we had avoided taking the lead' (Dale 2005, 150).

There were also changes in membership and leadership. The number of local activists increased enormously, and some local branches took pro-unity and pro-market positions, until pro-unity became the official line. Some of the previous intellectual leadership formed then a faction, Aufbruch 1989. The gap with the crowd reflected different attitudes towards the regime, but also the perspective on the survival of a GDR, especially when, after the fall of the Wall, the calls for reunification became dominant. By January, the Monday demonstration focused on unification, with marchers carrying German (rather than NF) flags, in February, protest marches were replaced by electoral rallies.

While Prime Minister Krenz still denounced NF as hostile and anti-constitutional, support for the group increased among party reformists in Dresden and Leipzig. In December, the victory of reformists within the party (Gregor Gysi was elected secretary general of the new party with ninety-five per cent of the vote) paradoxically challenged rather than helping NF and its reform oriented positions.

In the last phase, in any case, the horizontal structures preferred by the civil society organization seemed unfit to organize a large base. The number of NF supporters in fact dropped, from 200,000 in December to 30,000 in March. This might have contributed to the defeat at the elections of the Bundnis '90, which included many leaders of the opposition and received a mere three per cent of the vote, as compared to sixteen per cent for the successor of the regime party, renamed the Party of Democratic Socialism (PDS).

As this short account of NF shows, the influence of pre-existing or emerging social movement organizations in the development of eventful democratizations is a central issue. I will address it in this chapter, looking at the long development of mobilizing structures and the roles they played during the protest wave—but also the roles they could not play. At the same time, I will point at the effects of mobilization on the organizations themselves, looking at the formation of collective actors during the conflicts.

Traditionally, research on transition has focused, as mentioned, either on structural conditions or on elite choices. Social movements in authoritarian regimes have rarely been mentioned, while research has looked, at best, at the political opposition (often in exile). In the scant research on resistance against authoritarian regimes—for example, on the anti-Nazi occupation armed resistance in Italy and other European countries—little attention is paid to forms of citizens' mobilization or to conceptions and practices of democracy. When protests against dictators are mentioned, they are considered as a peculiar moment contributing to the breakdown of the regime, but they are not expected to play much of a role in the transition and consolidation of democracy.

Within transition studies, however, more recent empirical analyses have helped to bring the masses back in. First of all, attention has focused on workers and their organizations. As Collier and Mahoney (1997, 299) suggested, 'although it would be wrong to treat labor organizations as the principal force behind democratization at the end of the twentieth century, the literature as a whole has erred in the other direction in portraying transitions as primarily an elite project, a conversation among gentlemen, with labor protest having relatively little consequence'. Besides labour and the unions, a broad range of civil society organizations has also been singled out as mobilizing in various forms (see Chapter 1). Even if repressed, they were sometimes capable of winning concessions, even bringing about some liberalization.

Especially after the wave of democratization in Central Eastern Europe, literature on democratization in fact paid some attention to a (loosely organized) civil society. While the definition of social movements points at broad and long-lasting networks, mobilized in contentious forms to bring about social and political change, literature on civil society in authoritarian regimes points at a broader range of associations, or informal spaces of resistance, where opposition takes on more fluid structures and is only occasionally visible to the public.

Perhaps with some adaptation, social movement studies might be helpful in addressing this associational life developing in authoritarian regimes, as they have in general pointed at the importance of organizational structures, which allow for mobilization in times of protest and survival in times of abeyance. These studies have expected social movement organizations (SMOs) to develop when there are mobilizable resources in their environment. In the dominant approach, in fact, these organizations are considered as following an instrumental logic in adapting to their environmental context, but also in stimulating it. In Tilly's influential analysis (1978), what favours the mobilization of resources is 'cat-netness': that is, a combination of categorical similarities and intense nets of relationships. A (more or less explicit) assumption within this approach has been that freedom of association is a sort of requisite for SMOs to develop. In this sense, social movement organizations cannot be expected to flourish in authoritarian regimes. The assumption is that SMOs do not need to be bureaucratic, as reticular forms are often more efficient for powerless actors; nevertheless, research tended to focus on more or less structured organizational forms, with much less attention given to the everyday spaces in which activism is rooted.

However, there has also been some recent recognition within social movement studies that, while the Western types of SMOs are certainly difficult to find in non-democracies, the hybrid forms that have replaced totalitarian regimes (Morlino 2009) do tend to practice a modicum of tolerance towards various forms of non-governmental organizations. This leaves, therefore, some (variable) space for civil actors—individual or informal groups—that sustain democratic norms. Notwithstanding repression, these groupings often survive (or emerge), taking different forms than in so-called advanced democracies. So, even in authoritarian regimes, some (though very limited) free spaces, outside of state control, tend to be used as 'locales that lie outside the scrutiny of the regime and its agents' (Johnston 2011, 113). Social gatherings, neighbourhood associations, unions, study groups, recreational, intellectual, or religious organizations sometimes assume a duplicitous character, allowing for the development of sites of opposition. Usually (at least partially) secretive, these spaces do grant some freedom to express one's own mind, representing 'small islands of free thought and speech' (Johnston 2011, 103).

Within research on authoritarian regimes, as mentioned, the concept of civil society has been used to refer to groups that have little possibility to protest, but nevertheless form a sort of oppositional infrastructure. Development studies refer to a variety of grassroots associations, working as alternative developmental agencies, somewhere between modern associations and more traditional ascriptive groups. Sheila Carapico's (1998) research on Yemen brilliantly singled out many of these forms of civil society self-organization. Challenging the idea that an Arab civil society is an oxymoron, various types of civil society organizations flourished in Yemen in periods of liberalization, with a broad range of activism. The idea that in authoritarian regimes the dictator controls everything is therefore misleading. In fact, as democracies, authoritarianisms vary in terms of their capacity to steer the various institutions that are needed to govern.

If various forms of civil society were indeed present in our cases of eventful democratization, however, there are tensions between the fluidity of networks, which facilitate survival, and the coordination needed for action. During the various steps of mobilization, decentralized structures are in fact expected to increase resilience towards repression, but also to prefigure democratic decision making and to strengthen oppositional consciousness, through respect for diversity. Processes of coordination of broad coalitions seem in fact necessary for eventful democratization. How broad and cross-class these coalitions can/should be is another matter of debate.

Comparative analyses of non-violent revolutions have suggested that, in order to overthrow authoritarian regimes, the opposition must build multiple spaces and places of resistance with a capacity to disrupt the system's social reproduction in multiple settings (Schock 2005, 167), if possible creating liberated areas. These spaces must be put in contact with each other, often through long-lasting processes, and fluidity must be balanced by a need for coordination. In the cases studied by Kurt Schock (2005), democratization was promoted by social movement organizations characterized by decentralized networks, often based on local and grassroots groupings, with a large presence of affinity groups. Networks of civil society organizations might be politicized, especially under brutal violations of human rights and religious freedom, with early riser groups often playing a leading role in this process.

Finally, there is the tension between domestically rooted and transnationally sponsored dynamics. In democratization studies, the international system has long been a missing variable. O'Donnell and Schmitter's (1986) firmest conclusion was in fact that democratization was largely to be explained in terms of national actors and their calculations. Conversely, even if with exceptions, the international dimension of democratization processes has been considered to have little impact. While influenced by the tradition in comparative politics of considering each country as an independent unit of analysis, social movement studies have recently admitted the importance of supranational opportunities and constraints. This international dimension has multiple levels. First, international organizations or foreign countries might be the targets of social movement claims, as either enlarging or reducing the domestic opportunities. Second, social movements can themselves build cross-national or transnational coalitions at different geographic levels. In part as a cause, in part as an effect of these processes, ideas might diffuse cross-nationally and transnationally.

The transnationalization of efforts to bring about democratization from below has included the development of transnational campaigns as well as cross-national processes of diffusion. In many cases, in fact, mobilization has addressed domestic as well as transnational resources. In her research on Argentina, for instance, Brysk looked at the role transnational networks of activists had played through projective cognitive and affective information. As she observed, 'Identity based transnational alliances between Argentinean activists and their First World peers (such as mothers, lawyers, and members of religious communities) cut across national identities' (1993, 263). Civil libertarian, family-based, and religious groups succeeded in mobilizing peer lobbies through the mobilization of identity based on transnational alliances, which used varying means. Civil libertarian groups collected information on human rights violations, while family-based ones mobilized mediagenic symbolism. Their discourse on human rights resonated with the legitimated discourse of the international human rights regime as ally and arena. Challenged with multiple pressures, regimes often answered with some concessions (in Argentina, by opening an office to process complaints about *desaparecidos*). Moreover, new institutions that were established to address human rights continued to work after transition, even if with less success. As Brysk warns, however: 'Argentine human rights activists had access to the international system because they were politically but not socially marginal' (Brysk 1993, 281).

In what follows, I will apply social movement studies' definition of mobilizable resources to processes of eventful democratization. I will show that, while the waves of protest analysed in the previous chapter did accelerate and intensify organizational coordination, they built upon the mobilization of existing resources. I will look in particular at the creation of popular free spaces, up to the development of proper social movement organizations and coalitions. During the analysis I will single out the mentioned tensions between fluidity and structuration, cross-class and class-conscious actors, and domestic rooting and transnational connections. Here as well, I will suggest that mobilizable resources are not just preconditions for action but, to a large extent, they are created in action. New organizations tend in fact to adapt to new conditions, offering bases for coordination. Faced by a rapidly changing external context, they might however become quickly obsolete.

Resource Mobilization in 'Real Socialism'

Research on Eastern Europe paid particular attention to the ways in which some characteristics of the authoritarian regimes allowed, repression notwithstanding, for the development of free spaces and gradual development of social movements. According to some authors, repression thwarted civil society altogether. For instance, Killingsworth (2012) criticized the very idea of the existence of a civil society in communist Eastern Europe: given the level of repression, the dissident groups there were not autonomous, constituting, at best, a 'totalitarian public sphere' that was dominated by the party. Other scholars countered, however, that in 1989, 'Civil society has turned out to be the surprising protagonist of the East European transitions' (Di Palma 1991, 49).

As we will see, in fact, even if the Leninist state offered much reduced spaces for free expression to non-political organizations—with no access to policymakers, media, or courts—there did exist networks acting as mobilizing structures. Areas of opposition emerged in working class politics, as associations were often allowed in the workplace and the failure of official unions brought about demands for free unions (Lovenduski and Woodall 1987). Intellectuals—from students to artists—also publicly advocated freedom of expression. Churches mostly compromised with the regime, but some of their members also mobilized in independent peace movements. New social movements emerged, as in the West, on peace, environmental protection, women's rights, often exploiting some discursive space for their claims within the regime.

The term 'civil society' has often been used to describe these forms of opposition. As Giuseppe Di Palma observed, 'a civil society of sorts survived in Eastern Europe, not just as a conventional clandestine adversary but as a visible cultural and existential counterimage of communism's unique hegemonic project' (Di Palma 1991, 49). The organizational structure was very horizontal (see also Chapter 4). Concentrated in urban areas, highly educated, and politicized by communism, citizens needed little organization to mobilize (Goodwin 2001, 277), often staging their own contentious events in the spatial symbols of the mobilized regime. Coordination was then made possible through oppositional umbrella organizations, which were rather light and internally heterogeneous, as reflected in the self-definition as fora: the Civic Forum in Czechoslovakia, New Forum in the GDR, or Democratic Forum in Hungary.

The homogenizing characteristics of the regime have been said to be reflected in a homogeneous civil society, thus explaining why the demise of the Eastern European regimes was so sudden. 'Real socialist' regimes were, according to Di Palma (1991), 'legitimated from the top', as claims to legitimacy were authenticated by the party that justified command as bearer of a superior truth that did not require people's authentication. However, broken promises increased discontent, while the need to spend time and energy on the informal markets, as goods were in scarce supply, unexpectedly created networks and bonds of solidarity that brought together people of different backgrounds. Again, Di Palma observed that

> Western authoritarianism is largely 'class conscious'; its victims of material depri-
> vation are usually the poorer sorts. But impoverished communist markets treated
> everybody—with the exception of a pampered and highly select nomenklatura—
> with equal shabbiness.... The most articulate strata of society, the main activators
> of spillover effects, were no less affected than everybody else. As they pooled their
> ingenuity in the art of material survival, the informal but also socially homoge-
> neous and more resourceful microgroups that emerged assumed other functions.
> They became a potential source for various forms of dissent—more or less latent,
> more or less political. To begin with, the withdrawal into a circle of family and
> friends should not be taken as evidence of an atomized society that left a social
> vacuum which inadvertently fulfilled communist wishes (Di Palma 1991, 70).

The homogeneity of civil society in Eastern Europe varied, however. Oppositional networks were wide ranging in their composition: made up of intellectuals, industrial workers, and the church in Poland, of followers of Lukacs in Hungary, of new left intellectuals in the GDR, of human rights activists (mostly intellectuals) in Czechoslovakia (Lovenduski and Woodall 1987). Workers and intellectuals cooperated in some moments, but not in others: they worked together in Poland in the early 1980s, but not in the GDR in 1953, when workers remained isolated, or in Hungary where the 1956 rebellion involved mainly intellectuals and students.

Present in both the GDR and Czechoslovakia, experiences of protest, embedded in organizational structures, appeared as necessary (although not sufficient) resources for eventful democratization.

Czechoslovakia

Czechoslovakia has often been characterized by a particularly authoritarian regime and a weak civil society. In reality, however, various waves of past protest, even if often defeated, had left symbolic and organizational resources available for the peaceful revolution of 1989.

In the early history of the regime, free spaces had indeed been rather lim-ited in both religious and workers' mobilizing forms. The Catholic Church was under tight control by the regime, and some attempts at workers' protests were repressed in 1953. Dissatisfaction within the party itself was visible in the conflicts between hardliners and reformists. During the Prague Spring, mediating between the two more extreme positions, Dubček emerged as a moderate leader. He proposed socialism with a human face, maintaining the principle of party dominance, even if with some freedom of expression (espe-cially in the press). However, initiated from above, his moderate reforms, supported by seventy-five per cent of the population, were already too radical for the Soviet Union: they were in fact overthrown after the military invasion by Warsaw Pact troops on 20 August 1968. The Soviet tanks came as a shock—as a dissident recalled, 'we were ready to do anything, but we were told to do nothing' (Urban 1990, 107).

After one-third of the party was purged and seventy organizations disbanded, the first half of the 1970s were years of—at best—individual resistance. Some initial protests against Soviet occupation were in fact followed by a normalization. Nevertheless, a multi-faced, dissident community continued its activities until the so called Velvet Revolution of 1989. Opposition was kept alive in part by the old guard who had participated in the Prague Spring. One of them, Petr Uhl, recalled his participation in the revolutionary youth movement in 1968, followed by four years of imprisonment. After his release, he married a woman who had been in prison for two years and, along with other former political prisoners, signed petitions, collected money for unjustly persecuted people, and founded the committee K-231, a group of former political prisoners emerging from the ashes of the Prague Spring. A Club of Non-Party Engagés (KAN) would provide 'an important political example for a later movement of much greater importance and impact: Civic Forum. Not unsurprisingly, Vaclav Havel was a member' (Falk 2003, 76–7). These embryonic civil society organizations offered the 'closest approximation to, or surrogate for, political life' (Skilling 1991, 8–9).

Later on, the Helsinki accords between Western and Eastern countries (see page xxx) represented an important turning point. According to dissident Havel, 'they offered something that no one, probably, initially thought they were offering. They offered a basic argument, one that is difficult to dismiss, and that is the idea of human and civil rights' (cit. in Killingsworth 2012, 64). Although with difficulty, human rights groups developed along with some new social movements, especially on environmental issues. At the end of the decade, Charter 77 emerged, in fact, in direct response to the Helsinki agreements, from a small group of dissidents who signed petitions for democratization and human rights.

Charter 77 was founded in the aftermath of the trial against the rock band Plastic People of the Universe (PPU), a process that had shown particular disregard for human rights (Long 2005, 12; Saxonberg 2001, 153). Released on 1 January 1977, the organizational declaration for human rights was initially signed by 240 intellectuals. The Charter

> comprehensively details the litany of violations of both Helsinki and the UN covenants. Freedom of expression is described as illusory, given that 'tens of thousands of our citizens' are prevented from work in their professions because their views differ from those officially sanctioned and 'countless young people' are

prevented from attending university because of their own views or those of their parents. The document criticizes the 'centralized control of all the communications media and publishing and cultural institutions', the lack of freedom of religion, freedom of association, and the curtailment of civil liberties. Existing legal norms were condemned for their lawlessness, arbitrariness, and disrespect of civil rights (Falk 2003, 89).

The organization's mission was framed as 'helping the Czechoslovak government implement its own laws: the Universal Declaration of Human Rights and the 1975 Final Act of the Helsinki Covenant on Human Rights' (Tucker 2000, 124).

Not a mass organization, the Charter was made up of 'a few thousand people at the fringes, a few hundred near the center, a few dozen real leaders' (Stokes 1993, 149). It was a 'mainly Czech organization, grouping former communists, anti-communists and non-political intellectuals', whose main aim was 'to get Czechoslovakia to adhere to its obligations under the 1975 Helsinki Final Act' (Shepherd 2000, 31).

Even though heavy repression followed the foundation of the organization (with interrogations, home searches, beatings, arrests, and prison sentences), Charter 77 survived, building up a flying university that worked as an important public sphere. Human rights were the focal claims, and the main oppositional activities initially consisted of the production and distribution of samizdat. Typed on thin paper, in multiple copies, they had an illegal, and therefore risky, circulation.

Other organizations also focused on human rights. Established on 27 April 1978, VONS (Výbor na Obranu Nespravedlivě Stíhaných, or Committee for the Defense of the Unjustly Persecuted) was modelled on the Polish KOR (Workers' Defense Committee, Komitet Obrony Robotników; see Chapter 7) with the objective of (materially and legally) supporting the victims of state prosecution as well as spreading information about human rights violations (Falk 2003, 92).

Even after the foundation of Charter 77 in 1977, 'civic activities were relatively few and limited in scope but nonetheless, in spite of repression, persisted for more than ten years' (Falk 2003, 10). In fact, as the very history of the charter indicates, the old guard encountered another, emerging generation of dissidents. After the arrests of the members of the Plastics band, Havel declared: 'the objects of this attack were not veterans of old political battles; they had no political past, or even any well-defined political position. They were simply young people who wanted to live in their own way, make the music they liked' (Long 1996, 11). In fact, the group protested the attack against those young people who wanted 'to express themselves in a truthful way' (Saxonberg 2001, 65).

Networks of opposition between old and young activists were particularly important for the development of a dissident milieu. As dissident Daniel Kummerman recalled: 'Basically, I think I was kind of predetermined. I mean, actually it's a kind of theory of mine, that most of the signers, if you follow their personal history, were sort of pushed into it by the circumstances. This means, like among the original signers, there were quite a few people who I knew from school or other circles...and so, because I knew the signers, it was quite easy. Because for some people, it was difficult even to reach those circles' (Saxonberg 2001, 77). In fact, various networks converged in Charter 77: a group of Christians, with a strong moral appeal; former communists, who still believed in the reformability of communists; and young anti-establishment people, who entered in the mid-1980s (Long 1996). Environmentalists joined in as well.

In addition to about 2,000 human rights activists, another oppositional network developed around environmental issues. The official Czech union of nature conservationists, which had counted 26,000 members, was founded in 1969 and forced to disband in 1979 after its branches had participated in environmentalist campaigns and leaders had protested against the plans to build a hydropower plant. Later on, the group Brontosaurus, founded in 1973 by young members of the Academy of Science, organized up to 10,000 volunteers, later supporting Charter 77. In Slovakia there was also some freedom for conservationist groups, with various voluntary activities, and, from the mid-1980s, opposition to large dam projects. Managing to locate itself in the grey zone between permitted and forbidden organizing by focusing on the country's quite dramatic environmental situation, the movement was strengthened by the Chernobyl disaster (Heimann 2009, 294–5). Many activists evolved from an environmental to an oppositional consciousness in what was significantly called a *green*-velvet revolution—not by chance, the green party was the first to be founded, even if it was shaken by scandals later on for contacts with the secret police (Jehlicka 2001). Environmentalists had in fact a visible role during the mass demonstrations against the regime (Snajdr 2001).[1]

Even though the role of the Catholic Church was very limited, 'the dissident Catholic community played an important role in Charter 77 throughout the 1980s, as well as in the November revolution itself' (Judt 1992, 111). In 1987, in Slovakia, a petition calling for broader religious freedom collected somewhere between 300,000 and 600,000 signatures. While an 'unintended consequence of Catholic activism was one of the few instances of a broad civil

---

[1] Between the late 1980s and late 1990s, Czech environmentalism shifted from the two organizations recognized by the regime to a more complex network, and from established groups to dangerous radicals (Jehlicka 2001).

society developing among the Czechs and Slovaks' (Stokes 1993, 152), nevertheless, the protest on religious rights carried out by Slovaks was not considered as dissent by the Czechs (Innes 2001, 37). Some opposition also came from ethnic minorities: in 1978, the Committee for the Legal Defense of the Hungarian Minority was founded; its leader signed the Charter 77 document.

If social movement organizations were weak in terms of members and support, in 1988 and 1989 an increasing number of dissident groups emerged, along with growing sympathy from among the population. In 1987, the Democratic Initiative, which included members of Charter 77, was founded as part of an attempt to coordinate the opposition, with letters to MPs calling for democratic reform and the launching of a petition for democratization that gathered over 40,000 signatures (Judt 1992, 97). Organizations emerging in the late 1980s included MOST—which tried, with little success, to open a dialogue between the government and the opposition (Glenn 2001, 169)—and the Movement for Civil Liberties, which published its manifesto in 1988, announcing that the time was ripe to be involved in politics. These groups differed from Charter 77 especially in presenting themselves as explicitly political actors (Glenn 2001, 139; Stokes 1993, 153).

Coordination among all these groups grew during the protest. On 18 November 1989, the Civic Forum (CF) emerged from Charter 77, quickly becoming the umbrella organization of the opposition, where all recently created civic initiatives converged (Heimann 2009). CF was also extremely horizontal:

> There was a three-tiered structure to the coordinating center: the crisis crew, composed of Václav Havel, Jiří Križan, and Saša Vondra, which met every morning at 8:00 A.M. and made basic decisions that were discussed with the action group of approximately twenty people; later these decisions would be presented to the plenum of around 150 people, which was the final opportunity for discussion before the daily press conference. In explicit contrast to the hierarchical structure of the Communist Party and consistent with the civil society collective action frame, Civic Forum defined its structure as decentralized and local.... It was to have no hierarchy whatsoever but rather to be 'a horizontal network, with all local Civic Forums joined to one coordinating center' (Glenn 2001, 181).

On the same day as CF's founding, Public Against Violence (VPN) was created in Slovakia.

In addition, in the summer of 1989, 'student activists throughout Prague started an independent student organization, STUHA, with the goal of establishing a self-governing organ for the students' (Saxonberg 2001, 329). Indeed, students have been defined as the catalyst of the protest: 'although the known dissidents had become more daring and radical during the past year, their children at the universities outdid them in boldness. These young adults eventually became the catalysts of the revolution' (Saxonberg 2001, 328). Even the official student union, SSM, supported Gorbachev's politics.

Workers were present in the mobilization, although not as such. In fact, 'hundreds of little Civic Forums in the factories managed to mobilize huge support for the general strike. It was at this point that the credibility of the "Workers' State" collapsed and the confidence of the revolutionary leadership found firm ground' (Judt 1992, 101).

Civil Society in The GDR

The GDR is also considered a case of strong repression and weak civil society. Strong repression under Stalinism had for some time thwarted any opposition. The totalitarian regime did not remove conflicts, however: a few, small reformist circles survived on the periphery (see e.g. Muehlen 1995 on the Eisenberger Kreis), and factory strikes were sometimes effective in obtaining or opposing change, through quick agreements on specific demands (Huebner 1995). As a local history of the Saalfeld district from the 1940s to the 1970s shows (Port 2007), between 1945 and 1953 collective action on labour issues testified to the memory of pre-Nazi labour conflicts in protest and organizational forms, as well as in the geography of protests; but it also reflected the presence of a new generation of labour activists.

In particular, in this region, the Soviet exploitation of uranium brought about tensions in the mining areas due to compulsory recruitment and deplorable working conditions. In 1951, riots broke out after the police intervened in a fight: a prison was stormed and policemen wounded during violent confrontations, and there were rumours that miners had attacked SED and FDJ (Free German Youth) functionaries. Even though the police did not use firearms and the imprisoned miners were released, a semi-military occupation (state of siege) followed. Investigations were especially targeted at those who had recently moved into the area, as well as at 'outcast elements'.

In 1953, a broad, if short, mobilization of workers was heavily repressed. On 12 June, protests started in Berlin on working sites, then spreading everywhere, against a ten per cent increase in production quotas for all industrial workers. After a sit-in at a Berlin construction site, strikes spread on 17 June, asking for a reduction of the production quota, free elections, and freedom. A march to the council of ministers followed, with 10,000 protesters gathering in front of the house of ministers. They obtained the abolition of the quota increase that had prompted the mobilization, but without achieving the political recognition they had hoped for when they asked to talk to the party secretary general, Ulbricht, who refused to meet with them.

Various events took place on 17 July, following a somewhat common script. Typically, meetings were called in the factories by lower unionists or well-known militants. Then, ad hoc strike committees formed, often influenced by pre-existing networks in the Social Democratic party (SPD), unions, Vereinigung der Verfolgten des Naziregimes, or in the army. Strikers marched, joined by others, and rallied in the city centre. Initially, these marches were peaceful and joyful, communicating a sense of liberation; but there were also insurrectionary and riotous events such as takeovers of radio or television stations as well as occupations of Stasi headquarters, local courts, police stations, town halls, newspapers, SED, FDJ. Sometimes (for example in Leipzig, Halle, Bitterfeld, and Merseburg), inter-factory strike committees were created.

The claims were more political than in the earlier wave of protest in 1951. Protests developed on the issue of the quota increase, but also on other work related issues (wages, working conditions, eight-hour days, paid leaves, paid strike days and no reprisals), and free elections. They were politicized, as poor working conditions were linked to high military expenditures. Indeed, a slogan of 1953 was 'Wir wollen freie Menschen sein und keine Sklaven' (We want to be free persons, not slaves). Dissatisfaction was reflected in the re-election of only three per cent of incumbents as union representatives.

After the intervention of the Soviet troops and heavy domestic repression (see Chapter 5), only some individual or small group protests survived in the following years, subject to strong control. In the 1950s, the repertoire of everyday protests included leaflets and graffiti, but also rumours and jokes, as well as withdrawals of membership and membership dues or participation in party initiatives, and open opposition to paramilitary training. However, society was not united—rather the opposite. Notwithstanding repression, the art of resistance was evident in salary negotiations as well as in the use of some channels to present grievances, especially in moment of crisis such as in 1956, the early 1960s, and the late 1970s. Additional forms of resistance included emigration (from about 4,000 requests for exit visas in the 1970s to 16,000 in the 1980s) and youth rebellion (rock was repressed, as well as jazz and jeans).

Although in less massive forms than in the Polish case, a civil society did develop, especially in the 1980s. As a member of the oppositional movement recalls,

For years there had been dissidents in East Germany, just like those in Poland and Russia, but more hidden. Then in the early eighties we came to the surface. The new opposition was individualistic and bohemian, and composed of a kalei-doscope of 'counter-culture' social groups: hippies, Maoists, anarchists, human rights groups, greens, gays, lesbians, the protesting 'church from below'—a very colorful mixture, with lots of rock music; in fact, to professional people and academics, frankly somewhat alien! (Reich 1990, 71–2).

Since the 1960s, youth subcultures had been developing, stigmatized by the regime's pseudo-proletarian Puritanism (Wolle 2008), although there had been some opening in the mid-1960s when long hair and jeans started to be tolerated. On 7 October 1969, after rumours spread that the Rolling Stones would be singing on the roof of the Springer Haus, many young people converged, shouting 'Stones and freedom' and 'Dubček, Dubček'. In 1970, on the occasion of a festival of political songs in East Berlin, bands from the Third World (among them Mikis Theodorakis) sang songs of freedom against the regime. The authorities then feared similar moments of contestation during the X. Weltspiele der Jugend und Studenten in August 1973.

Some opposition also emerged within what novelist Günter Grass called a niche society, among others in work brigades, which functioned as the networks and informal exchanges needed in a shortage economy. Intellectual dissidence grew through open letters, petitions, and dissemination of information. Campaigns of protest on peace, women's rights, labour, nationality, and neighbourhood issues were sometimes not repressed 'for ideological reasons, for reasons of international politics or to provide a safety valve to reduce more direct antiregime protest' (Johnston 2011, 124).

In the late 1960s and 1970s there were some reflections on the Prague ideas of reformist communism, or socialism with a human face mixed with a Christian ethic. Protest followed the Soviet invasion of Czechoslovakia in 1968: 3,528 leaflets were found in 389 places, and there were investigations against 1,290 people, almost half of them under twenty years old (six per cent were school pupils, three per cent university students and seventy per cent workers). Of those, 1,400 were sentenced, among them children of high-level state functionaries who had been among the protestors. There were also collective statements in factories, with calls for press freedom. The 522 disciplinary procedures inside the party and 127 in the universities (for political activities) show the spread of the protest.

Important moments in the development of the opposition were the expulsion of the singer Wolf Biermann and the self-immolation of Oskar Bruesewitz, as well as the foundation of Solidarity in Poland in 1980 (Johnston 2011, 22). The prohibition to distribute an issue of the German translation of the Soviet magazine *Sputnik* produced protests (including work slow-downs and petitions, Pfaff 2006, 55), although these were not linked with oppositional organizations (Klein 1995).

In the 1980s, the regime's ability to control the media was limited by easy access to Western outlets. The opposition also started a rich list of publications, as well as writing open letters to important personalities (such as Christa Wolf), asking for their support. They could thus develop in a repressive environment, also importing ideas from abroad (Solidarity but also the peace and environmental movements).

New social movements also developed in the 1980s, along with a process of networking in the opposition. In that decade, a generation that grew up in the shadow of the Wall began to mobilize. Especially between 1979 and 1983, groups emerged on peace issues, but also around broader topics such as environmental and human rights concerns. Particularly important in the construction of an oppositional front was the peace movement of the early 1980s. According to Dale (2005, 101),

> From 1979 until 1983 the autonomous peace movement went from strength to strength. Communications amongst the disparate groups improved, and a national co-ordinating centre was established.... Events with a peace theme became increasingly popular. Thousands attended Rainer Eppelmann's 'Blues services'; 3 500 came to an independent peace event in Potsdam in 1982; and around 10 000 congregated at a Christian peace festival in Eisenach. Alongside burgeoning numbers, a minority began to express more radical opinions, arguing that activities should reach beyond the confines of the Church. A number of attempts were made to hold public vigils: by 'Women for Peace' in Berlin, and by activists around Roland Jahn in Jena, for example. The 'Berlin Appeal' of January 1982, launched by the dissident Communist Robert Havemann and by Reverend Eppelmann, raised taboo demands, a nuclear weapon-free Europe, the withdrawal of all occupying forces from both German states and freedom of expression; and thereby confirmed the regime's fears that the peace issue could stray towards explosive questions of the division of Germany, the GDR's reliance on a foreign power, and civil liberties. A signal event, it was the first direct appeal to the general public on behalf of an independent movement and, despite references to so many forbidden themes, gathered over 2,000 signatures.

Protests also exposed the division in the church. The Protestant Church had often found itself in opposition to state policy on issues such as conscientious objection in 1955, conscription in 1960, and the Soviet invasion of Afghanistan in 1980. Already in the late 1970s, informal groups were created in its milieu. Especially after the agreements of 1978, which gave the Church hierarchy some authority status, 'churches were permitted to act as arenas for the ventilation of dissent; their public meeting rooms and printing equipment became available to the groups that gathered within their walls' (Dale 2005, 101). In the 1980s, while the church hierarchy opposed the protests, individual pastors offered dissidents some shelter, free spaces for activists' meetings and publications (although they had to carry the designation 'only for internal use') (Poppe, Eckert, and Kowlczuk 1995, 21; Killingsworth 2012). So, even if with internal strains, 'the Evangelical church offered the oppositional forces the possibility to meet in their spaces and to network' (Poppe 1995, 252).

Activities developed especially on issues of conscientious objection, peace, environment, and human rights. In 1982, Deacon Günter Johannsen started to organize Peace Prayers every Monday at five o'clock at the Nikolaikirche in Leipzig (Maier 1997, 139). In fact, in the Church: 'an unrestive and critical "basis" of peace circles and friendly young priests became pitted against a more conservative and accommodating church leadership' (Joppke 1995, 87). The involved pastors provided cognitive resources (peace, non-violence) and human rights as a main frame, bridging it to the one on peace. Peace circles of the Evangelische student parish in East Berlin attracted dissidents, while, in the words of a dissident, 'Western publicity became our best protection' (Joppke 1995, 93).

The umbrella given by the Church however also tended to confine dissidents 'within an enclosed environment that was dominated by religious and ethical ideas, and in which they were subject to ecclesiastical control. It acted to contain dissent in both senses of the word: as host but also as steward of its boundaries' (Dale 2005, 106).

In the early 1980s, independent environmental activities began to develop, in part within the official society for nature and environment (with 60,000 members in 1989). Since the late 1970s, protests had already targeted the building of a highway, the destruction of a meadow, and toxic waste dumps (Dale 2005, 102). The environmental movement then grew, in part, out of the decline of peace protests in the mid-1980s. As Ritter (2012a) observed,

> Seemingly non-threatening to the regime, the environmental movement provided those keen to express their opinion with an avenue to do so publicly. In this way, one might argue that even semi-political protest contributed to the emergence of a protest culture in the mid and late 1980s. Towards the end of the decade, the environmental movements teamed up with churches to establish environmental libraries....By then it was clear that the movement was not as harmless as the regime had chosen to believe.

In 1988, the Umweltbibliothek developed as a civic initiative on peace and the environment, protesting against the growing spread of pollution in 1989. Two of its main campaigns opposed the construction of a silicon factory in Dresden and lignite mining in Leipzig (Rink 2001).

Women's rights organizations that considered themselves as part of the independent women's movement also mobilized. Some independent women's groups had been founded in the 1980s, mainly on peace issues and the rights of women and homosexuals (Dale 2005, 106); a first network meeting of women's groups was held in 1984. The group Frauen für den Frieden, established in 1982, mobilized on nuclear disarmament and the rights of conscientious objectors, but also criticized 'the educational system of the GDR [which] promoted gender segregation, traditional gender roles, and military themes' (Kranz 2010, 8). According to one of the leaders of New Forum:

Women played a fundamental part in making our revolution, and it, along with the role of young people, should be recognized. At an early stage, the sanctuary of the Gethsemane Church was the focus and the beacon of our movement. Every evening around the Gethsemane Church, people walked silently in the great ritual of our revolution. Women and young people enacted it, with candles, parading humbly and defencelessly but in awesome unity of purpose in front of the dreadful apparatus of State repression. The riot-police cordon, the armoured trucks, the water cannon. They demonstrated without any sign of fear. They quietly placed their candles on the street, sat down and waited until they were carried away or beaten up or arrested after Neues Forum had been declared illegal and unconstitutional (Reich 1990, 88).

During the 1980s, meetings on women's rights were held in state centres and university gender studies departments. Periodical publications started at the end of the 1980s (Miete and Hampele 2001). Women's groups called for dialogue with the state, using protest channels such as petitions (such as the one against the compulsory military draft for women in 1982) and critical church events (for example, politically motivated services, prayers of supplication, grassroots church councils). Through innovative actions, they claimed they wanted to break the circle of violence, linking the security politics of the GDR with human rights, as well as other politics (Kukutz 1995).

Between 1984 and 1986, repression brought about some resignation. Continued arrests resulted in sentences of up to four years in prison for leafleting (Neubert 1997, 503) as well as months in prison for even minor violations, such as writing graffiti. *Total-verweigerung*—that is, refusing to do civic service as a substitute for the military draft—was punished with prison sentences. In the peace movement, internal tensions were fuelled by Stasi agents, and tough repression targeted especially those who had applied for visas.

Repression did not jeopardize, however, but rather unwillingly fuelled the process of networking, which formed especially around the call for human rights. In 1986, the Initiative Frieden und Menschenrechte (IFM) was founded by peace and women's movements activists, and functioned as coordination for oppositional activities. In particular, IFM focused on calls for open society, democratization, and politics from below—resembling Charter 77, even though its leaders were not as prominent. Claiming to stand for democratic socialism, the group focused on democracy and human rights, rather than on social issues:

The achievement of a peaceful domestic polity, IFM argued, requires the creation of a 'critical public sphere' and this, in turn, requires guaranteed civil liberties. IFM's concrete demands—for democratic elections, freedom of association, and for a referendum on nuclear power—tapped into the concerns of many activists. Its magazine, *Grenzfall*, reached a print-run of around 1,000 but was read by a much wider audience than that figure would suggest. IFM was audacious, in that it openly articulated political opposition, but also because it dared to step outside the Church. Its publications, although often printed in church offices, lacked the usual imprimatur 'for internal church use only'. As such it was an especially troublesome thorn in the government's side, and one that was all the sharper for its concern to build bridges to other East European dissident movements, such as Charter 77 (Dale 2005, 127–8).

State repression of IFM members fuelled solidarization, along with the politicization of those groups that initially did not understand their action as political but were forced into a conflict with the state through repression (Poppe 1995). In 1987, to counter state repression, visa applicants formed their own Citizens' Rights group, later to affiliate with IFM: 'Before long it had attracted several hundred members, and began to spread nationwide and organize public protests in several towns and cities. Applicants were making their presence felt as the vanguard of public protest' (Dale 2005, 88). IFM members would then assume central positions within emerging organizations such as New Forum and Democracy Now.

Repression notwithstanding, also in the second half of the 1980s, some free space was carved out in churches, while some women's groups were still active; there was also a rapid increase in the publication of samizdat, especially between 1987 and 1989 (Neubert 1997, 517). Peace movement groups organized yearly seminars and conferences. Repressed punks also found free spaces in the church, as did gay and lesbian groups. In 1987, Kirche von Unten and Arbeitskreis solidarische Kirche were founded. Friedens konkret demanded the right to total conscientious objection and disarmament. Third World groups also mobilized. Grassroots groups proliferated from 1986, with up to 80,000 members. Women's organizations also played an important role. Frauen für den Frieden organized night-church services with up to 500 women. Many peace groups also started to address environmental issues, which were usually less repressed and reflected concerns among the citizens. There was resistance against the construction of a highway near a Jewish cemetery. Moreover, the oppositional discourse started to address human rights and democracy issues.

From 1987, there were also more and more protest events, with increasing politicization and coordination, to which the regime reacted inconsistently. People converged at the Branderburgertur during concerts, chanting slogans such as 'Mauer weg' ('Down with the Wall', Neubert 1997, 668). Protests against arrests were sometimes successful in obtaining releases. In 1987, a protest event was organized on the occasion of the official celebration at the Olof Palme peace march. Some demonstrations took the form of pilgrimages, involving up to 1,000 participants. In November, a repressive action against the Umweltbibliothek in the Ziongemeinde produced long-lasting reactions.

A few months later, in January 1988, oppositional groups participated in the official demonstration for the anniversary of the assassination of Karl Liebknecht and Rosa Luxemburg, with posters saying 'Freedom is always the freedom of those who think differently' (Neubert 1997, 697). There were pre-emptive arrests, but also solidarization and coordination of oppositional groups, with channels of coordination including telephone chains and crisis management units. Human rights groups organized protests, among them a candlelight march for the fortieth anniversary of the UN Declaration on Human Rights. In the same year there was also a peak in the publication of samizdat, notwithstanding attempts at pre-emption, including removing from the market the cheap paper needed for their production. The mentioned *Sputnik* affair—the suppression of an issue of the Soviet journal to which 180,000 DDR citizens subscribed, because of debates on the Hitler–Stalin pact and the end of communism in Soviet Union—also raised protests. In the autumn of 1988, at the Ossiesky School, a speaker's corner was organized, where criticisms of the military parade during the Fest der Republik were voiced. Collective action also targeted fascism and anti-Semitism, while solidarity church services were repressed in Berlin. Founded by Leipzig Pastors Führer and Wonneberger in 1988, the Initiative Group for Life (IGL) offered 'workshops and training in nonviolent direct action' (Nepstad 2011, 42–3).

Mobilization brought about increasing numbers of groups. In 1988, more than 300 groups were active, among them 160 on peace, eighty on the environment, forty-six on the Third World, and thirty on women's rights, with membership ranging between five and eighty (Neubert 1997, 705). At the beginning of the year, the Stasi counted 160 groups, of which thirty-nine focused on the environment, thirty-five on peace, twenty-three on peace and the environment, seven on women, ten on human rights, and thirty-nine on the '2/3 world' (Neubert 1997, 706), with a total of about 2,000 members. In 1989, 144 were counted, with 800 organizers (Neubert 1997, 707). In the late 1980s, 'the number of individuals engaged in some sort of (broadly defined) "active resistance" reached an estimated 20,000-25,000 each year' (Dale 2005, 124).

Even though the anti-regime forces were fragmented, weak, and even infiltrated by the state apparatuses, in 1989 the mobilization of citizens built upon itself with increasing coordination. On 12 January 1989, IGL activists 'quietly distributed thousands of leaflets calling for a demonstration at Leipzig's City Hall' (Nepstad 2011, 43); a crowd of 800 gathered on 17 January and was quickly dispersed by police, who jailed nearly 100 participants. In March and July, respectively, the Initiative für den Demokratischen Aufbruch (Initiative for a Democratic Awakening, or DA) and Initiative for a Social Democratic Party in the GDR were founded (Saxonberg 2001, 305). In

August, dissidents established Democracy Now (DN), and 'by late August at least seventeen initiatives existed that aimed to establish some sort of independent oppositional presence' (Dale 2005, 148). Finally, on 9 September there emerged what would become the most important of the opposition groups, namely NF (Maier 1997, 136; Reich 1990, 72; Stokes 1993, 139). By mid-October, a month after its formation, the organization had 25,000 members, and 200,000 had signed its manifesto (East 1992, 67; Nepstad 2011, 46). It has been noted that

> All of these organisations shared certain basic principles and goals, notably democratic transformation and ecological sustainability. That they did not formally unite was in part due to personal rivalries and the role of Stasi agents in exacerbating these, but it also came down to differences in philosophy, programme and strategy. Thus, New Forum, IFM, DA and DN drew more upon republican and liberal traditions whereas the UL gathered together reform-Communists, Trotskyists and anarchists. DN and DA were more affirmative of socialism and more explicitly opposed to the SED's 'leading role' than was New Forum. As regards organizational form, DA and the SDP quickly began to adopt party-political structures while New Forum, UL and DN developed along looser, 'movement-oriented' lines (Dale 2005, 148–9).

Interpersonal networks were relevant in this process. On 9 September 1989, a meeting at the cottage of the wife of a long-standing opponent of the regime, Robert Havemann, was organized. As a participant recalled, 'It was a more or less fortuitous collection: the principle we invited people who came was simple. We wished to ensure that we were properly representative; to ensure that Neues Forum incorporated not only clergymen, not only Berliners, not only young dropouts from the social ghetto' (Reich 1990, 72–3). New Forum (NF) then emerged, connecting activists of environmental, peace, and citizens' rights initiatives in a manifesto published on 21 September. Ten days later, the NF request for recognition as an association was denied, as the organization was labelled anti-socialist by the Minister of Security, Mielke (who had already been accused of harassing anarchists in the International Brigades in Spain) (Reich 1990). This even though its founding documents declared a commitment to socialist ideas, with calls for human rights within a democratically renewed socialism, also open to dialogue with the regime.

As mentioned in the incipit to this chapter, the extent to which these organizations were able to lead the protest is a contested issue. What emerged as important, however, is the role of past networks in the re-mobilization of protest, and their capacity to get new generations involved. Additionally, single issue protest, whether on peace issues or on the protection of the environment, tended to be bridged as coordination efforts multiplied.

Transnational Contacts and 1989

Transnational contacts among social movement organizations were very relevant in both countries and beyond. In general, it has been observed that the examples of the early risers reduced the costs for the latecomers. As Kuran noted,

> In the days following the fall of Czechoslovakia's communist regime, a banner in Prague read: 'Poland-10 years, Hungary-10 months, East Germany-10 weeks, Czechoslovakia-10 days'. The implied acceleration reflects the fact that each successful challenge to communism lowered the perceived risk of dissent in the countries still under communist rule....as revolutionary thresholds in neighboring countries fell, the revolution became increasingly contagious. Had this banner been prepared a few weeks later, it might have added 'Romania-10 hours' (Kuran 1991, 42).

During the 1989 events, decisions taken by neighbouring countries were clearly influential. In June, the elections in Poland, with Solidarity entering parliament, raised hopes for peaceful change in the Eastern bloc. During the 1989 wave, 'The success of antigovernment demonstrations in one country inspired demonstrations elsewhere. In early November, Sofia was shaken by its first demonstration in four decades as several thousand Bulgarians marched on the National Assembly. Within a week, on the very day throngs broke through the Berlin Wall, Todor Zhivkov's thirty-five-year leadership came to an end, and his successor began talking of radical reforms' (Kuran 1991, 39). As Saxonberg (2001) observed, while it took five weeks in the GDR for the size of protests to get beyond 100,000, in Czechoslovakia it took just a few days for the marches to involve over 500,000 people.

Beyond imitation, there were also transnational contacts from below. In the 1980s, transnational cooperation had developed across Eastern Europe. There were first of all contacts between oppositional groups in the various CEE countries, and common initiatives that resonated with a shared history between the East German, Polish, Hungarian, and Czechoslovakian opposition, such as protest action on the occasion of the various anniversaries of the Hungarian revolution or Prague Spring.[2] While hope in the support from Western parties and governments was followed by disillusionment (Poppe 1995, 256), peace activists in the GDR developed contacts with the peace movement in the FRG. Women for peace in the GDR were in contact with the other groups of women for peace; they wrote open letters in solidarity with the march against nuclear missiles from Berlin to Geneva (Kukutz 1995).

---

[2] There were, for instance, meetings between Hungarian and Polish opponents on the mountain bordering the two countries. A kind of political picnic, they were filmed and sent to the Western media (Urban 1990).

Work with Western pacifist organizations was pursued as 'detente from below'. Started by Charter 77, cooperation included in East and West Germany the Initiative for Bocks-Freedom in Europe. Relations developed especially with the Greens, via the peace movement. There were also close relations between the GDR opposition and FRG social movements, including solidarity against repression. Protest campaigns were carried out together by East and West German environmentalists against the export of West German rubbish in the GDR, with blockades and police intervention on both sides at the end of 1988. Films about pollution in the GDR were exported and circulated in the West. Counter-information included contacts with Western media, such as Radio Glasnost in West Berlin, collaboration with the Taz, and documentary films with the SFB.

Transnational social movement organizations were involved as well. In a comparative analysis of Latin America and Eastern Europe, Patricia Chilton (1995) suggested that peaceful and successful regime transformation is facilitated by civil society development and transnational exchanges. In particular, she pointed at the role of civil society development as détente from below. In international meetings, transnational human rights groups kept empty chairs for Eastern European delegates who were denied visas, as well as developing transnational communication and multiple bilateral contacts. In 1992, the END convention process developed meetings with hundreds of delegates each year in various European cities. The year-long preparation for each convention was even more important for transnational networking than was the event itself.

These transnational linkages acted as additional resources in legitimating the opposition. In Czechoslovakia and the GDR, even if national civil society was not particularly strong, it was embedded in very dense transnational networks. In particular, Hungarian activists contributed to this transnationalization, as they were more free to travel and to host meetings (thus, for example, when the preparatory committee of Helsinki's citizens' assembly was arrested in Prague, they reconvened in Budapest).

In sum, in both the GDR and the Czechoslovakia, various forms of resistance had developed at times, passing over resources to those who came later. A process of organization building and coordination was on its way, bridging different generations and concerns. The protest tide of 1989 helped consolidate these relations, as well as the creation of new groups. Especially at particular moments, these groups contributed important resources to the protest.

Resource Mobilization in The Arab Spring

Explanations for the lack of democratization in the MENA region oscillated between the weakness of a 'good' civil society and the strength of a 'non-democratic', Islamist civil society. In the late 1990s, in fact, as Cavatorta observed, 'in an interesting academic U-turn, it was then argued that democracy was not occurring in the region precisely because civil society was too vibrant and had an authoritarian nature, due in large part to the fact that much of the activism seemed to originate from Islamist movements' (2006, 204).

Both types of explanation were contested, however: first, by the observation of the presence of a rich civil society and, second, by the development of attention to democracy in Islamic civil society organizations. Several of them claimed, in fact, to follow democratic procedures, which they found important in both their internal life and for the state, and they often joined forces with other oppositional groups in denouncing state authoritarianism. Moreover, 'such associations have a rather precise understanding of social pluralism, and are increasingly tolerant of groups and associations that do not necessarily share their societal outlook' (Cavatorta 2006, 205). Even though Islamism is primarily a movement of the middle class, 'social Islam' represented 'a significant means through which some disadvantaged groups survive hardship and better their lives' (Bayat 2010, 78). Post-Islamism spread as a conscious attempt 'to conceptualize and strategize the rationale and modalities of transcending Islamism in social, political, intellectual domain with the aim of marrying Islam with individual freedom' (Bayat 2010, 243).

Moreover, informal networks were, here as well, considered as important mobilizing structures. In fact, 'informal networks may be a key to understanding both the quotidian struggles for survival and social reproduction that absorb the energies of the vast majority of the population in the region, as well as how undercurrents of anger and dissatisfaction may be mobilized' (Beinin and Vairel 2011b, 12).

A different issue, also at the centre of scholarly and non-scholarly debates, is the true independence of these associations. As Wiktorowicz (2000, 43), noted, 'Scholars, policymakers, and indigenous researchers alike hope that the growth of civil society in the region will promote democratic reform.... This optimism is encouraged by the United States, which now channels substantial resources to grass-roots organizations in the Middle East with the intention of promoting democracy.' He suggests, however, that, allowed to be founded and partially recognized in consultative function by regimes in search of legitimation after the shock of economic crisis in the late 1980s–early 1990s, 'Once created, these organizations were embedded in a web of bureaucratic practices and legal codes which allows those in power to monitor and regulate collective activities. This web reduces the possibility of a challenge to the state from civil society by rendering much of collective action visible to the administrative apparatus. Under such circumstances, civil society institutions are more an instrument of state social control than a mechanism of collective empowerment' (Wiktorowicz 2000, 43).

By other scholars, however, at least some of these associations have been seen as quite political and autonomous from the regime. Given the weakening/weakness of oppositional parties, a key trend in many Arab liberalizing regimes over the past decade has been seen in the rise of advocacy NGOs to the position of primary opposition to authoritarianism, against the almost complete marginalization of opposition parties (Langohr 2004). In fact,

> While insufficient or reversed liberalization measures have minimized the position of opposition parties, liberalization also created the conditions for Arab participation in a larger trend: the proliferation of human rights, women's, and environmental groups. With effective opposition parties all but nonexistent, advocacy non-governmental organizations have become the most vocal secular opposition in several Arab countries. They are also assuming roles, from defending the economic interests of workers and farmers to calling for the replacement of incumbent regimes, that typically are played by opposition parties (Langohr 2004, 181).

Given their organizational weakness in countries such as Tunisia or Egypt, the parties themselves promoted NGOs, and linked to them. Human rights organizations have been important in denouncing state repression (including torture) as well as defending groups that were hit by structural adjustments. Notwithstanding intense repression, labour movements also developed in the area, mobilizing workers on particular occasions, and riots protested regimes' decisions to cut subsidies on key goods.

Past experiences with mobilization were thus stressed against the image of a sudden 'awakening'. As Khalidi (2011) noted, people had also revolted in the past: citizens mobilized in Egypt against foreign rulers in 1800 and 1881, but also in 1919 and 1952; and Libyans revolted against the Italians in 1911. Even if within an anti-colonial approach, now overcome by a call for collective dignity, they had claimed democracy and constitutional reforms. Numerous protest campaigns in the 2000s played an important role in socializing to politics. In 2004, about one thousand activists occupied the palace of justice in Cairo to contest the prolongation of the presidency of Mubarak (el-Chazli and Hassabo 2013, 191), and in 2010 about one thousand activists welcomed the dissident and Nobel prize-winner Mohammad el-Baradei. In 2010, protests against the killing by policemen of the critical blogger Khalid Said included the readings of the Bible and the Koran by people dressed in black (el-Chazli and Hassabo 2013, 194).

Young people also participated through social media. The so-called Arab Spring was certainly not the product of new technologies, but such tools clearly helped in its spread. Howard (2010, 201) concluded his analyses of

Information and Communications Technology (ICT)'s influence on democratic change from 1994 to 2010 in seventy-five countries with large Muslim communities as follows: 'It is clear that, increasingly, the route to democratization is a digital one.' In fact, an active online civil society emerged as a most important condition for democratization during democratic transitions. It was also through Twitter, Facebook, and other social media that protest spread in the MENA region a participatory ethos that stressed individual over organizational involvement (Juris 2012).

Social networks certainly played an important role in the recent movements for democracy in Arab countries. As Postill (2012) noted, 'the combination of a politicised pan-Arab TV network (Al Jazeera), widely available mobile phones with photo and video capabilities, and the rapid growth of social media such as Facebook and YouTube since 2009, has created a "new media ecology" that authoritarian regimes are finding very difficult to control'. The information cascade generated through social media was impossible for the authorities to stop, spreading 'virally' through the simultaneous use of various means of communication. The Arab Spring has been defined in fact as characterized by 'the instrumental use of social media, especially Facebook, Twitter, YouTube, and text messaging by protesters, to bring about political change and democratic transformation' (Khamis and Vaughn 2011, 1). New media facilitated the development of free spaces, networking, and planning, as well as allowing 'citizen journalists' to document the protest activity and denounce police repression. As an activist declared, 'To have a space, an online space, to write and talk [to] people, to give them messages which will increase their anger, this is my favorite way of online activism. This is the way online activism contributed to the revolution. When you asked people to go and demonstrate against the police, they were ready because you had already provided them with materials which made them angry' (Aouragh and Alexander 2011).

As in Eastern Europe, religious places worked as (semi) free spaces. Holidays and holy days (Khosrokhavar 2012, 245), Fridays become central days for the protest, being named after specific slogans—Friday of anger, of determination, of the end of legitimacy, of defiance, of dignity, and so on. Already in the protests against the war on Iraq, marches started after Friday prayers and moved on from the mosques. Mainly mainstream in its religious leaning, the primary concerns of the Muslim Brotherhood (MB) at its foundation 'centered on the domination of Egypt by foreign powers, the poverty of the Egyptian people, and the declining morality they identified in both the Egyptian state and the lives of individuals throughout Egypt' (Munson 2001, 489). Participants in the MB were not the marginals, but rather the most modernized side of the society (especially urban students, teachers, and civil servants). The organization was successful in the building of a networked, three-layered structure, with large local autonomy and loose coordination, which—in contrast to hierarchical communist organizations—made it resilient to state repression. Its organization around mosques gave the movement the only space in which large congregations of people were tolerated, given protection and respectability, especially given its decision to involve each new branch in the construction of a mosque, a school, a clinic or a social club for the community (Munson 2001, 501). Additionally, its ideas resonated among the Egyptian population.

In general, Islamic social institutions—such as hospitals—have been defined as efficient networks for the building of an Islamist social movement (Clark 2004). Historically, religious networks had in fact been bases for protest against the imperfect functioning of clientelistic networks (Denoeux 1993). Middlemen sometimes became leaders of oppositional movements, escaping the control of their patrons. Professional bonds—for example in the bazaars—also helped in building networks that in some cases politicized. While the first generation of charities was mainly the work of clerics or notables, from the end of the nineteenth century they tended to be promoted by emerging educated middle classes, especially urban professionals, who felt they lacked career opportunities given their position outside the elite circles. As the International Monetary Fund (IMF) and World Bank (WB) sought the down-sizing of public institutions, Islamist ones acquired relevance as 'By offering successful social welfare services in the name of Islam to their fellow citizens, they represent an ideological and concrete or practical alternative to the present system' (Denoeux 1993, 15). Governments were therefore often forced to tolerate them in practice, even while constraining them in rhetoric and action.

In the mobilization of young people, in Egypt and beyond, football and music played a central role. As other gatherings were prohibited, football matches became occasions to express political claims (Khosrokhavar 2012, 226). Similarly, concerts were, in the words of a Tunisian activist, 'rare occasions when people could meet without feeling oppressed by the police or without the usual social barriers' (Khosrokhavar 2012, 238). Strongly repressed, heavy metal and hip-hop activists represented active counter-cultures.

Some technological support for coordination came from the mentioned rapidly increasing availability of new tools (in Egypt, there were 23 million broadband internet users, and eighty per cent of families had mobile phones) as well as some freedom in using the media arena. While satellite television channels had already introduced some media pluralism, the internet allowed for broader—if not equal—citizen participation through peer-to-peer communication between users and online networking. In fact, here as elsewhere, most of the user-generated content spread through social media (Khamis and Vaughn 2011).

The building of coalitions has been considered as particularly relevant in this area. As Goldstone (2011, 460) summarized, in Egypt and Tunisia, but also in Libya, 'a broad cross-class and cross-regional coalition was vital to overthrowing the regime. Islamists and secularists, residents of the capital city and rural towns; workers, students, teachers, lawyers; and defecting soldiers, all contributed to the revolutionary effort.' This made repression more difficult.

In both countries, moreover, diasporas and semi-diasporas (such as students of American University in Cairo or Tunisian students in France) were mobilized (Khosrokhavar 2012, 192).

Tunisia

The first country to rebel, Tunisia is a small and culturally homogeneous country with a strong national identity, long considered economically successful (only four per cent living below the poverty level), with a large and well-educated middle class and a weak military. Though the Jasmine Revolution started with an individual act of protest, social movement organizations had long been developing around issues of democracy and human rights, but also on labour and student rights.

Here as well, democratization struggles in 2011 had important antecedents. There was an important labour movement and a flourishing civil society, as well as the oldest human rights movement in the Arab world.

Strikes in the 1970s and anti-IMF riots in 1984 included claims for political reform, even meeting some temporary success. Also in Tunisia, between 1983 and 1992, the IMF had imposed structural adjustments, with privatization and an end to subsidies as well as price controls, plus lowering of trade barriers. These changes produced increasing unemployment, especially of young people. In the 2000s, there were street demonstrations and frequent activity by unemployed graduates. Pioneers of the movement were former student activists, who mobilized on the powerful frame of a right to work. In September 2006 there were daily demonstrations with up to 1,000 participants, followed by a de facto recognition by the authorities of activists as mediators on the labour market. In fact, one protestor explained that he 'used to be against these demonstrations. But then I realized that people who went out into the street were hired in the public sector' (Emperador Badimon 2011, 226).

Unions were in fact very important actors in protest campaigns. 'The unions' role in the Tunisian revolution was paramount. The intermediary grades of the General Union of Tunisian Workers (UGTT) managed to launch the movement, articulating the economic demands of workers and the lower middle class as well as the political demands for democracy of the middle classes and the younger generations' (Khosrokhavar 2012, 216).

While the main unions' umbrella organization, the UGTT, was rather controlled by the regime at the centre, there was some autonomy at the periphery (Joffé 2011). In 1978, the UGTT had called for a general strike in protest against the arrest of a union leader: fifty demonstrators were killed during the protests. After political liberalization in 1980 (when some unionists were released and parties legalized), the structural adjustments in 1984 fuelled bread riots in 1985. Harsh repression followed (with a ban on the communist party but also the repression of Islamist groups).[3] However, many local branches had gained independence, participating in various waves of labour activism. As Donker (2012b) recalls, 'Already before the 2010-2011 uprising... these local unions have been critical in translating direct material grievances (related to unemployment and regional underdevelopment) to more political demands of reform and better regional (economic) development.' The significance of the unions is reflected in the importance of strikes as a form of action.

In 2008, local unions supported the mobilization in the mining area against the clientelistic management of the Phosphate Company of Gafsa (CPG). Isolated, the workers were strongly repressed and their experience served as a warning to others. As Ayeb (2011, 470) summarized, as the CPG (Phosphate Company of Gafsa) recruited from outside the region, through practices considered corrupt, some local residents occupied the union office. During the protest, three people were killed and about a hundred arrested and charged. In December 2008, 'six leaders of the resistance movement received the maximum sentence, as they were accused in court "of leading demonstrations that undermine the public order by throwing stones and Molotov cocktails against the police"'. A transnational campaign was then launched, denouncing the torture and maltreatment of prisoners.

Young people protested as well, in different forms. One of them was the development of online protest groups. Exploiting the World Summit on the Information Society in November 2005, the 18 October Movement for Rights and Freedom saw an alliance of leftists, liberals, and Islamists, with hunger strikes against the Anti-terrorist Law of 2003. Even though this movement failed, as it remained secular and middle class, interactions between different groups increased later on. In 2008, a wave of strikes was accompanied by student protests. At the university, student representative bodies also mobilized, leading pupils from high schools to participate in the protests, which were in fact characterized by the very young age of the participants. In this, the uprisings initially built on young graduates who had not yet entered professional

---

[3] In the same year, fifty people were killed during an Israeli raid on the PLO headquarters in Tunis.

life and had low expectations of finding an occupation, given widespread youth unemployment (Ayeb 2011).

As reforms pushed for by the WB had increased unemployment, protest by unemployed but also by employed or precarious workers multiplied. Young unemployed coordinated via informal friendship networks, the unionists through pre-existing militant networks (Mersal 2011). Protests also mobilized unorganized under-proletariat and youth. Resistance came in fact from the subaltern classes, such as street vendors or unemployed, who called at the same time for integration in a consumer society, but also for freedom. Fights with police were carried out by unemployed and precarious youth, networks of friends that followed a set script. Young people organized quick attacks against the police in different places, while indiscriminate repression favoured solidarization. Urban dissidence also spread, with soccer ultras who declared, 'We leave the night, to avoid the society' (Allal 2012, 837). The use of cannabis had in this milieu an identifying function: it exposed protestors to police violence, which in turn produced radicalization. Young unemployed met in coffee shops, in informal groups like the 'BA for ever' (where BA stands of course for Ben Ali). Repression produced solidarization in this environment. Members of one such group recalled that a cousin called them during the protests in 2008 on the square—'We died from fear, but we wanted to know...' (Allal 2012, 836). The cousin was then arrested and tortured; his and others' repression spurred protests by relatives and friends in Nantes or Bellevue, as marches from every region converged on Tunis.

There was, moreover, increasing indignation against corruption (Hmed 2012). In 2010, strong protest spread from the southwest (Gafsa) to the southeast, the agricultural area of Sidi Bouzid and other regions against regional disparity in development. Corruption in the union hierarchies increased a sense of injustice. Even if there was repression, an activist declared, 'We are not going to stop. Now we know our strength' (Hmed 2012). While there were few activists among the protestors, there were many wives or widowers of workers, young unemployed with high school diplomas, high school pupils, rank and file unionists, and family members of the protestors who had been arrested (Allal 2012, 825).

In August 2010, people protested the closing down of the borders with Libya. Peaceful marches were brutally repressed, but there was also renegotiation on the reopening of the border. In Ayeb's (2011, 471) account,

> As a result of the frontier being closed between Tunisia and Libya, riots break out in Ben Guerdane. The official version explains this decision to close the frontiers by the need to control the very active informal trade between the two countries that feeds hundreds and even thousands of families, either by creating informal jobs, usually precarious and on the margins of legality, or by offering the local population expensive products cheaper than through formal channels. However

in fact it was due to the Trabelsi mafia realising that it had been missing its cut from this lucrative activity and now wanting to control it.

While collective protests targeted rampant nepotism, human rights activist organizations included the Ligue Tunisienne de Droits de l'Homme (LTDH, Tunisian league of Human Rights), the first human rights organization to be formed in an Arab country (Perkins 2004, 165). Unionized teachers supported local peasants against expropriation, and protests included demonstrations against the war in Lebanon in 2006 and the Gaza occupation in 2009. Already mobilized against Israeli aggression in Gaza, various groups—involving especially pupils, students, and teachers—organized solidarity caravans with the Palestinians, opposing the Tunisian government's support for Israel.

An additional network to mobilize was the Islamic one, including Hizb al-Tahrir (the Liberation party, or HuT) and Salafists. The latter 'generally build on very fluid and informal networks,... Within Tunisia they have mainly mobilized around issues concerning the freedom of religion (being allowed to wear a Hijab to university for instance) and in reaction to perceived attacks against the Islamic basis of Tunisian identity and public life.... General repertoires include marches, public prayers, sit-ins and—occasionally—arson attempts' (Perkins 2004).

These groups also mobilized at the onset of the Jasmine Revolution. Even if heavily repressed, all these protests allowed for the activation of oppositional networks, including young people, already mobilized in previous years. During the Jasmine Revolution, the protest tactics were inherited from previous mobilizations, among them the student movement of the 1980s (repressed first by Bourquiba and then by Bel Ali) but also of the repressed Islamist party Ennahda (which, however, did not take part in the uprisings). While Ben Ali's coup d'état reduced the spaces of politicization, people remained active, in the shadows.

What is more, these movement organizations had networked in recent times, bridging specific, material concerns with political discourse about their potential solution. In 2011, the demonstrations were organized, initially in Sidi Bouzid, by local members of the union, and radical leftists of Arab nationalist inspiration (Hmed 2012). As the mobilization proceeded, local councils were founded where activists from various movement organizations gathered. As in previous uprisings, these councils played a pivotal role in keeping the mobilization alive, as 'Local activists were experienced in building up cross-movement relations to channel, co-ordinate and sustain popular discontent' (Perkins 2004). It was from these coordinating committees that the councils for safeguarding of the revolution emerged after 14 January 2011.

Egypt

In Egypt as well, the sudden revolt was not so sudden after all, rooting itself in civil society networks similar to the ones noted in Tunisia, and to a similar process of coordination.

Some oppositional groups had developed through and around new technologies. Even though internet penetration was relatively low (only twenty-five per cent of the population was connected in 2011), the regime granted some freedom compared with other dictatorships in the area—presented by Mubarak to the West as proof of liberalism. The internet thus became an alternative to a heavily policed space (Gerbaudo 2012)—here, norms of linking, sharing, and remixing spread (Valeriani 2011). In the second half of the 2000s, Harvard-based NGO Global Voices had provided resources for online activism. Annual conferences, such as the Arab Technies collective in Cairo in 2008, the Arab blogger summits in Beirut in 2008 and 2009, and the Re:pubblica Digital media conference in Berlin were spaces where activists met (Tufekci and Wilson 2012).

The use of the internet for political purposes had grown during mobilizations in solidarity with Palestine and against the war in Iraq at the beginning of the millennium. Mobilization then spread in support of workers' strikes in 2008, and in the solidarity networks of the left-wing Youth for Change with farmers, fishermen, and local residents. Nobel laureate el-Baradei's calls for constitutional change and, in 2010, the killing by police of Khaled Said, a twenty-eight-year-old blogger who had exposed involvement of police officers in drug dealing, helped in the growth of a civil society rooted in loose networks and friendship cliques. In fact, Youth for Change staged several surprise protests, usually lasting less than thirty minutes, in popular areas in greater Cairo. Cyber-resistance supported these mobilizations through the use of mobile phones, mailing lists, blogs, and so on. Moreover, citizens' (or popular) journalism spread, also through workshops organized by international agencies and via the internet (Onondera 2011).

However, the focus only on the westernized, young, educated, middle class bloggers, writing mainly in English, has been criticized as a new Orientalist stereotype that sees modernization as coming from the West and denies actors their agency (Salvatore 2011). In fact, it was only when bloggers met with other social groups and organizations—including union activists and soccer hooligans—that the existing resources could be mobilized through a coordinated effort.

Notwithstanding a succession of authoritarian regimes, the history of Egypt is full of protests on social issues, especially since the 1970s, as the international financial institutions pushed towards cuts in state expenditure in order to reduce budget deficits. On 18 and 19 January 1977, bread riots, following cuts of subsidies on the price of basic goods, ended in the deaths of at least seventy-nine protestors; but Sadat was forced to reintroduce subsidies on basic foodstuffs (Mackell 2012). Later on, as Bayat noted, the streets were not deserted, even if heavily controlled, as 'Streets as spaces of flow and movement are not only where people protest, but also where they extend their protest beyond the immediate circles to include also the unknown, the "strangers" who might espouse similar grievances, real or imagined' (Bayat 2012, 76). The Egyptian Popular Committee for Solidarity with the Palestinian Intifada had brought together different groups, from nationalists to socialists, and from Islamists to women's rights protestors. Grassroots charity and boycotts of US and Israeli products had successfully spread, with Coca Cola losing up to forty per cent of its market (Bayat 2012). In 2005, during and after the elections, the judges protested against increasing constraints on their autonomy, bridging struggles for clean elections and judicial autonomy. As an ambiguous constitution had made judges responsible for supervising elections, the executive had since the 1990s increasingly attempted to control the judiciary (el-Ghobashy 2012b, 2012c). In 2010, new technologies helped with documentation, including disseminating abroad the evidence of electoral fraud (as phones were used to film pre-voted ballots) (Guibal and Tangi 2011).

From 1998 to 2009 over two million workers participated in more than 3,300 factory occupations, strikes, demonstrations or other collective actions. With quite democratic internal practices, union activism bridged specific claims to Arab socialist frames or Islamic notions of moral economy (Beinin 2011, 183). Much protest developed in the 2000s, usually on bread and butter issues but becoming later politicized (Beinin 2012). Labour protests followed each neo-liberal turn in the government's policies (WB ranked Egypt among the top ten reformer countries (Beinin 2011, 186)). As Beinin (2011, 181) observed, 'Egyptian workers have not received the message that class struggle is unfashionable.' Even though the Unified Labour Law legalized strikes in 2003, conditions were so restrictive (needing approval by official trade unions), and the Egyptian Trade Union Federation, ETUF (and its 1,751 local committees) so controlled by the regime, that all but one of the mentioned strikes were illegal (Beinin 2011). Supported by intellectuals and pro-labour NGOs such as the Center for Trade Union and Workers Services (CTUWS) and the coordinating Committee for Trade Union and Workers Rights and Liberties, workers mobilized in response to the privatization, throughout the 1990s, of 190 firms. In the second half of the 1990s, food prices increased, salaries dropped, and a sharp increase in inequality was also met by protests: between 1998 and 2003, workers' protests grew from an average of twenty-five in the previous ten years, to an average of 118, increasing to 265 in 2004 and 614 in 2007.

Indeed, protests exploded especially after, in 2004, a new government with several Western-educated ministers prompted a new wave of strikes during the privatization of what workers considered as their own firms. Labour and hunger strikes sometimes even won concessions (as in July 2006, after three days of work stoppage). The privatization of 312 enterprises in the Delta was met by brutally repressed protests. There were also struggles in public industrial firms, as at the Misr Spinning and Weaving Company, where women led the struggles to a victory, or at the private Ora-Misr company, using asbestos, which was then forced to close. Some of these events developed more politically, targeting the government and its neo-liberal policies. On 6 April 2008, the textile workers' strike in Mahalla, a large industrial town in the Delta, was also repressed. While a yellow union intimidated participants, on the day of the protest, Mubarak's picture was trampled on the ground. Demonstrations of tens of thousands on Labour Day 2010 testified to the continuous strength of labour conflicts, with the support of the 6 April coalition and youth groups (Mackell 2012).

Labour protests would also be very visible all through the uprisings, with three days of general strikes starting on 8 February. After Mubarak's fall, as well, an unprecedented wave of union activities with daily demonstrations continued until early October, with large national strikes of teachers, doctors, bus drivers. Union membership rose to two million, although jeopardized by threats of withdrawal of services by old unions (Mackell 2012).[4]

In the 2000s, there was a slow increase in the oppositional networks' size and density. Under Mubarak, as many as 30,000 organizations of various types existed, despite the persecution of human rights activists. Core opponents included independent NGOs, such as the Center for Economic and Social Rights, the New Woman Foundation, and the CTUWS (Teti and Gervasio 2012), while the parliamentary opposition—with parties such as the left-wing Tagammu, liberal al-Ghad (Tomorrow), and small Islamist groups (such as Wasat)—were quite discredited before the events.

Here as well, in the years immediately preceding upheaval, coordination increased. In the many protests carried out between 2004 and 2006, alliances were built (Khamis, Gold, and Vaughn 2012). As Abdelrahman's research (2011) demonstrated, there was even increasing cooperation between left-wingers and Islamists (even the MB), as well as Nasserists. There was certainly a long history of antagonism, fuelled when, in 1977, the Islamists supported Sadat's economic measures against the leftist protestors, accused

---

[4] Protest after Mubarak met with heavy repression and a demobilization effort by the MB and Salafists. While many groups opposed the proposal of further liberalization, the MB in Egypt supported them. The same is true of repression of protest after the revolution in Tunisia, and further structural adjustments and economic opening.

of conspiracy, and in 1993 the Left reciprocated by supporting the Unified Law for syndicates, which targeted the growing influence of the Islamists. However, some cooperation at the grassroots had developed already in the 1990s, with a major turning point in the 2000s, during the campaigns in support of the Palestinian Intifada. Popular Committees, with broad participation, also attracted Islamist groups, which had strong membership in the unions. Notwithstanding bitter divisions within and between each area, networks blossomed during waves of activism within the principle of cooperative differentiation, which meant working on the basis of consensus, avoiding divisive slogans, but also keeping independence.

Even if demonstrations remained small, they were important in the history of cooperation. The networked organizational structure was strengthened by the relations with the global justice movement, in particular through the work of the Anti-Globalisation Egyptian Group (AGEG). Conferences were organized together by left-wing and Islamic groups in Cairo, under slogans such as 'No to Capitalist Globalization and US hegemony', 'No to the occupation of Iraq and Zionism in Palestine', 'No to authoritarianism in the Arab regions'.

Notwithstanding internal conflicts, MB leaders participated in the protests, bringing with them some relevant networks.[5] Some characteristics of the organization had in fact allowed the organization to survive heavy repression. First, it was successful in the building of a networked, three-layered structure, with large local autonomy and loose coordination, which—differently from hierarchical communist organizations—made it resilient to state repression. Additionally, its ideas resonated among the Egyptian population. Mainly mainstream in its religious leanings, the MB's primary concerns 'centered on the domination of Egypt by foreign powers, the poverty of the Egyptian people, and the declining morality they identified in both the Egyptian state and the lives of individuals throughout Egypt' (Munson 2001, 489).

Additionally, MB members did not mainly come from the marginal strata, but rather from the most modernized side of the society, especially urban students, teachers, and civil servants (Munson 2001). Islamic social institutions—such as hospitals—worked as social movement organizations. Notwithstanding their expressed aims to help the marginal people, however, they tended to involve especially the middle class, towards whose need for

---

[5] The politicization of the MB had developed with their support for the Arab general strike in Palestine in the late 1930s and the increasing criticism of the Egyptian regime (Munson 2001). In 1941, the MB announced its own candidates at the elections, but they were banned after denouncing the British war effort. Tolerated de facto, in 1949, the MB had over 2,000 branches and about half a million members. A new wave of (this time strong) repression followed Nasser's assassination by a member of the MB.

jobs and services they are oriented (Clark 2004). This implied the risk of alienating the poor—their proclaimed constituency.

Also later on, the dominant organizational structure, which allowed for these collaborations, was no longer formal and bureaucratic, but rather networked and horizontal. Joint initiatives thus developed, excluding divisive issues (such as judgment on suicide bombers) but also leaving members independence in their respective activities beyond the coalitional ones. In both camps, this development arose from self-criticism and internal divisions, with a rethinking of Islamists on the Left (as potentially progressive, even near to the workers) and a shift—even in the radical Gamaa Islamia—towards consideration of democracy as more urgent than *sharia*.

Protests thus spread throughout the 2000s, in various waves including the pro-Palestine university mobilizations in 2000, protests against the US invasion of Iraq in 2003, the movements in Kifaya in 2004, the march of the judges for independence of the judiciary system in 2006, and workers' protests beginning in 2008. As el-Ghobashy (2011) noted, 'The reality was that Egyptians had been practicing collective action for at least a decade, acquiring organizational experience in that very old form of politics: the street action. Egypt's streets had become parliaments, negotiating tables and battlegrounds rolled into one. To compel unresponsive officials to enact or revoke specific policies, citizens blockaded major roads with tree branches and burning tires; organized sit-ins in factory plants or outside ministry buildings; and blocked the motorcades of governors and ministers.' Hundreds of protests have been registered at the workplace, in the neighbourhood, as well as on human rights, inside and outside Egypt (el-Ghobashy 2011).

These protests had a horizontal, loose coordination, with multiple hubs. Movements networked and changed the conceptions of collective action as plural and loosely coordinated. This was the case also for the Coalition of the Revolution's Youth during uprisings which, with its 50,000 Facebook members, worked as forums of discussion (el-Nawawy and Khamis 2012).

Initially, participation in these events was limited to a few hundred, with the exception of the demonstrations against the war in Iraq in February 2003, in which 40,000 people participated. The internet worked then as an arena for sensitizing young people to politics. As an activist recalled,

It was summer 2010 and I wasn't really into politics. I was reading the news, sometimes I would write something on Facebook. But that was it. I wasn't really caring much about politics. Then Khaled Said's page began, and it spread very fast. A friend sent me an invitation…and I started looking at the news and really caring about what is happening to my country. And I watched the pictures which were brutal. And the guy did nothing but ask why are you searching me. A lot of people like me started really caring about this after they saw the photo of Khaled

Said's face, which was very brutal, and I really thought sometimes that this could happen to me...That page is what got me into politics (el-Nawawy and Khamis 2012, 55).

It was in the early 2000s that protests on Palestinian issues brought about coordination efforts with the creation of the Egyptian Popular Committee in Solidarity with the Intifada (EPCSI), of which many activists of the 2011 protests had been members. As the war on Iraq started in 2003, the 20 March Popular Campaign for Change was formed, bridging claims on international and domestic issues. As an activist interviewed by Warkotsch (2012) recalled,

The main difference between the pro-Intifada mobilization and the 2003 mobilization was the level of radicalism. The pro-Intifada protests were something like a charity. The regime could easily say that it was in favour of the Palestinians as well. Even some activists were surprised when there were clashes with the police because they did not perceive their mobilization to be directed against the regime at all. 2003, by contrast, was a clear attack against the regime. The focus started to turn on Mubarak, people were tearing down his pictures and shouted slogans denouncing him. In general there was the feeling that Mubarak was the appropriate target of mobilization.

During the next year, in 2004, the Egyptian Movement for Change (Kifaya) started to mobilize against Mubarak, especially on the occasion of the presidential referendum and parliamentary elections in 2005. Even if failing to reach its aims, Kifaya's mobilization in 2005 inspired organizations such as Journalists for Change, Doctors for Change, Youth for Change, and Workers for Change (Khosrokhavar 2012, 46). Artists for Change developed from informal networks of dissidents that had kept the memory of activism alive (Duboc 2011). In 2005, left-wing and MB activists supported the mobilization of the judges for independence. The discourse on human rights—which had entered Egypt with Israel's invasion of Lebanon and the siege of Beirut in 1983, with a critique of the government that had failed to support the Palestinians—was taken up especially by left-wing activists. However, MB members also participated with EOR (Egyptian organization for human rights), and 'Islamists were key to the growth of the movement in one important way: they were the primary victims of state abuses' (Stork 2011, 93).

In the following years, young activists in particular moved towards more grassroots movement organizations, such as the 6 April movement. Young people, disillusioned by Kifaya, founded the new group, recalling in its name the date of the repressed textile workers' strike in 2008. Mainly very young, many of them had attended the same university: 'Thus, when talking about the initial mobilizers, those who put out the call for action, we are talking about young, educated, well connected activists mostly from the Middle Class' (Stork 2011, 93).

Other oppositional networks coalesced around parties such as the Social Democrats and Hizb al-Adl. As summed up by activist Noor Ayman Noor,

> The 6th of April set foundations for the fact that you can organise big protests online. Kifaya set foundations for the fact that you can go down on the streets and say 'kifaya Mubarak' [enough of Mubarak]. 25th of January didn't happen overnight. It was years of things building up, of people setting things in stone. And the best example of this is that on the 25th of January many of the chants that we were chanting were chants that we had been chanting in earlier demonstrations. Everything is a build-up, nothing happens overnight (Gerbaudo 2012, 54).

Finally, young participants also came from the poorer strata, which had indeed mobilized in the past. In the words of an activist: 'While groups of professional youth revolutionaries led the organization, what made it successful was that millions joined. If it had not been for the marginalized, the 3rd class of Cairo and its surrounding areas on the 28th things would not have moved. What united these people was that all of them hated Mubarak, but none of them was mobilized because of electoral politics, but rather because there are no jobs, they have no food' (cit. in Warkotsch 2012). Another added,

> ...on the 25th it was mainly middle class people mobilized through the internet. But on the 28th it was different. And people from the lower classes were essential for fighting against the police. I for example never even thought about attacking soldiers or police. Activists would just run away and collect themselves somewhere else and try the same again. The people who came with the idea of attacking back were not activists. The experience people make in encountering police in their daily lives is very different.... Political activists were not on those fronts defending Tahrir simply because they lack the skills. People from the Middle Class are not normally in contact with the police in their daily lives, and political activists encounter them but in a different way than lower class people (Warkotsch 2012).

Participation in the protests changed existing organizations. Although it waited until 27 January to officially join—fearing repression, but also (apparently) isolation of the mobilization as Islamists—the (technically illegal) MB allowed their youth wing to participate in the initial stages of the mobilization. When they did join, they efficiently contributed to the protection of Tahrir, against the police and violent Mubarak supporters: 'It was this superior degree of organization and discipline that allowed them to uphold the defence line of Midan Tahrir with an efficiency lacking from basically all other groups present during the protests' (Warkotsch 2012). In polemic with the leadership (especially when the leaders supported the military), many young MB members joined in the 6 April movement, which valued the encounter of people with different ideological and religious backgrounds converging on the common goal of increasing democracy, and the need to do it through protest.

The Tahrir revolution also transformed the workers' movement, especially since the general strike shifted 'the balance in favour of the protesters, thereby helping at least to speed up the process of bringing down Mubarak' (Warkotsch 2012). This happened thanks to the emerging independent networks of workers, who opposed the state-controlled union federation, ETUF. Workers did not only go on strike; they also articulated a political discourse. A politicization of the workers' movement had in fact developed since 2006 as, as an activist recalls, 'more than 1.8 million of people were involved in strikes and that's not including their families and friends who thereby heard about it. The breaking of fear like that cannot be called insignificant, if you have 1.8 million who have somehow contended with authority in some way' (cit. in Warkotsch 2012). Occupations and sit-ins were some of the workers' strategic contributions to the protest repertoire.

Thanks to the combination of old and new communication techniques, information overcame borders—as 'Egyptian activists were supported by the flow of information coming to them from abroad, while simultaneously influencing international public opinion abroad, through their own coverage of the Egyptian uprising and the information they provided on it'. When the mobilization began, messages from Tunisian protesters spread on the Egyptian blogs: they 'advised their Egyptian counterparts to protest at night-time for safety, to avoid suicide operations, to use media to convey their message for outside pressure, to spray-paint security forces' armored vehicles black to cover the windshield, and to wash their faces with Coca-Cola to reduce the impact of tear gas' (Eltantawy and Wiest 2011). They also advised: ' "Put vinegar or onion under your scarf for tear gas" and brainstormed with their Egyptian counterparts on how to evade state surveillance, resist rubber bullets, and construct barricades' (Khamis and Vaughn 2011).

As in the GDR, here as well, as the masses occupied the streets, previously existing social movement organizations lost their capacity to control the mobilization. In the first phase, the actions mobilized the young militant generation (leftist, Islamist, nationalist, liberal) which had networked in previous struggles. Debates developed on which place to choose for the protest (marches from the periphery?), its form (against just a meeting in a public space), the coordination of on-line and off-line communication, how to present oneself at demonstrations (slogans, signals, and so on) (el-Chazli 2012). Stand ins were in fact perceived as a weak form of protest, as they are isolated from the people by police and by media campaigns. As mentioned, the activists instead chose protests of proximity, such as marches in the small streets on the edge of the city, with demonstrators chanting slogans on social justice and against unemployment. However, the response exceeded their expectations, challenging strategic action as 'the militants realize they have a considerable difficulty to orient protestors, to control them, to impose a good sense to what happens' (el-Chazli 2012, 853). Their social capital and reputation was indeed useless in the square, with people who did not recognize them as leaders—their political capital did not work in Tahrir (el-Chazli 2012, 853).

In sum, in the Arab Spring as well, organizational resources had slowly been constructed during previous mobilizations. Coordination among different groups and movements had started well before the latest protest waves. In contrast to the Eastern European case, in the two MENA countries the workers contributed to this long-lasting accumulation of symbolic and organizational resources.

Resource Mobilization: A Summary

Unexpectedly for social movement studies, which have de facto considered social movements as a product of democracy, all of our four cases have shown the rooting of eventful democratizations in a growing social movement milieu. Unexpectedly for transition studies, which focused on elites, the development of civil society is a long-lasting process that shapes—not just catalyses—the democratization process.

Certainly, the groups we have analysed might be considered as wanting on some main characteristics of social movement organizations in a democratic context. Unions and labour activities were less than autonomous from the regime; non-movements were only temporarily politicized; human rights organizations lived a precarious life, barely tolerated by the authoritarian regime; new social movements found very limited space to develop their claims on issues such as the environment, peace, or women's rights, which were paid lip service by those in power. Nevertheless, oppositional milieus did exist, and did influence their environment much more than their size might lead us to expect.

A similarly broad range of associations was singled out in other authoritarian regimes as well. Among the forms of participation Carapico (1998) listed in Yemen were all those which emerged as important in our cases, including literary societies, labour unions, professional associations, village committees, sporting clubs, interest groups, political organizations, contributions to the third sector, free media—all developing when windows of opportunities were available. Even during British colonialism, there had been a blooming of public spaces (cafes, shops, parks, and so on) as marketplaces of ideas. In particular, the most militant Arab labour movement developed from 1956, in contact with British labour, substituting for prohibited political organizations. During the anti-colonial struggles, intellectual circles attracted *ulamas*, *shaykhs*, merchants and so on—several of the 'fathers of the revolution' were in fact poets (Carapico 1998, 98). After the National Liberation Front, with unions' support, eventually won independence in 1967, a self-help, cooperative movement developed, linked to 'small-scale, ad hoc improvements in community services; to liberal discontent with deliberately maintained backwardness; and to popular aspiration for better living standards, a measure of local autonomy, and rudimentary rights of association, expression, and investment....Community projects constituted political mobilization' (Carapico 1998, 118). Studies on development have observed how the struggles of subordinate people in action groups quickly developed in various regions of the world, as 'Action groups proliferate by the thousand in Latin America, Sub-Saharan Africa and South Asia' (Haynes 1997, 6). Often defensive, grassroots, and focused on sources of living, but also political, they are constitutive elements of civil society in authoritarian regimes.

In other cases as well, the story of opposition under dictatorship often involved an encroachment inside existing institutions that the dictators would have liked to, but could not fully subject to their will. Schools and universities, churches, firms, and factories are among the most important of such institutions, which are indeed (often in democracies as well) in uneasy relations with the state. In his comparison of Iran, Nicaragua, and the Philippines, Parsa (2000) points in fact at the role of students', clerics', and workers' groups in rapid transformations, not only of structures, but also of coalitions.

Not only did civil society organizations of various types exist in all our cases, but these groups had already started to network with each other in previous waves of—sometimes failed—rebellion. In particular, new generations of activists had emerged to integrate the older oppositional ones. If coordination, as mentioned in the previous chapter, intensified during eventful democratization, reciprocal knowledge and trust had already developed around previous contentious events. Not necessarily cross-class, pluralist organizational structures had developed as umbrella organizations in which different types of groups were connected. Churches, factories, and universities nurtured oppositional activities, and so did—especially in the Arab Spring—the street.

This research therefore confirms the emphasis we find in studies of revolutions on the important role of coalition building. Among others, Foran observed that,

> For revolutions to occur, an opposition must coalesce....To move toward revolution from the structural determinants of the grievances produced by dependent development and the repressive, exclusionary, personalist and colonial state (or channeled into electoral success in the open polity), broad segments of many groups and classes must be able to articulate experiences they are living through into effective and flexible analyses: capable of mobilizing their own forces and building coalitions with others (Foran 2005, 21).

In fact, labour was particularly influential when it sparked other actors into mobilization (Foweraker and Landman 1997, 213).

In South Africa (Schock 2005), mass protest was coupled with the development, in the 1980s, of local groups and social movement unionism involved in protest and persuasion, through, for example, education campaigns but also rent boycotts and non-cooperation through stay-away: decentralization helped with survival after strong waves of repression in the mid-1980s. Similarly in the Philippines, during the rule of martial law, a decentralized coalition was able to organize weekly demonstrations, accompanied by people's strikes (during which shops closed, barricades were built, and public and private transport was halted) and the withdrawal of funds from cronies' controlled banks and corporations.

However, the presence of networks of civil society organizations is only part of the story as, by definition, eventful democratizations involve masses of first-time protestors. This also means—as was especially clear in the GDR case—that protests and civil society organizations cannot be collapsed into one another. Eventful protests emerged as less spontaneous than transition studies would have expected, but also less organized than social movement studies would have predicted. In particular the degree of control of protests by social movement organizations varied in time and space. Civil society organizations played important roles in the mobilization, but they were also transformed by it. They led protests at times, but were also sometimes contested. And these complex interactions shaped the destiny of eventful democratizations. Similarly, in Eastern Europe the protest politicized those very informal networks that had until then functioned more to soothe than to fuel dissatisfaction with lack of freedom and poor working conditions.

If the mentioned characteristics were similar in the two waves, some differences are nonetheless worth noting. First, social movement organizations as well as protest appear as better developed in the MENA region than in Eastern Europe. Even if repression was more brutal in the former than in the latter, a longer process of (even if interrupted) liberalization had allowed for the growth of semi-autonomous spaces. Additionally, if communication was a challenge in both areas, as authoritarian regimes thwarted freedom of speech, the presence of new technologies, more accessible and more difficult to control, gave the second wave a different dynamic.

A main difference also emerged in terms of the social actors who mobilized. In Eastern Europe there was frustration at the declining economic performance and unfulfilled promises of economic growth. In the MENA region, market liberalization had been met with intense—and often violent—protests. In particular, while in Eastern Europe the coalition was built around human rights organizations that evolved in connection with various types of new social movements, in the MENA region (especially in Egypt) the unions and professional organizations played a more pivotal role. Even though in all cases workers participated in the eventful democratization, their presence took on more organized forms in the MENA region. If both Christian and Muslim clerics have at times supported the protests, the relations within the organizational fields were more strained between Islamic and left-wing organizations in the MENA countries than between Protestant or Catholic and lay people in Eastern Europe.

In addition, in the MENA region there was a more visible mobilization of marginal peoples. There, in fact, the poor had built passive networks, by occupying the same street, and coming together under common threats. So,

conflict originates from the active use of public space by subjects who, in the modern states, are allowed to use it only passively—through walking, driving, watching—or in other ways that the state dictates. Any active or participative use infuriates officials, who see themselves as the sole authority to establish and control public order. Thus, the street vendors who proactively spread their businesses in the main alleyways; squatters who take over public parks, lands, or sidewalks; youth who control the street-corner spaces, street children who establish street communities; poor housewives who extend their daily household activities into alleyways; or protestors who march in the streets, all challenge the state prerogatives and thus may encounter reprisal (Bayat 2010, 11).

While in street demonstrations one found the middle class in particular, sometimes endowed with a nationalist discourse, some forms of action were based instead on what Bayat (2010) defined as the encroachment of everyday life with a sort of cosmopolitanism of the subalterns. Free spaces were also constructed here by self-help activities among the poor and marginalized groups, which so often play an important role in resisting authoritarian and semi-authoritarian regimes. It was through the politicization of various forms of resistance that the streets then became a space for mobilization. As Bayat (2010, 220) noted, the Arab street was neither irrational nor dead; rather, the regimes' attempts to depoliticize social ties instead had a hyper-politicizing effect. Football supporters accumulated an important savoir faire in their fights with police (Bennani-Chraibi and Fillieule 2012).

Saxonberg (2012) has stressed that different social groups bring to democratization processes different interests: while workers tend to rebel when their conditions worsen, intellectuals dominate dissident movements independently of economic conditions, and professionals join only when rebellion is already strong. Intellectuals are expected to rebel especially because of regime expectations that conflict with their own vision. They are considered as the most likely to lead the opposition, as their voices are more likely to be heard, being more sophisticated and having better access to international audiences. Having more to lose, professionals are expected to join later.

While Parkin (1968) assumed that they would lead the opposition in socialist regimes, given their incongruence of status, this expectation was balanced with their interest in keeping their posts.

Less present in 1989, workers are considered as less frustrated as they 'do not have to worry about hammering out product in a socialist realist manner' (Saxonberg 2012, 166). Workers are then said to be under less pressure, as they do not have to perform their work in particular ways, and are discouraged from protesting by threats of job dismissals and lack of promotion. Even if they have little to lose, they also have little protection: if arrested, they do not make international news. They—as peasants—are therefore expected to protest during economic crisis or waves of starvation.

Built on Eastern Europe, this picture needs some correction, however, especially when moving to the MENA region. In Tunisia, but also in Egypt, the workers were in fact main actors in various waves of protest that reacted to parallel waves of economic liberalization, with a related increase in inequalities. These struggles had slowly politicized not only industrial workers, but also precarious workers and unemployed that had perceived the state as betraying the promises that the nationalist elites had made to the population. While intellectuals and middle classes were also mobilized in both cases, the impetus came more from the excluded class.

In this sense, rather than the position in the productive cycles, a sort of class consciousness seems to have played a most important role. The cognitive processes of construction of the self and the opposition will be addressed in the next chapter, looking at the framing of the protest as well as the interaction within and without the social movements' organizational field.

In addition to domestic organizational structures, transnational connections were relevant as well. These were both intra-area connections among countries that faced similar regimes, and transnational connections beyond the involved areas. The first were particularly important in spreading the frames and structures of the revolt, as well as helping create an assessment of similarities that favoured cross-national diffusion of ideas. The second type of connection was relevant in order to gain symbolic recognition and international support against repression. In this sense, human rights movement networks played a role in both 1989 and 2011, through the mobilization as well the support of diasporas from the various countries, which helped create solidarity for protestors abroad but also at home.

In the Argentinean case addressed by Brysk (1993), the reframing of the Argentinean regime as a fascist rather than a traditional authoritarian one helped in increasing solidarity. So, 'In addition to the traditional sanctions of diplomacy and economic linkages against the repressive regime, International actors directly provided the Argentinean movement with publicity, legitimacy, information and material resources' (Brysk 1993, 272). Similarly in our cases, mobilized actors were effective in stopping specific instances of repression, opening communication offices for victims of abuse, educating the public, increasing the perceived costs by the elites, and challenging the legitimacy of those in power.

Beyond adding or subtracting constraints, other national or transnational actors can provide material resources for associations involved in democratization processes. This mechanism became particularly visible as Western-supported NGOs played a role in the so-called orange revolutions (McFaul 2010a), spreading an electoral model consisting of registering voters, getting them to vote, and persuading them to vote for the opposition (Bunce and Wolchik 2010b). In this sense, in the post-communist world, the international system was in fact not only permissive, but also acted as a promoter (Bunce and Wolchik 2010b). This help sometimes came however with strings attached: support for a human rights discourse, but not necessarily for a participatory alternative to representative democracy.

This was only partially the case in our two waves. In Eastern Europe, the Helsinki agreements offered symbolic rather than material support (which came, instead, after the transition). In the MENA regions, economic support went to the least politically committed organizations. Thus, the US Agency for International Development donated to Egyptian NGOs $410 million between 1976 and 2001, but international pressures and NGO mobilization did not stop very restrictive laws on associations (such as Law 153 in 1999), while dependence on foreign funds deprived those organizations from an important basis of accountability: paying membership.

4

Framing Democracy: The Cognitive Dimension of Mobilization

Introduction

Freedom is always the freedom of those who think differently,
  Rosa Luxemburg
Democracy
Privileges away: We are the people
Freedom, equality, fraternity
Wiedersehen-Ja; Wierevereinigen-nein [seeing each other again yes,
  being again united, no]
Germany: one fatherland
Free elections: Now
            (slogans of the GDR protests, reported in Lindner 2010, 128–9).

Never again forgotten, never again marginalized
Lawyer and unemployed, together for the revolution
Unemployed citizens, let's participate in the revolutions
Employment, Liberty, Dignity, Citizenship
Citizens, join us against repression and humiliation
We will never forget you, Mohamed Bouazizi. We are going to make
  cry those who made you cry
                    (slogans of the Tunisian protests, reported in
                            Bettaieb and Bettaieb 2011, 128–9).

These slogans, in their variety and differentiated temporal emergence, reflect cognitive processes at work during eventful democratization. Successful when resonating with widespread thinking and feeling, they are, once again, constructed in action. During waves of protest, in fact, actors (individual and collective; from above and from below) assess present situations, often relying on past experiences, but also on new ideas, sometimes coming from outside the country.

As mentioned, during the eventful processes of democratization we have analysed there was a growth in generality of the scope of action, a politicization of
claims, a perception of empowerment. Memories of past situations played a role
in the appreciation of the external reality, while mobilization changed the frame
of everyday reality, through cross-fertilization with other movements.

Democratization studies have paid limited explicit attention to cognitive
processes. Although elites' predispositions have been taken into account, and
the rootedness of democratic values has been considered as a pre-condition for
democratic consolidation, research on the development of ideas, narratives, and
discourses has been sporadic. In the 1980s and 1990s, with the shift of attention
from socio-economic structures to political negotiation, democratic norms were
no longer considered as preconditions but rather as emerging from the democratization process itself. As Adam Przeworski (1991) explained, in fact, face-to-face
contacts make individuals more oriented to bargaining; he in fact insisted

> ...on the importance of understanding actors' motivations and expectations as critical
> forces intervening between structural conditions and institutional outcomes. What
> Przeworski teaches us is that macro-historical comparison must be supplemented by a
> historical hermeneutics of political action, developed within a 'cognitive political sci-
> ence'. Only within a framework of structural and cognitive analysis does it make sense
> to explore the extent to which game-theoretic rational-choice analysis illuminates the
> actual process and outcome of democratization (Kitschelt 1993a, 425).

In social movement studies, a central concept to address cognitive processes
has been that of *frames*, defined as the dominant worldviews that guide the
behaviour of social movement groups. The social science literature on frames
has taken two different paths (Johnston and Noakes 2005). With a focus on individual cognitive processes, some authors have analysed the way in which normal people try to make sense of what happens by framing events into familiar
categories (see Gamson 1988). Looking instead at the meso, organizational level,
other scholars have considered the instrumental dimension of the symbolic construction of reality by collective entrepreneurs (Snow and Benford 1988).

Frame analysis focuses on the process of the attribution of meaning, which lies
behind any conflict. There are three types of frames that are particularly important
for collective action to develop: diagnostic frames, corresponding to the recognition of certain occurrences as social problems; prognostic frames, which help in
identifying possible strategies to resolve these problems; and motivational frames,
which raise motivations for acting on this knowledge (Snow and Benford 1988).

A crucial step in the social construction of a problem consists in the identification of those responsible for the situation in which the aggrieved population finds itself. As della Porta and Diani (2006, 76) summarized,

> the identification of social problems and those responsible for them is, inevitably,
> highly selective....Cultural development places actors in the position of being

able to choose, from among various possible sources of frustration and revenge, those against which they should direct all their energies and action, not to mention their emotional identification. The process can, in this sense, be seen as a reduction of social complexity. At the same time, however, once solid interpretative frames have been established, the possibility of identifying other potential conflicts becomes limited.

Collective framing also involves the suggestion of a prognosis, identifying new social patterns, new ways of regulating relationships between groups, and new articulations on consensus and the exercise of power. Finally, the symbolic elaboration must also aim at producing the motivations and the incentives needed for action. In order to convince individuals to act, frames 'must generalize a certain problem or controversy, showing the connections with other events or with the condition of other social groups; and also demonstrate the relevance of a given problem to individual life experiences. Along with the critique of dominant representations of order and of social patterns, interpretative frames must therefore produce new definitions of the foundations of collective solidarity, to transform actors' identity in a way which favors action' (della Porta and Diani 2006). In a similar vein, Gamson (2011) suggested that framing has an injustice component (usually linked to national/local concerns), an agency component, and an identity component.

In general, framing processes that allow for mobilization are innovative. As they aim at producing a break, they need to present the established situation in a new light. At the same time, however, it is important that their diagnosis be shared by a broader public, resonating with their everyday experiences. In addition, although aimed at justifying a drastic change, the new vision does not have to produce (too much) shame about one's own past behaviour.

Cross-country diffusion of ideas has been considered as particularly relevant during waves of democratization. In their respective analyses of the coloured revolutions, Bunce and Wolchik (2011) as well as Beissinger (2007) noted that they developed a modular strategy, that is, they produced a model as an example to emulate. Their spread was not predicted by either analysts or activists, as they 'failed to take into consideration the power of example' (Beissinger 2007, 260). Imitation but also learning then applied to a repertoire of action consisting of massive mobilization after stolen elections, foreign support for democratic movements, mobilization of youth movements using unconventional tactics, united opposition, election monitoring, international pressure, transnational networks, mobilization after announcement of fraudulent results. There is, in fact, between proximate units, the working of what Beissinger defined as a tipping model, with rapid spread through active promotion as well as contagion. In the coloured revolutions, on the one hand, contagion was spontaneous, based upon a power of conformity; but, on the other, there was also active promotion as, for those who were successful, the attempt to reproduce themselves was also a way to consolidate support as well as to express their ideological belief in the rightness of their own behaviour.

The diffusion of the electoral model was facilitated by objective and subjective similarities—the continuity in dissent communities facilitating this perception—as well as dissatisfaction with the regime (economic crisis, leaders corrupted by very long permanence in power). There was also the exporters' self-interest: 'What we find, in short, is a network composed of an assembly of transnational actors promoting the diffusion of electoral change through implementation of the electoral model' (Beissinger 2007, 300); 'as the model moved from place to place, this group expanded' (Beissinger 2007, 301). Promoters organized voter registrations in order to increase turnout, also facilitating networking among civil society organizations that shared common perceptions and common identity. The electoral model diffused because it was successful, but was often 'amended to make its cross-national journey'.

Diffusion happens cross-space, so that what is initially constrained by structures becomes potentially a causal variable in a further chain of events. In this sense, 'A tide is not only a powerful, substantively related stream of mobilization within a mobilizational cycle, but also a transcultural and transnational phenomenon' (Beissinger 2002, 31). Even though ideas spread cross-nationally, especially to nearby countries, early risers enjoy advantageous structural conditions. Mutual empowerment is shaped in fact by some structural pre-conditions, such as some economic growth, presence of a middle class, education, political rights and a robust political culture of opposition (see Foran 2005, on revolutions).

In this chapter, we shall look at the ways in which diagnostic, prognostic, and motivational framing developed and spread in defining the enemy as well as the self. In particular, we will pay attention to the dynamic processes through which framing develops via tensions between innovation and path-dependency, instrumental and normative concerns.

As we will see, in eventful democratization, the corruption of the political class (or the elite) emerges as a diagnostic frame that denounces the growing degeneration of a situation, pointing at the same time at the lived experience of a large part of the population, which gives this frame empirical credibility. The framing of the corruption of elites is also powerful in creating broad support in the population at large by suggesting a dichotomy between 'them' and 'us'.

If diagnosis points at the 'them', against whom one mobilizes, prognostic frames also need to identify the group in the name of which one acts. Here, common to processes of democratization from below is a broad and inclusive definition of the 'us', often linked to a regeneration of the people and the nation. In both waves, the people were indeed recalled in slogans (from the

"Wir sind das Volk" in the GDR to "the people want...", which travelled from one Arab country to the next during the Arab Spring). Moreover, appeals to patriotic values, as embedded in flags, anthems and national celebrations, contributed to define as a community those with whom the protestors identified. If nationalism is said to undermine democratization, it has also been the basis of several movements for democratization (Bunce 2000; see also Chapter 9 in this volume).

Prognostic framing includes some definitions of the democracy-to-be. In eventful democratizations, conceptions of democracy are also, of course, particularly relevant for the framing processes, even if this does not mean that they are explicitly theorized. The framing of democracy usually bridges, in different equilibria, different conceptions. In classical theories, institutional decision making is usually considered as democratic when power positions are assigned on the basis of free, competitive, and frequent elections. In political science, this mainstream definition (see, among others, Dahl 1998) has been called minimalist, since it ensures only the minimal conditions for democracy: on the input side, in that it operationalizes democracy on the basis of electoral procedures alone, irrespective of the way in which power is used; and on the procedural side, in that it focuses on the respect of formal procedures. Such electoral conceptions of democracy are increasingly challenged by evidence of citizen disaffection, and the need to be supplemented by other conceptions (Rosanvallon 2006). In normative theory, balancing the understanding of democracy as representative institutions, *participatory* conceptions of democracy have long stressed the need for channels of citizen access to decision-making arenas (Pateman 1970). In more recent theorizations and practices, the conceptions of participatory (and direct) democracy have been linked with *deliberative* democracy, challenging the definition of democracy as majoritarian decision making and stressing instead its discursive quality and the importance of building multiple public spheres in which decisions on the public good can be made on the basis of reason (Habermas 1996). Democratic deliberation is capable of producing new preferences, rather than just counting or negotiating pre-existing ones (Elster 1988).

While 'minimalistic' conceptions of electoral accountability usually dominate elites' discourses on democratic institution-building, social movements tend to bridge participatory and deliberative visions (della Porta 2009a, 2009b). Social movement organizations in eventful democratization in fact often nurture participation, as well as constructing free spaces where conceptions of the public good are discussed based on an exchange of reason (e.g. Cohen 1989; Mansbridge 1996; Dryzek 2000). In the most recent wave of protest on global justice in particular, conceptions of deliberative democracy have appealed to many organizations and individuals, especially through an emphasis on consensual decision making and high quality discourse, as well as the building of free spaces (such as the camps in Tahrir), where 'normal' citizens can speak up. Movements active in mobilization for democracy developed, in fact, some specific visions of their role, which motivated participants to action.

Corruption of elites, patriotism, and resistance of the (national) civil society, through a mobilization from below, were widespread frames in all of our cases. While freedom was invoked, democracy was seen as broadly participatory, also involving the creation of open and pluralistic public spheres. Although representative democracy was the outcome, the conceptions of democracy that developed in the struggle against dictatorship were critical of delegation and majoritarian visions, supporting instead—more or less explicitly—direct and deliberative practices of democracy. This was true, with different emphasis, in both Eastern Europe and the MENA region. Identities also remained in flux in our cases, since, as Calhoun observed about the Chinese case, protesters 'went through a series of experiences that shaped and reshaped the identities of many' (1994, 269).

Framing 1989 in The GDR and Czechoslovakia

During the eventful democratization in Eastern Europe, we noted cognitive mechanisms such as a growth of cognitive generality and a discourse politicization. These built upon diagnostic, prognostic, and motivational frames that had developed in previous years and were then transformed in action.

Within an initially moderate discourse of reform of the system, the corruption of those in power was contrasted with the honesty and commitment of civil society. As we are going to see, in the GDR in particular, socialist values were initially supported by the dissidents, that challenged however their betrayal by the incumbent elites. In Czechoslovakia, where the reformist wing had been defeated after the Prague Spring, there were however still continuities with those ideas, embedded in the role played by the dissidents of 1968 in keeping alive the criticism to the degeneration of the original ideas of equality and solidarity. References to corruption, in terms of both the enrichment of the party privileged elites and of their the opportunistic abandonment of the communist original ideals in 'real socialism,' indeed allowed the protection of an 'original' idea of society as a positive point of reference, which had been betrayed by those in power. In fact, given the traditional Communist asceticism, even relatively small signs of enrichment of the elites produced indignation. This was all the more true when economic difficulties made the internal inequalities not only more visible, but also more symbolically offensive. In both the GDR and Czechoslovakia, especially for those who had believed in the reformability of real socialism, the frame of corruption allowed the maintenance of some loyalty to past beliefs. For others, corruption was proof of the inherent dysfunction of the communist system.

The appeal to the nation against those whom this nation and its ideas had betrayed was an important moment in the definition of a mobilizing discourse. The politicization of ethnicity was particularly relevant during and after some transitions in Eastern Europe, where democratization was accompanied by increasingly ethnic-based politics. This happened especially in countries that were ethnically heterogeneous and in which elites competed through the adoption of a nationalist discourse, in a search for alternative identities (Harris 2002; see also Chapter 9 in this volume). This was, however, not the case in our two instances of eventful democratization. While not an issue at all in the GDR, ethnic divisions did exist in Czechoslovakia, but were initially kept at bay. In both cases, however, there was reference to a national history, reflected as we saw in the mobilization of the theatres in Czechoslovakia, but also in the debate on German identities in the GDR. In both, there was a frequent use of national celebrations.

In both countries, the opposition had initially taken mainly a moderate tone, appealing not for a breakdown of the regime, but for reforms that would allow for challenges to the corruption of its essence. Either instrumentally or because of a deeper belief, the calls were for a defence of some proclaimed principles, against the lies of the regime. A combination of appeals to the nation and stigmatization of corruption helped in finding a common denominator among disparate social groups and political ideas, at the same time allowing them to build upon legitimated ideas and widespread symbols. Calls for freedom and against repression became louder and louder.[1]

In Czechoslovakia, CF defined itself as 'the representative of the nation by presenting speakers from all parts of society'. Its leader Havel stated that 'after forty years, citizens are beginning to meet freely. It has happened after what we all called for—dialogue with the powers that be!' (cit. in Wheaton and Kavan 1992, 89, emphasis added). The local branches of CF had to be 'self-administering and independent representatives of the common will

---

[1] The movement for democratization thus acquired a broad base during the mobilization itself. A survey of a representative sample of Leipzig's population, plus an extra-sample of oppositionals (Opp, Voss, and Gern 1989), show that respectively thirty-three per cent and forty per cent of them had refused to vote or to become party members; twenty-seven per cent had participated in peace prayers and other church related activities, even if only four per cent worked for oppositional groups (Opp, Voss, and Gern 1989, 21). There were high levels of discontent on environmental pollution, SED's control over life, lack of freedom of speech, Stasi surveillance, and unfair political trials as well as economic problems; less widespread were concerns on sexual equality, childcare, or educational opportunities. Political dissatisfaction was an important reason for participation in demonstrations, and (together with social dissatisfaction, but not economic concerns) in other protests: ninety per cent of protestors declared that they demonstrated for more democracy, free elections, the dissolution of the Stasi; sixty-eight per cent for a market economy; fifty-eight per cent for democratic socialism; and fifty-six per cent for reunification.

throughout the republic'. As with Solidarity in Poland, CF presented itself as the embodiment of the nation, a nation which was in turn embodied by the striking theatres (Glenn 2003, 113). As for the GDR, Joppke (1995) suggested that while in other countries (inclusive) nationalism took a unifying role (Solidarity as national rebirth; velvet revolution as creating feelings of belonging to a nation), this was not possible in the GDR because of the East–West division and the struggle against fascism as fundamental myth. Nevertheless, here as well, reference to a 'Volk' was important in establishing the broad base of reference of the movement. In fact, in the evolution of the protest, 'paradoxically, the "wir sind das Volk" message helped to overcome the sense of being part of an anonymous mob and soon implied emergent rules of cooperation' (Pfaff 2006, 131).

Joppke (1995) singled out two types of intellectuals: revisionists, striving for reformed, democratic socialism, and (true) dissidents. In Czechoslovakia, Dubček clearly built upon previous attempts to bridge socialism with democracy. If his discourse of a socialism with a human face was weakened by the repression of the 1968 attempt to implement it, reformist attitudes were still widespread. Calls for participation in the general strike stressed improvements over the past: 'We do not want to destroy, on the contrary, we want everything to work better'. The general strike itself was considered as resonant with CF's constrained political ambitions, as:

> From the beginning, Civic Forum declared that the general strike was 'a political protest strike [which] has no other aims'. In a demonstration of orderliness, the strike excluded the health, public transportation, and service industries which Civic Forum called upon to manifest 'the strike in a suitable way'. The strike was not directed by the center in Prague but rather, consistent with Civic Forum's informal structure, manifested as local strike committees wished (Glenn 2003, 111).

The demands were initially limited: resignation of some individuals, a parliamentary commission into repression, sixty minutes on television, new television directors. CF refused to make recommendations for the government, as it did not consider itself as a political party but rather 'a spontaneously emerging movement of citizens united in their efforts to find a way out of the crisis in our society' (Glenn 2001, 181). The new government therefore included fifteen members of the communist party and five non-party members. Even when, after the strike, the regime capitulated (the Central Committee resigned), the opposition asked for a government of national understanding. Calls for immediate elections failed, also because many in the opposition did not want to form parties, which they saw as instruments of the past (Glenn 2001, 139).

A discourse of moderate changes also prevailed in the GDR, linked to a debate about the destiny of the country, whose survival depended on the survival of a socialist Germany. Many dissidents, even if defending the right to leave, were critical of those who decided to migrate, whom they saw as renouncing the struggle for change in their country. Even if with different declinations, there was in the opposition a preference for dialogue, rather than confrontation with the regime, and a tendency towards reforms (Fehr 1995). In addition, the new generation, which had not lived through the division of the two Germanies, in fact saw some advantages in that division— as compared to, for example, the growth of one, too powerful Germany.

For many years, even the dissidents considered socialism as a positive metaphor for social justice. As Biermann declared, 'we named us communists, and attacked in the name of true communism the Bonzen' (Wolle 2008, 134). According to Joppke (1995), this is why East German oppositional leaders saw themselves as losers. However, there were also discussions about the reformability of the system. Besides common calls for pluralism, there were divisions on economic questions, as well as theological ones. Demokratischer Aufbruch was critical of real socialism, but still not against socialism, while Demokratie Jetzt called for direct democracy against socialism (Eckert 2011). Participation in the anti-IMF protests in West Berlin brought attention to anti-capitalist declarations.

Still debatable is the degree to which this moderation was a strategic move to maintain some space for expression. Even though reformist framing allowed for finding some interstices inside the regime,[2] an instrumental justification is not fully satisfying given the articulation of the framing processes themselves. In fact, throughout the transition process, identities of participants were not fixed, but contested. A call to govern in the name of a united society did not help in revitalizing socialism. In Czechoslovakia, 'identity claims on the basis of the unity of society offered little guidance for how to resolve conflicts within democratic institutions' (Glenn 2001, 195). Similarly, in the GDR, conflicts among the individuals referred to in the slogan 'Wir sind das Volk' (We are the people) were quick to emerge, especially after the fall of the Wall.

Movements for democracy in Eastern Europe have been accused of having too easily embraced Western capitalism. In a reactive fashion, leaders of the opposition were said to support ideologies fundamentally at odds with the regime's, while the idea of reformed communism survived only in the 'exceptional' case of the GDR (thanks to large opportunities for exit). Jeff Goodwin thus summarized, 'The reason for this absence of ideological innovation is undoubtedly quite simple: "Bourgeois" liberalism and free market capitalism were appealing in Eastern Europe principally because—like Marxist-Leninism

---

[2] Another dissident, Benda, proposed a salami tactic, based on taking advantage of the vagueness of existing law to gradually expand freedoms (Tucker 2000, 128).

and the "Society model" in the Third World of the recent past—they seemed to represent the most visible alternative social order' (2001, 271). That no new ideas came from 1989 is, however, open to challenge.

While clearly no new ideology was created, the framing of the 'self' of the oppositional groups of 1989 was quite innovative. As Ulrich Preuss noted, these movements did not try to impose a common will of the people, but rather promoted the principle of self-government, citing 'the idea of an autonomous civil society and its ability to work on itself by means of logical reasoning processes and the creation of appropriate institutions' (1995, 97).

In an original conception of civil society, informal 'micro-groups' allowed for the spread of 'horizontal and oblique voice', with 'the development of semantically coded critical communication'. This coded communication included 'political jokes, innuendo, emphases and mannerisms of language, and choice of topics that encode one's own political preferences' (Di Palma 1991, 71). Horizontality was in symbolic contrast with the verticality of the regime, as

> ...voices are horizontal because they offer an alternative to 'vertical voice', that is, to the communication of petition and command that dictatorships prefer. They are oblique because they are coded. Coding, though, is more than just a way of hiding from the authorities. Particularly in Eastern Europe, the aspiration to reject the system's opacity, to be public and transparent, was powerful. Coding created an emotional and cognitive bond among opponents of the regime, who came to recognize that they were not alone (Di Palma 1991).

In fact, they built upon a moral opposition to the vanguard politics associated with communism (Goodwin 2001, 277). Later on, even though participating in roundtables, a dissident declared, 'We were deeply mistrustful of power' (Joppke 1995, 169).

These visions were in part rooted in previous frames. Attempts to reform Eastern European economies through social (rather than state) property and workers' self-management in 1968 were often referred to in 1989. While those attempts had failed—see defeat of the Prague Spring, but also some attempts in Yugoslavia and Poland (Stokes 1993)—the emphasis on self-organization remained.

An embodiment of a horizontal, participatory vision was the samizdat, that is, illegal publications, which were however circulated in public. Di Palma (1991) stressed three of their features, linking them to a specific conception of civil society:

> First, the publications—typically, personal political and parapolitical testimonials—were authored, reproduced, and circulated through self-generated, improvised networks, in which the authors and the disseminators at each step were often single individuals. Second, this meant that in certain cases, though the

publications were illegal and alternative, they were not strictly clandestine. Full clandestinity would have defeated the testimonial function. Third, the individual nature of samizdat also meant that organizational infrastructures to sustain publication were, strictly speaking, not necessary. Instead, where infrastructures did not already exist, the production of samizdat was a unique additional factor that brought people together. In sum, there was more to sustain opposition to communism than oblique voice and collective ingenuity in the art of personal survival (Di Palma 1991).

The samizdat thus reflected, and at the same time helped to spread, a particular organizational culture. First of all, there was a rejection of underground conspiracies for power, as dissidents rather 'sought to build, slowly and by the power of example, a parallel society'. In fact, in this environment, oppositors of both countries consciously avoided conspiratorial forms of action, instead engaging in the spreading of a different culture by

> ...challenging the official counterparts of unofficial organizations; collecting information on, reporting, and denouncing government activities and misdeeds; demanding redress of grievances; holding the authorities accountable; proposing alternative policies; negotiating with the authorities, if it came to that. In turn, this unselfish mode of contestation, contrasting as it did with the reclusive and offensive opacity of nomenklaturas, gave organized dissent a popular credibility not dissimilar from that enjoyed by the more heroic examples of individual dissent (Di Palma 1991, 72).

In symbolic differentiation from the regime, the choice of transparency brought about an emphasis on the recovery of the truth. This explains why the organized opposition chose the form of civic forums, which were conceived as broad in scope and ambition as they mainly aimed at the development of civic values and the construction of critical public opinion as the basis for a transparent democracy (Di Palma 1991). The cultural effects of the mobilization of the civil society implied, therefore, 'the breakthrough in pursuing a new civic culture—a culture that wishes to deny the historical prophecies that stem from regional retardation and fragmentation—.... Uncharacteristic of intellectual mobilization in backward countries, the East European movements made an anti-Leninist (hence, anti-Jacobin) choice, one that entrusts progress to the proper constitution of citizens' relations to one another rather than to a guiding state' (Di Palma 1991, 80).

A specific view of civil society was developed by intellectual dissidents, with cross-fertilization among different countries. Future president of the Czech Republic Havel took from philosopher Patocke the conception of living in truth as realization of human quality. For Havel, dissidents were not only the intellectuals in the opposition, but all those 'who act as they believe they must' (Tucker 2000, 116), striving for a society in which they could live in truth and share that truth with the other members of the society. Living in truth was a moral act that allowed one to regain control over one's own sense of humanity: it corresponded to the building of authentic relations between the person and the universe. The essence of life was in 'plurality, diversity, independent self-constitution and self-organization' (Tucker 2000, 142). Differently than in the eighteenth-century Scottish enlightenment, civil society was therefore defined as something that was not naturally given, but rather needed to be constructed, exploiting a natural tendency for autonomy, but also based on pastoral art (Tucker 2000). From Czechoslovakia, these ideas travelled to the GDR and the other countries of Central Eastern Europe.

Conceptions of civil and human rights were linked to the conception of the self. The ideas of self-organization were rooted in an ethical discourse on a second society built around values such as truth and openness. Going back to some groups involved in the Prague Spring, the appeal to the creation of a parallel polis as democratic society spread also in the GDR.

With a focus on horizontality, Charter 77 defined itself as 'not an organization'. In one of its documents, one reads that 'It has no rules, permanent bodies of formal membership. It embraces anyone who agrees with its ideas, participates in its work, and supports it'. Significantly called by an activist a 'school for diversity' (Stokes 1993, 151), in its own words, it was 'a loose, informal and open association of people of variable shades of opinions, faiths and professions united by the will to strive individually and collectively for the respecting of civil and human rights' (Tucker 2000, 124). On the same principles of pluralism and tolerance, in 1988, a loose network of grassroots organizations was formed.

Civic education played a central role in this self-understanding. The mobilization of moral power had to help in producing changes through dialogue, rather than by seizing government. According to Eyal (2003), two groups of counter-elites, both coming from the purges after the Prague Spring, developed in Czechoslovakia. One was composed of intellectual humanists who—dismissed from journals and universities (especially Charles University in philosophy, phenomenology, and law)—then accepted minor jobs, keeping a dissident attitude. Another counter-elite was made up of technocrats (monetarist economists), demoted but not dissident, interested in western style economy, but with some more dirigistic attitudes when in power. Notwithstanding their differences, some similarity existed between the two groups in perceiving their task as primarily oriented to a civic education, aimed at self-governing (Eyal 2003, 89).

Dissidents linked the importance of possessing the truth about oneself to dignity and morality, and the value of an authentic life of sacrifice. An anti-political frame resonated with the New Left *nouveaux philosophes'* criticism of political power as oppressive, appealing to moral resistance as a duty and reaction to the state's interference in everyday life. It bridged a critique of power, defined as a specific type of politics pursued by state power—in fact, Havel advocated an 'antipolitical politics' (Jorgensen 1992, 42)—in a 'detotalizing' attempt against the fusion of politics and economics. This discourse substituted categories of left and right with moral categories of right or wrong, lie or truth (Jorgensen 1992). In Havel's definition, 'politics outside politics' is ethical and existential (Flam 2001).

In the GDR, as well, transparency was a main value in the opposition. In fact, 'In their activities, the groups tried, differently than in the 1970s, to stay open and visible, to all' (Poppe 1995, 257). The idea of publicity, pluralism, citizens' and human rights, autonomy, self-organization of society, and tolerance gained relevance in opposition to a mono-centric and hierarchical structure of power. The strategy evolved to openly developing collective action, in public (Fehr 1995).

In fact, theorists like Havel considered self-organized structures from below as fundamental loci for and of democracy. As dissident Konrad observed, 'workplace and local community self-government, based on personal contact, exercised daily, and always subject to correction, have greater attraction in our part of the world than multi party representative democracy because, if they have their choice, people are not content with voting once every four years.... When there is parliamentary democracy but no self-administration, the political class alone occupies the stage' (Baker 1999, 4–5).

Similarly in the GDR, the democratic opposition expressed a criticism of liberal democracy, stressing instead participatory and deliberative democratic qualities (Olivo 2001, 2–3). The basis groups' document on 'Mehr Gerechtigkeit in der DDR—Unsere Aufgabe, Unsere Erwartungen', later to be defined as a bible of the opposition (Neubert 1997, 791), asked for freedom and exchange of opinion, with reference to the human rights declaration of the UN; division of tasks between party and state; judicial control over administrative decisions; electoral reform (with more candidates); equal opportunities in the educational system, regardless of ideological belief; freedom in art and culture. While not aiming at conquering state power, dissidents wanted to build autonomous spaces to develop what they defined as 'a culture of dialogue', 'a culture of plurality and the free public domain' (cit. in Olivo 2001, 14). There was also a commitment to a politics of consensus, 'Not based on partial interests, because tackling an issue without the consent of the opponents would only bring harm' (Joppke 1995, 180).

In these free spaces (or parallel polis, in Havel's words), as dissident Ulrike Poppe put it, 'members learned to speak authentically and to relate to each other...to engage in social matters and to put up resistance' (Olivo 2001, 14). According to a dissident of the time, the groups that formed the citizen's movement in the GDR were in fact characterized by values such as 'openness and publicity...grassroots democracy rejection of patriarchal, hierarchical, and authoritarian structures, non-violence, spirituality, unity of private and public consciousness' (Joppke 1995, 88). The citizens' movement (calling for 'democracy now') aimed at constituting public forums for deliberation, open to all citizens, self-organizing with a commitment to participatory democracy (Joppke 1995, 92). Local roundtables and citizens' committees reflected this conception.

Social movement organizers imagined, in fact, the development of 'a fully open citizen movement in the grey zone of legality in the SED state, which existed in the periphery of the churches. We thus did without formal membership and let ourselves be guided by the principle of participation through collaboration' (Olivo 2001, 94). Not by chance, the appeal of Demokratie Jetzt presented a draft of theses to be developed through participation—including through the 10,000 letters received during the Ecumenical Assembly (Olivo 2001, 95). In addition, at its founding conference, NF adopted non-centralized but rather grassroots structures. As an activist declared, 'there should be no group of elites; there should be no circle of specialists who instruct the rest of the population on what should be done' (Pfaff 2006, 198). IFM also stressed that it was no party and had no membership.

Together with horizontality in the movement organizations, a fundamental principle was the self-organization of the society. One of the leaders of NF, Sebastian Pflugbeil, thus declared, 'We do not want to make the mistake of...trying to lead other people, when we know quite well that we do not have the solution...it is important to analyse the situation together...that's a path from below to above, in contrast to what otherwise happens in parties' (Pfaff 2006, 96). Another activist talked of the need to change society starting from below (Pfaff 2006). In Leipzig, the organization was especially horizontal. According to one activist: 'In Leipzig, no centralized structure existed in most groups. A lot happened in groups of friends who were active in a variety of circles, and a lot of things were done together besides the political. One did not sit in darkened cellars and promote "the revolution"; we laughed and partied together. Many people shared apartments' (Pfaff 2006, 94).

The search for a basis for democracy brought about long discussions about how this should look (Schoene 2011, 44). For instance, IFM founders aimed at creating a critical public sphere for which human and civil rights were needed, a second public sphere in competition with the official one (Pfaff 2006). Dissident Guntolf Herberg called for a 'societal model based upon a decentralized economy', as in Yugoslavia (Neubert 1997, 523).

The oppositional groups in the GDR stressed horizontal structures as reflecting the refusal of a vertical power. Reformism and nonviolence, in the works of a German activist, resonated with the fact that 'The opposite force to power is a grass-roots movement' (Poppe 1995, 261). A socialization process to alternative values developed within informal groups. According to a former activist, 'the groups are also a training field for social relations. Peaceful attitudes, tolerance and solidarity can be practiced in the groups' (Fehr 1995, 315). A founder of Democracy Now declared, 'our model was the democratic decision-making process within the Church' (Fehr 1995, 142).

Political commitment was located in everyday life. Activists considered working for peace as a political commitment, and stressed the importance of living in a responsible way, in contrast to the delegation of responsibility to state or church (Neubert 1997, 524). There was a utopia of an alternative civilization. Some of these ideas were indeed resonant of the new social movements' critique of Western civilization. Spanish basis democracy and anarchist thinking drew attention as sources of potential alternatives. So, for instance, Kirchentag von Unten included papers on topics such as 'Jesus from below', or 'Jesus, an anarchist?'. The Kirche von Unten, within a self-definition oriented to basis democracy against hierarchy, promoted an anarchist ideology, non-violent and community oriented (Neubert 1997). A critique of civilization also developed in the environmental movement.

Critics found particular fault with the Western identification of democracy with parliamentarism, advocating instead for 'the growing political competences of a broad, not party-member basis, and therefore the need for grass roots democracy' (Poppe 1995). As an activist observed, 'the West German democratic model has no attraction for us. For us, parliamentary democracy was only one possibility, perhaps an intermediate step, but certainly not a model to strive for' (Pfaff 2006, 199).

The organization of roundtables and related citizens' councils represented, in fact, moments of participation and deliberation. Conceived as spaces for debate among equal participants, they built upon the ideal of an open discourse, free from domination (Preuss 1995, 108). The *Buergerkomites*, formed by citizens that occupied public buildings, were similar 'forums for direct democratic participation in public matters' (Preuss 1995, 112) oriented at fostering a plurality of ideas.

If this framing helped in mobilization against the regime, it also appeared problematic to sustaining mobilization after the transition to democracy. As Baker rightly noted, the radical view of the civil society that had developed in the opposition in Eastern Europe (as in Latin America) was 'tamed' after the transition, when a liberal conception of democracy prevailed. As he summarized, 'For the opposition theorists of the 1970s and 1980s, civil society was an explicitly normative concept which held up the ideal of societal space, autonomous from the state, wherein self-management and democracy could be worked out. That is, the idea of civil society was political and prescriptive' (Baker 1999, 2). Civil society theorists, such as Michnik and Kuron in

Poland, Havel and Benda in Czechoslovakia, and Konrad, Kis, and Bence in Hungary, 'in addition to their calls for a more liberal politics of checks and balances, also saw civil society originally in the more positive, or socialist, terms of community and solidarity. Indeed, for many such theorists civil society indicated a movement towards post-statism; for control of power, while not unimportant, would be insufficient for the fundamental redistribution, or even negation, of power itself. If this was to be achieved, self-management in civil society was necessary' (Baker 1999, 15). The appeal to the construction of a community from below did not resonate with the delegated and majoritarian conceptions of democracy that dominated the institutions built after *die Wende*.

The consolidation of a model of democracy based on a liberal conception, focusing on elected elites, in fact denied civil society a political role—a role that was instead monopolized by political parties. Procedural democracy thus obscured the substantive claims of the radical conception of civil society, contributing to reduce the participation of the citizens.

Nevertheless, oppositional groups' ideas survived, keeping alive alternative visions of democracy. After unification, Bündnis 90 tried to carry on these principles by proposing instruments for participation, such as referendums, forums, citizens' councils. In contrast to existing party models, NF looked for 'open structures'. If the attempt to build a constitution from below failed, some roundtables survived nevertheless, developing 'an ability for communication that is open to integration', as 'the survival of democracy will not be decided in the state sphere but in the society' (Preuss 1995, 170). Houses of Democracy created during the rebellious months continued to host a plurality of groups. The citizens' movement thus continued to have relevance for alternative democratic visions (Preuss 1995, 177).

Framing The Arab Spring in Tunisia and Egypt

With reference to the Arab Spring, the importance of framing has been stressed by Jeffrey C. Alexander, who reminded us that 'Social facts enter into history as meanings, not only to outsiders but to revolutionaries themselves' (Alexander 2011, 3). As he observed, 'The Egyptian revolution was a living drama whose political success depended on its cultural power' (Alexander 2011, x). The framing within the Arab Spring has been defined as post-national, post-ideological, civil, and democratic (Nigam 2012). Denunciation of corruption and patriotic appeals were also present here, together with visions of democracy from below.

The Egyptian events were in fact framed as aiming at re-establishing a lost dignity. Activists stated 'This is not a political revolution, This is not a religious revolution, This is an all Egyptians revolution. This is the dignity and freedom revolution' (cit. in Nigam 2012, 7). The uprising is carried out 'In the name of my brother's dignity', as 'It isn't a question of politics, it is a question of dignity' (Nigam 2012, 7). The events were presented as part of a moment of epiphany: as a 'truly historical moment', a 'revolutionary moment'—in the words of an activist, 'everybody understood that it was, in fact, a moment' (Nigam 2012, 54).

Activists as well as observers noted the extraordinary social diversity in the protestors' backgrounds. *The New York Times* wrote that 'Friday's protest was the largest and most different yet, including young and old, women with Louis Vuitton bags and men in *galabeyas*, factory workers and film stars.... The protestors came from every social class' (cit. in Alexander 2011, 9). Similarly, Al Jazeera noted in the street, 'not the 50 or 60 activists that we have been seeing protesting in Egypt for the past five or six years', but rather 'normal Egyptians, older women, younger men, even children'; also 'children, the elderly, the ultra-pious and the slickest cosmopolitans, workers, farmers, professional, intellectuals, artists, long-time activists, complete neophytes to political protest, and representatives of all political persuasion' (Alexander 2011, 10).

This diversity found a composition in a broad self-definition, as the people fighting against the oppressor: a frequently used slogan was 'Our people, our people, come and join us' (el-Ghobashy 2012a, 35). If for Mubarak, protestors were foreigners, spies, irrational, primitives, outlaws, chaos, for the protestors the regime was barbaric and arrogant, brutal, a modern day Pharaoh, while they themselves were the people, spontaneous and leaderless, youth, Egyptians, democratic (Alexander 2011).

Appeals to the nation increased, in fact, during the protest. In the words of a protest leader, 'we have been a cowardly nation, We have finally to say no', in the name of 'Egypt, the land of the Library of Alexandria, of a culture which contributed groundbreaking advances in mathematics, medicine, and science' (Alexander 2011, 25). Slogans read 'raise your head high, you're an Egyptian', 'We shall die for Egypt to live', 'our country has been humiliated so much', 'Wake up, Egypt' (Alexander 2011, 26–8), 'We are all the Egyptian people' (Alexander 2011, 42). As an Al Jazeera journalist observed, in fact, 'despite the number of teargas canisters fired at protesters and the number of those who have been beaten and detained...a long dormant patriotism and pride has been awakened' (Alexander 2011, 30). In fact, a change was noted in Tahrir Square, with reference to national symbols increasing in time:

Liberation was a word with several meanings in the square. People arrived demanding free elections, regime change, an end to police brutality, improvement in their economic lot, or all of the above. As the days passed, the discourse was slowly taken over by expressions of patriotism. The people's art in every corner of the square became less visible in a staggering mass of Egyptian flags. The consensus against Mubarak developed into a jubilee of national pride. Following Mubarak's resignation on February 11, Tahrir erupted in joy. 'Hold your head high', chanted hundreds of thousands, 'You are an Egyptian' (Shokr 2012, 45).

Also in Tunisia, the emphasis on national pride was visible in the use of national symbols. In particular, the national flag was reminiscent of the anti-colonialist movement—as an activist noted, "the flag was a symbol we had especially used [when playing] against the French [national team], but now it means that the politicians have no right to wave it, it has come back into the people's hands" (Sergi and Vogiatzoglou 2013, 228). The use of national symbols did not, however, imply an exclusive identity: rather, there was an inclusive reference to the citizens of the other countries who were also struggling against dictatorship.

Rather than pure nationalism, a new pan-Arabic trend has been observed as one of the products of the Arab Spring, which mainly developed by differentiation from what was perceived as a New Orientalism. This is visible in the critique of a 'westernized' vision of the Arab Spring as the product of (Western) modernity, with Gene Sharp (author of *From dictatorship to democracy*) credited with having offered the winning strategy. The reading of the movement as one led by techno-savvy students (Nigam 2012), as well as the metaphor of an awakening built upon a stereotyping of the Arabs as quiescent (Salaita 2012), were seen as Orientalization, as 'othering' (traditional versus modern) and exoticizing (see also Chapter 3). Similarly, the American media rallying in defence of Israel, with the stigmatization of a 'Fall after the Spring' when criticism of Israel increased in Arab countries, were noted as confirming the widespread idea that Arabs have to guard against their inner barbarism and laziness (Salaita 2012). Orientalism was also identified in the role given to Wikileaks or in singling out Mark Zuckerberg, founder of Facebook, as the hero of the revolt. So, as Burris noted (2011, 2), 'To construct the Arab spring as a response to Facebook and the new media is not such an innocent gesture as it might initially appear'.

In opposition to this stereotyping, the call for dignity against domestic autocrats loyal to the West, rather than to their people, allowed the identification of a pan-Arabic self. Pan-Arab reaction brought about the construction of a cross-border Arab identity (Gause III 2011). Pan-Arab (Bayat 2012), the movement in fact took the Palestinian *intifada* as role model, mixing forms of protest that included civil disobedience, strikes, demonstrations, withholding of taxes. The discovery that there is no Arabo-Muslim exceptionalism paradoxically created a growth of pan-Arabism. Even if national symbols were also displayed, there were also similar slogans (*degage*, that is, go away, addressed to Western leaders, or "the people want …") as well as the development of cross-border solidarity (Khader 2012). It has been suggested that 'All this designs a new pan-Arabic sentiment whose core is less ethnic (and even less racist) than political: the refusal of the foreign control, aspiration to freedom and at the same time the possibility of change' (Temlali 2011). As an activist declared, 'finally, I'm proud to be Arab' (Khader 2012).

Appeals were inclusively oriented to the people, with 'reference to civil society, to the national community instead of sectarian identities' (Khosrokhavar 2012, 233). Indeed, the most widespread slogans started with 'the people demand…', followed by the reform of the regime, the trial of the dictator, and so on. Not by chance, the Arab Spring has been presented as a revolution for dignity against the humiliation of Western powers who supported the dictators: 'The Arab spring forces the United States and especially Europe to rethink their politics of complacence, or collusion with Arab dictators. Because it is probably over the time in which the Arab regime were just puppets, manipulated at pleasure, with the only function of control their populations and serve International interests: police of the status quo and guards anti-migrations' (Khosrokhavar 2012). The Arab world was reconciled in the contestation (Badie 2011).

If the Arab Spring was about democracy, social justice was also tightly bridged here with claims on freedom. In Tunisia, the demands of the protestors included opposition to unemployment, underemployment, low wages, growing inequality, corruption of elites (Shahshahani and Mullin 2012, 87). Protestors denounced increasing inequalities in welfare and insecurity among young people, as well as a nineteen per cent rate of unemployment in the population overall—twice as much for young people, even the highly educated (Shahshahani and Mullin 2012). A main slogan was, in fact, 'freedom, justice and national dignity'.

Also in Egypt, strikers in Mahalla had called not only for individual freedoms but also for strong state sectors and collective rights, especially the right to collective bargaining as well as a minimum wage, rises in food allowances and better working conditions, decreases in food prices. The framing of the protest converged on calls for social justice and political inclusion, opposing the effects of the liberalizing reforms of the past (continued by the military junta, even if it then granted a seven per cent increase in public sector salaries). Requests included a minimum and a maximum wage, land redistribution, and renegotiation of the 'odious debt' of Mubarak's regime. Main slogans were not only 'the people want the downfall of the regime', but also 'bread, freedom, social justice' (Teti and Gervasio 2012).

Claims for freedom were bridged to demands for equality. Following a series of wildcat strikes in the industrial and tourist sectors, demonstrations in 2011 in Tunisia called for 'bread', as synonymous for jobs—challenging the widespread idea of a Tunisian economic miracle (Hibou 2011, xv). Increasing unemployment was in fact one reason for the weakening of the regime control machine, with jobs being created only in greater Tunis and on the coast. This grievance was then linked to other streams of dissatisfaction, such as discontent with corruption in the business class, with political dependence in the justice system, or the end of upward social mobility among the middle classes (Hibou 2011, xvii). In fact, 'The protest movement, with its broad extent and its deeprootedness in society, was also and perhaps above all born out of the sense of injustice and humiliation' (Hibou 2011, xvi).

This bridging of calls for democracy and social justice differentiated the Arab Spring from the Iranian Green Movement. In particular, 'The two founding revolutions of the Arab Spring fought for two things: social justice and political democracy' (Khosrokhavar 2012, 216). Would-be middle class members, but also other classes, were drivers of the revolts where dignity, decency, and recognition were central claims (Khosrokhavar 2012, 68). In 2011, a popular Tunisian rapper sang: 'my president, your country is dead/people eat garbage/look at what's happening/misery everywhere/nowhere to sleep' (Khosrokhavar 2012, 238). Immediately banned, the song spread quickly. In fact, 'The major claims were freedom of speech, dignity, a graft-free society, the rule of law rather than the arbitrary reign of a despot (be it Ben Ali, Mubarak, or Kharnenei), the end of social injustice based on wild cronyism of the ruling families, and a new system respectful of the citizens' vote' (Khosrokhavar 2012, 21).

The Arab Spring movements also stressed a participatory and deliberative vision of democracy. Rather than the USAID-sponsored model of representative institutions, the movement pushed for 'real', direct democracy, against corruption and crony capitalism (Nigam 2012). Since the very beginning, Kifaya saw political parties as part of the problem rather than the solution (Shorbagy 2007). In addition, the ultras culture talked of a joyful liberation, a politics of fun based on values such as dynamism, flexibility, a group mentality, rebellion, and refusal of patriarchy and traditionalism.[3] The (apparently sudden) upheaval that brought about the fall of dictators in Tunisia and Egypt has been linked by political commentators, with some apprehension, to the Iranian revolution. However, while the Iranian revolution was Third-Worldist, anti-imperialist, and headed by a religious leader, recent events have been defined as moved by 'post-national, post-ideological, civil and democratic' popular movements in a post-Islamist MENA region (Bayat 2012). More similar to 1989 in their calls for freedom, the Arab Spring

---

[3] Defined as the only organized group capable of resisting police violence, they developed an expertise about how to attack and defend themselves, reducing losses, which was clear in the Battle of the Camel (el-Sherif 2012).

protests have been notable for a lack of chants and slogans 'against foreigners, westerners or Americans'. Immanuel Wallerstein (2011) praised, in fact, components deriving from the world revolution of 1968, with its emphasis on horizontality, participation, non-violence. The Arab Spring movements have been said to be based on a utopia that is 'modest, measured, not absolutized in a holistic way, renouncing a conflict-free society, and rejecting the idea of an absolute moral order that could create a golden age in any fashion' (Khosrokhavar 2012, 19).

Democratization movements in the MENA region have in fact been described as leaderless, fragmented, and atomized, relying on new media for coordination. They are characterized by avoidance of violence, lack of specific ideology (after the death of holistic utopias, such as nationalism or Jihadism), declining political centrality of religion, and the emergence of a new pan-Arabism. In fact,

> On the whole, democratic movements in the Arab world have changed the subjective framework of society, creating new expectations and demands in terms of social justice (blue-collar workers ask for better wages and more favorable working conditions in the name of a regained dignity, building on a relative absence of power) and political freedom (the reign of charismatic strongmen is over). They have also endowed citizens with a desire to be politically relevant, not marginalized and excluded, as it was in the past. These dimensions—social justice and political democracy—have become the major manifestation of the sense of reconquered dignity through a new definition of the individual (Khosrokhavar 2012, 113).

A participatory ethos prevailed. Egyptian activist Ghonim declared in an interview, 'A revolution is like Wikipedia, okay? Everyone is contributing content, [but] you do not know the name of the people contributing it.... There is no hero in that picture' (Khosrokhavar 2012, 192).

The movements expressed strong demands for participation in political decisions, while the Internet made party organization superfluous (Badie 2011). A deliberative vision stemmed from experiences in the global justice movement. For example, the AGEG, an Egyptian anti-globalization group, represented between 2002 and 2005 an arena for coalition building, favouring networking among small groups and also searching for contacts outside (see also Chapter 3). The aim of the group was to disseminate information on global capitalism through, for example, seminars with guests such as Waldon Bello and Samir Amin, but also via campaigns in support of social groups that were more negatively affected by globalization. The participation in the Cairo Conference against Zionism and Imperialism supported the development of contacts with Nasserists and MB members, as well as Leftists of various currents, professional syndicates, and NGOs. The oppositional group favoured loose, transnational networks of action, with a particular interest in contacts in the South, especially with Lebanese, Moroccan, and Syrian activists. The idea was that networking must come in action, also through overlapping membership (Abdelrahman 2011).

Within a similar conception, Kifaya succeeded in bringing together leftists, nationalists, Islamists, and liberals. If AGEG's social basis remained mainly confined to middle class, rooted cosmopolitans, and then disappeared, an emphasis on pluralism and alternative tactics ultimately remained. As an activist stated, 'I carried AGEG with me'; 'We all continue to carry its principles and ideas' (Abdelrahman 2011, 422). After Mubarak's fall, divisions in the movement addressed issues such as the focus on parliamentary versus extra-parliamentary activities, the collaboration with pro-regime GONGOs, independent coordination for unions, and relations with MB.[4]

Dynamics of diffusion have been noted in the recent wave of protests for democracy that moved from Tunisia to Algeria, Libya, Jordan, Yemen, Sudan, Egypt, Bahrain, Morocco, Iraq, Iran, Oman, Saudi Arabia, Syria (Bunce 2011). Here as well, cross-national diffusion moved from early risers, based on proximity, similar (regime) conditions (authoritarian homogeneity), and transnational networks. The Arab Spring has in fact been defined as going viral, spreading across frontiers, attaching itself to hospitable bodies (Nigam 2012). The idea and practice of the camps spread as a particular form of protest, which also embodied a conception of democracy: from Kasbah in Tunis and Tahrir in Egypt to al-Chajara in Benghazi, Green Square in Tripoli, Taghyir in Sanaa. The camps in fact allowed protestors to overcome fear in a liberated space and helped to construct a unified image of the movement—creating a revolutionary identity as well as small group solidarities (Bennani-Chraibi and Fillieule 2012, 789). They were also spaces for exchanges of ideas, where non-activists took the floor, facilitating inter-class relations and the development of new practices.

Similarities in movements among the various Arab countries include, in fact, an emphasis on (multi-generational and gender diverse) participation, the call to citizens (rather than party members), and the absence of charismatic leaders. Common themes were also calls for the end of dictatorship and corruption, for free elections, for trials against those responsible for brutal repression, for increases in salaries and creation of jobs; but there were no religious slogans—civil or secular (Corm 2011). Collaboration with Tunisian activists, as well as the previous oppositional experiences of the MB, were both important in the organization of the protest in Egypt.

Cross-national diffusion—often described as a domino, snowball, or tsunami effect—built upon a community of language and civilization, even

---

[4] Who now denounced the foreign hands on oppositional work; some MB members left, while others followed the tried and tested tactic of compromising with the regime.

though the 'attribution of similarity is largely the product of political work by agents' (Bennani-Chraibi and Fillieule 2012, 782). While the frame Egypt-is-not-Tunisia was spread by Mubarak with pride, but also by oppositionals with sadness, the cross-national diffusion built upon an emphasis on similarities—as poetry was quoted to say, 'we are the same'. In fact, poetry became a source of inspiration. A commonly cited verse was the one by Ahmed Fuad Negm on the occasion of the Iranian revolution, which stated, 'oh Egypt, is like us. Self same there, self same here. . . . Whichever way you wish to view it, that which happened over there will certainly take place here' (Saad 2012, 64). And as one activist wrote, 'get rid of the experts and listen to the poets—we are in a revolution' (Saad 2012, 65).

The Muslim diaspora in the West also played a role in generating a transnational collective identity through a 'significant amount of politically critical content via mass media such as radio, television, film, and newspapers', which is more and more accessible in Arab countries (Howard 2010). Thus, 'the internet has a causal and supportive role in the formation of democratic discourse in the Muslim communities of the developing world' (Howard 2010, 40).

Framing Democracy: A Summary

While literature on transition pays little attention to cognitive processes, assuming some rational calculations among elites, social movement studies have long regarded frames as an important concept in their toolkit. Considered in part as instrumental, framing processes also emerged in our analysis as constrained by historical experiences, memory, cultural background. While cognitive processes helped to address the context, they were limited by an existing repertoire of ideas. At the same time, however, eventful democratization produced some rapid changes with tradition, allowing for fast innovation. Moreover, during waves that involved several countries, cross-national diffusion played an important role in spreading innovation.

As we have seen, eventful democratization implied a growth in generalization of claims and the politicization of claims. In this chapter, we saw in which discursive contexts these mechanisms operated. In particular, we have looked at diagnostic, prognostic, and motivational processes.

In both waves, actors presented themselves as civil society organizations, opposed to a regime that had betrayed what was perceived as the initial social pact on which the nations had been built. In both waves, corruption was stigmatized as an evident and offensive sign of the crisis of the regime, of its lies and injustice. In Eastern Europe it was the corruption of the original, socialist ideas; in the MENA region the betrayal of pan-Arabic socialism and its modernizing pacts. Frames of corruption allowed for the narrative construction of a symbolic, positive origin, followed by decadence and then rebirth. Similarly, in the 1989 uprising in China, Jiping Zuo and Robert D. Benford (1995) noted the successful oppositional framing processes that developed over time. Initially, in fact, the 'students advocated more democracy, an end to the persecution of political dissidents, and other political reforms they believed would better suit the emerging social and economic structures' (Zuo and Benford 1995, 142). Later on, however, they did align this request with people's widespread concerns with rising corruption, as:

> By displaying posters with slogans such as 'STOP POLITICIANS FROM ENGAGING IN ILLEGAL TRADE!' and 'ELIMINATE CORRUPTION!' in more conspicuous places (e.g., along main vehicular and pedestrian arteries) and by aligning their frames with the vocabulary of the masses, student activists hoped to expand the movement's populist appeal. The student framing, bridging growing profiteering with growing inequalities, in contrast to communist asceticism had empirical credibility and experiential commensurability as it tended to fit with widespread observation and experiences (Zuo and Benford 1995, 140).

Defining the incumbents as corrupt, in all our cases the opposition built upon a broad definition of the self as the people, the civil society, the masses of citizens oppressed by the state. A reference to broad and all-inclusive identities could be noted also in other cases of fights for democratization. Remaining with the example of the Chinese protests in 1989, in their framing, protestors succeeded in reaching a delicate balance between denouncing corruption and appealing to national sentiments: 'First, they constructed cogent critiques of the injustices and improprieties resulting from the economic reforms. These framings tended to resonate because they were consistent with citizens' observations and experiences. Second, students grounded their claims in three Chinese cultural traditions or narrations: Confucianism, communism, and nationalism' (Zuo and Benford 1995, 139). While increasing contacts with the West brought uncertainty about the cultural definition of the self (Calhoun 1994), the students' emphasis on patriotism as well as alignment with some of the main national cultures found resonance in the population. In fact, 'Students' subsequent actions and framings, which were consistent with both traditional and communist culture, represented attempts to demonstrate further their patriotism' (Zuo and Benford 1995, 144).[5] Presented as an act of sacrifice for China, the mass hunger strike in Tiananmen Square was also extremely successful in winning the students the

---

[5] The student petition during the funeral service for the dead leader Hu Yaobang—with student representatives on their knees, holding petitions above their heads—has been interpreted 'as a dramatic recreation of traditional encounters in which subjects sought to persuade an emperor

support of the population, to which they appealed by presenting themselves as part of the people and the country. In their 'Statement of the May 13th Hunger Strikes', the students wrote:

> We commence our hunger strike in the lovely May sunshine. In the full bloom of youth, however, we leave beautiful things behind, but with great reluctance. Yet the condition of our country is one of rampant inflation, economic speculation by officials, extreme authoritarian rule, serious bureaucratic corruption, a drain of products and people to other countries, social confusion, and an increase in the number of criminal acts. It is a crucial moment for the country and its people. All compatriots with a conscience please heed our call: The country is our country. The people are our people. The government is our government. If we do not cry out, who will? If we do not take action, who will?...We do not want to die....No, we are not seeking death; but if death could lead to improved conditions and prosperity for our country, then we ought not to shun it....Death awaits. Farewell. To our colleagues who share our loyalties. To our loved ones, whom we would rather not leave, but whom we must. To our mothers and fathers, for whom we cannot be both patriotic and filial at the same time. To the people of our country, from whom we ask permission to pursue this final act of loyalty.

As in our cases, references to patriotism, which allowed the students to speak for China as a whole, developed in action. Demands started out as particularistic student claims (including autonomous association, improvement of life conditions at universities, meritocracy); 'yet, once the protest took root, a variety of deeper, longer range ideas came to the fore. Grievances specific to students and intellectuals flowed together with a discourse about democracy, modernization, and China's cultural crisis' (Calhoun 1994, 240). Patriotic appeals helped in building alliances: while students started out showing arrogance against peasants and workers, they ended up invoking the nation. In fact, 'The consciousness of the students changed in important ways during the course of the protest' (Calhoun 1994, 265).

While the corruption of the enemy and identification with the people were themes common to the two waves, some differences between them are also worth noting. Fairly homogeneous in 1989, the vision of the self seemed more differentiated in the most recent wave, with a stress on the positive value of plurality and diversity. In addition, issues of social justice now came to the fore, reflecting the participation of unions as well as the characteristics of the regime. While there was not an anti-colonial discourse, issues of dignity were clearly linked with the stigmatized dependence of the dictators from the help of superpowers, and their submission to their diktats.

---

to adopt just policies....Beneath a large photo of three students kneeling on the steps of the Great Hall, the poster's caption read: CRYING FOR FREEDOM; KNEELING FOR DEMOCRACY; THE REPUBLIC WILL NEVER FORGET' (Zuo and Benford 1995).

In our cases, if in 1989 the regime was mainly considered as failing to meet its promises of development and well-being, in the Arab Spring the claims against social inequalities were very audible. Activists in both cases saw democracy as something different from representative institutions, resonating instead with participatory and deliberative visions. The core of democratic processes was located in society rather than the state, and direct participation of the citizens was a fundamental value. Outside of state institutions, and beyond delegates or experts, citizens had to take their destinies in their own hands, constructing spaces, horizontal and open, for deliberating on the common good. The roundtables in Eastern Europe, as well as the camps in the Arab Spring, embodied the reconstruction of a public sphere—the latter allowing, however, for a broader participation of the citizens who occupied the street.

First and foremost, social movements during democratization processes often developed grassroots conceptions of mobilization. Often emerging with a criticism of the hierarchical, authoritarian, and occult power of the regime, the insurgents proposed a vision of democracy of participation by the citizens, constructing alternative public spheres. The samizdat in Central Eastern Europe and the blogs or Facebook accounts in the Arab Spring, the assemblies in the Czech theatres and the camps in the squares represented free spaces in which new frames developed. As the Eastern Europeans invoked a civil society, the Arab protestors called for freedom, but also practised other conceptions of democracy that, if not completely contradictory, are certainly different from liberal representative democracy, resonating instead with ideas of participatory and deliberative democracy. Concepts and forms of actions then spread transnationally, adopted and adapted by national movements that perceived themselves as part of broader territory than the national ones. The assessment of similarities among the enemies and the struggles developed over time, intensifying during the protest. In the case of the Arab Spring, ideas spread beyond the MENA region, being adopted and adapted by social movements that challenged indeed (neo)liberal democracy. Austerity measures in Iceland, Ireland, Greece, Portugal, and Spain were in fact met with long-lasting, mass protests. Directly inspired by the Arab Spring, the Spanish and then the Greek Indignados occupied hundreds of squares, not only to protest austerity measures in their respective countries, but also to ask for more, and different, democracy (della Porta 2013a).

Also in other cases, those who struggled for democracy have tended to present themselves as horizontal groups of people who wanted to take their destiny into their own hands. In Yemen, for instance, protestors called for decentralization, autonomy, self-governance, and self-taxation, using in their decision-making a modification of the traditional Yemen gathering (*qat*-chewing session) in discussion circles, tribal conferences, rural open-air meetings, and urban mass-conferences (Carapico 1998, 162). In fact, 'There was an expanded sense that public policy decisions should be subject to public, press and scholarly debate, a widening sense of political efficacy, unprecedented if still not unmitigated eagerness for participation' (Carapico 1998, 169). This was also the case, for instance, in Brazil, with the important role of the urban popular movements that developed with the liberalization of the 1970s. Even if they were fragmented along class lines (middle class versus popular classes), related with social and political identity rather than basic interests, and were at risk of being co-opted into clientelistic networks, they were particularly influential in introducing a participatory ethos rather than functioning as an enlightened vanguard. As Mainwaring (1987, 149) noted, 'The movement has helped redefine the parameters of political discourse in subtle but significant ways. Perhaps most important has been the change in discourse, away from the technocratic elitist discourse that permeated all sides of the political spectrum in the late 1960s and first half of the 1970s, to a new discourse that emphasized popular participation'. Even the Chinese students, who sang the Internationale song, stated that 'we want to take our destiny into our hands. We want no more god or emperors' (Calhoun 1994, 239). In fact, protestors conceptualized democracy following Rousseau's ideals of direct participation: they saw in democracy a process of education (Calhoun 1994).

In our cases, as in others, the democratic framing that was spread by the social movement organizations mobilizing for democracy was different from the representative one that came to dominate after the transition. This lack of resonance with the framing of the new regimes can contribute to explaining the declining relevance of democratic movements after transition. In fact, as had been observed in the cases of democratization in Sub-Saharan Africa, after transition democracy came to mean representative democracy, while no space was left for forms of direct democracy and consensual decision making (Bratton and van de Walle 1997, 11).

5

Repression and Challengers

Introduction

Tunisia: 'Yet we should not lose sight of the fact that the first cause of the fall of this dictatorship was in its rigid and brutal nature. It was a dictatorship that hermetically closed down all potential spaces for expression, such as the media, research centres and civil society organisations, and exercised terror as a privileged strategy of government. On the pretext of struggling against religious fundamentalism and terrorism (particularly against Islamists) and therefore of protecting Western countries but also local secular elites from the risk of having political power seized by Islamist movements, the dictatorship progressively and methodically succeeded in crushing any political, individual or organised opposition and in reducing all the media to silence. Frequent political procedures and condemnations, usually heavily disproportionate, were the systematic response to political activity or actions considered political, including minor actions. The anti-terrorist law, rapidly drawn up after 9/11, freed security forces from any legal and 'technical' restrictions. Systematic torture was almost the standard welcoming ceremony for young men, even when the accused answered investigators' questions. Foreign newspapers were often banned, their websites censored, and, more widely, the homepage of the vast majority of websites that provided any information about the Tunisian political system was generally replaced by the infamous '404 not found' message. Finally, books that might have been useful to Tunisian readers rarely crossed the frontiers legally. Carrying books not specifically permitted by the authorities led the owner directly to jail.... To this oppressive regime should be added the corruption and patronage system built by the Ben Ali-Trabelsi clan. Whether it involved a job, a bank loan, buying a car with credit facilities, importing machinery or raw materials, exporting or even just marketing any product, getting your electricity connection, drinking water or a sewage system installed, or building a house, bribery was the rule and, in most cases, membership of the RCD (ruling party) was useful if not indispensable, especially in marginalised regions such as Sidi Bouzid. (Ayeb 2011, 469–70).

Egypt: 'Like his predecessors, President Husni Mubarak deployed the resources of a high-capacity state to cement his power. He handily eliminated all threats to his rule, from a riot police mutiny in 1986 to an armed Islamist insurgency in the 1990s. . . . He presided over the transformation of the economy from a command model with the state as primary owner to a neoliberal model with the state as conduit for the transfer of public assets to cronies. He introduced an innovation to the Egyptian authoritarian tradition as well, attempting to engineer the hand-over of presidential power to a blood relative, rather than a military subordinate. To manage social opposition to these big changes, Mubarak used the political arena to coopt critics and the coercive apparatus to deal with those who would not be incorporated' (el-Ghobashy 2011).

Both quotations point at a paradox: brutal repression is a cause of survival of the repressive regime, but also a cause of the development of democratization movements. High levels of repression increase fear, but high levels of repression also produce indignation. This is a puzzle addressed in this chapter, by looking at the repressive traditions of the four countries I analyzed as examples of eventful democratization, but also at their transformations.

Transition studies have linked the chances and forms of democratization to moments of liberalization, which bring about some openings of space for the opposition as well as reducing human rights violations, especially in the repression of political and social protest. Social movement studies have long considered repression a relevant barometer of the opportunities and constraints that are available for challengers (della Porta and Reiter 1998). The expectation is that closed opportunities will bring about a greater use of coercion—as expressed in more brutal and escalated styles of protest policing. In reverse, the opening of opportunities should be reflected in more tolerant, negotiated policing of protest. Political choices refer not only to the policing on the street, but also to the ways in which protest is prevented by the police or the judiciary, as well as the forms of surveillance of the opposition and the citizens at large.

While research on protest policing has focused especially on democracies, repression is even more relevant in authoritarian regimes. Social movement studies have long assumed that, given high levels of repression, there is little opportunity for mobilization in such regimes. As Hank Johnston (2011) has observed, however, there is wide variability in authoritarian regimes' capacity and willingness to repress, as well as in the focus of that repression. Decisions by the state to repress are complex, as the state is diversified and different groups have different visions and interests. In making such choices, dictators have to guess how much repression will suffice to control dissent without producing backlash effects. But 'calculations will change as the events progress and context changes', for example with increasing international pressure, elite defection, or economic crises (Johnston 2011, 128–9). In particular, the style and amount of repression change over time, with periods of liberalization alternated with periods of increasing repression. In addition, liberalization is supposed to favour an increase in protest, but also a moderation in its forms, while the more brutal the regime the more radicalized the opposition is expected to be.

This does not mean, however, that there is a simple correlation between the amount of repression and the amount (and forms) of protest. Research on the use of repression in authoritarian regimes has pointed at the 'dictator's dilemma', as repression has sometimes been found to be effective in keeping law and order, at other times working as a main trigger for solidarization and further protest, in either non-violent or violent forms (Francisco 2005). Moreover, the effects of repression have been linked to the moment in which it develops during a cycle of protest, as once resources are mobilized and mobilization has spread, police brutality risks increasing mobilization rather than curbing it, becoming yet another grievance that fuels contentious politics (Brockett 2005). Indeed, what is needed is a more subtle analysis of styles of repression and their evolution over time.

In what he defined as a state-oriented approach to revolutions, Jeff Goodwin (2001) suggested going beyond modernization approaches (stressing rapid changes) and Marxist explanations (in which revolutions are the mobilization of coalition of peasants and workers against the penetration of Western capitalism; see e.g. Paige 1997; Wolf 1969) by focusing on the opportunities faced by revolutionary groups—opportunities that not only fail to expand, but actually contract. In so doing, he looked at challengers' perceptions of the strength of the dominant coalition: they choose to revolt, he suggested, when they see 'no other way out'. In line with assumptions used in approaches to political opportunities in advanced democracies, in authoritarian regimes as well, people are not expected to support revolutions if they believe that the state has little to do with their problems, if by doing so they will become more vulnerable to state violence, and if there are other ways out (Goodwin 2001, 25–6). Relevant characteristics that affect the answers to these questions are related to the political regime (liberal/inclusive versus repressive/exclusive character); the type of state organization (bureaucratic/rational versus patrimonial/clientelistic); and the infrastructural power of the state (strong versus weak). Revolutionary movements are more likely to develop where there is high repression combined with weak state power; and they are more likely to be successful when there are also patrimonial/clientelistic relations. Repression is considered to be particularly important as 'popularly supported insurgencies have persisted when and where the armed forces of weak states have committed massive and indiscriminate abuses against civilians suspected of collaborating with the insurgents' (Goodwin 2001, 33).[1]

---

[1] Revolutionary movements are expected to be especially resilient to repression in peripheral societies, when they build large coalitions with strong international support (Goodwin 2001).

Besides the amount of repression, its forms are also relevant in influencing the repertoires of action of democratizing actors. In his in-depth comparison of Burma, Indonesia, and the Philippines, Vincent Boudreau (2004, 1) noted that analysts 'have seldom attempted to understand modes of protest in authoritarian settings—or indeed elsewhere—via its relationship with styles of state repression. More often, we have been concerned with quantitative associations between the degree of repression and the extent of protest'. His research shows, in fact, that the style of repression—as 'coercive acts of threats that weaken resistance to authority will' (Boudreau 2004, 3)—is relevant in explaining how changing collective actors are able to bring down an authoritarian regime. In general, the stronger the repression, the more difficult it was to sustain movements for democracy. But styles of repression also had different effects according to their degree and type of selectivity: some modes of repression marginalized all activists, pushing them to build coalitions, while others more selectively distinguished between forms and actors; some eliminated activists, and with them the memory of previous protests, while others let them survive, even if at the margins.

Specific histories of repression thus influenced the forms that mobilization for democracy took, as well as its outcomes. As Boudreau suggested,

> First, events that encouraged democracy movements acquire significance as political opportunities only in connection with ongoing modes of contention. Opportunities that attract our greatest concern do not merely encourage mobilization, but encourage specific modes of mobilization with particular power to undercut established state-society relations; second, interactions between state repression and claim making (i.e. contention) influence who will be available for the democratizing coalition, and on what terms. Third, the political character of alliances of democratizing forces in turn influences movement power, coherence capacity—factors that all matter immensely in the post-dictatorship settlement (Boudreau 2004, 239).

State repression affected protest through three main legacies. In his reconstruction:

> The first is institutional and material. State repression killed, bruised, imprisoned and terrified citizens, but seldom indiscriminately. Most focused on specific targets, and so shaped the material and organizational resources that survived, promoting political forms that escaped the state's most direct proscription. Often, forms that authorities judge least threatening survived—as with student protests in 1970s Indonesia. Elsewhere, forms survived because the authorities had neither the capacity nor the will to defeat them—as with insurgencies in both the Philippines and Burma. Activist forms and organizations, however, do not exist independently of activists. Repression shapes the

duration, direction and intensity of activist careers in ways that profoundly influence political contention. Where activist forms and organizations survive state attack, generations of experienced dissidents bring their accumulated wisdom and leadership to the struggle; and provide a thicker and more complex network of support for new protest. Elsewhere, authorities may eliminate entire activist generations and deprive new claim makers of experienced leaders....

The second legacy is interpretative....Movements under authoritarian regimes must always anticipate state repression and explicitly incorporate this anticipation in their plans....

Third, historically patterned modes of contention create distinct movement culture in each setting (Boudreau 2004, 11).

Memories of repression remained important, as they 'also shaped movement strategies and mobilization patterns by suggesting the costs and consequences of collective action' (Boudreau 2004, 161). Especially, they worked as a filter between existing opportunities and activists' perceptions of them. If repressive styles had long lasting effects, eventful democratization grew out of changes in the repressive capacity of the regime, at the same time contributing to those changes.

In this chapter, discussing the effects of repression in our four cases of eventful democratization, we shall indeed detect some impact of repressive styles on the timing and forms of the transition. In all cases, eventful democratization happened after long (even if by no means linear) periods of liberalization—as testified by the use of labels such as 'post-totalitarianism' in Eastern Europe's post-Stalinist period, and 'liberalized authoritarianism' for the two Arab countries. This does not mean, however, that protest was not met by repression. Not only had liberalization often been reversed in de-liberalization moves when protests had emerged in the past; but especially at the beginning of the waves of protest for democracy, regimes used their coercive force to crush the opposition. Nevertheless, there were limits to the amount of blood dictators could plan to spill without losing their domestic legitimacy and international supports. Moreover, during the protests, the loyalty of the various coercive forces—military and non-military, public and private—was put to the test, eventually unsuccessfully. While attempts (or discussions) to mobilize the army or party militia failed, the police proved unable, even if willing, to face (unexpectedly) large masses. As repression suddenly filled rather than emptied the streets, coercive apparatuses proved indeed too weak and fearful to embrace heavily repressive solutions. While some more freedom existed in the liberalized autocracies of Egypt and Tunisia, repression of street demonstrations was however more brutal there than in GDR and Czech Republic.

The Dynamics of Repression in GDR and Czechoslovakia

Throughout the history of the 'real socialist states', repression played a role in constraining protests, but also in increasing indignation toward the regime. Saxonberg (2012) noted that the repressive tactics in Eastern Europe catalysed rebellion, as they were perceived as outrageous acts. Thus, in Czechoslovakia, protest spread as rebellion against repression on 17 November 1989; a similar process took place in the GDR after heavy repression at the beginning of October. In this reaction, one should consider the effect of the gradual, differentiated, and often reversed dynamics of liberalization. Some steps were taken in the direction of decreasing brutality in repression, in fact, as Eastern Europe moved from Stalinist to post-Stalinist (or post-totalitarian) regimes. Nevertheless, liberalization then often reverted into intense repression following waves of mobilization from below.

In the post-World War period, repression had been so strong as to effectively thwart any open opposition. In the GDR, as in other countries in the Eastern Bloc, any dissent was brutally suppressed. After the war, camps were established under Stalinism in 1945, for spies, Nazis, and so on: as many as 220,000 were interned, 43,000 died in detention, and 736 were executed (Killingsworth 2012, 86). Between 1948 and 1950, about 200,000 social democrats who had entered the regime party SED after the compulsory unification with the Social Democratic Party (SPD) were expelled; more than 5,000 were imprisoned and a few hundred ended up in *Arbeitslager* (Poppe, Eckert, and Kowlczuk 1995, 17). The strong repression targeted in particular the 'foreigners from the West' (Yugoslavia-supporters and social democrats), but also members of the former KPD (the Communist Party of Germany). Anti-Soviet propaganda or leafleting could be punished by death (Poppe 1995). In the universities as well, especially since 1952, controls became extremely stringent. After the Berlin Wall was built to seal off the Eastern-controlled sectors from those controlled by the Allies, shoot-to-kill orders were issued against those who tried to escape to the other side. This explains the survival of only a very small and conspiratorial opposition.

Forms of repression tended however to change in post-totalitarian Eastern Europe, although with moments of intensified repression after some major crises. In the GDR in 1953—as in Hungary in 1956 and Czechoslovakia in 1968—perceived challenges to the dominant regimes brought about military repression, implemented with the support of the Soviet army.

In the 1950s in the GDR, uncertainties about post-Stalinism seemed to open up some political opportunities and a new course was announced. However, as security forces proved unable to contain the unexpected revolt,

Soviet troops came in on 17 June 1953. The Soviet army then cracked down on the about 500,000 participants in the protest, arresting 13,000. During the events of 1953, sixty to a hundred civilians were killed by police bullets or tanks. Between 12,000 and 15,000 were arrested, and thousands received prison sentences (Dale 2005). As more strikes and unrest followed for about a week, the regime party SED conceded that the working class was made resentful, but also stressed the need to build a state security apparatus. There was in fact a compromise on the protest claims (with a salary increase of about sixty-eight per cent over the following two years), but also brutal repression. As many as 1,400 received life sentences, while about 2.5 million fled the country before the Wall was built in 1961. The Stasi secret services increased the numbers of collaborators and its capacity for control (Nepstad 2011).

In Czechoslovakia, as well, the ebbs and flows of repression were influenced by the evolution of the Soviet Union, with some liberalization following the shift from Stalinism to post-Stalinism, but also brisk closing down of windows of opportunity when the Soviet Union feared changes were going too far. This was the case particularly in 1968, with the abrupt end of the process of reform that had brought about some hope in the building of 'socialism with a human face'. Citizens had resisted the Soviet military occupation mainly through songs, graffiti, placards, petitions, jokes, and poems; but initial reactions had also been confrontational, with stones thrown at the occupying army. Even though demonstrators tried to fraternize with the Soviet soldiers, it was the national police and the army who were most often supportive, helping to diffuse tensions (Williams 2011). Repression was less harsh in Czechoslovakia in 1968 than it had been in the GDR (and Hungary); but still, about a hundred died during the events, 172 were arrested, and eight remained in detention (Ekiert 1996).

In the late 1980s, the effects of previous crises were visible (Ekiert 1996). In all countries, memories of past repression also affected the peaceful evolution of the protest at the end of the 1980s. Specific recollections of repression in these highly symbolic moments then played an important role in influencing the forms of protest chosen.

Although with some differences, repression changed therefore in all countries after Stalinism, generally becoming less tough. Although repressive, the police state left more free spaces than usually recognized, moving from the mass arrests of the post-war era to heavy surveillance afterward.

Later on, repression was more likely to take legal paths. For instance, in the GDR, following the protest in solidarity with Czechoslovakia in 1968 (3,528 leaflets were found in 389 places), there were judicial investigations against 1,290 citizens. There were moreover 1,400 criminal investigations related to these protests, involving also the children of high state functionaries. There were also 522 disciplinary procedures inside the party, many among workers; in universities, there were 127 disciplinary procedures for political action.

In the 1960s, the emerging youth counter-culture was repressed, through the official stigmatization of long hair, blue jeans, and the youth movement Gammler Bewegung, as well as campaigns of repression of rowdies that targeted especially the *Szene* in the Berliner district of Prenzlauerberg. The anti-authoritarian nature of the 1968 youth protest in the West scared the regime into a critical attitude that targeted repression on them. Among others, 430 were arrested during the gathering that had followed rumours of the Rolling Stones playing on the other side of the Wall.

Even with some increasing tolerance for long hair and jeans, youth cultures also continued to be repressed in the following decade. In 1970, a festival of political songs was organized in East Berlin, with bands from Third World and resistance movements (among others, Mikis Theodorakis) whose songs on freedom evolved into songs against the regime. In just the first half of 1973, there were 6,635 procedures for endangering the political order through asocial behaviour. Sometimes, young people were sent to psychiatric clinics; often to juvenile institutions—2,720 in July alone. During the X. Weltspiele der Jugend und Studenten in August 1973, there were controls against '*asoziale, geisteskranke, Vorbestrafte und HWG-Personen*'—that is asocial, psychologically disturbed, with criminal records; HWG stood for 'haeufig wechselndem Geschlechverkher', which could be rendered as 'people who often change partners in their sexual lives'. As many as 26,000 youngsters were put under surveillance and about 20,000 were contacted by the police to discourage them from travelling to Berlin.

In various periods, especially but not only in the GDR, leaving the country has been an aspiration for those who did not support the regime—a choice the regime punished as they could. The construction of the Wall in Berlin allowed for the brutal repression of illegal exiting, with the mentioned shoot to kill at the borders. In the 1980s, however, there was a shift away from killing those who left the country, towards an increasingly permissive attitude that brought the number of those who travelled to the West from 46,000 in 1982 to 1.3 million in 1987 (Pollack 2009). In 1989, the economic crisis, together with changes in other countries of the Eastern bloc, led 100,000 to leave the GDR; eighty per cent of them were less than forty years old.

Prison sentences were often used against opponents; so, for instance, Wolfgang Herig, philosopher at the Humboldt University, was imprisoned for seven years; another oppositional intellectual, Robert Havemann, was put under house arrest in 1977 after he protested the expatriation of Biermann. In the mid-1980s, however, arrests became rarer; the risk for activists was not so much prison time but especially jeopardizing their careers or having to pay high fines (up to 500 marks, or half a month's salary). Prison sentences were in fact limited, as they risked creating a bad image for the regime (for this reason, there was also the order to no longer shoot at those who leave the country) (Poppe 1995).

Surveillance developed, however, thanks to the 90,000 employees of the Stasi and its 300,000 informal collaborators (Joppke 1995, 109). State archives contained six million individual dossiers, on 125 miles of shelves (40,000 pages for Wolf Biermann alone). In an activist's words, 'The Stasi was always with us, always. We lived under permanent surveillance' (Joppke 1995, 111). Notably, eight of the sixteen founding members of the IFM were Stasi agents (Joppke 1995, 112). Informers were sometimes reformers, others cynics or true believers. When protests developed, the SED regime, overestimating its degree of public support, reacted mainly with propaganda. In the 1980s, repression then increased on church-linked publications, with forty-three interventions and twenty-three prohibitions to publish, as well as ensuing solidarity demonstrations but also tensions with the church hierarchy.

Similar evolutions happened in other countries in Eastern Europe. So, activists described the conditions in Czech prisons in the 1980s as 'not too bad'. Some moderation in the repression, which here as well became, if not lenient at least less brutal, was also linked to the fear among the elites that, as in 1968, archives could be opened (Long 1996).

Thus, the very forms of repression tended to create a division into a public, conformist self, and a private, more rebellious one. This *Nischengesellschaft*, even though discouraging protest in the short term, also increased the chances in the long term, once a few mobilized, showing the potential for discontent and protest. So, given divided elites, 'islands of autonomy begun to develop, particularly where a more liberalized political environment was joined with comparatively high levels of economic development and public resentment of communism' (Bunce 1999, 32).

In the 1980s, indeed, in the transition in Eastern European cases, the non-violent development of mobilization was explained by the constrained forms of repression: 'Had the civilian leadership or the top brass attempted to resist the opposition, the transfer of power would not have been so swift, and certainly not so peaceful. One of the most remarkable aspects of the East European Revolution is that, with the partial exception of Romania, the security forces and the bureaucracy just melted away in the face of growing public opposition' (Kuran 1991, 40).

In 1989, after some attempts at repression, even the less liberalized regimes in fact mostly avoided violent tactics. This was the case in the GDR, where a major demonstration on 5 October was brutally charged by the police; but from 7 October demonstrations were tolerated, therefore becoming increasingly larger. This was also true in Czechoslovakia after the repression of the demonstration on 17 November.

Goodwin (2001) gives four reasons for this: a) Gorbachev's abandonment of the Brezhnev doctrine; b) the belief among elites that they would win elections (and sometimes did); c) the fact that the ruling elites were not physically threatened, but rather d) had the opportunity to make personal gains (after 'privatization from above' had brought about an 'en-bourgeoisement' of socialist elites). In fact, international dynamics had reduced, for all Eastern European countries, the potential of repression, while economic difficulties had favoured various forms of liberalization.

Certainly, repression strategies changed along with protest, as early attempts at repression during eventful democratization failed or backfired and mass demonstrations made old tactics ineffective. So, for instance, in Leipzig, the spread of protest was met by a police strategy based on containment: controlling speeches in the church and harassing demonstrators outside, arresting up to half of the participants at demonstrations. However, these tactics only worked on small numbers. So while there were more than 3,000 arrests around the country in the first week of October, there were proportionally fewer in Leipzig where the demonstrations were larger (only about two per cent of participants were arrested there against, for example, almost thirty per cent in Magdeburg and more than ten per cent in Berlin).

So, as it became clear that the Soviet Union had no intention of interceding, the masses of protestors proved too large for coercive interventions by police and security forces. Moreover, the party militia—called to intervene—refused to charge peaceful demonstrators: many of its members did not show up when called, or resigned. Considered as unreliable in its rank-and-file troops, the military was not a practicable option for repression. The emerging dissidents inside the party thus preferred to declare the dissident not as hostile to the state, but rather as expressing diffuse concerns (Pfaff 2006, 185).

Repression was similarly constrained in the Czechoslovakia case. As it did not really lose control of its security forces (the military, the People's Militia, the regular police force, and the secret police), the government could indeed have been tempted to use them against the protests. While investigations revealed that tanks and soldiers were to be deployed to Prague, the Central Committee of the party opted instead for a political solution (Glenn 2001, 133). However, later on, 'a branch of the People's Militia proclaimed that it would "not take steps" against "working people" or "working youth, including the student community," but instead work "to build socialism in common and work towards perestroika"' (Heimann 2009, 303). Additionally, although security forces had been mobilized, no order was ever issued to deploy them (Saxonberg 2001, 338).

In sum, while repression had been particularly evil in the Stalinist years, both regimes became less brutal, if not more tolerant, following strategic turns in the Soviet Union. It was especially the loss of the support of the Soviet Army against potential opposition that represented turning points in both countries, eventually leading away from brutal repression before and during the eventful democratization.

The Dynamics of Repression in Tunisia and Egypt

The level of repression was traditionally very high and widespread in the MENA region, where—not by chance—the police became a main target of the protests. Even within a trend of liberalization, in part stimulated from the outside, regimes resorted to brutal methods, including torture. The first state reactions to the wave of protest for democratization costed many demonstrators their lives. However, in both Egypt and Tunisia, once the rebellions started, the army kept a neutral stance, refusing to implement the regime's requests.

Authoritarian regimes in the MENA region had a tradition of brutality. According to Bellin (2004), the resilience of authoritarianism in the MENA region is determined less by failing preconditions than by an existing resource: the capacity and willingness of security apparatuses to repress. Resilient authoritarianism was, that is, produced by a robust coercive apparatus, which could rely upon sufficient resources (the ratio of police-person per inhabitant was sixteen per 1,000 in the region, against, for example, six in France) as well as international support (granted presumably in exchange for oil, gas, and control of the Islamic threat), as well as patrimonial (rather than institutionalized) administration. Not by chance, the institutionalized military, as in Egypt and Tunisia, proved less willing to repress than the patrimonialistic military in Syria.

While some liberalization had provided a rather selective tolerance for journals and associations, the emergence of violent Islamism—in part itself out of repression—brought about an increase in the dictators' coercive means, as well as in the tacit permission, by international allies, to use them. In Egypt, political repression produced a politicization of the MB, which typically oscillated between comprehensive efforts at cultural renaissance, charity activities, and more political action. Already in the 1940s, some radicalization had followed the government's repression of Islamists, who were growing in numbers and becoming more oppositional. In the early 1950s, after some initial cooperation with Nasser, a wave of repression followed a presumed plan to assassinate the president. This brought about mass arrests in 1954, and a further turn in radicalization. With the end of the liberalization period—which had allowed for the growth of the MB and the election of their representatives to parliament, as well as increasing influence in the civil society—the repression by the

Nasser regime radicalized elements of the Brotherhood and led individuals to transform the ideology of modernist Islamists into a 'rejectionist call to arms' (Esposito 2002).

In the 1970s, confrontations with state institutions accompanied and fuelled the quickly rising influence of Islamist groups in the universities. In the early 1970s, an Islamist student movement had been used by Sadat to counterbalance the Left. Initially apolitical, it had concentrated on Islamic book fairs, selling of Islamic clothes, provision of services to the community. Violence then started with clashes with left-wing students, and, in the words of an activist, 'this then evolved in the concept of changing the bad by the hand, which became essential to the movement' (cit. in Meijer 2011, 149). In the 1980s, a second generation of militants, often radicalized by torture in prison, grew devoted to paramilitarism in the implementation of religious precepts by violence, extending control on fifty-two villages (Meijer 2011).

In the 1980s and 1990s, the repression of the Islamic movement brought about new waves of radicalization, with splinter groups emerging from the Muslim Brotherhood. Al-Jamaa was strengthened by the repression of the MB, as activists, frustrated by the lack of results from peaceful protest, chose more radical forms of action, eventually founding clandestine organizations. As a militant jihadist declared, 'what is astonishing is that every time the Muslim Brotherhood rushes to issue their statements of moral condemnation, denunciation, and disavowal of all that is jihad—they call it terrorism— the more the government redoubles its constraints against them' (cited in Hafez and Wiktorowicz 2004, 75).

Violence erupted in fact when, at the end of the 1980s, the regime closed down other channels of institutional access and peaceful opposition that had slowly opened up at the end of the 1970s. It was in the first half of the 1980s that violence escalated, from 120 deaths between 1970 and 1989 to 1,442 between 1992 and 1997 (Hafez and Wiktorowicz 2004, 71). Here, indeed, 'the cycle of violence began largely in response to a broad crackdown on the Islamic movement that ensnared moderates, radicals, and a number of tangential bystanders. The crackdown included arrests, hostage taking, torture, executions and other forms of state violence' (Hafez and Wiktorowicz 2004, 62).

Torture as well as shoot-to-kill policies became widespread, along with the storming of mosques, mass arrests, and executions. Repression was not only brutal, but also indiscriminate, hitting the militants of the violent organizations as well as their families, and even 'anyone wearing a beard with a trimmed mustache' (Hafez and Wiktorowicz 2004, 78). Especially indiscriminate forms of repression 'antagonized hitherto inactive supporters and sympathizers and intensified the moral outrage of the activists' (Hafez and Wiktorowicz 2004, 70).

149

In the early 1980s, the government reacted to sectarian clashes with the arrests of 1,500 opponents and the dissolution of thirteen organizations (Malthaner 2011, 74–6). The assassination of President Sadat was the radicals' response to those arrests, and the execution of the death penalty against four Islamists fuelled further radicalization. As Malthaner writes, 'While they appreciated martyrdom, the attackers also rationalized the assassination in political terms, as an act to punish Sadat for the harm he had done to Muslims and for the preceding crackdown against the Islamist movement. They hoped to "give a lesson" to his successor and that their deed would be a step towards an Islamic order: "...they thought that now the sharia would come"' (Malthaner 2011, 74).

Later, President Mubarak alternated tolerance with repression. In the 1980s, al-Jamaa had been allowed to form bands to repress 'immoral' behaviour in upper Egypt, but also to organize welfare services (from food distribution to clothing and school supplies for the poor) and 'mediation' institutions to peacefully solve local disputes (Hafez and Wiktorowicz 2004).

However, a new escalation occurred in 1987 and 1988, with frequent confrontations during police interventions on the university campuses in Assiut and in some particular neighbourhoods (Malthaner 2011). Again, repression did not stop the conflict but instead escalated it. Between 1992 and 1997, al-Jamaa would be responsible for about 1,300 fatalities targeting police and government officials, as well as intellectuals, artists, tourists, and Coptic Christians. In turn, violence escalated repression.

More recently, as well, particular characteristics of repression that facilitated escalation were not only its brutality (including shoot-to-kill policies and torture), but also its indiscriminate nature. Since the mid-1990s, the authorities intervened 'moving ruthlessly against the militant groups and arresting tens of thousands of alleged members and supporters' (Malthaner 2011, 80). Here, too, some events played a transformative role. In 1990, the death of al-Jamaa leader Ala Mohieddin was perceived by activists as 'the threshold to all-out confrontation, to which they responded by assassinating the speaker of parliament two months later. It marked the beginning of a violent insurgency which would torment Egypt for the next eight years' (Malthaner 2011, 80).

Research on the Egyptian case also shows how radicalization developed at the local level, involving Muslim activists in violent clashes with police. In August 1988, such clashes followed police irruptions in several mosques in Ayn Shams, as they 'interrupted sermons, and arbitrarily arrested young men wearing a beard and *galabiyya*' (Malthaner 2011). In one of these events, activists built barricades and threw stones at police officers, who responded by killing five people, wounding dozens, and arresting more than a hundred.

Support for violence was heightened, in fact, by the military occupation of entire communities. In the mid-1980s, for instance,

> ...a milieu had formed in Ayn Shams which identified with and supported the Islamist movement, including their political criticism against the Egyptian government—a milieu to which, at that time, a considerable part of the area's residents seemed to belong. Their support for the Islamist groups included protests against the police operation, which was regarded as unjustified repression against all Islamist groups and against the entire neighborhood. People in Ayn Shams, another resident emphasized, never informed the police about members of the Islamic groups, and nobody cooperated with the police, with the exception of criminals and drug traffickers who had been paid for their cooperation. People even provided refuge to members of the Islamic groups when members were pursued by the police. The Islamist groups, Ahmad's father emphasized, were just the young people from the neighborhood, and they did nothing wrong. They had just defended themselves against the arbitrary attacks by the police: 'And because of what happened, the arrests [...] and the torture, and the suffering, and they were humiliated and tortured to death—it turned into some kind of revenge between the victims' families and their friends [and the police].' He added that: 'I myself don't regard what has happened as terrorism because the word terrorism was an invention of the police. The events started in the form of revenge' (Malthaner 2011, 135–6).

Street battles involved, in addition to members of various Islamic groups, 'teenagers, and, as witnesses recounted, many ordinary residents, including elderly women throwing stones at the police from their balconies'. New riots followed police intervention after the assassination of a police officer, again with mass arrests (of about 300 people) and several killings. Additionally, the area was put under curfew and the Adam mosque remained closed for more than a year. As Malthaner recalled, when interviewed as many as fifteen years later, the anger and indignation against the government and its police was well alive. People still remembered 'several neighbours who were arrested in 1988 and had never returned', as well as tortured sheikhs. In particular, there was still the perception that repression had targeted 'not only the Islamic groups but also the entire neighborhood, without reason or justification, and had used violence far out of proportion to the alleged offenses. The clashes, they said, were between police and all the people of Ayn Shams, who also suffered under the effects of the curfew and the closure of the market' (Malthaner 2011).

Escalation continued then, fuelled by people's mistrust in the state, which in turn favoured indiscriminate police repression (della Porta 2013b). As Malthaner recalled, in the 1990s, 'Police operations also took the form of collective punishment against the militants' families and the general population in alleged strongholds. After violent incidents, any male person wearing a beard was arrested, houses of alleged al-Jamaa members were destroyed, and, according to human rights organizations, their parents, sisters, or wives were detained in order to force fugitives to surrender' (Malthaner 2011, 237). During curfews, 'Hundreds of residents were arrested, houses of alleged members of al-Jamaa were destroyed, and their families were taken into custody. With electricity cut off, markets dissolved, and sugar cane fields were eradicated because militants used them to hide during ambushes. Economic activities in the villages were almost brought to a standstill' (Malthaner 2011, 240). In the early 1990s, in addition to the imposition of curfews and police occupations of entire villages (such as Imbaba, Dairut, or Mallawi), repression hit family members of suspected Islamists and, especially after violent confrontations, male persons wearing a beard. Again in Malthaner's reconstruction,

> ...the Egyptian security forces' repressive and violent reaction severely affected living conditions and put towns and village communities under enormous pressure. From the early 1990s on, Egyptian police deployed a large number of forces in Upper Egypt and carried out brutal and arbitrary arrest operations against alleged strongholds in a manner which resembled, as one observer remarked, punitive expeditions in the tradition of Cairo's semi-colonial rule over its southern provinces. Suspects could be held without trial under emergency law, and in the mid-1990s human rights organizations put the number of political prisoners in Egypt at an estimated 20,000 to 30,000, most of them alleged Islamist activists. Military courts handed out a large number of death sentences (more than 80) and several hundred alleged al-Jamaa members were killed during arrest operations by the police (Malthaner 2011, 167–8).

However, repression in the form of collective punishment produced waves of solidarization with those who were perceived as defending the community, as the state responded to disturbances by militarizing the territory of the suspected groups. In fact, if collective punishment aimed at terrorizing the local population, discouraging support for radicals, it had initially an opposite effect as it fuelled sympathies towards radical Islamists and indignation at the police, accused of 'starting the terrorism, which prevented cooperation with the security forces rather than furthering it' (Malthaner 2011, 237).

Even when the Islamist violence subsided, the police remained as powerful as it was corrupt. With power increased by the so-called 'war on terror', and little to no accountability, the police became feared but also hated as representatives of a brutal regime. Police brutality hit not only political opponents but also normal citizens, in forms that raised more and more indignation. As el-Ghobashy (2011) noted,

> Doing politics outdoors brought citizens face-to-face with the caste that rules the streets: Egypt's ubiquitous police. Mubarak's was not a police state because the coercive apparatus routinely beat and detained people. It was a police state

because the coercive apparatus had become the chief administrative arm of the state, aggregating the functions of several agencies. Police not only deal with crime and issue passports, drivers' licenses, and birth and death certificates. They also resolve local conflicts over land and sectarian relations; fix all national and sub-national elections; vet graduate school candidates and academic appointments at every level; monitor shop floors and mediate worker-management conflicts; observe soccer games and Friday prayers; and maintain a network of local informants in poor neighborhoods, to ensure that dispossession is not converted into political organization. Officers are free to work out their own methods of revenue extraction, sometimes organizing the urban drug trade. Patrolmen routinely collect tribute from taxi and microbus drivers and shopkeepers, while high-ranking officers partner with landowners or crony businessmen. When there is a riot or a road accident or a natural disaster, Egyptian police personnel are the first responders, not to aid the victims but to contain their rage.

Repression was high in Tunisia, as well. Under Habib Bourghiba, a main event was the national strike of 1978, when hundreds of protestors were killed by police. Nevertheless, there was also some political liberalization, including the legalization of a number of leftist oppositional parties. Although quickly reversed, liberalization had supported the rise of some Islamist actors, such as the Movement of Islamic Tendency, inspired by the Islamic revolution in Iran and the MB in Egypt (Esposito and Voll 2001). Bourghiba's rule ended in 1987, as he plotted the execution of Islamist leaders.

His successor, Ben Ali, disillusioned hopes of democratization and an opening of the political sphere (Alexander 1997). Some political liberalization was again reversed, after the Islamist party Harakat Ennahda (the Renaissance Movement) achieved good results at the 1989 elections (Allani 2009, 263). Between 1989 and 1992, thousands of Islamist activists were arrested and leaders forced into exile (Esposito and Voll 2001). With the passing of time, the regime became increasingly authoritarian and the Ministry of Interior and its political police more powerful. Unions were co-opted or disbanded, and the oppositional leaders harassed or forced into exile. In 2003 an anti-terrorist law—which according to human rights organizations brought about securitization, criminalization of Muslim practices, even also allowing for torture—received enthusiastic support from the US (Shahshahani and Mullin 2012). In prison, torture was not rare, and mistreatment common, including tortures that

> ... have sometimes led to the death of the victims or their suicide; solitary confinement that sometimes lasts for years on end; overcrowded prisons; the absence of any bed or space to lie down; sleep deprivation; poor food and malnourishment; lack of sufficient water; the difficulty or impossibility of maintaining any contact with the outside world; poor hygiene and the spread of diseases; negligence or laxity in medical monitoring and sometimes even the complete absence of this or any

medical care; development of drug addiction, the use of psychotropic and neuro-leptic drugs; forced labour in conditions of near-slavery; the banning of prayer; systematic and humiliating body searches; promiscuity, sexual aggression and rape; a ban on studying or receiving letters or parcels; isolation, restrictions of visit-ing rights and 'basket' rights (food and clothes brought by one's family), and so on. Everything is done to grind people down and dehumanize them (Hibou 2011, 4).

Repression also continued when a prisoner was released from prison, as all official papers were withdrawn from him or her for years, and constraints on freedom were imposed—for example, the obligation to report to a police station, even several times a day. Interference in private life continued even longer (Hibou 2011, 4–6). In what Hibou called a 'meticulous grid', the omni-present police (about one policeman per sixty-seven citizens, as compared to, for example, 1 per 265 in France and 1 per 380 in the UK) was joined in the task of surveillance by party cells, neighbourhood committees, and other municipal services (Hibou 2011, 83), as well as national organizations (such as the Union Tunisienne de Solidarité Sociale) and many of the about 2,000 private associations that 'constitute one of the main means of con-trolling and subjecting the population to a network of surveillance' (Hibou 2011, 98). Independent civil society organizations—such as the LTDH, or Ressemblement pour une Alternative international de Development-Attac—were instead considered 'bad' associations. Not recognized officially, these groups were at the same time infiltrated, and persecuted also from the finan-cial point of view. Through these means, for instance, the union confed-eration, the UGTT, was controlled, at least at the central level: in fact, the organization was mainly considered as an institution of social peace and repression, as well as distribution of favours (Hibou 2011, 124).

During the waves of protests for democracy, with a widespread critique of police violence, repression fuelled radicalization. In Tunisia, as a partici-pant declared about 14 January: 'It was my first demonstration, I didn't like to be member of a union, usually when there is a strike I stay at home. But that was too much, they kill children. It is necessary to change things' (Allal 2012, 831). Protests often targeted the Ministry of Home Affairs, defined as the heart of a Tunisia without heart. In Egypt, also, the moral shock for epi-sodes such as the 'camel battle' fuelled moral indignation. The police were indeed, from the very beginning, a main target in a rebellion which—not by chance started with the contestation of the regime-proclaimed police day (see Chapter 2). Even later on, when seventy-four people died in violence related to a football match in Port Said in February 2012, the police were accused of having ignited the events (Khamis, Gold, and Vaughn 2012).

In sum, while there were some formal openings, with very limited, selec-tive, and contingent tolerance for oppositional actors, both Egypt and Tunisia were characterized by high levels of repression, including torture and killing. The actual experience with radical Islamist groups in Egypt, and the fear of them in Tunisia—together with support for illiberal laws by the US in the name of the war of terrorism (see Chapter 6)—helped to sustain police brutality.

Repression and Challengers: A Summary

The regimes protestors addressed in both waves of eventful democratizations were undergoing some—although inconsistent—liberalization. They were still authoritarian regimes, but post-Stalinist ones in the two East European cases, and so-called liberalized authoritarianism in the two MENA cases. In fact, slowly and with reversals, some free spaces had been achieved, with some selective tolerance for the samizdat autonomous publications in Eastern Europe and (although very limited) press freedom in the MENA region.

This did not mean, however, that there was no experience of repression in the recent past or that there was no attempt by those regimes to use their force to brutally stop transition. Repression in Eastern Europe had moved from the death penalty and long years of incarceration to strict controls, fines, and harassment. In the MENA region, while some organizations and parties were tolerated if they moved within strict boundaries set by the regime, waves of arrests but also torture and killings were used to address increasing dissatisfaction and protest.

Moreover, when mobilization for democracy intensified, the autocrats in both areas reacted in repressive ways, initially attempting to use all of their armed power to crush opponents. While the lack of support by the Soviet army as well as international and domestic pressures pushed the East European regimes to leave power peacefully, this was not the case for the Tunisian and Egyptian dictators, who tried to deploy all the strength of their repressive apparatuses, killing and wounding their people, before being forced to surrender by the sheer force of the number of protestors as well as by their army's refusal to comply with their orders.

Our research confirms, in fact, the complex effects of repressive strategies on forms of resistance. In his studies of three different countries, Boudreau (2004) had already noted that forms and dynamics of democratic movements varied, as they were influenced by a long history of contention and its harsh repression at the onset of their respective authoritarian regimes. In Burma, extremely high levels of repression long thwarted any opposition. The military takeover led by Ne Win in 1962 followed student protest and state massacres: the university union building (symbol of the independence struggle against Great Britain) was dynamited, killing thousands of the students who had sought refuge there. Burmese students then escaped into the rural areas and often joined the communist party, while the authorities focused on keeping protest out of the urban areas. As a consequence of this brutal repression, no more than six demonstrations (in 1968, 1974, and 1975) took place in the country between 1962 and 1988. In Indonesia, the military coup of 1965 was also followed by brutal repression, with the killing of between 300,000 and one million suspected communists, perpetrated, especially in rural areas, with the help of Islamist groups and CIA support for General Suharto. The effect was the destruction of the communist organization, while sporadic and fragmented protests (for example, student protests in the 1970s) did emerge in the urban areas. In the Philippines, President Marcos' 1972 declaration of a state of emergency—here as well, with US support—brought about the suspension of the Supreme Court and imprisonment of 30,000 oppositional and social movement activists. Marcos hit both organizations and protest, but with less vigour than in the other two cases.

In these, as in our cases, more repression brought about more violent protest in the long run. If 1989 could become the perfect illustration for non-violent revolutions while violence spread at times in the other two cases, this was in fact related with a more constrained reaction by the Eastern regimes, both before and during the events, than in the Tunisian and Egyptian cases. Nobody died in Czechoslovakia or the GDR, hundreds in Egypt and Tunisia. In the first two cases, it was especially during Stalinism that very heavy repression had impeded the expression of dissent, while later on, slowly and with reversals, both the GDR and Czechoslovakia had reduced the use of the most brutal oppressive forms. In comparison with these two countries, in 1989, Egypt and Tunisia had kept a heavier negative record in terms of violations of human rights. While protests did not disappear, torture and shoot-to-kill orders created a more radicalized climate in 2011 than in 1989.

The interactions between repression and protest involved different mechanisms: adaptation, but also learning. First, repressive styles reflected some characteristics of the movements the states faced. In all three countries Boudreau studied, anti-colonial struggles had politicized social networks, while 'institutionally weak and resource poor, post-colonial states had comparatively little prestige or authority with which to meet opponents' (Boudreau 2004, 21). The challenges were, however, different: in Indonesia, there were myriads of local and autonomous militias; in Burma, there was an ideologically diverse leadership and ethnic antagonism; in the Philippines, left-wing challenges increased with fiscal crisis. The perceptions of the opponents also differed: 'Movement participants' selection of contentious forms occur against larger issues of power, informed by risk hierarchies associated with different modes of repression' (Boudreau 2004, 27). Post-war Eastern Europe had different characteristics from the post-colonial MENA region in terms of mobilization of the society and perception of risks by elites.

The past, however, also held experiences to be reflected upon. In South-East Asia, memories of repression had an impact on the challengers. In fact, Boudreau noticed, 'Oppositional cultures are at least partial consequences of interaction between authorities and may serve to reproduce authoritarian proscriptions even as state power weakens' (Boudreau 2004, 28). Repressive styles had deep historical roots in the colonial power arrangements, which then influenced the post-colonial ones and, in turn, 'the state and ferocity of state repression'. So, different repressive strategies developed, and played a role through memory: 'From these fears and from the movement accommodation with state proscriptions, a political calculus emerges' (Boudreau 2004, 86). Over and over again, 'State attacks restructure opposition vehicles in each state' (Boudreau 2004, 153). In Burma, strong insurgency challenged a state that was weak but armed with a large anti-insurgent force, thus succeeding in scattering the opposition, similarly to the Communists after the anti-Chinese riots. The regime eliminated entire generations of activists, so that new cycles had to start again from the beginning. In Indonesia, the New Order destroyed or co-opted mass organizations (through, for example, the creation of a few student associations). The limited aims of the protest allowed for some tolerance of it, but only as long as it remained fragmented, preventing movement accumulation over time. In the Philippines, liberalization left free spaces for dissent after the crackdown, also favouring links between moderates and radicals. Protest was more frequent, more organized, and better coordinated, and a protest culture developed with songs, slogans, symbols. While no strong economic elite joined the protest in the other two countries, in the Philippines economic elites mobilized against Marcos' cronyism. As the regime relied upon a definition of the opposition as communist, it lost support when it became evident that those who protested did not conform to that image.

The evolution was in part similar in our cases. Memories of 1953 in the GDR and of 1968 in Czechoslovakia influenced both incumbents and opponents in discouraging violent solutions. Even under totalitarian Stalinism, the regimes were unable to totally eradicate any opposition. Especially, however, the path of repression was blocked by the changed strategy of the Soviet Union, which refused in 1989 to help the allied regimes, after having contributed in the past to their very weakening through an intransigent opposition to any reformist paths. In the MENA region as well, memories of police massacres played a role in pushing the opposition towards mainly peaceful strategies. However, here, brutal repression had also contributed to an escalation of the forms of action, as well as to the development of techniques to resist, and react to, police brutality.

If repressive styles had long lasting effects, however, democratization processes developed from changes in the levels of repression, as civil society grew with political liberalization. This is also visible in Yemen, where Carapico (1998) has shown that a non-profit non-state sector developed especially when the regime was less repressive. A weak state, Yemen was dependent on foreign aid, unable to control its border, plagued by widespread banditry that lived through secession and reunification, and a civil war in 1994. Nevertheless, civil society emerged through mutual help, as rural services were very modest; voluntary associations in the cities helped the poor, the orphans, the elderly, and made donations for education. In the three moments of political openings Carapico singles out in the history of modern Yemen:

> In each case a fledgling administration tried to rally opinion and investment around its governance project by relaxing the restrictions on autonomous projects. The main findings have been, first, that civic participation quickly fills any space ceded to it by the state; second, that this participation takes different forms depending on economic and political circumstances; and third, that activism materially affects broad trends in political and economic development. In the colonial port city labor and merchant interests organized syndicates, clubs, and political parties. In the second opening, and indeed for much of the twentieth century, voluntary energies and donations supported projects rather than organizations. The third opening, Yemen's most democratic experience, saw more specifically political participation in parties, intellectual seminars, conventions, and lawsuits as well as a surge of charitable activity (Carapico 1998, 207).

Our cases confirm that if moments of liberalization were indeed important for the growth of the opposition, the relations were neither simple nor linear. In fact, protests went in waves, which also preceded the successful eventful democratizations. These waves were often allowed by moments of (domestic and/or international) openings, but also sometimes contributed to new closures of opportunities. Moreover, mobilization often emerged from outrage at the repression of moments of protest. Even within eventful democratization, tipping points included successful mobilization and repression thereof. The killings of protestors at demonstrations created martyrs, and their funerals often provided occasions for further protests.

Paradoxically, in the MENA region we can note, at the same time, more 'controlled' liberalization as well as co-optation and divide-and-conquer strategies, but also more brutal repression, especially on labour conflicts and the Islamists While in both waves the economic failures of respective regimes fuelled political crises, in the MENA region neo-liberal reforms had created deep grievances, breaking with the symbolic basis of legitimation through modernization (and integration of the population in it) that had represented the basis of the socialist and/or nationalist authoritarian regimes in the area. Political struggles were entrenched with social ones, with some more resistance on the side of the regimes and their allies than in Eastern Europe.

In all cases, attempts at repression eventually failed. When protest became massive, the regular police forces proved insufficient to curb them. Regimes then resorted to militias and the army—but were unsuccessful. In part, this failure was linked to the respective regimes losing international support, something that was, to a certain extent, a consequence of protest itself. East European regimes could indeed no longer count upon the Soviet army, while the national military in both MENA cases remained neutral in the conflict. As Kruzman (1996) observed about the Iranian revolution of 1979, the challengers' interpretation of the potential for radical social change was transformed by emotional reaction to repression: so, 'as protestors' perception of political opportunities clashes with the state's structural position, the structure of the state gave way. . . . thus, the collapse of the military followed, rather than preceded, mass mobilization of the protest movement' (1996, 163). Then, 'the strength of the revolutionary movement induced even nonrevolutionary liberals to join in' (1996, 164). In fact, critical repressive events galvanized the masses, increasing spatial diffusion (Rasler 1996).

As we shall see in the next chapter, their disalignment from the regime, as well as the withdrawal of international support for the autocrats, were consequences rather than preconditions of the protests.

In sum, eventful democratization seems to have developed in settings in which regimes were far from lenient on protestors, but domestic and international constraints worked to diminish the state's repressive strength. Police, armies, and militias were all potentially important actors whose structures and choices influenced the dynamics of the transition. The regimes' capacity and willingness to use force were tested during the protest waves, however, with trial and error on both sides.

6

Appropriation of Opportunities

Introduction

'[In personalistic regimes] the absence of any social contract linking the despot's right to rule to the will or well-being of the people reduces the impact of mass challenges to the regime on regime stability. Absent any implicit link between the public interest and regime legitimacy, popular uprisings are more likely to play out as raw power struggles. Not surprisingly, regimes built explicitly on the use of coercion or terror usually perform well in such struggles, and bystanders, who generally recognize the regime's extreme commitment to power maintenance, are less likely to bandwagon. The despot's palace rivals are also unlikely to ally themselves with popular challengers because under all circumstances the expected payoffs from sustaining the regime exceed the expected payoffs from a popular victory. Whether those rivals are in or out of the despot's favor, so long as the regime remains intact, they can expect positive gains either from sharing directly in the leader's spoils or from side payments intended to sustain their loyalty. By contrast, all regime insiders can expect to do worse should the regime topple through mass mobilization' (Ulfelder 2005, 316).*

'The practices of neopatrimonialism cause chronic fiscal crisis and make economic growth highly problematic. In addition, neopatrimonial leaders construct particularistic networks of personal loyalty that grant undue favor to selected kinship, ethnic, or regional groupings. Taken together, shrinking economic opportunities and exclusionary patterns of reward are a recipe for social unrest. Mass popular protest is likely to break out, usually over the issue of declining living standards, and to escalate to calls for the removal of incumbent leaders....Endemic fiscal crisis also undercuts the capacity of rulers to manage the process of political change. When public resources dwindle to the point where the incumbent government can no longer pay civil servants, the latter join the antiregime protesters in the streets. Shorn of the ability to maintain political stability through the distribution of material rewards, neopatrimonial leaders resort erratically to coercion which, in turn, further undermines the regime's legitimacy. The showdown occurs when the government is unable to pay the military' (Bratton and van de Walle 1992, 460).*

If there is agreement on the importance of political and social conditions in facilitating and constraining democratization, these two quotes, from two interesting pieces of empirical research on protest events, suffice to indicate the degree of disagreement in the field. Without pretending to single out general laws that could tell who is right and who is wrong in this controversy, in this chapter I do wish to revisit some theorization in social movement as well as democratization studies, focusing on the interaction of political and social conditions during eventful democratization.

Social movement studies have traditionally looked at contextual opportunities and constraints, with particular attention to political systems. In democracies, sets of conditions considered as particularly relevant in explaining the degree and forms of protest have included both more stable and less stable situations. The former refer to the functional divisions of power as well as the institutional channels open to citizens; the latter instead to the contingent availability of allies. The characteristics of different types of democratic regimes in fact have been related to the intensity and forms of protest. In general, the more inclusive and pluralistic the democratic model, the more it will facilitate moderate forms of protest. In an inverted U trend, contentious politics is expected to grow especially after a certain threshold of pluralism is reached, but when access is still limited, at least for some social or political groups. Tilly (2006) specified this set of hypotheses, pointing at the combination of facilitation and constraints that each regime poses to various actors.

There has been criticism of the structuralist vision of opportunities and constraints, however. Stable, long-lasting characteristics have actually proved unfit to explain changing levels and forms of protests and social movements that are in permanent flux, and whose intensity and forms vary over time. Additionally, the initial approach to political opportunity structures has been considered as too deterministic, underestimating the role of social movements' strategic thinking (and acting) (Goodwin, Jasper, and Polletta 2001). Structuralism has then been nuanced through attention to actors' perceptions as a filter between structures and action, and determinism through recognition of the social movements' capacity for agency, with related consideration of strategic dilemmas. Additionally, in a relational perspective, contingent contextual changes—in part produced by the social movements themselves—have been considered as effects of long chains of interactions, rather than just preconditions. In their *Dynamics of Contention*, McAdam, Tarrow, and Tilly (2001) suggested looking at the mechanism of appropriation of opportunity, as activists take note of some windows of opportunity and act upon them.

As mentioned, a move from structure to action characterized transition studies as well. Initially deterministic in their orientation, scholars of democratization tended to look at the economic, cultural, and geopolitical context as constraining the very potential for democratic development. However, the results of this type of research remained inconsistent. If economic development emerged as correlated to the presence of a democratic regime, the causal direction was still unclear (e.g. Bunce 2000).

Dissatisfaction with contrasting evidence led, in fact, to several theoretical turns. One most important direction developed with the work by Guillermo O'Donnell and Philippe Schmitter, who defined transitions as underdetermined political changes, as the available structural or behavioural parameters are insufficient to predict the outcome. In Bratton and van de Walle's synthesis,

> Compared with the orderliness of authoritarian rule, transitions are marked by unruly and chaotic struggles and by uncertainty about the nature of resultant regimes. Analysts cannot assume that the transition process is shaped by pre-existing constellations of macroeconomic conditions, social classes, or political institutions. Instead, formerly cohesive social classes and political organizations tend to splinter in the heat of political combat, making it impossible to deduce alignments and actions of any protagonist. Political outcomes are driven by the short-term calculations and the immediate reactions of strategic actors to unfolding events (1994, 456).

Going beyond economic or cultural determinism, then, new waves of research also seemed less pessimistic about the chances for democratization in poor countries (Kitschelt 1993a).

Underdetermined does not mean, however, entirely undetermined. Addressing the risks of excessive voluntarism, Terry Lynn Karl defined structured contingency as an approach that relates structural constraints to contingent choices. In her words: 'Even in the midst of tremendous uncertainty provoked by a regime transition, where constraints appear to be most relaxed and where a wide range of outcomes appears to be possible, the decisions made by various actors respond to and are conditioned by the types of socioeconomic structures and political institutions already present' (Karl 1990, 1).

Bridging together these various trends, therefore, one can adapt the more dynamic version of the political opportunity approach to social movements to the analysis of authoritarian regimes. In parallel to the stable political opportunities of the social movement tradition, one could look at the structural constraints, which, as we shall see, are related not only to the political institutions but also to state–society relations. Second, potential allies could be expected to play a role even in authoritarian regimes. In a dynamic perspective, however, we should look at the context as sets of relations rather than at given preconditions.

Transition studies devoted particular attention to the way in which the *characteristics of the authoritarian regime* that a movement addresses impacts the magnitude and forms of contentious politics. In general, 'The authority patterns, elite bargains, and corporate interests on which different types of autocracy are based make those regimes differently vulnerable to different kinds of public challenge' (Ulfelder 2005, 326–7). Linz and Stepan (1996) have authoritatively suggested that the type of non-democratic regime influences the potential for democratization. In *totalitarian* regimes, which are the most repressive, it is particularly difficult to develop the autonomous organizations and networks that could then be the promoters of democracy. *Sultanistic* (or personalistic) regimes, due to the high personalization of power, promote a manipulative use of mobilization for ceremonial purposes and through para-state groups, while discouraging and repressing any kind of autonomous organization that could sustain resistance networks. *Authoritarian* regimes, thanks to their higher degrees of pluralism, are instead expected to experience more massive mobilizations and better organized underground resistance, based on networks that either predated the regime or were formed later. One can further assume that in authoritarian regimes, mobilization opportunities differ for *bureaucratic–authoritarianism*, with a technocratic civic–military elite that promotes the depoliticization of a mobilized society in view of capital accumulation (O'Donnell 1973), and *populist–authoritarianism*, where elites mobilize civil society from above, attempting to legitimate the regime by incorporating the lower classes (Hinnebusch 2006).

Focusing on authoritarian regimes, Barbara Geddes (1999) had distinguished strategies of cooperation and conflict among elites in military, single-party, and personalistic autocracies, linking their characteristics to the dynamics of their breakdown. *Single party regimes* are regimes in which 'the party has some influence over policy, controls most access to political power and government jobs, and has functioning local-level organizations' (Geddes 1999, 20). *Military regimes* are 'governed by an officer or retired officer, with the support of the military establishment and some routine mechanism for high level officers to influence policy choice and appointment' (Geddes 1999, 20). Similar to what others have defined as sultanism or neo-patrimonial regime, a *personalist regime* is one in which 'the leader, who usually came to power as an officer in a military coup or as the leader of a single party government, had consolidated control over policy and recruitment in his own hands, in the process marginalizing other officers' influence and/or reducing the influence and functions of the party' (Geddes 1999, 20). There is in fact a fusion of the private and the public, with family control over economic and political resources, and little use of ideological justification. As Geddes suggested (1999, 1),

> Different forms of authoritarianism break down in characteristically different ways. They draw on different groups to staff government offices and different

segments of society for support. They have different procedures for making decisions, different characteristic forms of intra-elite factionalism and competition,
different ways of choosing leaders and handling succession, and different ways
of responding to society and opposition....These differences...cause authoritarian regimes to break down in systematically different ways, and they also affect
post-transition outcomes (Geddes 1999, 6).

In general, Barbara Geddes noted lower survival rates for military regimes (only
sixteen per cent of those that emerged since 1946 still existed in 1998), as well
as their tendency to end up in negotiated transitions. A bit more stable than
military regimes, personalistic regimes are however affected by the death of
the leader (1999, 132) and are more likely to be overthrown by popular uprisings. Personalistic regimes are said to be at low risk of internal splits, but are
instead vulnerable to the death of the leader and/or economic crisis; single-
party regimes show high degrees of resilience, thanks to diffuse incentives for
party cadres to cooperate; military regimes are the most fragile, given different
visions of the proper role of the army. Single-party regimes survive longer as
they tend to allow for larger participation and popular influence on policies.

In addition, the *longer* the life of the authoritarian regime, the more difficult is the mobilization during democratic consolidation. In general, 'The
authority patterns, elite bargains, and corporate interests on which different
types of autocracy are based make those regimes differently vulnerable to different kinds of public challenge' (Ulfelder 2005, 326–7).

While these hypotheses make intuitive sense, however, they have rarely
been systematically tested. One exception is Ulfelder, who referred to a similar typology of non-democratic regimes. Using an event history analysis on
riots, general strikes, and anti-government demonstrations, he has shown
that contention has no relevant effects on personalistic regimes, while
single-party and military regimes are more likely to break down following
non-violent anti-government protests, and military regimes are less likely to
break down in cases of violent protest. He concludes, in fact, that, 'These
distinct patterns highlight key differences in the underpinnings of different
kinds of autocracy, and thus their vulnerabilities to contentious collective
action. The durability of personalistic regimes depends largely on bargains
among cliques with no claim to grass roots, so ruling elites are freer to ignore
popular challenges or to suppress them vigorously when they occur' (2005,
314). Single-party regimes, which tend to search for ideological justifications,
according to Ulfelder (2005, 318), are instead 'more likely to break down in
response to contentious collective action, either by acquiescing to out-of-type
change or as the result of a conservative coup that replaces the old order with
a military or personalist regime'. In military regimes, the corporate interest
of the military makes the regime more fragile, as well, while in personalistic
ones, mass challenges tend to be absorbed or repressed.

The idea that personalistic regimes are more resilient to protest has been contested, however, even before the Arab Spring. Michael Bratton and Nicolas van de Walle (1997) concluded from a comparative research project on Sub-Saharan Africa that as neo-patrimonial elites fragment over access to material resources and pacts among the elites are unlikely, transitions are mainly driven from below. Neo-patrimonial rule, dominant in Africa, is based on personalized exchanges, clientelism, and political corruption, structured in institutions such as presidentialism (derived from military or party). Absolute power is linked to an image of paterfamilias and of omnipotence, although tempered by the need to maintain various balances. Personalized clientelism is based on the use of state resources for coercion and favouritism. Even though personalistic regimes often failed to keep effective control, as the large state apparatus was undisciplined and ineffective, rent-seeking increased public expenditure while there was also a weak capacity to collect revenues. This was the condition, in the 1990s, of a wave of protest for democracy in Africa, prompted by the 1989 events in Eastern Europe. Peaks of protest in 1991 were followed by liberalization in 1992, competitive elections in 1993, and improved democratic scores in 1994. Between 1990 and 1995, the number of African countries that held competitive legislative elections more than quadrupled, so that in 1994, not a single de jure one party state existed in Africa (Bratton and van de Walle 1997).

Even a cursory look at militaristic, single-party, and personalist regimes suffices indeed to challenge easy generalizations and ad hoc explanations. Among single-party regimes in Eastern Europe, the role of mobilization from below varied. The same was true of militaristic regimes in Latin America and South-East Asia, or of personalistic regimes in the Middle East. As protest moved in waves, affecting different geopolitical areas at different times, we saw contestation becoming effective even against types of regimes that had previously defeated challengers.

What seems relevant in defining the very characteristics of episodes of democratization is not the (relatively) stable regime, but rather the mutable system of alliance between political and social elites. Besides and beyond the type of regime, there is another dimension that seems in fact of the utmost importance in determining contextual constraints on social movements in authoritarian regimes: the strength versus the weakness of the dominant coalition itself.

As mentioned, social movement studies have often looked at contingent opportunities, related with the opening and closing of the political arena. Particularly in times of electoral instability, social movements might win over allies inside political institutions. In fact, social movements' emergence, forms, and effects are influenced by the strength and strategies of alliances as well as oppositional fields: allies help social movements, reducing the cost of mobilization and increasing the chances that they obtain what they seek; in reverse, opponents aim at increasing the costs of mobilization and thwarting the chances of success. Focused on established democracy, research on social movements has addressed especially the position of political parties, as expression of consolidated social cleavages.

Even though political parties are unlikely allies in authoritarian regimes, here as well, the dominant coalitions shift, opening and closing opportunities for social movements. Some research has shown that, even in these systems, mobilization is influenced by the political opportunities created by divided elites and the emergence of potential allies, with different effects at different moments of the protest cycle (Osa and Cordunenanu-Huci 2003). Authoritarian regimes, like democratic ones, are supported by specific politically relevant elites (PREs), defined as

> …those people in a given country who wield political influence and power in that they make strategic decisions or participate in decision-making on a national level, contribute to defining political norms and values, and directly influence political discourse on strategic issues. The PRE thus encompasses the political elite, defined as those top government, administrative, and political leaders 'who actually exercise power' or 'persons whose strategic position in large and powerful organizations and movements enable them to influence political decision making directly, substantially, and regularly'. The PRE reaches, however, beyond the political elite to include groups and segments that contribute to political processes or influence them from various sidelines (Perthes 2004, 5).

Democratization emerges, in fact, as an outcome from the convergence of elites' exit strategies and challengers' entrance strategies (Oberschall 2007). In addition, according to Schock's research (2005), challengers are facilitated when a coalition of oppositional, decentralized networks, using multiple types of non-violence, succeeds in producing a withdrawal of elite support for the regime and an increase in international support for opposition to human rights violations. Repression then proves particularly difficult for dictators to manage, especially as it produced divisions among elites.

Elite coalitions in authoritarian regimes might indeed include, according to Slater (2010, 15): '(1) state officials, from the top leadership to mid-level bureaucrats, including the police and armed forces; under conditions of colonial control or foreign domination, external patrons as well; (2) economic élites, such as major industrialists, financiers, merchants, and landowners; (3) middle classes, including professionals, petty merchants, university students and intellectuals; and (4) communal elites, especially leading religious and nationalist figures, as well as top figures in ethnic associations'. In his work, democratization is linked to changing perceptions by members of the elite coalition, as 'contentious politics also profoundly shapes authoritarian

Leviathans' ultimate fates, when political crises call their continuing survival into question' (Slater 2010, 197). In general, 'the emergence of a cross-class urban protest movement, willing to risk repression by confronting a dictator's repressive apparatus at a polity's geographic and symbolic center, serves as the most powerful stimulant for an authoritarian retreat' (Slater 2010, 197).

Attention to elites' coalitions is also central to Elisabeth Wood's analysis of democratization through insurgency. Differently from Slater, Wood considers troubled cases that involved violent rebellions. As she writes, some democracies have been forged through sustained mobilization that 'convinced hitherto recalcitrant elites to negotiate an end not only to civil conflict but also to authoritarian rule... this enduring insurgency was the principal reason for the political pact that led to democracy in these two unequal societies' (2000, xiii). Insurgencies for democratization happened, she suggested, especially in very unequal societies, where 'elites long opposed democratization not only for the usual reason—that the many might expropriate or heavily tax the wealth of the few—but because the economic privileges of the elite depended on state-enforced procedures unlikely to be sustainable under democratic rule' (Wood 2000, 4–5). Both cases she studied, South Africa and El Salvador, were oligarchic societies, in which 'economic elites rely on extra-economic coercion of labour by the state for the realization of incomes superior to those possible under more liberal, market-based arrangements' (Wood 2000, 6–7). In these societies, relations are, in Barrington Moore's terms (1966), 'labor-repressive', and extra-economic coercion includes gross violations of rights and freedoms.

Here, cohesive elites were not challengeable by cross-class coalitions. As democracy was considered a threat for the entire economic elite, challengers were not to be found in elite groups. However, the exclusivist ideology of the regime created strong resentment that could be mobilized by the opposition. As Wood stated, 'In oligarchic societies, the exclusivist ideology of economic and regime elites (whether racially coded or not) toward subordinates (indeed, its explicit disdain for members of subordinate groups), together with the experience of repression, fuels deep resentments that can be mobilized by an insurgent group, providing a collective identity based on their claim to common citizenship that lessens the costs of collective action and contributes to the emergence of its leadership as an insurgent counter-elite' (2000, 11).

Opportunities and alliances are far from being limited to the domestic arena. In the 1990s, attention began to focus on the role of international actors, including the potential support (or lack thereof) by international institutions and superpowers. In general, superpowers constrain the range of possible activism, while international regimes might support democratization (for instance, through the development of human rights norms) or coerce it (through, for example, the imposition from outside of economic conditionalities that reduce welfare and freedom). The alliance with transnational human rights coalitions has emerged as especially helpful when it is consistent, uni- and multilateral, and supported by a strong civil society within. As Kathryn Sikkink observed, 'it is at exactly this point of decision within the authoritarian regime, when civil society is still severely repressed and not yet actively able to mobilize, that international human rights efforts might help to affect the calculation of actors internal to the regime, giving weight to arguments that the soft-liners are making in favour of liberalization' (Sikkink 1996, 115). In general, human rights organizations had consciousness raising effects (Brysk 1993, 268).

Multilateral human rights forums were provided by, for example, the UN Human Rights Committee or the Organization of American States (OAS) human rights commission. In particular, the United Nations was often used as a forum for the denunciation of human rights violations (with varying effects according to the power of the denounced state). International financial institutions, such as the WB or the IMF, have been seen instead as privileging free markets even at the price of widespread social crisis, often resulting in reduced liberalization and imposition of emergency laws or even coups d'état.

In what follows, I will look at the ways in which the characteristics of the political regime, also in the relations between (domestic and international) political and other elites, influence the dynamics of eventful protests, thus singling out some similarities but also differences between the Eastern European and the MENA cases. In doing so, I will pay particular attention to the ways in which protests produce alliances, by changing the assessment of pros and cons by potential allies. Beyond the role of agency in capturing existing structures, I shall also point at the ways in which opportunities are constructed in action, emerging from the protest itself. I will therefore address regime types as equivalent concepts for stable, functional opportunities in democracy as well as changing opportunities, in terms of the strength of opposition and allies. Beyond the regime characteristics, I shall also stress the specific dynamics of the interactions between social movements and their context.

Appropriating Opportunities in GDR and Czechoslovakia

Authoritarian one-party states, the Eastern European countries shared a specific ideology, which combined with formal institutions in determining the context for the opposition. In particular, scholars have looked at the complex political culture and societal networks of 'really existing socialism' in order to explain the specific dynamics of contention during democratization. As Valerie Bunce pointed out, a main characteristic of Eastern European socialism that influenced regime development was the ideological mission of the ruling elite: 'Unlike most dictatorships, which tend to be concerned with stability, if not a version of cultural and class nostalgia, and which operate within a capitalist economic framework, socialist regimes were future-oriented, avowedly anti-capitalist and premised on a commitment to rapid transformation of the economy, the society, and, following that, in theory at least, the polity as well' (1999, 21). These ideological concerns took the late developer and import substitution models to the extreme, creating autarkic economies and depressed agriculture and consumption, while increasing savings. In parallel, growth became a fetish, and production was concentrated on the markers of modernization. Linked to this was the Communist Party's construction of a compact economic and political monopoly (Bunce 1999, 22). As party and state were fused, with the state relying on the party for its personnel as well as for its resources, the result was an extraordinary penetration of the state by the party.

If this created a very powerful elite, its strength was temporary, as those characteristics fuelled a vicious circle: 'Over time and certainly by accident, the institutional framework of socialism functioned to deregulate the party's monopoly and to undermine economic growth. This set the stage for crisis and reform—and, ultimately, for the collapse of all of these regimes' (Bunce 1999, 26). This happened especially through inter-elite conflicts along vertical and horizontal lines that developed especially during leadership succession. At the same time, conflicts among elites strengthened the role of the society, as intra-party conflicts interacted with moments of protest (Bunce 1999, 27), such as the ones in the GDR in 1953, in Hungary in 1956, and in Poland in 1956, 1968, 1970–81, and 1980–1.

The fusion of the state and the party also tended to produce a broad potential base for the opposition through the creation of a large and homogeneous group of discontented, as 'the party's economic, political, and social monopoly, its commitment to rapid socioeconomic development, limited wage inequalities, and stable prices for consumer items, its preference for large enterprises and large collective forms, and its creation of consumer-deficit societies all worked together to give publics in the European socialist systems a remarkably uniform set of experiences' (Bunce 1999, 28).

Faced with a potentially unified challenger, the all-powerful party functioned, in turn, as a unified target. Fusion of functions also meant convergence of claims, as

...the party did not just orchestrate elite recruitment, attendance at rallies, and the content of the mass media. It also functioned in the economy as the only employer, the only defender of workers' rights (through party-controlled unions), the only setter of production norms, and the only allocator of vacation time (while being the builder and maintainer of vacation retreats). At the same time, the party allocated all goods and set all prices. Finally, it was the party (sometimes through enterprises) that was the sole distributor of health care, transportation, and opportunities for the leisure-time activities (Bunce 1999, 28).

A bias towards systemic uniformity also contributed to this target unification, as shared experiences produced uniform interests and a shared definition of the target.

A similar argument is put forward by Jeff Goodwin (2001), who explains the 'refolutions' (mix of reform and revolution) in Central Eastern Europe as the product of a dependent and authoritarian state, characterized by unfulfilled promises of economic development. Neo-patrimonial in their fusion of political and economic power, the regimes in the 'second world' controlled important economic sectors; were economically and politically dependent upon supports by foreign powers; and were disembedded from civil society. As in the Third World, repression, dependency, and clientelism facilitated the development of broad multi-class (and even multi-ethnic) coalitions (of intellectuals and producers), targeting the party apparatus. In fact, the fusion of power induced politicization and nationalization of initially local struggles. As an opposition member in the GDR explained, 'Always the state was to be blamed, even in intimate matters: in people's midlife crisis.... There was an all-pervading conviction that "They", the State, the Party, the authorities were responsible. They had to provide a flat. They had to organize a builder to repair the house or a plumber to unblock the drains. They allocated place at the university to the children who had kept quiet about their true political convictions' (Reich 1990, 78–9).

Linking the characteristics of civil society to those of the regime it was fighting, Di Palma noted that the very repressive connotation of the regime created, as a reaction, spaces for an opposition to emerge: 'since the notion of a civil society is fundamentally antagonistic to communist doctrine, communism, unlike Western authoritarianism, should supposedly leave no space for civil society. Yet already for many years East European social scientists, most of them dissidents, have paid much attention to the fate of civil society during the period of normalization'. First of all, the stated aims were not achieved in reality—so the regime claims 'to a monopoly of public discourse, and related cognitive removal of increasingly degraded realities... is also the spark that ignited both societal resistance and then cathartic rebounding when the crisis of communism exploded'. Civil society then emerged from this failure (1991, 63). In a similar vein, Christian Joppke (1995) pointed at the gap between promises and realizations, defining the Leninist regime as based on incorporation of the masses into the polity and mobilization of those masses towards an abstract and distant goal (Joppke 1995, 5). This became a source of discontent especially in the post-mobilization phase, when the totalitarian intentions could not be implemented.

Even though civil society was weakened by the party's cognitive monopoly on public discourse and citizens' cooperation with the system, the regime's monopoly on public discourse was challenged by the dissidents. While Stalinism was successful in removing dissent through force, cognitive dissonance re-emerged during the normalization of the post-Stalinist period: 'Thus, the reassertion of reality and the recovery of community imbued dissent from communism with a moral justification and an impetus beyond that of most other movements against dictatorship. For the discrepancy between communist doctrine and reality showed that the responsibility for the degradation of reality stemmed from communism's refusal to learn' (Di Palma 1991, 67).

The narratives about the characteristics of the regimes in the cases of eventful democratization do not show a particular sufferance in comparison with those cases of democratization from above (see Chapter 7), but rather a lack of capacity and willingness of the respective political elites to address the slowly deteriorating economic conditions. In both cases of eventful democratization in Eastern Europe, the political opportunities were closed. Nevertheless, in both, the one-party regime had slowly liberalized its policies, especially under the pressure of changing international opportunities. The protests then brought about realignment within and without the party, which favoured the opposition. Indeed, opportunities were created and appropriated in action, as elites dealignment happened in action.

International opportunities and constraints played a particularly important role, as the spread of international norms (and treaties) supported first liberalization, then democratization. Often mentioned, including in the very name of Charter 77, is the Helsinki Final Act, which institutionalized the Conference on Security and Cooperation in Europe and created an international framework for negotiations. In the Helsinki agreement, thirty-five European governments committed to respect 'civil, economic, social, cultural and other rights and freedoms, all of which derive from the inherent dignity of the human person' (Glenn 2001, 51). Especially as the European institutions started to use it for trade negotiations on a country-by-country basis, the formal commitment to respect for human rights could be made more effective (Smolar 2011, 134).[1] In fact, it

> ...functioned to undermine regime and state in the socialist world by legitimating international intervention in domestic affairs; by providing an international

---

[1] According to some observers, however, the European Community (EC) was less effective in pushing for democratization in East-Central Europe than it had been in southern Europe (Whitehead 1996). Even if welcoming German reunification and launching PHARE (Programme of Community Aid to the Countries of Central and Eastern Europe) for technical assistance, it

norm on human rights and the possibility of organizing oppositional activities within socialist states around that norm (which proved to be particularly important in hard-line regimes, such as the Soviet Union and Czechoslovakia...), by legitimating the right of nations to self-determination, a consequence that was particularly influential in the story of state dismemberment. Through the Helsinki process and through other mechanisms, then, the larger dynamic of détente introduced new ideas, new allies, and new resources into the socialist region. In reducing the party's control over international boundaries, détente qualified the monopoly upon which Communist Party rule and the socialist system itself rested. This in turn weakened these regimes while altering in significant ways the calculus of political protest in the Soviet Union and Eastern Europe (Bunce 1999, 61).

The removal of some international constraints on democratization clearly influenced the 1989 wave of mobilization for democracy. For the whole area, transformations in Soviet politics and policies were of most fundamental value; in particular, 'The sweeping political reforms introduced by Gorbachev in the late 1980s completely altered the Soviet government's response to civil resistance both in east-central Europe and in the Soviet Union itself' (Kramer 2011, 101). The wave of transitions in Eastern Europe was in fact strictly linked to the impact of the Soviet *glasnost*—especially after, in 1988, liberalization began to turn into opportunities for democratization (Whitehead 1996, 367), with Moscow's acknowledgment of the lack of realism in attempts oriented to avoid democratization through liberalization and reform.

Among the events often cited as turning points in the mobilization for democracy in Eastern Europe are particular statements by Gorbachev. Kuran (1991) mentioned in particular his declaration during the visit to Finland in October 1989, after the first non-communist government since the 1940s had been created in Poland and the Hungarian Communist Party had endorsed free parliamentary elections and changed its name to the Hungarian Socialist Party:

> With the world wondering whether the Soviet Union had reached the limits of its tolerance, Gorbachev declared in Finland that his country had no moral or political right to interfere in the affairs of its East European neighbors. Defining this position as 'the Sinatra doctrine', his spokesman jokingly asked reporters whether they knew the Frank Sinatra song 'I Did It My Way'. He went on to say that 'Hungary and Poland are doing it their way'. Using the Western term for

then failed to maintain this momentum (Whitehead 1996, 381). If democratization was facilitated by access to the EU, the condition of full acceptance of *acquis communitaire* made the EU the only principal, with a de-empowerment of national publics and often contradictory incentives, especially on the rule of law (see Mungiu-Pippiddi 2010 on the Balkans).

the previous Soviet policy of armed intervention to keep the governments of the Warsaw Pact in communist hands, he added, 'I think the Brezhnev doctrine is dead.' Coming on the heels of major communist retreats in Poland and Hungary, these comments offered yet another indication that Gorbachev would not try to silence East European dissent. If one effect of this signal was to embolden the opposition movements of Eastern Europe, another must have been to discourage the governments of Eastern Europe from resorting to violence unilaterally (Kuran 1991, 38).

So, as in the Third World, where revolutions developed when colonialist powers started to feel the costs of repression were too high, in the Second World they occurred when the Soviet Union withdrew military help. As Goodwin concluded, 'what collapsed in Eastern Europe was not socialism but a type of dependent authoritarian socialist—just as what collapsed in the Third World had not been capitalism, or even "backward" capitalism, but authoritarian models of "colonial" and "crony" capitalism' (2001, 274).

These opportunities and constraints can be seen at play in both the GDR and Czechoslovakia, as it is their development in action during eventful democratization.

GDR

In the GDR, no powerful domestic ally was available before the upheavals that brought about democratization. As for the elites' position, the party had its leading role written into the country's constitution. Additionally,

> The nationalization of all industries meant that there were no economic elites that had an interest in promoting the status quo. Similarly, the armed forces, including the military, the Stasi, the police, and the militias, took their orders directly from the party. Orders on how to deal with demonstrators were supposed to be issued not by military commanders, but by the political leadership in Berlin. In short, the diversity of elites present in other authoritarian systems simply did not exist in the GDR, since the party sought to incorporate every element of society (Ritter 2012a).

Even though the GDR was quite rich in comparison with other Eastern European countries, the economic situation deteriorated especially in the 1980s. While in the 1970s the country had long been represented as an economic success story, planning and centralization did not work. Additionally, the dependence on the Soviet economy and bloc trade was reflected in the use of lignite and the production of dioxin, as well as problems with the chemical industry. This situation challenged the promises of maximum satisfaction of material and cultural needs, as well as unbroken growth and technological advancement (Pfaff 2006, 37). Beyond material difficulties, it was especially 'because it undercut its stated goals, [that] economic decline tugged at the fabric of party rule in the GDR' (Pfaff 2006, 46).

The deterioration of economic conditions certainly contributed to increasing dissatisfaction—as 'the most damaging and counterproductive aspect of this dictatorship was its bureaucratic stranglehold on the economy' (Grieder 2006, 159). In the early 1970s, the state had completed the nationalization of privately and semi-privately operated enterprises, which started to experience supply problems, while growth and productivity rates declined steadily. The army, the Stasi, and the state bureaucracy were heavily funded (Grieder 2006), absorbing public resources. From the tenth industrial power in the world, the GDR had fallen to the twenty-sixth by 1988, and in 1989 the foreign debt had reached $26.5 billion (Nepstad 2011, 44).

A long-lasting trend, economic decline cannot be considered as a direct cause of the crisis that brought about the end of the regime. Rather, by the late 1960s, SPD leader Willi Brandt had recognized the potential advantages of providing economic assistance to East Germany. As Chancellor, in 1972, he signed the so-called 'Basic Treaty' that acknowledged the existence of 'two German states in one nation' (Grieder 2006, 160–61).

A most immediate indicator of the loss of regime support was the increase in the number of aspirant 'exiters', that is, in those who applied for visas to leave the country. An important step in the détente process was the GDR participation in the CSCE talks, culminating in the Helsinki Declaration which 'bound signatory states to mutual recognition of territorial integrity, including respect for existing borders' (Dale 2005, 86), but also committed them to respect human and civil rights. Considering the right to movement as one of those rights, an increasing number of citizens applied for exit visas: from about 7,200 first-time applications per year (of which about 4,000 were approved) in the late 1970s to 12,600 (7,000 accepted) per year in the early 1980s and up to 57,600 applications and 29,800 visas in 1984 (Dale 2005, 87). Applicants in fact often cited 'the Helsinki provisions that guaranteed the right of free emigration' (Naimark 1992, 78–9). As Ritter (2012a) recalls,

> Some of those opting to exit the GDR in the late 1970s and throughout the 1980s were political prisoners for whom the West German government in Bonn paid its East German counterpart around 70,000 Deutschmarks each. This questionable 'trade' brought the GDR leadership 3.4 billion Deutschmarks, a significant sum that helped mitigate some of the accumulating economic losses of the country. Yet despite these benefits for the state one must not fail to recognize that on the whole the wave of exits made for a dangerous precedent.

The Helsinki agreements also more broadly brought about attention to human rights and freedoms, creating potential breaks within the party itself.

Especially in the 1980s, 'East German dissidents found that human rights messages resonated with Western journalists and humanitarian organizations, whose attention afforded some protection. And with so many East German households watching German television, coverage of dissidents expressing human rights claims often "boomeranged" back into the GDR on the nightly news' (Pfaff 2006, 90). In 1985, the Stasi had in fact warned about a 'growing interest in the "demagogic", "bourgeois-liberal" conception of human rights and feared that dissidents might mobilize a "democratic mass movement"' (Pfaff 2006, 90–1).

Faced with economic crisis, the elites lost support as they proved unable to find solutions. While some state advisers suggested reforms, they were consistently blocked by conservative politicians in the politburo, particularly the aging party cadres (with one-third over fifty years old). A declining of identification among new generations, even SED members and students, followed. Some emerging tensions were testified for by the expulsions of party members, often linked to defection while travelling abroad or signing petitions for exit visas (Pfaff 2006). Additionally, the East German leadership was

> ...desperate to maintain stable relations with the Federal Republic, not only because they craved international recognition, but also because they became more and more dependent on it for economic assistance. The result of this increasingly lopsided relationship was a reduction in overtly oppressive measures taken against the East German population.... When the regime abstained from using force to crush the revolution of 1989, this was partly because it feared losing its hard-won international status and economic aid (Grieder 2006, 163).

Gorbachev's reforms then had a particularly high impact on the GDR because of the absolute dependence of the SED on the Soviet Union (Dale 2005, 121)—not by chance, its revised constitution in 1974 emphasized the 'forever and irrevocable' alliance with the Soviet Union. In fact, country 'leaders knew that they could no longer rely on the type of military intervention that the Kremlin provided during the 1953 uprising. Thus Soviet withdrawal of economic and military support decreased the regime's power and increased the opposition movements' leverage' (Nepstad 2011, 43).

Even though the Perestroika wing in the SED had remained weak, the party leadership collapsed as the protests developed, while a new leadership endorsed a reformist course. In sum, while there was initially little division among the elites, it was the wave of protest that transformed the perceptions of the incumbents, pushing them to surrender. The party then quickly transformed itself, in order to compete in democratic elections, with noteworthy results.

Czechoslovakia

Czechoslovakia was also a highly industrialized country with a relatively developed economic infrastructure in comparison with other countries in the Eastern Bloc. It was thus 'much more sensitive to the extreme unsuitability of the centralized Communist planning system than were the other East European countries managed by Communist governments after the war. There was also a lot more to squander. In comparison with its neighbours, the economy was not damaged by war' (Urban 1990, 103).

Here as well, however, while the country's development had long allowed for decent living standards, by the late 1980s there was increasing awareness of economic stagnation (Judt 1992, 96–7). Additionally, as in the other Eastern European countries, complaints about the economic situation interacted with increasing dissatisfaction with the lack of freedoms, including the inability to choose one's profession (Falk 2003, 89).

Considered as a most Stalinist and repressive regime (Judt 1992, 108), the Husak government had been put in power by Soviet troops after the defeat of the Prague Spring. As they were no longer ready to intervene, the opposition felt a political opening. Even though the effects of Gorbachev's reforms would not be felt until later, 'By 1988, there had been some cadre changes, a loosening of the limits of what it was permissible to publish or say in public and, most dramatically, an end to the jamming of foreign broadcasts' (Heimann 2009, 295).

Closely connected to the Soviet Union, the Czechoslovak government would also resent particularly the changes towards liberalization in that country's politics and, especially, the withdrawal of any pretention to intervene to militarily defend allied governors. As Heimann (2009, 282) observed:

> the one Communist leadership in the world that could not afford to retreat even an inch from the official line as officially broadcast from Moscow in the summer of 1968 was, of course, the Czechoslovak one. The Husák leadership had justified its rise to power on two ideological pillars: the need to oppose reforms of the kind proposed during the Prague Spring; and moves towards an ever-closer 'friendship' (political, economic and diplomatic ties) with the Soviet Union. But just as Khrushchev had created problems for the [country]...leaderships in the mid-1950s with his denunciations of Stalin, twenty years later the Soviet Union again pulled the rug out from under the Czechoslovak Communist leadership. This time, pressure came in the form of the US-Soviet policy shift known as détente, which required the Soviet Union to make at least some concessions to improve its human-rights record in exchange for slowing down the nuclear-arms race.

The Helsinki agreement was important here as well. As an anonymous dissident stated, 'If we disregard our subjective feelings and views...we must admit that the results of the European security conference, although no more than a beginning, are still promising. Even the few new things that the West succeeded in incorporating into the document could represent a step forward, provided they will be complied with' (Kusin 1978, 293). So, the signing of the Helsinki Final Act gave to a small group of Prague intellectuals hope that they had finally found a breach in the regime (Heimann 2009, 284), by requesting that the government respect the existing laws on human rights. So, 'this process, more than any single political, economic, or military event, is what doomed the Communist regimes of Eastern Europe' (Stokes 1993, 23). As Ritter (2012b) observed, in fact, 'The Helsinki Accords did indeed provide the opposition with its first political opportunity to challenge the regime, but until the mid-1980s Charter 77 and other similar organizations made minimal progress on the path to democratization. It was not until Mikhail Gorbachev became the new General Secretary of the Communist Party of the Soviet Union in 1985 that the human rights framework the opposition had tried to employ for the past 8 years began to show signs of effectiveness'.

Given the lack of either economic or military elites, the most important interaction for protestors was with the political elite of the Communist Party. Until the protests spread, the political elites seemed quite united—in fact, after the defeat of the Prague Spring and the purging from the party of Dubček's supporters, the Czechoslovakian communist party no longer experienced any relevant internal cleavages.

In January 1989, however, the Communist Party of Czechoslovakia recognized the need for economic and political reforms, particularly the decentralization of economic decision-making as well as a constitution that would not mention the 'leading role' of the party (Heimann 2009, 295). It was then that the fear of the conservative part of the elites increased, together with the hopes of the reformists and the population at large (Saxonberg 2001, 137)—especially as it became clear that the Soviet Union no longer intended to militarily impose compliance abroad (Saxonberg 2001). In the beginning of 1989, those former party dissidents formed Obroda, a network of former communists that had been purged after 1968, with whom the Communist Party met in order to discuss the development of a sort of perestroika in the country (Glenn 2001, 136–7).

So, in Czechoslovakia as in the GDR, no significant division among the elites was visible before the protest wave; instead, it was created through action. Short but intense mobilizations were perceived by the incumbents as increasing challenges. In action was revealed their lack of capacity to repress protest, as well as the disengagement of the Soviet Union from its role of enforcer of law and order in the Eastern bloc.

Appropriating Opportunities in The Arab Spring

The narrative about 1989 shows the embeddedness of political opportunities in political economies that assume specific characteristics in a socialist one-party regime, but also vary by country. A similar conclusion can be drawn if we look at the regimes targeted by the episodes of mobilization for democracy in the Arab Spring. It has been observed that Egypt and Tunisia had a number of characteristics in common: both had an homogeneous population, both were considered as neo-liberal champions, and both suffered from growing inequalities, high corruption, and daily abuses of power. This tends to explain why the protest claims bridged political rights with economic justice, with labour playing a pivotal role in both. Moreover, in both cases the regime reacted with carrots and sticks (for example, Ben Ali promised 50,000 new jobs) (Gelvin 2011).

Similarly, in the MENA region in the 1970s and 1980s, a degradation of social conditions followed economic liberalization, breaking the social compromise the national populist regimes of the FLN (National Liberation Front) in Algeria, Nasser in Egypt, Ba'ath in Iraq and Syria had built upon (Amin 2012). The upheavals targeted especially the leaders, accused of having betrayed their role. Traditionally considered as a broker, a mythic figure that expressed the *vox populi*, leaders like Nasser represented the unanimity of the religious community, the Umma. However, this image entered in crisis with the economic openings, when the grievance spread that social contract was broken (Camau 2011). If former leaders, even if authoritarian, tended in fact to support a Third Worldist as a project of non-aligned movements involving calls for peace, bread, and justice, this project lost ground to face the neo-liberal policies sponsored by international financial institutions. The debt crisis of 1980s was then a turning point, with imposition of dramatic cuts in welfare and education (Prashad 2012).

The 2000s were thus characterized by an increase in the number of people living below the poverty line, unemployment rates, and food prices (Salt 2012) by up to seventy-five per cent in 2010 (Joffé 2011). Unemployment, demographic pressures, and lack of housing spread dissatisfaction, contributing to mobilizing young people. Economic difficulties were exacerbated by the focus on a few sectors (for example, tourism in Tunisia, oil in Libya) as well as corruption by clan oligarchies. MENA economies have been said to have resisted the 2008 crisis, as they had low levels of international integration and began implementing anti-cyclical interventions. There were, in fact, advances on the index of human development between 1970 and 2010—life expectancy increased from fifty-one to seventy-one years old and young people with school achievement from thirty-seven to seventy per cent. With the destabilizing impact of neo-liberal policies, however, inequalities, clientelism, corruption, and emigration of qualified people remained high (Mouhoud 2011–12).

In both Tunisia and Egypt, 'cartel states' relied on the increasing integration of political and business elites (Bennani-Chraibi and Fillieule 2012). Research on the MENA region before the Arab Spring has been criticized for having underestimated revulsion to rampant crony corruption (Gause III 2011). With privatization, political elites and their offspring had become economic elites themselves, with resonant policy preferences and lifestyles (Haddad 2012, 122). Deepened relations with business challenged increasingly the former social contract with labour and popular actors.

Neoliberalism went hand-in-hand with waves of market liberalization, but also with political deliberalization. In order to explain the survival of authoritarian regimes in the MENA region, Eva Bellin (2004, 140) talked in fact of their 'robust authoritarianism' and 'robust coercive apparatus'. Others have pointed also at a strategy of *divide et impera* on the part of the liberalized autocracy (e.g. Cavatorta 2007, see also Chapter 5).

International conditions are relevant also for the Arab Spring, but differently than in Eastern Europe. Here, in fact, protest was considered as a cause of the changing alliances in the international system, rather than being helped by them. For the MENA region as well, the US institutions' increase in investment in civil society support has been mentioned (Bunce 2011), and international actors have been said to have offered training and technical assistance as well as funding. However, this interpretation has been strongly contested. While in 1989 the change in the Soviet Union's policies facilitated democratization, there were no changes in dictators' international alliances in the MENA region prior to the Arab Spring (Badie 2011), as foreign Western powers consistently supported authoritarian leaders. In general, the US and EU did little or nothing to implement the principles of good governance and respect for individual rights that they had written into various treaties. Especially when securitization became dominant after 9/11, they preferred what they considered as stability over democracy and human rights (Joffé 2011). There was in fact little support for oppositional movements by EU or US governments—which helped the dictators to the very end (Joffé 2011), even though the spread of an international regime of human rights was important here as well.

As for the US' promotion of democracy, not only did it receive far less funds than did military help to dictators, but funds went to NGOs approved by dictators, oriented to class cooperation and the fostering of entrepreneurial spirit, working with authorities or so-called modern unionism. Of $70 million given in 2006–10, only a quarter went to democracy promotion, the rest to military and security assistance—e.g. the Egyptian army received $1.3 billion per year from the US (Beinin and Varel 2011a, 248). While Obama's changes in foreign policy towards the Middle East were accused of being merely rhetorical, conflation of democracy and the free market was observed (Shahshahani and Mullin 2012). The Arab revolts have been therefore said to testify to the failure of the American empire, which allowed aid to be recycled into subsidies to the US arms industry (Baker 2012). Significantly, on 25 January 2011, Secretary of State Hillary Clinton declared, 'Our assessment is that the Egyptian government is stable and is looking for ways to respond to the legitimate needs and interests of the Egyptian people' (Reuters, 25 January 2011). US ambiguity—between support for dictators and calls for democracy—was in fact stigmatized by the very young people the US wanted to socialize, as US policy remained mainly oriented to 'protect Israel, freedom of oil transport in the Persian Gulf, encirclement of Iran and its protection for Hezbollah, Hamas and Syria' (Khosrokhavar 2012, 282). This position notwithstanding, Egyptian activists tried to sensitize US institutions. One of them, from the April 6 Youth Movement, recounted that, when he met with US State Department officers, he had 'asked them no longer to support Moubarak, to freeze his foreign accounts, of no longer closing their eyes on the violations of the human rights, to stop selling means of repression such as the tear gas used against the protestors materials'. Activists also distributed the list of political prisoners to foreign power, pleading with them to intervene on their behalf. In a telegram revealed by Wikileaks, the American ambassador in Egypt defined these requests as unrealistic (Guibal and Tangi 2011, 75).

The EU was also surprised by the events, after it had helped unpopular authoritarian leaders for fear of Islamists, betrayed its ideals by not implementing what it had promised on human rights, and tolerated high levels of corruption (Martinez 2011). As Wallerstein (2011) noted, France and Great Britain, in particular, were 'badly caught with their pants down in Tunisia and Egypt. Their leaders had, as individuals, been personally profiting from the two dictatorships'.

After having supported dictators as long as they could, the US and EU were then accused of attempting to contain the Arab Spring, which they considered as a risk for stability given some anti-US characteristics (as testified by activists' refusal to meet with Hillary Clinton and slogans such as 'Clinton; degage!' shouted during her visit), as well as a stigmatization of previous Western support for dictators (Salt 2012; Shahshahani and Mullin 2012). The Arab Spring was indeed defined as a call for collective dignity against the subordination of the Arab authoritarian regimes to US and Israel.

This set of characteristics played a role in both Tunisia and Egypt. Appropriation of opportunities here meant in fact a growing disengagement for regime support by the professional middle classes and, later on, from the military. No longer controlling resources for consolidating clientelist consensus through distribution of favours, the regimes had also concentrated richness and power in the hands of a very restricted elite of dictators' cronies, so increasingly alienating the non-protected part of the business community.

Tunisia

Since independence from France in 1956, Tunisia had lived under two authoritarian leaders: Habib Bourghiba (until 1987) and Zine El Abidine Ben Ali (until 2011). The struggle for independence against the French, since the early 1930s, had been relatively peaceful (Perkins 2004). A relatively small country of about ten million inhabitants and, besides a few phosphate mines, poor in natural resources, Tunisia had in fact a limited strategic value. The armed forces never gained much power as compared to other Arab armies. As has been noted, however,

> To answer the other recurring question of why Tunisia was the first Arab country to experience this revolutionary process that ended what many called a 'mafia dictatorship', it was often argued that this related to the level of education in the country, considered the highest among the countries of the Arab League; to the freedom of women and the family code, adopted in 1956; to the general economic level; and to the middle classes and the youth 'networks' that had sprung up as a result of the spread of computers and the Internet, the latter desired by Ben Ali himself, and even turned against him by hundreds of thousands of bloggers and 'Facebookers', despite widespread censorship and the famous web error message 404 Not Found, known to young Tunisians as Ammar (Ayeb 2011, 468).

Several of the main Tunisian organizations had their roots in the anti-colonial struggle. It was during the mobilization for independence that the dominant party, the Rassemblement Constitutionnel Démocratique (Constitutional Democratic Rally, or RCD), was created. The main union (UGTT) was founded in 1946 (Alexander 2010, 1041–58), and its participation in the struggle then gave it leverage to ask for a key role after independence. It was thanks to the leftist and secularist parts of the UGTT that Habib Bourghiba could win the internal struggle with a more conservative and religious wing (Perkins 2004, 124). Once he achieved power, however, he used a mix of repression and clientelism to keep it, as well as ensuring secular reforms. He also engaged in conflicts with labour and student movements, to which he responded with the co-optation of the main union, although without succeeding in pacifying the country.

Socio-economic policies affected the complex model of societal control. As Béatrice Hibou observed, 'obedience was, much more profoundly, the result of a link forged between, on the one hand, the latent violence relayed by the police and the tight supervision of the single party, and, on the other, various powerful mechanisms of inclusion' (Hibou 2011, xiv). The members of Ben Ali's clan accumulated money by working as mediators in privatization and import–export operations, as well as through access to public markets (Hibou 2011, xx). In this sense there was a politicization of the economy, put to the use of political clans. The movement then developed thanks to the weakening of social integration and the security pacts that neo-liberalism brought about.

The economic liberalization demanded by international financial organizations and pursued in the 1990s and 2000s increased the power and wealth of Ali's family members: 'The practical result was that the ruling family, the RCD party structure, state organizations (specifically the Ministry of Interior) and economic structures became increasingly interconnected. It seemed that, also in the context of worsening political climate, these political–economic networks provided the regime with the necessary political alliances needed to stabilize its rule' (Donker 2012b). In 2010, Wikileaks' revelation (spread by Al Jazeera as well as Tunisian bloggers) that the US embassy consider the regime as not reformable, as well as the broadcasting of images of corruption of the dictator and his family contributed to increasing dissatisfaction. Interestingly, this hit particularly former strong-hold of the clientelistic power machine of the regime party, the RCD, such as Sidi (Begir Ayari 2013, 245–7). Discontent in the periphery was addressed by a mix of repression and co-optation: forceful dispersal of protests but also attempts at buying off local activists. First reactions by the regime to the 2011 upheaval included in fact the promises of investment in the most affected regions, as well as symbolic gesture, such as visit to families of self-immolation victims. The spread of the internet, blogs, and social media was considered as dangerous for the regime's stability, in fact resulting in attempts at repression.

Despite the corruption and clientelism, the Tunisian economy was better off than those of its Arab neighbours. Development was unequal, however, also at the geographical level, as it left aside the periphery inside the country. Economic development had not reduced social and territorial inequalities. It had rather made feelings of injustice emerge as, 'since independence and even before it, the south, centre and west of the country have suffered from the economic and social consequences of the unbalanced and unequal developmental policies that were particularly concentrated on the capital Tunis, the Sahel, some big coastal cities, such as Bizerte and Sfax, and tourist zones, including Djerba and Hammamet-Nabel' (Ayeb 2011, 471).

As income inequalities grew and economic and political business increasingly overlapped, labour organizations gained support. Additionally, while 'social policies had resulted in an outwardly strong secular minded society, with one of the lowest birth rates of the region, highest levels of educations, and a progressive family law' (Donker 2012b), neo-liberal policies challenged this equilibrium.

Before the upheaval, domestic political opportunities looked however quite closed: elites were united and no ally was available for the opposition. Also, as mentioned, little foreign pressure was exercised on the regime. Divisions emerged, instead, during the uprisings, as some of the elites started to consider Ben Ali as a risk rather than an asset. Donker (2012b) singled out three perceived opportunities with opening up:

> The first was the learning process in which opposition figures started to cooperate with (wildcat) strikers and protesters in the periphery; and the realization that these types of cooperation could be successful in sustaining popular mobilization. Second, the logic of domestic political/state elites in engaging with protests made that protests were repressed at the start, but often bought off at the end. This type of 'carrot' tactic taught activists they could go into the streets, get away with it and gain some government concessions. Third, because of a changing media landscape, news about protests spread faster and became increasingly uncensored. Also, related, activists understood that when protests happened in one town, one could help them by going to the streets in a neighboring town: it forced police to spread over a larger region. As such, it can be said that the combination of increased cooperation between unionists and (human rights) activists, the perception of regionally weakened repression and a changing media landscape, would prove the basis on which the uprising built.

The very type of relations between the regime and the society made control all the more difficult once challenged by protest. As Mehdi Mabrouk (2012, 626) noted,

> At the social level, the country experienced 'social peace' through a policy of negotiation between government and the UGTT, the only labour organisation that continued to be recognised by the regime after it had been cowed in 1978, which was based on the principle of automatic increases in salaries every three years at the behest of the government itself—a typical corporatist approach. The 'social peace' that resulted was undisturbed, except for some isolated individual and minor group protests from time-to-time, in the form of sit-ins and hunger strikes. Indeed, this weapon of protest was so popular that Tunisia earned the title, in some commentators' eyes, of being 'the capital of hunger strikes'! In general, all such events were connected to relieving political and social suffering such as the deprivation of travel visas or dismissal from work for political, union or social reasons or because of unfair treatment. Such initiatives, of course, usually ended without achieving their objectives.

However, as young people remained excluded from these arrangements, 'abrupt and unpredicted protest began to grow as the officially tolerated political society lost its linkages with the social sphere so that political and social structures which normally formulate intermediation frameworks in moments of crisis had been dispersed or taken over by the state. This was particularly true of human rights associations in Tunisia as well as other organisations such as the Union Générale des Etudiants Tunisiens (General Union of Tunisian Students—UGET), the journalists' union or the association for judges and magistrates. The result was that, when the political system lost control of the growing protest, it had no access to any alternative mediatory mechanisms' (Mabrouk 2012, 627).

An additional element then reduced the chance for repression of the protest, once it had begun to spread. While the political police was too small for effective control, the army did not intervene. So,

> When on 8 January 2011 police forces retreated after heavy clashes from Thalla it was perceived as a direct victory for the protesters over the police and Ben Ali's regime, and sent shock waves through the country. The 14th was set as a national strike. As the 14th approached and the police forces had to focus all their strength on the capital—thereby effectively retreating from most other towns in the countryside—it was a clear sign for many that the regime was on the verge of collapse: fanning protests even more (Mabrouk 2012, 627).

That the Tunisian army is relatively small but institutionalized and professional, in an ethnically homogeneous country without great economic resources, could account for General Rachid Ammar's refusal to repress protestors as mobilization spread to the capital. The army's lack of compliance was also explained by the suspicions of government involvement in a helicopter crash in which several generals lost their lives.

It was protest, then, that 'brought about on one side a complete opening of opportunities: in the sense that repression decreased and the political sphere was completely open; at the other side ensuing chaos meant that particular *configurations* within the political sphere were not of any influence—because they were to a large extent nontransparent and unknown by the larger public' (Donker 2012b).

During the protests, the UGTT (umbrella organization of the labour unions) progressively detached from loyalty to the regime. Relying on their relative independence, the local branches had often since the very beginning supported the protests at the periphery, joining in coordinating committees with human rights associations; but later in the rebellion even the central UGTT abandoned the dictator. As an observer stated,

> The union's influence was limited, and therefore the power of the union against the regime weak. But this concerns the central union. When we consider the branches of the union things are different. The branches in the region had some independence. Because unionists in the regions were close to the people, they knew what were truths and what were lies. It made them crucial in mobilization.

For instance, the uprising in Sfax—at the start of the revolution—did not come from the UGTT. 50.000 people were there. Who organized them? The local Union in Sfax (in Donker 2012b).

While the UGTT did not issue any statements on the protests in the first three weeks, with the escalation after 8 January, pressures multiplied from rank and file members for taking positions, premises followed by a call for a strike on 14 January 2011.

While religious leaders remained silent about the protest, either for fear of repression or of stigmatization of the protests as Islamist, intellectual elites often expressed support for the uprising. What especially emerged in action was the disalignment from the regime of one of its main instruments of co-optation: the official union. Not only blue collar, but also white collar workers converged in the protests which focused at the same time on social justice and democracy.

Egypt

Like Tunisia, post-colonial Egypt had also been subject to the power of dictators, although with different characteristics. While the first one, Gamal Abdel Nasser, had been a leader of Arab socialism, strengthening the state's function as provider of a modicum of welfare, the second ruler, Sadat, had brought Egypt into the Western sphere, implementing a project of economic opening that had implied relevant cuts in public services. These policies were continued by his successor, Hosni Mubarak, with an increasing spread of crony capitalism.

When Nasser came to power in 1952, he rooted his power in the incorporation of some main sectors of society:

> Under Nasser, what has commonly been described as a social contract between the regime and the people was instituted that guaranteed basic social standards, jobs, and food in exchange for political acquiescence via the route of corporatist incorporation coupled with strong repression against those that did not accept the boundaries of the system. Thus, Nasser's regime while initially being ruled by a clique of military men, in order to sustain and deepen its rule turned to what were essentially populist–corporatist mechanisms, enacting land reforms to redistribute land to poor farmers, which were aimed at disempowering the previously influential landholding classes, building corporatist labor unions that imposed tight controls on labor activity, while at the same time increasing the living standard of workers by establishing a job guarantee for university graduates (Warkotsch 2012).

By 1970, the public sector accounted for seventy-four per cent of industrial production and forty-six per cent of production overall, as well as ninety per cent of investments and thirty-five per cent of the national GDP (Ayubi 2001, 199–200). In fact,

> All foreign enterprises and large and medium-sized Egyptian enterprises were nationalized. Their workers became state employees whose standard of living, along with many middle class Egyptians, improved markedly. Public-sector workers received extensive social benefits, such as health care; access to consumer cooperatives, which sold subsidized food and other basic commodities; subsidized housing; pensions; the right to elect representatives to management boards of all public enterprises; and an annual cash distribution of 3 percent of the profits of public-sector firms. The minimum wage of many workers was doubled. Real wages increased by one-third from 1960 to 1964, while the number of weekly hours of work declined by 10 percent. The government guaranteed all university graduates a white collar job and all high school graduates a blue collar job. Firing a public-sector worker required a review by a committee including representatives of the union, the Ministry of Labor, and management (Solidarity Center 2010, 11–12).

In the 1970s, Sadat drastically changed these policies by opening the economy to the global market, with a consequent dismantling of welfare services and the public sector and the emergence of a crony capitalism strictly linked to the political elites (Baker 1990; Beattie 2000; Kienle 2003). In the 1990s, pushed by an agreement with the IMF, the government launched a plan of structural economic reform, with a first wave of privatization.

Nasser's policy had brought about some economic improvement, later to be reversed. As Amin (2012, 31) observed, 'Egyptians began the decade of the 1950s poor and the ended the decade in the 1960s poor, but the revolution of 1952 offered them hope for better conditions'—thanks to agricultural reform, minimum wages, free education, employment of college graduates, progressive taxation. Inflation remained low until the war, and the economy developed. With Sadat, entering under US influence also meant abandoning Nasser's project of growth, giving up Arab nationalism and opening the borders to foreign goods and investments (which remained however quite small). It also implied cutting taxes and state expenditures for welfare, with consequent emigration and unemployment.

The open door politics under Sadat and the IMF requirements since 1987 brought about a reduction of public services as well as national cultural institutions. Cuts notwithstanding, Sadat left a huge foreign debt and a high rate of inflation, with structural imbalance in the gross national product (Amin 2012, 3). Mubarak, in a short honeymoon, invited economists of various tendencies to discuss possible ways out of the crisis, opening space for freedom of the press. In his first ten years in power, however, Mubarak continued to increase foreign debts (Amin 2012, 57). Between 1986 and 2006, following drops in oil prices, there were pressures by the IMF towards cuts in state budgets (Amin 2012). In 1991, a new agreement with the IMF brought even more cuts in public spending. In 2004, the neo-liberal vision received new strength in the new government.

The middle class—which had grown under Nasser, thanks to expansion of education and employment in the public sector—remained a victim of neo-liberal policies, between the pauperization of the many and the enrichment of the few. The cost of accommodations increased, as the quality of drinking water declined. Per capita income dropped, from among the highest among Arab countries (second only to Lebanon) to among the lowest (Amin 2012, 161). With it declined Egypt's prestige in the Arab world. Intellectuals fluctuated between co-optation and frustration.

Hosni Mubarak's Egypt has been considered as either military regime (Gandhi 2008), limited multi-party regime (Hadenius and Teorell 2007), or personalist regime, as power laid with those most loyal to the leader, in particular his relatives (Eisenstadt 1973, 15). While multi-party elections took place beginning in 1979 (Beattie 2000, 241), the ruling party always got a large (over seventy per cent) majority, often through repression and fraud. As for the other twenty-one parties, the only ones that kept any importance were the liberal Hizb al-Wafd, the leftist Hizb al-Tagammu', the Nasserist Hizb al-Nasseri, and the liberal Hizb al-'Amal, as well as Hizb al-Ghad (Stacher 2004, 216–17). While political opportunities remained quite stable, 'the socio-economic basis of the regime support changed quite significantly over the years, with profound consequences for regime survival' (Warkotsch 2012).

While patriotism had enforced moral attitudes and Nasser led a cult of asceticism, after the war the defeat had a strong impact: not only economically, but also morally. Egypt thus remained the soft state it had become after Nasser, passing laws it did not enforce, with widespread corruption (Amin 2012, 7). Under Nasser, a sense of belonging had kept the tendency to corruption low (Amin 2012, 34); this changed, however, after the 1973 war and following hyperinflation, during which Sadat (and family) amassed a huge fortune. This increased further under Mubarak when, 'little by little throughout the 1980s, corruption became routine and was no longer thought shameful' (Amin 2012, 38).

Political and economic power became in fact more and more intertwined under Mubarak, especially since the early 2000s. At the core of the regime, the people close to the President were in leading positions in the ruling NDP, including as ministers or personal advisers to the president. In particular, the Ahmed Nazif government in 2004 included several members of the Mubarak-affiliated business elite (Collombier 2007; Hassabo 2005). Privatization increased quickly from 2004 onwards, while there was instead a de-liberalization in the political sphere. Summarizing, 'Nasser limited political liberties and participation while increasing economic incorporation, Sadat

shifted this balance towards more participation for less economic incorporation, and Mubarak in the end circumscribed both, leaving not only the lower
classes, but even the Middle Classes increasingly impoverished, while height-
ening repression significantly, to a degree where it seemed arbitrary even to
people not usually involved with the political sphere' (Warkotsch 2012).

As in Tunisia under Ben Ali, the Egyptian case under Mubarak testifies for
an intrinsic relationship between political and economic elites. As Warkotsch
(2012) noted,

> while the political conditions of authoritarian rule remained largely unchanged
> in the last decades, and thus represented a rather static image of the structural con-
> ditions, the socio and political economic conditions underwent rather profound
> transformations, in their wake altering the socio-structural make up of regime
> support and incorporation. These changes left the regime of Husni Mubarak
> increasingly vulnerable to challenges to its rule by alienating it from most sectors
> of society, save a small circle of business elites, which in the end turned out not to
> be sufficient to sustain its rule.

Each neo-liberalist turn produced revolt (Javial 2011), while the global crisis
had repercussions in terms of reductions of exports, with increasing deficits,
as well as reduction of migrants' transfers (Daguzan 2011). The development
of Mubarak's regime was in fact based on a pact with rampant business interests as a main component of the politically relevant elites.

Politically, in Egypt as in Tunisia, the regime oscillated between liberalization and de-liberalization moves, using selective tolerance and co-optation as
additional arms for coercion. As it was observed,

> Government officials, pundits and academics, foreign and domestic, thought the
> regime was resilient—not because it used brute force or Orwellian propaganda,
> but because it had shrewdly constructed a simulacrum of politics. Parties, elec-
> tions and civic associations were allowed but carefully controlled, providing
> space for just enough participatory politics to keep people busy without threat-
> ening regime dominance. Mubarak's own party was a cohesive machine, organ-
> izing intramural competition among elites. The media was relatively free, giving
> vent to popular frustrations. And even the wave of protest that began to swell in
> 2000 was interpreted as another index of the regime's skill in managing, rather
> than suppressing, dissent. Fundamentally, Egypt's rulers were smart authoritar-
> ians who had their house in order. Yet they were toppled by an 18-day popular
> revolt (el-Ghobashy 2011).

During the protests, opposition to cronyism and corruption began to
spread to the business community, as well as among parts of the state
institutions. Splits even developed within the business elites, which
included a younger guard made up of foreign educated business cronies
of the President's son, Gamal Mubarak (himself an investment banker

in London), who had entered the NDP ranks since the beginning of the 2000s. This latter group pursued policies of liberalization, with an increasingly tighter overlapping of economic and political power as business elites occupied more and more political positions. This rise produced tensions between the new elites and the old guard as well as the military: 'While for the old guard, Gamal Mubarak's rise was a rather political threat, whereby one part of the elite threatened to push aside or at least diminish in influence another one, for the military, whose vast economic holdings depended and still depend on the state, it was an economic, as well as a political one' (Warkotsch 2012).

Another organizationally important elite was in fact located in the military (Blades 2008, 2), and deeply intertwined with the political and economic elites. It has been noted that:

> Until this very day, the role of the military establishment in the economy remains one of the major taboos in Egyptian politics. Over the past thirty years, the army has insisted on concealing information about its enormous interests in the economy and thereby keeping them out of reach of public transparency and accountability. The Egyptian Armed Forces owns a massive segment of Egypt's economy—twenty-five to forty percent, according to some estimates. In charge of managing these enterprises are the army's generals and colonels, notwithstanding the fact that they lack the relevant experience, training, or qualifications for this task. The military's economic interests encompass a diverse range of revenue-generating activities, including the selling and buying of real estate on behalf of the government, domestic cleaning services, running cafeterias, managing gas stations, farming livestock, producing food products, and manufacturing plastic table covers (Abdul-Magd 2011).

Retired generals were also appointed governors (twenty-one, of a total of twenty-nine). Nevertheless, the military kept some autonomy from the political power. As in Tunisia, moreover, the army has a comparatively (for the region) high level of institutionalization and no dominance of specific ethnic groups. This might explain the lack of intervention of the military in some central moments of the revolt. So, 'While old guard and young guard thus tried to stave off the protests by all means possible, the army played a more ambiguous role. Whereas the former stood to lose unambiguously should the regime fall, the latter, due to its high prestige within society, as well as the not quite ironclad hold on its lower and middle ranks faced a more complex payoff balance' (Warkotsch 2012).

Even after the formal end of Mubarak's regime, repression remained high. Overall, a contraction in terms of citizens' rights and freedoms as well as violations of human rights has been denounced by Amnesty International. In particular, since 1981 the state of emergency was continuously in force and Emergency Law (Law 162 of 1958) was extended to criminalize protests such as blocking roads or 'assault on freedom to work'. Freedom of expression and association, as well as the rights to assembly and to strike, were constantly under attack. A Law on Thuggery was passed in 2011 to increase, up to death sentences, the penalties for disturbance of the peace. Permission was required before writing articles critical of the military forces as well as for NGOs to receive funds from abroad. Military prosecutors and military courts were used against dissidents. Some of these measures 'reinforced long-standing patterns of serious human rights violations, while others—such as subjecting women protesters to forced "virginity tests"—represented disturbing new forms of abuse. From the end of February onwards, the armed forces used violence to forcibly disperse protesters on several occasions. They used tear gas and rubber bullets and fired into the air with live ammunition and accused those they detained of looting or damaging public or private property or other crimes' (Amnesty International 2012, 12–13).

In Egypt, as in Tunisia, the protests prompted the disalignment from the regime of important social institutions, with dissident voices being raised in unions and among professionals. Wave after wave of neo-liberal reforms had brought about increasing inequalities, with dramatic impoverishment of not only the working class but also the middle classes. Rampant corruption of the core elites was thematized by the protestors—and perceived by public opinion—as all the more offensive, given the suffering of increasing numbers of social groups (see Chapter 4). Most important, the spread of protest fuelled elite divisions about how to face the challenges, culminating in the military's decision not to defend the dictators.

Appropriation of Opportunities: A Summary

Political opportunities were quite closed in all the cases of eventful democratization I have analysed. In different ways, political and economic elites were entrenched with each other in both waves, with growing overlapping of political and economic power. Corruption spread in both, with the use of political power for personal enrichment. From the political point of view, the one-party versus patrimonialist nature of the respective regimes in the CEE and the MENA regions made an obvious difference in terms of the role the incumbent parties played, and in their breakdown. Although the two types of regime were similar in terms of the dynamic of the personalization of power and its concentration in a few hands, the differences in their socio-economic bases played an especially important role in the development of the incumbent coalition. While in both areas economic difficulties accompanied the protests, in the CEE 'real socialism' had brought about a large and homogeneous group of almost a petite bourgeoisie, frustrated by limited opportunities for consumption, while in the MENA region neo-liberal reforms had instead contributed to a dramatic shrinking of the middle class. Poverty, unemployment, and the precarity of life for growing parts of the population had an impact on the elites' dynamics during the fall of the regime.

Given this lack of allies, protests in the street might have followed citizens' belief that there was 'no other way out'. In both waves, in fact, the politically relevant elites appeared united until the protest emerged, with a process of defection developing only after protestors showed their strength and determination. In both waves, only then might changes be detected inside the regime coalition.

During the protest waves in the one-party regimes of real socialism, tensions emerged especially in the political party, which in fact, after weak attempts to resist, underwent the most dramatic changes. In the Arab Spring, the cronyism of the ruling leaders, with rampant corruption and increasing inequalities, had raised discontent among the excluded (and declining) middle classes, but also within the parties and their collateral organizations (such as the unions in Tunisia). In both waves, a determinant role was then played by the army inability to repress issued by authoritarian leaders. This disalignment further strengthened reformist forces within political parties and political institutions as well.

In line with what Elisabeth Wood (2000) has observed in her two cases of democratization from below, protest is to be seen, therefore, in a dynamic way, as capable of producing a change in elites' perceptions of their very interests rather than being pre-determined from already existent elite alliances. Even if the elites are initially recalcitrant, insurgency can change their strategic calculations:

> First, sustained mobilization eventually constituted the leadership of the popular opposition as an insurgent counter-elite, by which I mean representatives of economically subordinate and socially marginalized actors that are a necessary party to negotiations to resolve an enduring crisis of the political regime. This insurgent counter-elite is 'elite' only in the limited sense of being a necessary party to the negotiations if the ongoing conflict is to be durably resolved. Second, the accumulating costs of the insurgency (and the various counterinsurgency measures) transformed the interests of economic elites, eventually convincing substantial segments that their interests could be more successfully pursued by democratizing compromise than by continued authoritarian recalcitrance (Wood 2000, 5–6).

Protest thus fuelled itself: it did not so much respond to emerging political opportunities as it created and broadened them in the struggle (Wood 2000, 12). Insurgents, in turn, given the exclusionary nature of the regime, learned to value democratic participation. While no new elite might emerge, prolonged insurgency alters elites' perceptions. As Wood predicted, 'Political mobilization may affect the proximate determinants of investment in anyone of three ways. It may depress present profit rates (because of extended strikes or subsequent wage increases, for example), dampen expected profit rates (if mobilization is seen as likely to recur), or render expectations so uncertain that investors suspend investment' (Wood 2000, 151).[2]

Processes of democratization are indeed complex, their dynamics being difficult to assess in terms of dependent versus independent variables. Similarly, Schock criticized 'the tendency of social movement scholars to focus on how challengers respond to opportunities' as causing them to overlook 'how dynamics of collective action may recast the political context to one that is more favourable to challengers. Divisions among political or military elites, for example, might be the outcome of rather than the precondition for mass mobilization' (2005, 162). In Sub-Saharan African democratization, as well, it was protest that forced the elites and other actors to take sides. As Bratton and van de Walle noted, a common sequence of democratization processes involved in fact a continuous interaction between protestors and elites as, first, protests signalled the need for reform, with a twin crisis of the political and economic systems; afterward, protest tended to produce fractures in the elites, especially with regard to the perceived fate of dictators.

Context still plays a role, of course, defining the borders of what is possible. The differences in the socio-economic bases of the one-party, 'real socialist' regimes in Eastern Europe and the neo-liberal cronyism in the MENA region had clear effects on the elites' alignment and disalignment during eventful democratization. In Eastern Europe, the party elites had enriched themselves thanks to their political power—but much less so than in the MENA region, where, strong and privileged, the protected business elites did support the authoritarian regime, while the middle class in decline was in part involved in the opposition. In fact, in both cases, as in the wave of democratization in Sub-Saharan Africa, there was a crisis of legitimacy linked to the economic one which undercut the material foundation of the regime (Bratton and van de Walle 1997, 100). In our cases as well, transitions often started with popular protest (Bratton and van de Walle 1997, 101), initially on non-political issues, usually addressed with a mix of repression and co-optation. Protest became

---

[2] As Wood observes: 'In El Salvador, prolonged rebellion together with counterinsurgency measures taken to undercut mobilization reshaped the political economy, transforming elite economic interests (as well as elites' perceptions of their core interests) and thereby inducing hitherto recalcitrant elites to negotiate a democratic compromise with the insurgents. In particular, the civil war led to a dramatic transformation of the structure of the economy, as the commercial sector fuelled by migrants' remittances boomed and the export agriculture sector declined. In South Africa, sustained mobilization by trade unions and to a minor extent by township organizations—despite repressive measures by the apartheid state and repeated National Party efforts to develop a moderate black opposition—contributed to a climate of general uncertainty, declining investment, and a gathering perception that apartheid rule was unsustainable' (Wood 2000, 14).

politicized, however, as well as building up coalitions of various groups. The more political the protest, the more the repression grew; but resources often became scarce, not only to buy out protestors but also to repress them.

The compactness of the elites has been considered as path dependent on how the state was formed. Social movements are seen as conditioned by the type of regime they challenge, but one must also consider the opposite relationship in addressing the question of how regimes change. Analysing 'Why [some regimes] are more prone to act collectively in some political system?', Dan Slater (2010, 4–5) suggests that it depends upon 'historically divergent patterns of contentious politics' as social movement challengers—as wars—can contribute to making the state. 'By treating elite collective action as the keystone of political order', he then systematically links 'the mass politics of extraordinary times with the elitist politics of ordinary times' (Slater 2010, 176). His assumption is that 'people support a dictator when he provides with economic benefits'. If Hobbes had already observed that individuals tend to more easily organize in collective action against shared adversaries, Slater linked this observation to the perceived risks for elites that derive from the 'variations in the type and timing of contentious politics', which he assumes explain 'national variation in elite collective action, and hence in the robustness of postcolonial state'. The risk of the challenge, as perceived by the elites, defines the ordering power as the command of a steady flow of resources towards the leviathan, so that it can apply coercion in a sufficient and targeted manner. According to Slater, 'Outbreaks of contention are especially likely to be perceived as endemic and unmanageable by an extremely wide range of elites when class conflict afflicts urban areas and exacerbates communal tensions' (Slater 2010, 14).

In general, urban and class conflicts are perceived as threatening, because they are more difficult to appease through patronage. It is not only the amount, but also the type of contention that explains the specific forms authoritarian regimes took. The central idea is in fact that 'How well authoritarian leaders fare at capturing the strategic resources that elite groups possess depends on the types of contentious politics that presage the birth of the authoritarian Leviathan. Where such conflicts are widely perceived as endemic and unmanageable...authoritarian regimes enjoy an excellent opportunity to craft a protection pact: a pro-authoritarian coalition linking upper groups on the basis of shared perceptions of threat' (Slater 2010, 15).[3]

---

[3] In his comparative analysis of South-East Asia, Slater distinguishes three pathways to state formation. The first path, emerging in Malaysia and Singapore, is *domination*. Here, 'Endemic and unmanageable (left plus ethnic) conflicts brings the elites together; as movements preceded the rise of authoritarian Leviathans, stinted radical demands, penetrated the polities' urban core, and provoked ethnic and religious tensions. New elite coalitions arose in active support of both state centralization and open-ended authoritarianism, as the imperative of re-stabilizing what appeared to be an endemically destabilized social and political order outweighed the perceived risks of giving free rein to a potentially predatory authoritarian Leviathan' (Slater 2010, 23). The second

In our cases, in both areas, the creation of smaller and smaller elites of privileged people was an effect of the development of the dictatorship. In different forms and degrees, the original ideas of socialism and national solidarity were lost against the increasing corruption of those in power. The mirror effect of this restriction of the circles of power was the broadening of the circles of those excluded. While in times of adaptation exclusion could increase the power of those who could provide for even minimal doses of integration, in times of revolt the coalition of the excluded tended to become broader and broader. Particularly in the different classes, claims against the regime emerged. In our cases, the higher levels of repression in the MENA regions testified of a larger fear in the elites face to religious and class conflicts.

Also in our cases, however, elite disalignment was an effect of the protest. Mass mobilization emerged, in fact, as a major and often essential stimulant of regime collapse, not only pushing undecided or weakly committed elites to change sides, but also transforming their very assessment of advantages and disadvantages. A similar development happened in the Philippines, as Marcos did not succeed in maintaining a supportive class coalition. So, 'Intensifying social conflict during the run-up to Ferdinand Marcos' declaration of martial law neither mobilized radical demands among the working class against upper class, nor worsened communal tensions in the process. This explains why Marcos continued to face such implacable elite opposition in the days before he definitively destroyed democratic practices in the Philippines' (Slater 2010, 163). The lack of a (perceived) challenge gave him no capacity to order power from economic, religious, middle classes, and even state officers. The Church—even in its leadership—supported democratic protest: priests and nuns participated in the demonstrations, protecting the demonstrators with crucifixes and statues of the Virgin Mary. Middle and upper classes also came to be involved in the demonstrations against Marcos—as 'while the middle class provided much of the biomass for protests, economic elites provided funding, and religious elites provided inspiration' (Slater 2010, 199). Opposition emerged even in the military, which was disillusioned by mounting corruption, as a Reform the Armed Forces Movement grew with contacts to Aquino's family mobilized young officers. A cross-class mobilization brought a million people into the streets.

path is *fragmentation*: characterized (as in Thailand and South Vietnam) by challenges that were perceived as episodic and manageable as challengers lacked urban roots and communal implications, keeping a purely rural character. *Militarization* dominated the third path, for example in Burma and Indonesia, where contentious politics was characterized by regional rebellions against the establishment of central authority. As rebels aimed to escape the state, they were perceived as a threat by the military. Their very repression, however, made the conflicts appear not endemic.

In addition, during the protest waves, international opportunities opened up. In general, the role of superpowers has been observed closely. During the Cold War, the US had often supported dictatorships. Among others, the bilateral agreement with the US in 1953, renewed in 1963, 1970, and 1976, had integrated Franco's Spain in the Western Defence system, and the US had even supported Spain entering NATO (blocked by the Scandinavian countries) (Powell 1996). In addition, authoritarian regimes ruled by their allies have been supported in Asia, Africa, and Latin America, while democratization was promoted only if it did not involve mass protests, as 'mass actors scared Washington as did socialists' (McFaul 2010b, 19).

Reduced by Cold War concerns, prospects for pro-democratization interventions increased in light of public opinion's interest in specific situations (Donnelly 1983). Transnational mobilizations aimed at shaming democratic regimes about their alliances with dictators especially impacted on the Carter administration, which represented a turning point with regard to the national security doctrine that had justified help to military regimes. So, in 1977, the US cut support to Argentina's dictatorship and then withdrew all military aid while promoting multilateral sanctions. In Latin America more generally, the Carter administration put pressure on human rights violations, through annual reports on violations and elimination of military aid. Integration into the world market is said to increase the influence of international pressures, as in the case of Iran in 1976, when the Carter administration pressed for liberalization after human rights violations had been documented by Amnesty International. With the change in government, Reagan proved less concerned with human rights, for instance keeping support for the Philippine dictator Marcos even after Aquino's assassination. Even if, for a period after 1989, US officials seemed to worry less about stability, this was not the case with the Arab countries, as Islam replaced communism as the feared enemy. Of course, the attitudes of the other superpower, the Soviet Union, also played a most relevant role in supporting incumbent strong military allies, but also in the withdrawal of that support.

Macro regional organizations were also at times important players. Especially research on southern Europe and, later on, Eastern Europe, has addressed EU interventions. Research on Spain pointed, for example, to the role of potential membership in what was then the European Community in pushing towards democratization through convergence with democratic states (Whitehead 1996). In the dynamics of the Spanish transition, together with the Portuguese revolution and the changes in the Catholic Church after Second Vatican Council, the EC had an influence: even if pressures were not always effective against death penalties, in 1976 the European Parliament had adopted a text that explicitly linked membership by Spain to democracy (Powell 1996).

What our cases indicate is that the process of naming-and-shaming the respective regimes for their lack of compliance with international agreements was not automatically successful: rather, it required the action of the opposition, and their transnational ties. This was the case in Eastern Europe, where the willingness of Gorbachev's Soviet Union to step down from its policing role in the Warsaw Pact was tried and tested during the upheavals. And it was even more the case in the MENA region where, especially after 9/11, Western powers had supported—or at least turned a blind eye toward—autocrats' repression in exchange for what they saw as stability against the assumed risks of Islamists. It was indeed the protest, and the international solidarity it received from below, that pushed reluctant governments in the US and the EU to offer some words of support for the insurgents.

Going back to the two opening quotes, patrimonialism helped the survival of the authoritalian regimes, but also their breakdown. Especially in the MENA region, but also in CEE, support for despots' declined as they restricted more and more the groups of those privileged, increasing the feeling of exclusion of the others. Additionally, as economic crises or changes in economic policies reduced the capacity to meet the needs and expectations not only of citizens in general, but also of clients and party members, alienation from the regime increased.

7

Participated Pacts and Social Movements

Introduction

> *It is the interaction between mobilization and bargaining that must be analyzed to explain democratization.... First, mobilization in collective action influences bargaining among elites by introducing new actors into political arenas, by altering the bargaining power of representatives of social movements, and by articulating new demands that shape the range of outcomes considered. Second, bargaining structures opportunities for mobilization by influencing the aims and scope of political competition, as well as the acceptable participants in the political sphere* (Glenn 2003, 103).

Mobilization was very visible in the cases of eventful democratization I have just analysed. However, it was also present, in different timings and forms, in other cases, which have been often praised as pacts among moderates of both the incumbents and the opposition.

According to traditional approaches, in order to succeed, transitions are expected to be smooth, and actors to moderate their aims. Samuel P. Huntington has been one of the strongest supporters of this moderation view. He suggested, in fact, that third wave transitions were complex political processes involving several actors—including the standpatters, liberal reformers, and democratic reformers in the governing coalition, and the democratic moderates and revolutionary extremists in the opposition (1991, 588). He thus presented Spain and Brazil as prototypical instances of change from above, with Spain becoming a model for subsequent processes of democratization in both Latin America and Eastern Europe (Huntington 1991, 592).

The assumption was that moderates have to be sufficiently strong within the opposition to be credible negotiating partners with the government. As Huntington recalled,

At one point in the Brazilian transition, General Golbery reportedly told an opposition leader, 'You get your radicals under control and we will control ours'.

Getting radicals under control often requires the cooperation of the other side. In transplacement negotiations, each party has an interest in strengthening the other party so that he can deal more effectively with the extremists on his side. In June 1990, for instance, Nelson Mandela commented on the problems F. W. de Klerk was having with white hard-liners and said that the ANC had appealed 'to whites to assist de Klerk. We are also trying to address the problems of white opposition to him. Discussions have already been started with influential sectors in the right wing.' At the same time, Mandela said that his own desire to meet with Chief Mengosuthu Buthelezi had been vetoed by militants within the ANC and that he had to accept that decision because he was 'a loyal and disciplined member of the A.N.C'. De Klerk obviously had an interest in strengthening Mandela and helping him deal with his militant left-wing opposition (Huntington 1991, 614).

In his 'Guidelines for democratizers', Huntington in fact recommended:

> Like democratic rulers, authoritarian rulers over time alienate erstwhile supporters. Encourage these disaffected groups to support democracy as the necessary alternative to the current system. Make particular efforts to enlist business leaders, middle-class professionals, religious figures, and political party leaders, most of whom probably supported creation of the authoritarian system. The more 'respectable' and 'responsible' the opposition appears, the easier it is to win more supporters....Cultivate generals. In the last analysis, whether the regime collapses or not depends on whether they support the regime, join you in opposition to it, or stand by on the sidelines (Huntington 1991, 607).[1]

Similarly, O'Donnell and Schmitter (1986) also pointed at the importance of tactical moderation. They warned, indeed, that 'if the opposition menaces the vertical command structure of the armed forces, the territorial integrity of the nation-state, the country's position in international alliances, or the property rights underlying the capitalist economy or if widespread violence recurs, then even bland regime actors will conclude that the costs of tolerance are greater than those of repression' (O'Donnell and Schmitter 1986, 27). Democratizing actors are therefore advised to avoid explosive redistributive issues, moderate their aims, and queue requests, circumscribing the agenda.

Parties—not movements—are considered to be pivotal in these efforts at moderation, acting as instruments of social and political control as well as effective demobilization. As Bermeo summarized, the main message of the series of studies edited by O'Donnell and Schmitter is that 'political party leaders are the key players in the transition gamble. They set the stakes; they

---

[1] Suggestions to moderate in opposition also included '(1) Be prepared to mobilize your supporters for demonstrations when these will weaken the stand patters in the government. Too many marches and protests, however, are likely to strengthen them, weaken your negotiating partner, and arouse middle-class concern about law and order. (2) Be moderate; appear statesmanlike. (3) Be prepared to negotiate and, if necessary, make concessions on all issues except the holding of free and fair elections' (Huntington 1991, 616).

work out the compromises; they act as the forces for moderation that the successful transition process requires.... The distinction between a compromise and a sell-out is often debatable, and the line between pragmatic and unprincipled behavior is sometimes difficult to draw' (1986, 369). There seems to be consensus in this stream of literature about the positive role played by political parties. In Venezuela, Spain, or Peru, political parties negotiated pacts, mediated conflicts, and quelled revolts.

All these assumptions are disputed, however. Scholars have noted that not only did protest emerge during transition and consolidation, but it did not have the negative effects some 'transitologists' expected. Among others, Nancy Bermeo criticized the claim that 'too much popular mobilization and too much pressure from below can spoil the chances for democracy', suggesting that 'fear of the masses lies at the root of this cautionary argument. For some, this fear emerges from the conviction that the general citizenry may not have the values a sustainable democracy requires'. Instead, she noted that, 'In many cases, democratization seems to have proceeded alongside weighty and even bloody popular challenges' (Bermeo 1997, 314).

As we shall see in this chapter, moderation and radicalization are not absolute values. In fact, equally successful democratization paths could emerge either from disruptive and contentious movements, or from movements oriented to bargaining. Contention or moderation, protest or bargaining are not choices that are made once and for all, but rather tend to follow each other in waves, protest creating resources which are then invested in negotiation. Moreover, even in pacted transitions, contentious politics—or the threat of it—is an important chip that opponents can put on the game table, to overcome stalemates and obtain better bargains. Thus, if previous examples of disruption by a well-developed civil society are important pushes in participatory pacts, these tend to develop when there are, on the other side, fractures among the elites, and thus potential allies for the opponents.

As we have seen in the previous chapters, in eventful democratizations a central role was played by disruptive social movement organizations that had developed in previous years with an empowering discourse and broad civic and national self-definition. Political opportunities were relatively closed at the onset, but protest itself brought about some realignment among elites, changing their perceptions and interests. These realignments did happen very late in the process. In this chapter, I will show that a significant presence of social movements also characterized participated pacts, where preexisting civil society negotiated change mainly by threatening mobilization rather than practicing it. In fact, the expectation that stronger social movement organizations would more likely bring about eventful democratization would be misleading, as would be the opposite claim that democratization is always driven from above. Strategic choices of social movements, but also of elites, will emerge as relevant in the two main pacted transitions in 1989.

As we will see, facing economic crisis accompanied by falling legitimacy, East European elites reacted differently, with more of an orientation to negotiate when confronted by stronger political societies (Saxonberg 2001). So in Poland and Hungary, reformists within the elites allied with moderates in the opposition in pushing for market and political liberalization. Following Przeworski's expectations, elites in the two countries seemed indeed willing to compromise, as it allowed them to maintain some power. In particular, reformers among incumbents and moderates in the opposition could control, respectively, hardliners and radicals. While no participated pacts have yet emerged from the Arab Spring, we will turn to the spreading of protests to Morocco and Yemen as well as to the Turkish case to discuss the potential for participation in this path of transition in the MENA region. I will show that, here as well, mobilizations from below represented important moments in the (often interrupted) path towards liberalization.

Participated Pacts and Social Movements in 1989

With the partial exception of Romania and (even less) Albania (see Chapter 8), the 1989 wave of mobilization for democracy in Central Eastern Europe remained peaceful. There was, however, a different mix of mobilization and bargaining in the different cases: mobilization followed by bargaining in Czechoslovakia and East Germany; bargaining followed by mobilization in Poland and Hungary. Negotiated cases indicated that relatively strong civil societies constitute important bases for moderation and participated pacts. These cases are, in fact, not easily defined as democratization from above, as the intervention of social movement organizations of different types was important in the various steps of the transition process.

According to Saxonberg (2001), the communist regimes based their legitimacy on the monopoly of truth and the capacity to improve living standards (see also Chapter 6). Communism was a political religion with eschatological and messianic qualities, as well as claims of superior economic performance. The regimes followed a basic pattern of one-party rule, party–state control over the economy, coherent Marxist–Leninist ideology. However, there were different declinations of 'real socialism'. With the end of the Eastern European Stalinist messianic phase and its totalitarian aspirations, as the regime institutionalized and lost support, post-totalitarian regimes followed, divided into mature (like Hungary and Poland) and frozen types (as in the GDR and Czechoslovakia). While at the beginning of post-totalitarianism, the regime still enjoyed some ideological support (although it becomes pragmatic acceptance later on), the post-totalitarian communist regimes fell either through pacts (in mature cases) or due to non-violent insurgencies (in frozen ones).[2]

Especially in mature cases, as the economic crisis deepened, conflicts developed within parties, as well as between party leaders and bureaucracy. As Gorbachev took power in the Soviet Union and outrage and indignation pushed people into the streets, reformist regimes negotiated with the opposition, while orthodox ones remained paralysed. While, as we have seen, the impetus for change came from mass opposition using protest in Czechoslovakia and the GDR (Saxonberg 2012, 25), when reformers supported opposition against the centre or hardliners the result was pacted transition.

Changes developed notwithstanding the resistance of the nomenclature, which Saxonberg defines as composed of 'all members of the Party apparatus and state bureaucracy at or above the level of factory manager or head of the factory party organization' (2001, 51). Faced with economic crises linked to inefficiency, oil price increases, growing military spending, modernization, and economic change, while all regimes pragmatically accepted Soviet dominance, reforms also began, involving some liberalization. This happened not only in Hungary, where liberalization had gone further in the 1960s, including some freedom for travel, but even in Poland, where Jaruzelski had tried to placate the public, for example by disbanding the old communist union, setting up a consultative council, and granting a few amnesties.

So, given the economic crisis, reformist forces in the two countries saw an opportunity when Gorbachev took power in the Soviet Union. They then negotiated with the (moderate) opposition. While the Hungarian reformers were more popular than their Polish counterparts, the opposition was weaker there. Differently than in the GDR and Czechoslovakia, in Hungary and Poland the respective regime leaders feared rebellion (based on past experience) and acted to secure a compromise.

Although its strength varied, an autonomous civil society did exist in these two countries. While in Poland we found in Solidarity a mass movement, in Hungary, there were hundreds of groups and twenty new political movements.[3]

---

[2] Sultanistic cases (such as Romania), which are characterized by patrimonialism and personalized leadership, tend to collapse under more violent circumstances, as do failed totalitarian regimes (for example, Ethiopia, Nicaragua, Grenada).

[3] An annotated survey of independent movements in Eastern Europe, mentioned in Radio Free Europe on 13 June 1989, reported about 100 groups (Ekiert 1996).

Poland

In Poland, as in the cases of eventful democratization, there was a long process of building up civil society, through waves of protest, followed by various degrees of repression. In contrast to those cases, however, this strong civil society pushed elites towards a negotiation.

A) THE MOBILIZATION OF CIVIL SOCIETY

Poland is a good example of a strong civil society in Central Eastern Europe. Based on research on members of oppositional organizations (how many members are jointly shared by any organizational pair), Osa (2003a and 2003b) observed an increasing capacity for networking by those who mobilized against the regime. Here as well, networking between different types of actors happened during protest.

Protests against price increases in 1966—a year that marked an important anniversary for Polish Catholicism, but also the tenth anniversary of the 1956 oppositional action and attempt at de-Stalinization by leader Gomulka—used religious symbols, adapted from religious ceremonies. Initially, according to Osa, the 1966–7 protest involved four Catholic civil society organizations, well connected in a clique; a year later she also found three student organizations, two of them linked to the Catholic groups.

In 1968, there was in fact some limited oppositional activity at Warsaw University after the regime banned a play by the most famous Polish romantic, Adam Mickiewicz. As two students were expelled, 5,000 students mobilized in their support. Brutal police charges followed, with hundreds expelled, jailed, and sentenced. While party opponents to Gomulka orchestrated anti-Jewish as well as anti-student campaigns,[4] reformists in the party were marginalized or expelled.

Workers' protests developed in different moments. In December 1970, strikes against price increases turned violent: forty-five people were killed, 1,165 wounded, 3,161 arrested. In 1976, Gierek's attempt to increase prices was met by factory walkouts and violent demonstrations. In June 1976, strikes against price increases resulted in 2,500 arrests, 500 indictments, and up to 20,000 dismissals. Even though price increases were suspended, activists were arrested and beaten up in custody. Initially, however, workers had no connection with other networks (Osa 2003a).

The 1970s saw also the consolidation of a circle of independent intellectuals who were active in public protest and support for political prisoners. Although with internal tensions, the Catholic Church, historically a symbol of national resistance, offered free spaces to protestors. Wojtyla's election to

---

[4] Demonstrations called for 'Students to their studies, writers to their pens' (Osa 2003a, 86).

Pope in 1978 and his pilgrimage to Poland in 1979 strengthened the opposition, as did the successive visits in 1983 and 1987. In 1978–9 new organizations, including liberal and nationalist ones, joined the oppositional network; the number further increased in 1980–1 when a dense network fuelled mobilization capacity (Osa 2003a).

The Helsinki agreements functioned also in Poland as a point of reference for dissidents who 'continually demanded respect for fundamental human rights. They also revived the national and religious traditions' (Kenney 2002, 20). It was especially between 1976 and 1980 that networks between previously scattered groups were established (Fehr 1995, 302). Links developed when, similarly to Charter 77, the Workers' Defense Committee (Komitet Obrony Robotników—KOR) was founded in 1976, after the repression of workers' strikes in Ursus and Radom. This organization was formed to provide activists with legal aid, with particular reliance on the Helsinki agreements (Killingsworth 2012, 123–5). It focused initially on human rights violations, aiming at reform within the limits of the existing regime, through open and unconspiratorial public action—not by small elites, but rather from below—with the goal of forcing the system to respect legality. Similarly to Charter 77, KOR planned to contribute to the organization of a public sphere to bypass the state. It certainly helped in networking various oppositional actors, representing an initial alliance between workers and intellectuals (Flam 2001).

In the early 1980s, the labour movement became particularly strong. Protests grew, once again, with claims against price increases and for higher salaries, the erection of monuments to victims of the 1970s strikes, family subsidies (as there were for policepersons), free Saturdays, limitations on censorship, and free media. The Inter-Factory Strike Committees (Międzyzakładowy Komitet Strajkowy, MKS) emerged to coordinate the protest committees that mushroomed in numerous workplaces in the summer of 1980. After the government's decision to increase food prices, 'For more than two weeks about three million Polish workers took part in the occupation strike in more than 1,500 plants' (Barker 2001, 264). Especially in August, massive strikes ended in the signing of the 21 August Gdansk Agreements (Porozumienia Sieprniowe). There were also protests of 40,000 full-time employees and students (Independent student union) as well as artisans, craftspeople and small businesspeople, as 'The civil fever, sparkled by Solidarity, spread to all social groups, cities and villages in the country, and to all organizations and institutions of the Polish party-state. Even the police and the military were not immune, and their members attempted to organize independent trade unions' (Ekiert 1996, 242).

The creation of an independent trade union confederation was granted on 17 September 1980, and confirmed on 10 November 1980, when the Solidarity trade union was registered in a Warsaw court. On 12 May 1981 the farmers' section of the union, the Niezależny Samorządny Związek Zawodowy Rolników Indywidualnych Solidarność, was also registered in a court. Claims included, besides salary increases, better working conditions, amnesty for imprisoned colleagues, an end to the harassment of activists, and a decline in censorship, as well as the right to build an independent workers' movement, party pluralism, freedom of speech and religious practices (including the right to building new churches, which was often opposed by the authorities). Strikes continued, as activists believed the terms of the Gdansk agreements were not respected—thus 'the conflict intensified and spread to the whole social system. It became a real cycle of protest' (Osa 2003a, 231).

These actions were followed by increasing politicization of Solidarity, which was in fact the main movement organization: nearly one-quarter of the population joined during the protests (between nine and ten million people). Officially a trade union, it also extended its scope to include respect for human rights as well as freedom of speech and of the press, political pluralism, freedom of assembly (most importantly, the right to establish independent trade unions). Very varied, it was composed of different groups united as citizens, part of a Polish nation, endowed with fundamental and inalienable rights. Important was the alliance with the Church, historical bearer of national identity during partition, which had bargained for some autonomous spaces with the state. Relying on the Church for support, the union emphasized legal means for change.

Solidarity in fact bridged different types of concern. First, Solidarity was a movement of workers, which linked economic concerns with concerns for democracy: especially in the beginning of the cycle of protest, the call for self-management indicated the will to eliminate the party from the enterprise. As Alain Touraine and his collaborators noted, 'A labour movement, strengthened by economic failures, started in Poland the re-conquering of the society' (Touraine, Dubet, Wieviorka, and Strzelecki 1982, 59). However, workers' consciousness was also bridged with nationalist appeals: 'against the International that was referred to by leaders in the factory, the militants sing "God save Poland"' (Touraine et al. 1982, 67); militants spoke of the superiority of the 'interest of the Polish nation' (Touraine et al. 1982, 77) and accused the party of wanting 'to make of Polish people Russian ones' (Touraine et al. 1982, 245). The three components of the workers' movement, the nationalist movement, and the democratic movement were linked in the idea of an autonomous civil society, as 'in Solidarity, the national movement is less the exaltation of the nation than the will to separate the society from the state, to give citizens their freedom back' (Touraine et al. 1982, 84). Religion comes in as a component of the nationalist appeal, as 'the link between national action and democratic action so articulates the will to live in a free society, liberated from the almighty power of the Party–State, and a national consciousness defined in opposition to foreign domination. But it is also a link between the democratic will and a national affirmation which goes through religion and appeals to the grand values proper to Catholic Poland' (Touraine et al. 1982, 91).

After pressure from the Soviet Union, however, martial law was declared in 1981, and leaders were arrested. Under threats of Soviet invasion, softer leaders in the Politburo were replaced by General Wojcich Jaruzelski. Notwithstanding repression, there was still protest in the streets in 1982—in sixty-six cities in August, with two people killed, hundreds wounded, and thousands arrested (Osa 2003b).

While the workers took the lead of the protest cycle, new social movements were present as well, mobilizing especially on environmental issues. The first national environmental organization, the Polish Ecological Club, was founded in 1981, and several youth groups developed in the late 1980s. About 135 organizations, some with international contacts, existed in 1989 (Glinski 1996).

In addition, in September 1980 an independent student's union (Niezależne Zrzeszenie Studentów—NZS) was formed. Even though initially functioning under the auspices of Solidarity, with time the university students became increasingly radicalized, expressing sympathies for, for example, the Confederation of Independent Poland (Konfederacja Polski Niepodległej, KPN), asking for exit from the Warsaw Pact and the creation of a multi-party democracy, but also for new social movements of various types (Kenney 2002, 50). As Piotrowski (2012) summarizes,

> The shift towards more conservative positions of the dissidents (especially after the killing of Solidarność's chaplain, Jerzy Popiełuszko, in 1984), together with the support of Pope John Paul II, resulted in the emergence of many small youth-based groups that were critical of the communist authorities as well as of the pro-democratic dissidents. Because of their anti-systemic attitude, they were rejecting the communist authorities, but also claimed that the dissidents were too eager to compromise with the state. Another criticism was that the mainstream opposition had made a sharp turn to the right and had too close connections to the Catholic Church.

Among the more radical youth organizations was the Orange Alternative (Pomarańczowa Alternatywa), established in Wrocław (cf. Kenney 2002, Tyszka 1998), which made extensive use of street actions. These youth groups criticized Solidarity's moderation as well as its disregard for issues such as compulsory military service and environmental protection, particularly with regard to the building of nuclear power plants in Żarnowiec and Klempicz and of a dam in Czorsztyn.

Also important were the Peace Marches (the Easter marches in particular), as well as the protests against the war in Afghanistan and for the abolishment of compulsory military service. Pacifist groups and groups against compulsory drafting, such as Wolność i Pokój (Freedom and Peace, WiP) or Ruch Społeczeństwa Alternatywnego (Movement for an Alternative Society, RSA), mobilized especially young participants through hunger strikes, takeovers of trams, and short-term occupations of scaffoldings. Again in Piotrowski's (2012) words,

> Many of the groups were associated and connected to subcultures and counterculture and many of their leaders were musicians, theatre actors and movie directors. Lots of activists did not join any organized groups relying on small, locally based collectives and groups that picked up particular topics and campaigns....They also stressed the rejection of conservatisms: the Catholic one (represented more and more by the Solidarność movement) and the communist one. This opposition to the dissidents and the Church was seen at its best at cultural events: music concerts, street performances etc. Many artists and musicians began to support these grassroots groups (Piotrowski 2012; see also Kenney 2002, 82).

Additionally, the intellectual elites increasingly opposed the regime in more or less straightforward ways. As Piotrowski (2012) summarizes,

> Academics in humanities and social sciences, but also many lawyers, medical doctors, architects, artists participated in protest. Although quotations from Marx and Engels were quasi-obligatory in academic writings (and courses in Marxism–Leninism or materialist dialectics were compulsory for almost all students and soldiers), many intellectuals were supporting the dissidents. A whole industry of underground publishing—similar to soviet *samizdat*–developed, printing both works of Polish intellectuals and classics that were prohibited by the censors office (collected works of Karl Popper for instance were published in thousands of copies).

When this new opposition emerged in the 1970s and 1980s, it no longer aimed at a revolution but rather at a strategy of 'living in truth'. Refusing the regime's lies, 'the new strategy of the opposition relied on the assumption that the emergence of an archipelago or new islands of autonomy would be gradual and sufficiently limited so as not to push the communist authorities to a confrontation. It aimed at exploiting the possible interest of the authorities in tolerating the 'lesser evil' of an...enlarged sphere of social autonomy, thus avoiding a perhaps bloody full-scale confrontation with the emergent opposition and its likely domestically and internationally negative effects' (Smolar 2011, 133).

The conception of a civil society was—here as well—fluid and non-hierarchical. In the late 1970s the dissident Adam Michnick suggested the creation of an independent, self-governed organization. The KOR was established on this basis: stressing horizontality, it renamed itself the Committee for social self-organization (Garton Ash 2011). Mixing Catholic and secular political culture, it located citizens' rights within an ethical discourse, proclaiming the independence of the civil society and its self-organization. Following a similar organizational model, Solidarity was structured as a decentralized federation of local unions with a national coordinatory committee, which was seen as resonant with elements of utopian socialism. The self was defined here through negation: non-violent, non-utopian, non-party (Jorgensen 1992).

However, despite the contentious tradition of post-World War II Poland, this rich civil society did not produce an eventful democratization, but rather a participated pact. In this process, the different souls of Solidarity would clash with each other. Politicization, pushed by repression, fuelled internal conflicts, which developed in particular on internal democracy. In fact, 'mechanisms of differentiation crystallize first of all around the theme of democracy, opposing those who, in the name of democracy, aim at leaving free course to local and regional initiatives, imposing a control by the rank-and-file, and those who, in the name of the efficacy of the negotiation, want to keep a strong and centralized control' (Touraine et al. 1982, 211). In addition, tensions increased on some main axes of Solidarity's identity: 'workers' consciousness is the claiming of workers' rights, but also the populist defence of the small people against the big ones...; national consciousness is affirmation of a cultural identity but could also become aggressive nationalism; the very democratic will, almost always associated with the defence of freedom, may come to appeal to the people, the rank-and-file, against all leaders, and imposition of a semi-military discipline to save the threatened nation' (Touraine et al. 1982, 231). In fact, a wave of strikes in 1988 and 1989 would take Solidarity by surprise, scaring the leadership.

Moreover, as negotiation started, Solidarity was no longer the eight-million-member organization of 1980–1, but had seen its members drop to 1.5 million when re-legalized in 1989. Distancing itself from power, during the transition Solidarity worked in fact on the framework of an honourable compromise (Glenn 2003). Accepting participation in politics, it agreed on partially free elections, which then saw a large victory for Solidarity (ninety-nine out of a hundred seats in the senate and 161 of the competitive seats in the lower chamber). Solidarity leader Walesa then declared, 'Too much grain has ripened for me, and I can't store it all in my granary' (Glenn 2003, 125). After the election, Solidarity went for a broad coalition with former satellite parties, and a Communist as president of the parliament.

Negotiation developed then at the roundtable, as well as at an informal level. As it has been observed,

> The result, unforeseen by regime and opposition bargainers, was the outcome of the interaction between bargaining which determined the rules of competition

and the successful mobilization of voters by Solidarity, drawing on preexisting mobilizing structures in the Catholic Church and employing collective action frames justifying an 'honorable compromise'. In this manner, Solidarity transformed what was to have been their co-optation into Parliament into a competition for votes in which they could demonstrate their trustworthiness to the Polish public (Glenn 2003, 109).

B) APPROPRIATION OF OPPORTUNITIES

A strong civil society was therefore able to influence and appropriate emerging political opportunities, through a slow accumulation of resources, that made it resilient to further repression.

In the 1940s and 1950s, there had been in Poland several instances of brutal interrogations, death sentences for political prisoners, kidnappings of activists. The secret police was powerful and feared. With post-Stalinism, however, repression gradually softened in Poland as well. At the end of the 1980s, although demonstrations were still dispersed, the courts became more lenient towards participants. The Security Service (Służba Bezpieczeństwa; SB, the secret police) used less and less brutal actions (even if in 1984 two of its officers received prison sentences for kidnapping and killing a priest, Jerzy Popiełuszko, who was the chaplain of Solidarity). Furthermore, 'Over the years, the police (both the secret and the normal ones) went from beatings at the stations (during interrogations or as a preparation for interrogations) to infiltration and the use of collaborators. . . . In the 1980s, under international pressure, the authorities went from prison sentences for the activists to fines' (Piotrowski 2012).

The regime's oppression could, however, still be observed at different levels. There were beatings, arrests, and imprisonments for 'hostile propaganda' or 'conspiracy to overthrow the regime', house searches, and so on. Moreover, many activists lost their jobs, students were thrown out of universities and schools, and psychological harassment was used. In fact, many activists 'felt fines more painfully than jail. In 1987, when the average monthly wage varied between fifteen and twenty thousand, the typical fine for participating in demonstrations or distribution of underground publications amounted to fifty thousand zlotys' (Kenney 2002, 41). The secret police also collected data on the private lives of the activists, including information about sexual orientation or involvement in petty crimes. Visas were selectively given to those who agreed to give information about the Polish diaspora. Continued harassment notwithstanding, 'in 1980–81 the repressive capacities of the state as a result of social mobilization capacities were significantly reduced, partly influenced by the low morale of the party apparatus and government as well as the depletion of declining state resources and organizational effectiveness' (Osa 2003a, 237).

In fact, the implementation of martial law after the wave of protest did not achieve the expected results. Indiscriminate repression of the opposition rather backfired—as a member of the opposition in Poland declared: 'If martial law was a setback for independent society, it was a disaster for the totalitarian state' (in Goodwin 2001, 266). In addition, attempts by the regime to gain support—less and less on an ideological basis, and more and more pragmatically through clientelistic distribution of resources—failed, producing frustration and disaffection. This was all the more the case since the 1970s, when increasing economic stagnation and dependence on the West brought about experiments at liberalization and decentralization.

The 1980–1 protests have reflected a crisis with institutional and ideological dimensions: a crisis of political authority strengthened by the opening of a second economy and rampant corruption (Ekiert 1996). After the short legalization of Solidarity, and then the military operation and martial law in December 1981 (lifted two years later), power shifted from the party to the state, and from the civilian institutions to the military. Under Soviet pressure, the banned Solidarity was crushed by the military. Thousands of activists (about 7,000) were arrested, union buildings seized, and borders closed (Ekiert 1996, 257). Repression was, however, weaker in Poland in 1980 than it had been in the previous crises in the GDR, Hungary, Czechoslovakia. Fewer people were killed (thirty-seven) than in the other cases—although there were 10,000 internments of Solidarity activists, and more than 4,000 of them were arrested (Ekiert 1996, 23). In part thanks to strong international support, sentences rarely exceeded three years.

The wave of repression thus did not thwart social movements, as a (semi-underground) civil society survived. Fines for activists were paid by the Church or by committees for the victims of repression; other networks were active in the collection of union dues, the defence of victims, the organization of boycotts of official institutions, but also in demonstrations—for example, on labour day 1982 or the anniversary of the Gdansk agreements. There were frequent street protests in 1982 and 1983, together with the formation of an independent educational system and underground publishing and distribution networks. After the heavy crackdown on protest, there were amnesties in 1983, 1984, and 1986. Following a decline in 1984, in 1986 some liberalization, with de facto recognition of the opposition, opened spaces for action. Solidarity then resurfaced, while the party suffered a massive loss in members.

The crisis of 1980–1 left, then, a weak party state to deal with a strong civil society that had survived repression (Ekiert 1996). The mobilized society did not allow for the regime to recover its power, with ideals of self-organization, within a free public sphere with a plurality of movements but also relying upon the well-established organizational structure of Solidarity.

The economic challenges had brought openings for reforms within the party. From the economic point of view, Poland was a success story at least until the mid-1970s, thanks in part to international loans. Economic decline then became all the more frustrating, as 'growing familiarity with the West among the citizens of Central Europe (because more people were traveling or met with Western products or have been in contact with the Western media) resulted in the awakening of the need of the benefits of the Western markets' (Kenney 2002, 19). Economic reforms were initially limited to some liberalization of regulations on private entrepreneurship, notwithstanding pressure for reforms coming from the London Club, a consortium of over 500 privately owned banks that helped authorities to pay the debt in 1976.

In the 1980s, the economic crisis worsened, with rationing of food and goods and increases in food prices; rampant corruption became a widespread public concern. Great dissatisfaction emerged over the shortages of supplies on the internal market, while at the same time, the Soviet Union forced the selling of goods, such as coal, below its production costs. State owned farming cooperatives experienced mismanagement and lacked the flexibility needed to meet market requirements. As Piotrowski (2012) summarized,

> by the late 1980s many of the daily needs (such as sugar, meat but also alcohol and shoes) were rationed and hard to find in stores. People had to queue for almost everything; the supplies in stores were irregular and often chaotic (toilet paper—a highly demanded and scarce good—could be bought in bicycle shops or obtained only after bringing recyclable materials such as paper or bottles to special meeting points). More luxurious goods like furniture, TVs, household appliances etc. were available through complicated system of pre-payments, official queues, waiting lists and recommendations from workplaces. Waiting times for flats, cars or even telephone lines were measured in years.

In response to these economic problems, from 1980, negotiations for market reforms also took place within the Paris Club, composed of the ministers of finance from the nineteen wealthiest countries in the world; an initial agreement with the IMF was signed in 1986. According to Piotrowski (2011), 'the government, aware of the poor condition of the state and its weak position, decided to open up debates with the leaders of the opposition and began implementing changes that broadened individual freedoms. These included economic reforms (since 1987), allowed private entrepreneurship to boom, and the citizens to buy foreign currencies (before these transactions were limited and every attempt to buy foreign currency had to be justified, by for instance a trip to a conference abroad)'.

Economic decline increased the influence of reformers in the party. In fact,

> By late 1970s (which already signaled a crisis coming) many of the party elites were pragmatic apparatchiks that understood that party membership was a gate towards a

better career or business opportunities. These people were much more open towards discussions about Marxism-Leninism and communist dogmas. At the same time, a new class of intelligentsia was rising—educated people living in large cities that travelled around the world (it was much easier since the early 1970s). Many members of university faculties were supporting the opposition (Piotrowski 2012).

In the 1980s, together with martial law, a project of economic reforms developed. Given the dramatic economic crisis, negotiations with the opposition appeared a necessity. As no new loans from abroad were granted and no funds were available to repay the previous ones, Poland went bankrupt. Political liberalization (including amnesty for political crimes) was then perceived as necessary in order to gain international funds. In a top secret memo to the Political Bureau on September 1986, experts from the Ministry of Interior stated that an act of amnesty 'will allow us to develop broader international politics, which should bring an improvement in many areas and result in positive outcomes for the country' (Piotrowski 2012). In 1986, new laws opened spaces for private entrepreneurship, and in the following years more and more economic sectors were deregulated.

Attempts at co-optation addressed members of the Patriotic movement for national rebirth; a consultative council was established with fifty-six specialists on social and economic policies, seventy per cent of them without party membership cards. The wave of strikes (and wildcat strikes) in 1988 produced fear of drawing support away from Solidarity, prompting negotiations in which Jaruzelski played the neutral patriotic officer (Saxonberg 2012). This situation created favourable conditions for the negotiations, which developed after a new wave of strikes in 1988 with the proposal of a roundtable that was opened in February 1989. As mentioned, after the semi-free elections in June, the Parliament elected Jaruzelski as president of Poland in July.

Hungary

While certainly not strong as in Poland, a civil society did exist in Hungary as well, favoured by some liberalization and the relative international openness of the country. As in Poland, however, oppositional resources were built up during waves of protest, constructing networks and memories of resistance that could be activated during the negotiated path to democracy.

A) THE MOBILIZATION OF CIVIL SOCIETY

In contrast with Poland, 'At the end of 1988, the independent organizations of Hungary's civil society were neither large nor cohesive nor fundamentally committed to challenge the legitimacy of the Communist regime' (Stark and Bruszt 1998, 28). Reformers in the regime were also weaker than they were in Poland, and hardliners tried to incorporate the civil society (for example, by accepting a constitutional process but demanding that only socialist-oriented organizations be admitted, or asking for seventy-five per cent of those elected in parliament to be party members). At the roundtable, attempts at co-opting the opposition failed, however, and, here as well, a process of participated pacts brought about democracy.

Hungary's civil society was weaker than Poland's, although stronger than in Romania, Albania, or Bulgaria—probably comparable to the GDR and Czechoslovakia. Until a few months before transition started, while independent civil society organizations did exist, also thanks to a relatively liberal attitude by the regime, they were however weak and non-political (Stark and Bruszt 1998). In fact, even though a civil society eventually mobilized in the second half of the 1980s, it never reached the strength of the Polish one at the beginning of that decade (Saxonberg 2001, 211–12).

After some hopes of reforms from within the communist party, in 1956, the upheavals were followed by some concessions but also a brutal repression that left initially little space for the development of a strong civil society. Repression notwithstanding, Hungary soon became one of the most open of the Eastern European countries.

As in the other Eastern European cases, however, a civil society developed especially with the Helsinki accords, which allowed for the emergence of 'an identifiable opposition movement, as opposed to dissident individuals' (Stokes 1993, 88; Falk 2003, 128). At the end of the 1970s, attempts at mobilization remained organizationally weaker than in Poland. A main organization was Szeta, a self-help initiative, and there were informal groups of social scientists, journalists, social workers, and writers. A sign of increasing oppositional activities was, in 1979, a declaration signed by 250 people to protest the sentence against a Charter 77 activist in Prague (Fehr 1995).

Intellectual opposition also developed slowly. In 1976, the first samizdat was published, and in September 1978 the first lecture of the 'Flying University' took place; in 1981, the most important opposition journal, *Beszélö* (Speaker) was founded. In contrast to Poland, however, 'there were no systematic efforts on the part of Hungarian intellectuals to "reach out" to independent worker organizations, as no such organizations existed' (Falk 2003, 129). So, until 1987, opposition groups were limited to 'a few dozen individuals, maintaining contacts with a few hundred others among the intellectuals of research institutes, university departments, editorial offices and student circles' (Kontler 2002, 461).

Subsequently, however, the oppositional groups started to voice more overtly political demands (Bruszt and Stark 1991, 211). As Ritter (2012d) summarized,

> The composition of Hungary's opposition reflected the country's pre-communist political divisions between urbanists and populists. The urbanists, often referred

to as the 'democratic opposition' made up the faction most similar to opposition groups in East Germany and Czechoslovakia, emphasizing as they did human rights and democratic principles in the civic sphere. The populists, on the other hand, were more restrained in their outlook and preferred to focus on less politically charged issues, such as the situation of ethnic Hungarians in neighboring countries, crime, religious issues, and demographic problems.

They also developed nationalist visions (Kontler 2002, 462). It was this populist wing—including the Hungarian Democratic Forum (*Magyar Demokrata Fórum,* MDF or HDF)—that enjoyed 'official acquiescence' (Falk 2003, 139).

On 1 May 1988, the Network of Free Initiatives emerged as a representative of the urban opposition; on 13 November it transformed itself into the *Szabad Demokraták Szövetsége* (SZDSZ), that is, the Alliance for Free Democrats. Finally, the Young Democrats, known also by the acronym FIDESZ, came to represent a generational student rebellion (Tőkés 1996, 312). Moreover, at the end of 1988 'there were twenty-one new or recently founded political associations that identified themselves as "society," "league," "association," or "front" and the Independent Smallholders' Party (ISP)' (Tőkés 1996, 308). These groups all played a major role in the democratization process through their participation in the Opposition Round Table (ORT, or *Ellenzéki Kerekasztal,* EKA, in Hungarian).

As for new social movements, in Hungary as well the environmental movement was the most visible. Since 1984, environmental groups had emerged in the city but also in rural areas, protesting against air and water pollution, industrial and nuclear waste, forest destruction. During the decade, they often encountered each other, although no umbrella organization was founded. Green Future, in Budapest, was an example of a club that emerged to denounce environmental problems in a specific district and then evolved into a social movement organization, with some support from business as well (for example, public transport). According to Sajó, there was in fact 'no mass support for the opposition except in one respect. Ecologists managed to mobilize an increasing number of people against the Danube dam project, which was considered disastrous in ecological as well as in business terms' (1996, 70). In September 1988, 30,000 people demonstrated before Parliament against the construction of the dam in 'the first major public questioning of the legitimacy of the Parliament' (Bruszt and Stark 1991, 220); in October over 70,000 citizens signed a petition; in 1989, more than 100,000 petitioned for a referendum on the issue. In May of that year, the government declared the project suspended (Falk 2003, 143; Kis 1995, 43; Stokes 1993, 95). Future political activists joined the protest against the dam issue, which was also of interest for less politicized people (Stokes 1993, 94–5). According to Stokes (1993, 95) 'the contrast with Czechoslovakia, which tolerated little or no opposition to the dam, suggests how far Hungary had come by the end of 1988'. Not seen as a major threat by the regime, dozens of groups existed in 1989.

Autonomous peace movement organizations were also important in mobilizing especially young people, growing quickly in the early 1980s (Falk 2003, 143). Peace activists bridged their traditional issues with concerns for the respect of human rights. In the early 1980s, students created the Anti-Nuclear Campaign Hungary (ANC); founded in 1982, the Peace Group for Dialogue even tried to set up a peace camp modelled on Greenham Common (Falk 2003, 143; Lomax 1982). Against the advice of their church hierarchy, Catholic priests such as László Kovács and András Gromon delivered pacifist sermons and supported conscientious objection to the required eighteen months of military service (Falk 2003, 143). While the official church supported the regime, some Catholics 'found inspiration within their beliefs to oppose it' (Falk 2003). Human rights organizations also grew in the 1980s, with increasing production and distribution of samizdat, characterized by the use of human rights language and an emphasis on democratic renewal, individual autonomy, and free emancipated citizens. Legally minded behaviour was the basis for legal protection; with the advocacy of local democratic fora, activists emphasized a lack of orientation toward power, having no desire for it. Organizations such as the MDF mobilized in support of Hungarian minorities, especially in Romania (Stokes 1993, 95; Tőkés 1996, 309–10). In June 1988, 30,000 people demonstrated in Budapest for their rights in 'the largest demonstration in Hungary since 1956' (Stokes 1993, 95).

As in the GDR, the labour organizations did not play any relevant role in the revolution, although workers were present in the protest events in 1989. It was not until the mobilization that the Democratic League of Free Trade Unions was established as an umbrella organization for the independent unions that were now forming, campaigning to encourage workers to exit from the official National Council of Trade Unions (Falk 2003, 145; Hankiss 1990, 20). As Hankiss summed up, the unions, which had mobilized against the regime in 1948, remained in 1990 a last bastion of communism (1990, 25).

The students' role was also limited, even if some independent student organizations such as Polvax developed as discussion clubs for political issues (both international and domestic), including economic reform and human rights. Finally, on 30 March 1988, FIDESZ was founded by a few dozen students, mobilizing on issues such as political reform, the Danube Dam, and conscientious objection to military service (Falk 2003, 144–5).

The frames of the opposition remained moderate, even if undergoing a process of politicization. The aim declared in many Hungarian samizdat publications was strengthening social autonomy rather than taking power. Together with the self-determination of society, there was a search for consensus, within anti-state and anti-authority frames, and a denunciation of repression on the part of the regime. The opponents defined themselves as torchbearers, who wanted to 'tell the truth. The louder, the better' (Bozoki 2010, 9). The organizational spaces of civil society were defined as the world of informal relations (Bozoki 2010, 19), although there was debate about how political the civil society was. The civil society was presented as an antidote to the state. Criticisms of the regime focused on its superpower ambitions, the opposition to military service and to censorship at universities, and support for peace and environmentalism. There was also attention to art (punks and new wave), as well as avant-garde groups with alternative lifestyles (yoga and so on). These dissident circles thus formed a critical public sphere (Bozoki 2010), referring to the works by Adam Michnik and Vaclav Havel, which were translated in a number of samizdat publications.

So, at the end of 1988, that 'the category of "opposition" could be used as a collective noun to refer to such a set of weak, diverse and fragmented organizations would scarcely have occurred to anyone active on the Hungarian political scene' (Bruszt and Stark 1991, 218). While usually described as weak, the Hungarian social movements did enjoy however more free space than in neighbouring countries—so that in the 1980s, about one per cent of the population was involved in independent political organizations (Bruszt 1989, 369).

Here as well, civil society then grew in action, through the networking of these scattered organizations. If the mentioned environmentalist demonstrations against the dam on the Danube 'illustrated the potential gains of more active mobilizations, the hard-liners' threats provoked recognition of the potential costs of failing to do so. That is, it was the hard-liners' confrontational policies that determined the urgency and the timing of the opposition's shift to popular mobilization' (Stark and Bruszt 1998, 29).[5] In 1988, the Hungarian Democratic Forum and the Alliance of Free Democrats were formed, with 10,000 and 1,500 members respectively. Radical reformers, they did not exclude cooperation with communists in a 'positive opposition'.

These developments in the civil society were not devoid of influence on the events in 1989. As Laszlo Bruszt (1989) observed, in Hungary the transformations occurred without strikes (with the exception of a so-called sausage strike against meat price increases), and without any mass nationwide demonstrations. Nevertheless, when the regime tried to weaken the opposition through separate dialogues with various groups, there was an increase in coordination within the civil society organizations. The EKA was established in March 1989 at the initiative of the *Független Jogász Forum* (FJF, Independent Lawyers' Forum), founded in November 1988 with the aim of introducing

---

[5] After the transition, however, they would lose their oppositional character, and thus part of their appeal (Pickvance and Gabor 2001).

'legislative changes in the democratic tradition' (Sajó 1996, 71). Civil society organizations then 'called for bilateral negotiations between the power structure and representatives of the opposition, rejected all legislative proposals that would remove from the hands of a future, freely elected parliament the opportunity to formulate a state and a social system, and declared a willingness to enter into negotiations only in regard to laws directly related to the holding of free elections' (Bruszt 1989, 375). The attempt by the party to limit negotiation was thus defeated as civil society organizations built an opposition roundtable, calling for bilateral negotiations and a freely elected parliament. Eventually, the roundtable, which began in June 1989, included 500 experts from nine oppositional organizations, the party, and six linked organizations; many informal negotiations also took place.

In 1989, some protest accompanied the negotiations, at crucial moments pushing for more inclusive participation and more radical change. On 15 March 1989, the official commemoration of 1948 was challenged by a demonstration organized by the opposition which, with its 100,000 participants, overshadowed the official event. This demonstration was in fact defined as a 'performative action that made possible a mutual self-recognition of an oppositional identity transcending the boundaries of the various participating organizations' (Stark and Bruszt 1998, 31). On 23 March, under the auspices of the Federation of Independent Lawyers, the Opposition Round Table (EKA) was established in the law faculty by the representatives of eight organizations, who committed themselves 'to resolving differences in a framework of equality'. Rejecting the regime's proposal of power sharing, they asked for power legitimacy through elections, while citizens continued to demonstrate for democratic change.

Reform circles inside the party also grew at this contentious time, in open criticism of the hardliners, and the government separated itself from the party. New polarization emerged on 1 May, as the League of Independent Unions staged a demonstration which was (with 60,000 to 100,000 participants) between six and ten times bigger than the official one. The next planned demonstration was on 16 June, on the anniversary of the regime's 1956 execution of former Prime Minister Imre Nagy. On that occasion, 250,000 protestors filled the square, while the prime minister, the minister of interior, and the president of the parliament took part in the ceremony. According to some interpretations, it was eventually the very weakness of challengers that forced them to refuse a compromise, as there was no representative of the civil society as there had been with Solidarity in Poland (Stark and Bruszt 1998, 38).

Reformers then became hegemonic in the party, although (in contrast to Poland) there were still doubts about a possible compromise with the opposition. For the elites, competition seemed appealing, as opinion polls gave them thirty-six per cent, the highest percentage, while the opposition was neither well-known nor much trusted (Stark and Bruszt 1998, 39). Thus, 'The Hungarian Round Table negotiations that opened on June 13, 1989 were ambiguously-framed: Civic principles dominated, but they co-existed with elements of late paternalism, reflecting the persistent but by now minor role of the hard-liners on the political stage' (Stark and Bruszt 1998, 41). Eventually, no agreement was reached at the roundtable; there was instead a referendum, which the communists lost, and with it the opportunity to go to elections before the opposition could strengthen. In the first free election in 1990, the Hungarian Socialist Party won only thirty-three out of 386 seats, while the Hungarian Democratic Forum got 164 seats and the Alliance of Free Democrats ninety-two. A weak civil society thus won its partial victory through a mobilization in action.

B) APPROPRIATION OF OPPORTUNITIES

In this evolution, political opportunities opened up, at various moments. Socialist Hungary had a relatively liberal history, especially after the end of Stalinist totalitarianism. In 1956, after Stalin's death, the collapse of the forced industrialization scheme and the ensuing economic decline increased internal struggles between Stalinist and anti-Stalinist elites (Ekiert 1996, 37). In that year, the old Stalinist regime 'experienced almost complete institutional breakdown and was de facto overthrown by the revolutionary popular movement from below', and divisions within the communist parties facilitated mass mobilization (Ekiert 1996). Apparently, only the Soviet invasion prevented a fundamental political transformation from taking place.

Repression of the 1956 upheaval was extremely brutal, with 4,000 people killed and 20,000 wounded by Soviet troops, of which 669 were killed. Later on, 35,000 people were arrested and 22,000 sentenced; about 300 people were sentenced to death, including the Hungarian leader. The reformist Imre Nagy, who had briefly assumed leadership of communist Hungary for the few days between the old regime's collapse and the Soviet invasion, was in fact executed in the revolution's aftermath.

Memories of these events certainly played a role in 1989, by discouraging radical moves on both sides:

Although suppressed publicly, memories of the lost revolution of 1956 were never forgotten across the decades, and signs of crisis were the surest stimulus for recalling this haunting past. For the Communist elite, the ghosts of 1956 were the memories of the fury that can be unleashed when society has been pushed beyond its limits. It was above all the fear of society that simply imbued the Communist leadership with the instinct to do everything to avoid another 1956. As the economic and political crisis deepened throughout 1988, the references to

> 1956 in party leaders' speeches increased.... It was the fear of society—the fear of the transformation of the economic crisis into social and political crisis similar to that of 1956—that pushed the leaders of the regime to seek a compromise with the organized forces of society; it was the lesson of the Russian intervention in 1956 that made the leaders of the newly emerging social and political groups hesitant to question the legitimacy of the regime and to seek instead a compromise with its leaders (Stark and Bruszt 1998, 23).

In terms of degree of repression, patterns of cleavages within the party and the elites, the density of networks in the opposition popular mobilization, and the duration of the rebellion—as well as international constraints—the crisis in Hungary had different effects from those in the GDR or Czechoslovakia (Ekiert 1996). Here, in fact, upheaval and ensuing repression produced a strong party–state that used repression but also concessions.

After the intense repression of the upheavals, in 1957 Moscow installed János Kádár as Hungary's new leader, destined to remain in government until 1990. Coming to power as Nikita Khrushchev was consolidating a more liberal form of communism in the Soviet Union following Stalin's death, Kádár was not reform-minded, but he was no Stalinist either. No major purges thus took place within the post-revolutionary communist party, which thereby became 'the only East European [communist party] which after 1956 and 1968 not only abstained from liquidating the reformist wing but integrated it' (Kende 1982, 7). As an outcome of the rebellions and post-Stalinism was the expulsion of both Stalinists and reformers from the party, Kádár could then rebuild the socialist state, leaving some autonomous space (Ekiert 1996, 101–4). Loyal to Khrushchev and following his reformist vision, Kádár was said to have made Hungary the most liberal of the Central East European countries—as he 'never forgot his indebtedness to Khrushchev and found his de-Stalinization policies admirable. To prove his loyalty, Kadar never made any major decisions without Khrushchev's approval. Thus, the sixty-three-year-old Khrushchev and forty-five-year-old Kadar gradually grew fond of each other. As a consequence of this personal and working relations, Hungary received favourable economic considerations from the Soviet Union, while Kadar was granted more freedom to manage the country's domestic affairs' (Felkay 1989, 113). As Bruszt (1989, 383) observed, 'among all state-socialist systems it was Kadar's system that removed itself most from the basic model established in Stalin's time', and, as Stokes confirmed (1993, 79), 'of all the Communist parties in Eastern Europe, the Hungarian was the most reform minded'.

Reforms were especially visible at the economic level as, already in the 1960s, cooperatives experimented with auxiliary business schemes, and a 'second economy' developed (Stokes 1993, 81–3; Hankiss 1990, 15). The New Economic Mechanism (NEM), enacted in 1968, provided industrial firms some autonomy in their search for profit maximization, decentralized economic planning on the local level, and enacted price and wage reforms (Falk 2003, 113–14). The results were encouraging, and in the late 1960s and early 1970s, 'Hungarian grain yields exceeded the average in the EEC countries, per capita meat, fruit and vegetable production came second only to the most advanced economies of the world, and in terms of the general standards of agriculture Hungary was esteemed to rank closely behind the eight most developed countries of Western Europe' (Kontler 2002, 440).

This initial success notwithstanding, the oil crisis of the mid-1970s imposed loans on the international market, with a related increase in the country's debt from $1 billion in 1970 to $9.1 billion in 1979. In 1982, as Hungary joined the IMF, the party continued its economic liberalization processes. As Ritter (2012d) summarized, 'Shops could be leased from the state, and by 1986 ten percent of the country's restaurants were privately owned and turning a combined profit equal to that of the remaining (state owned) 90%'. This did not solve the economic problems, however, and by the mid-1980s, 'the second economy was so extensive in Hungary that virtually the entire citizenry engaged with it in the routines of daily life' (Falk 2003, 117). At the party congress in 1985, the party secretary admitted to a decline in the standard of living, while party leaders blamed the government for inflation and inadequate housing (Stokes 1993, 87). By 1988, the economy appeared bankrupt (Bruszt and Stark 1991, 214). These difficulties were resented by the Hungarian population, as testified by high rates of suicide and consumption of alcohol (Kontler 2002, 458).

The economic crisis (with growing indebtedness to Western creditors) strengthened the reformists' call for negotiation with the opposition and, as new parties emerged, young reformers in the communist party pushed for Kádár's removal (Saxonberg 2012). Differently from their colleagues in the GDR and Czechoslovakia, Hungarian reform communists saw a controlled transition as necessary for addressing economic problems. Technocrats had in fact found their way inside the party since 1986–7. As Bruszt (1989, 381) observed, reformists were helped significantly by changes in the Soviet leadership:

> In Hungary, just as in other East European countries, the dramatic change in the external environment enabled factors within the country to play a decisive role in formulating the system. For the first time since 1948 an opportunity presented itself to openly suggest a change in the model, and for the first time it became possible to make a fundamental change in the power structure. While previous Soviet leadership groups almost instantly sanctioned any deviation from the basic model by way of direct and indirect pressure and interference, the new leadership under Gorbachev let it be known to Hungarian leaders that its primary objective was not to upset social peace in Hungary, and that it regarded social stability as more important than adherence to the Soviet model.

219

With the opening—and pressures for opening—by Gorbachev, Kádár 'could no longer claim the Soviet Union was preventing him from going further with reforms. Since the Hungarian Communists had based their pragmatic acceptance on testing the borders of what the Kremlin would allow, the younger Communists were willing to go even further and to democratize society' (Saxonberg 2001, 284). The reformists thus prevailed, to the point that, as Stokes (1993, 91) noted, 'by 1987, the question was not so much reform versus recentralization, but rather what sort of reform to implement and how fast it should proceed'.

Additionally, Western loans brought about pressures to meet the human rights criteria set by the Western powers (Bruszt and Stark 1991, 211), as well as further reforming its economy. In fact, after the indebtedness repayable in dollars had doubled in 1987 and 1988 and Hungary risked insolvency,

> Western creditors gave increasingly direct indications that they would be willing to continue financing the Hungarian economy only in exchange for significant changes in the economy. In other words, as Gorbachev stabilized his position, a situation evolved in which Hungary was subject to simultaneous pressure from both the East and the West. Pressure from the East aimed for political changes to prevent societal crisis, while the forceful 'pull' from the West called for a radical transformation of the economy, also implying changes in the political structure (Bruszt 1989, 382).

Thus, the rapid economic decline contributed to agreement among the elites that, if not democratization, at least radical market reforms were needed (Saxonberg 2001, 284). However, belief in the need for democracy was growing as well. Already at the party congress in March 1980, the head of the trade unions' national council, Sándor Gáspár, had argued that Hungary could 'best strengthen the country's economic power... if we rely on democracy, on the clash of opinions and interests, and on the increased participation of the working population' (Stokes 1993, 84). In the second half of the 1980s, reformers in the elites converged on the belief that economic progress was linked to democracy: 'In short, it seems clear that the aim of the reforms was not democracy per se, but rather an avenue towards economic recovery. Democracy was simply seen as a way to accomplish this more important goal' (Ritter 2012d).

Political liberalization thus accompanied economic reforms. In 1985, for the first time, citizens had the ability to choose the candidates they wanted to elect in a party list, with the effect that all incumbents were removed. In 1986, economists produced a document for reform, which spurred debate in the party. A party-commissioned official report addressed 'the squandering of labor, energy, raw materials, and capital; the inability to adjust to world trends; and wasteful investment allocation. It went on to make a startling proposal to fix them: introduce the profit motive through marketizing reforms.... For this to happen, the report concluded, political change was needed. No party should be above the law, individual rights should be protected, and an independent judiciary should be introduced' (Stokes 1993, 91).

In 1988, the struggle internal to the party resulted in the removal of party leader Kádár and his replacement by centrist Károly Grósz, with reformers entering the new Politburo (Saxonberg 2001, 285). As Grósz took over from Kádár in 1988, he stressed the need for an acceleration in liberalization reforms, as Hungary would otherwise have risked losing millions of dollars and Deutschemarks in foreign aid, in a period in which its hard currency foreign debt had doubled in just two years (Bruszt and Stark 1991, 211). In November of the same year, the Central Committee adopted a less ambiguous position for political pluralism, including the lifting of censorship and abolition of most party privileges. Grósz then relinquished the premiership to Németh and, in July, Pozsgay submitted a 'democracy package' to parliament (Swain 2006, 146). Reform Circles developed, as groups of party members from the local branches pushed for controlled change from below. The first meeting of the National Council of Reform Circles took place in May 1989 (Bruszt and Stark 1991, 225; Swain 1992, 20–21).

Besides the fear of retaliation, party elites also started to hope for economic gains from reforms: 'In the late 1980s a substantial part of the Hungarian party and state bureaucracy discovered a way of converting their bureaucratic power into lucrative economic positions and assets (and indirectly also into a new type of political power) in the new system based on market economics and political democracy' (Hankiss 1990, 30). So, as Ritter (2012d) summarized, 'Without strong incentives to defend the Party, and thanks to a long history of gradual reforms, the HSWP collapsed in the fall of 1989. On September 7th, the Party ceased to exist, and transformed itself into the Hungarian Socialist Party (HSP). However, at its congress a month later it became obvious that little enthusiasm existed for the successor organization. For example, most party members serving in congress failed to join the HSP'.

Democratizations from Above? The MENA Region

If participated pacts characterized some Central European cases, no similar path emerged during the Arab Spring, when in some countries, such as Morocco or Yemen, protests brought about some liberalization, but no democracy. Even in these cases of liberalization conceded from above, social movements affected, however, elites' decision making. This is also the case with the long lasting and troubled process of democratization in another main country in the geopolitical area: Turkey.

The Spreading of the Arab Spring

After the emergence, and success, of protests in Tunisia and Egypt, learning and imitation brought about similar mobilizations in other countries, although with different evolutions. In some of these cases (but not in Libya and Syria, which will be addressed in the next chapter), peaceful protests obtained some liberalization, but fell short of achieving regime transition. This was the case, in particular, of Morocco and Yemen.

From Tunisia and Egypt, protest quickly spread to Morocco, where on 20 February 2011, large demonstrations against absolutism and for political freedom and human rights remained peaceful. Tunisian and Egyptian rebellions prompted a process of attribution of similarities by the protestors, to which the elites responded by stressing instead the Moroccan exceptionalism. After some solidarity demonstrations in January and early February, with almost daily frequency in Rabat, a call for demonstration on Facebook produced protests in at least fifty-three localities in Morocco on 20 February 2011. This was the start of the so-called 20 February Movement, bringing together very heterogeneous actors (Bennani-Chaibri and Jeghllaly 2012, 872), from the Islamists of al Adl to the youth groups of the left-wing parties.

Here as well, the traditions of street demonstrations were rejuvenated in the 1990s with marches in solidarity with Palestinians and Iraqis as well as sit-ins against repression during the years of inflation and declining social services (Vairel 2011, 31). In addition, human rights organizations had emerged from the actions of relatives of political prisoners in late 1970s, with ties to the diaspora. In 1999, the new King Mohamed VI agreed to discuss compensations for victims of repression and, in 2003, an Equity and Reconciliation Commission was appointed, although with no steps towards punishing the perpetrators. Many NGOs, some of them independent like the Association Democratique des Femmes du Maroc, emerged from this liberalization turn.

Although referring to a similar, middle-class basis, left-wing groups and Islamist ones such as al Adl had a long history of confrontations on issues of *laicité* and religion. Cooperation between Islamist and left-wing actors had however grown over time, with common campaigns against unemployed in 1991 and on social and political issues also later on. During the mobilizations of the global justice movement, ATTAC-CADTM worked as a point of aggregation, and coordinating groups like the Espace Casablanca were formed in the late 2000s to offer a common space to the fragmented Left.

The protests in 2011 were initially called for by activists from the Espace du Dialogue de la Gauche, but also from campaigns against the increases in costs of living, the alter-mondialist ATTAC, as well as student activists. Also Islamist groups participated in the mobilization. The term *camarakh*, bridging the term camarade used in the Left and the one of brother used by the Islamists testified to attempts to bridge the religious versus secular cleavage (Smaoui and Wazif 2013, 65). While the regime was accused of corruption, the dissidents stressed their Moroccan identity, against accusations of supporting the independentist Polisario Front. Following the Tunisian and Egyptian examples, camps were organized in squares, and assemblies formed as decisional bodies, while political parties remained marginal. Formerly apolitical youth participated with groups of friends, relatives, neighbours (Vairel 2011, 882).[6]

After initial attempts at criminalizing them, the king promised reforms, which did not stop the protests.[7] The regime reacted to the first protests with some openings, such as the intensification of the negotiations with unemployed and trade unions, as well as increases in public expenditures. Stressing Moroccan specificity, the monarch addressed the nation on 9 March, promising reforms. Various committees had indeed been created or made more inclusive during the protests: an Economic and Social Council, a consultative committee for the revision of the constitution, and a National Council of Human Rights were founded, the latter under the presidency of a former political prisoner from the Left. At the same time, the media discourse moved from stigmatizing the protestors to praising them as heroes of the nation.

National marches were then organized on 20 March and 24 April, by hundreds of groups and mobilizing hundreds of thousands, in a cross-class coalition that included not only secular and religious groups, movement organizations and parties, but also artists, businesspeople, street vendors, and shantytown inhabitants. The protests remained peaceful, with no coercive intervention by the police (and political prisoners were released). On 22 May, marches were however strongly repressed and NGOs that receive state funds were menaced (Smaoui and Wazif 2013). On 29 May, further mobilization followed the killing of a demonstrator by the police, with denunciations of the formally constitutional monarchy, heavily controlled secret services, and repression of protesters (Hoffmann 2011). While 'Adlist' and leftist activists cooperated, the royal discourse of 17 June was followed by the development of internal cleavages in the movement, with disengagements of moderate

---

[6] Protests emerged also in Bahrain, where they were however heavily repressed (Louer 2013), and in Jordan, where fights with loyalists and some social concession discouraged further mobilization (Ronsin 2013). In both countries, internal divisions—with Shiites in Bahrain and Palestinians in Jordan—jeopardized the development of a coalition for democratization.

[7] Reforms—or at least promises of reforms—were common in the eight monarchies in the area, with the exception of Bahrain, where the Sunni minority in power feared the rebellion of the Shi'a majority. Here as well, little international reaction followed the police killing of four protestors as they slept at the protest camp in Pearl Square (Gelvin 2011).

forces as well as middle class participants and, then, of the Islamists towards the end of 2011.

The protests brought about some liberalization in a regime that wanted to present itself as increasingly inclusive. In Morocco, in fact, the monarchy had co-opted some of the opposition, although repressing the radical left-wing movements that had developed in the post-colonial period with urban revolts (as in 1967). In 1997, after a period of political violence and repression, there was partial inclusion of Islamist parties in parliament, as well as some freedom of the press. Taking Morocco under Hassan II and Mohammed VI as an example, Cavatorta had singled out a strategy of co-optation and division of opponents as 'certain sectors of society are awarded privileges in exchange for support or at least tacit assent to authoritarian rule'. In fact, this strategy is facilitated by the presence of multiple (linguistic, ethnic, religious and class) cleavages. Fearing the dominance of an Islamist civic society, left-wing as well as ethnic and religious minorities have indeed trusted the rulers as authoritarian but yet more liberal than their main antagonists (Cavatorta 2007, 193). Many civil society organizations were therefore forced either to remain apolitical, or to reproduce the stereotype of Islamism as incompatible with democracy (Cavatorta 2007, 198). Also, according to Lust-Okar, the division of the opposition between a legal and an illegal one creates a special dynamics: 'As a result of these very different linkages with incumbent elites and the masses, opposition elites have divergent preferences concerning mobilization. Legal opponents want to mobilize in order to gain their demands, but they do not want their mobilization to become out of control.... In contrast, excluded opposition elites prefer to use more radical methods of challenging the status quo' (2005, 89). So in Morocco, the legal opposition feared radical demands by outsiders, and this radicalized, and at times strengthened, the outsiders; this was even more the case as, in 1993, the king even invited the opposition to join the government and cooperated with moderate unions.

This had an effect on oppositional groups, which are in fact expected to be more likely to develop coalitions when incumbents do not attempt to create divisions by co-opting loyalists and repressing radicals. More specifically,

> In divided environments loyalists who previously mobilized popular movements may become unwilling to challenge incumbents when crises continue, even if their demands have not been met. Because loyalists have organizational structures and lower costs of mobilizing an independent protest, they are often able to exploit the early stages of crises to demand reforms. However, as crises continue, radicals gain strength and become more likely to join in demonstrations, even if they are unwilling to mobilize independently. Thus, to avoid the possibility that radicals exploit unrest to demand radical reforms, moderates choose not to mobilize. The very same elites who previously exploited economic discontent to

demand political change now remain silent, while radicals who might take to the streets if the moderates mobilized are unwilling to do so alone. Thus, in a divided environment moderates who previously challenged incumbent elites may choose not to continue to do so when radical groups join, even if incumbents have not accommodated their demands (Lust-Okar 2004, 161).

In this way, the protests in Morocco against neo-liberal reforms in the late 1980s and early 1990s were discouraged by an alliance between the king and 'certified' opponents, while, in contrast, Islamic and left-wing oppositions, both repressed, converged in common campaigns in Jordan (Lust-Okar 2004). In line with this long-lasting strategy, the monarchy then responded to the protests with some repression but also some negotiation on reforms as well as economic concessions, supported and praised by Western powers.

Protest also spread in fragile Yemen, the poorest Arab country, where about 100 protest events were counted since the beginning of 2011 (Heibach 2011), resulting in the negotiated departure of the dictator. Here, a liberalized regime had taken an authoritarian turn in recent years, while facing clandestine Islamist political violence as well as the ethnic armed rebellion of the Zaydists in the Sa'da region. Clientelism and patronage were used to fuel the traditional resentment between Palestinian Jordanians and Trans-Jordanians.

In the wake of the rebellions in Tunisia and Egypt, on 3 February 2011, Yemen's oppositional groups coordinated through the Common Forum called for a demonstration in support of reforms. It also included young people and students who criticized the reformist attitudes of the parties, calling for regime change through the peaceful revolution of youth. The founding fathers of Yemen were referred to as symbols of a civic state, with legal rights and social justice, against a tribal state, with armed tribes. On 11 February, the day Mubarak stepped down, oppositional party members and youth gathered outside Sana'a University, also supported by some tribes. Modelled on Tahrir Square, a camp was organized at Sana'a's Place of Change beginning on 19 February, with convergence of heterogeneous groups: students, unemployed, human rights activists, tribal people, women, and children, with a variety of political ideas and ideological affiliations (Bonnefoy and Poirer 2012, 902). The driving force was here as well the 'revolutionary youth' (there was fifty per cent unemployment for people between 18 and 28). They managed the camp, which was run by an organizational committee, one on security, one on the media, one on health issues. Conceived as 'a microcosmos of change, where a new conception of "making the society", the one of the civil (or civic) state...develops' (Poirer 2013, 47), the camp was also rich in cultural activities, from concerts with traditional music, but also rap and rock, to theatres, painting ateliers, poetry reading. Activities on the square also included *qat* parties, where socialization and conversation centred on the use of a traditional drug. Solidarity developed in this intense space, with calls for participatory democracy, justice and freedom in opposition to the military and hierarchical power (Poirier 2013).

Within a move towards de-sectorialization, the occupied space allowed for 'encounters and unprecedented cooperation among actors traditionally considered as rivals. It is the case of the militants and the cyber-activists of the civil society and of the tribal men (*quabili*), originally from the Northern high plains and central regions, who came to Sana'a, and were previously stigmatized by the formers as hostile to modernization' (Bonnefoy and Poirier 2012, 904). The reconstruction of collective identities went through the development of inclusive discourses, also on the part of radical actors, such as the young activists of the *zahidi* groups. The self-management of the camp also supported the development of internal solidarity, while the alternative media developed a pedagogical function. The intense emotions of the extraordinary moment were accompanied by the development of everyday habits, such as the 'tea of freedom', or the prayers.

When the mobilization peaked in March and April, hundreds of thousands met on the square, with activities continuing in the following months and even after the negotiated departure of the dictator, Ali Abdallah Saleh, in February 2012. During these months, especially since May 2011, however, the official opposition, in part already incorporated in the regime, gained space, presenting themselves as negotiators. This was particularly true of the Islamic networks, linked to traditional tribal structures and coordinated by al Islah, which in fact gained increasing power and visibility in the camps, as with the MB. A re-sectarianization ensued (Poirier 2013). This was visible particularly in the increasing gender segregation of the spaces in the square. The oppositional parties then negotiated an agreement with the counsel of cooperation of the Gulf for the departure of Saleh, after thirty-three years in power. After the dictator left, the political parties, the Islamic authorities, and the army took over. With Yemen considered as a loyal ally in the war on terrorism, there was no Western support for protestors (Gelvin 2011).

Similarly, protest developed in Jordan (Bouziane and Lenner 2011), as well as in Algeria (Belakhdar 2011). In the latter, in January 2011, mobilizations of young demonstrators against price increases escalated into violent clashes with police but also evolved into protest activities (mobilizing about 3,000 protestors) of a coordinatory committee for democracy, including independent unions, human rights organizations, an association of the unemployed, and a young people's association. Consequences of the failure in 1992 of one of the first experiences of democratization in the region, followed by the state of exception and the trauma of the civil war, was a generalized mistrust in the political class, but also a tendency to self-censorship (Bamaare 2013). There had nevertheless been many demonstrations at the local level since

2001, which multiplied in 2011, with some success in obtaining economic and political concessions. While protest subsided, after a show of force by the regime that also confirmed the loyalty of the military, the 2011 mobilization did trigger new organizational dynamics within the oppositional groups, which had been internally divided.

In all these cases, elites seem to have learned from their peers' failure in Tunisia and Egypt. In different equilibria, they therefore combined the carrot and the stick, granting (or at least promising) some political and economic reforms (especially, clientelistically distributing money), while at the same time hitting the opposition hard. Although social movements in these countries remained ineffective in reaching their stated goals, they did make a step in that direction. Even if they did not sit at any roundtable, they were not negligible actors either.

Turkey

The long and troubled history of democratization in Turkey comprises the different forms of social movements' intervention, even in democratization processes that are driven from above. Democratic transitions and authoritarian relapses in fact followed 'a strong centralist state and an elite tradition', which is 'dominated heavily by a bureaucratic structure and culture' (Sunar and Sayari 1986, 166). Especially in the first transition, after World War II, regime changes came mainly from within the regime itself, in particular from the military-bureaucratic elites in Turkey, with some influence at times from Western allies. However, mobilizations from below played a role in imposing pressures for democratic reforms.

Since the 1920s, statism and authoritarianism had jeopardized labour protests, on the one hand providing some protection for state workers and on the other prohibiting any class-based organized activity. When economic conditions deteriorated in the 1930s, while private enterprises increased their market share, the National Defense Law (in 1940) augmented working hours to eleven per day, enforced obligatory work, and introduced a ban on leaving the workplace (Güzel 1993, 166–73).

The emergence of civil society had long been thwarted by very restrictive laws. The law No. 3512 in 1938 prohibited the formation of organizations based on locality, family, religion, and class, while existing trade unions had already been outlawed under the Law on the Maintenance of Order in 1925, which was meant to repress Islamist and Kurdish rebellions. Some journals, such as *Vatan* (Homeland) and *Tan* (Dawn), were, before 1946, the only vehicles for the expression of some oppositional views.

Some liberalization after the 1938 law on associations had brought about the emergence of several student organizations, with an important influence of ultra-nationalist groups such as the Turkish Culture House (*Türk Kültür Ocağı*), Turkish Association of Culture Studies (*Türk Kültür Çalışmaları Derneği*), and Turkish Youth Organization (*Türk Gençlik Teşkilatı*), which also physically attacked weaker left-wing adversaries, eventually forced into semi-clandestinity.

Since the foundation of the republic, some protests had targeted the de-Islamization of public life in the name of a secular state, as was prominently the case with the Sheikh Said rebellion in 1925, which merged Islamic and Kurdish resentment. Mobilization—sometimes violent—addressed the wearing of hats and the outlawing of the veil (B. Toprak 1981, 69). Even during the liberalization period, there were still 'criminal charges and heavy sanctions against actions aiming at the restructuring of the state according to the Islamic principles' (Duman 1999, 33). Opposition was mainly expressed in printed media such as *Sebilürreşad* or *Büyük Doğu* (Great Orient). In sum, 'Islamic opposition both under single party rule and during transition was limited, and did not directly challenge the very idea of autocratic rule but its secularist agenda. Their relationship with democracy took the form of positioning themselves vis à vis competing political actors once the multiparty game has been introduced. Yet, this positioning at times pronounced an outcry for Shari'a rather than a deliberate request for democracy' (Atak 2012).

Liberalization started, slowly, in 1946, and in May 1950 the first free and fair elections resulted in the first transfer of governmental power to the parliament. However, civil power was often interrupted by military interventions, even if they 'have not been directed against democracy itself..., but rather the resumption of democratic politics is nearly always explicitly contemplated by the military and, what is more, does eventually take place' (Giner 1986, 38). These coups d'états were in general oriented to defend Kemalist principles such as a unitary state, secularism, and a free market. This happened during the breakdown of the multi-party regime on 27 May 1960, followed by a new constitutional draft and the reinstallment of electoral democracy in October 1961. Similarly, the coup d'état of 12 September 1980 was followed by a return to multi-party democracy three years later. Additionally, 'in 1971 and 1997, the military involvement undermined democracy's survival without dissolving its main representative institutions' (Atak 2012).

If the military supported Kemalism, it also intervened however when some economic interests were at stake. After World War II, although Turkey had avoided the war, economic conditions were very poor. They were addressed through compulsory work for peasants around mining areas as well as heavy taxes on the income of the affluent classes—especially for non-Muslim minorities such as Greeks, Armenians, and Jews (Akar 2009; Okutan 2009). A broad use of martial law and heavy repression discouraged protests (VanderLippe 2005). Although a military–bureaucratic identity dominated among political elites (Karpat 1964, 51), an orientation of foreign relations towards the West pushed them to a commitment to 'determinedly progressing on the way to modern democracy' (Karpat 1964, 51). As some members of the dominant party, the Republican People's Party (RPP), also advocated freedom and human rights, they were expelled from RPP and founded the Democratic Party (hereafter DP), while the Republicans split between the hardliners and the (dominating) moderates. More than twenty parties were established between 1945 and 1950, including a Turkish Socialist Workers Party and an Islamic Protection Party. A new Association Law also allowed labour unions to emerge, although they were forbidden from calling strikes.

Still, liberalization was selective and inconsistently implemented. Challenged by increasing dissatisfaction, the regime prohibited even the publication of the weekly *Sendika* (Syndicate), which was closed in December 1946. In the same year, some liberalization (including the right to form unions) was brought about by the so-called 'Syndicalism of 1946' (Öztürk 1996; Z. Toprak 1996; Çelik 2010). Ensuing union activism, however, brought about a new ban on unions and socialist parties in the very same year (Çelik 2010, 107). While the RPP established its own labour unions, the right to strike was denied, even when the Democrats came into power in 1950.

Protest events therefore remained rare, mainly confined to the celebration of DP founding events or the contestation of alleged electoral frauds (for example, on 25 July 1946, about 30,000 protestors converged in Izmir; on 27 July, another 20,000 mobilized in Bursa, and other protests developed days later, culminating in the 40,000-person protest in Ankara on 1 August) or DP-led protests against the increasing costs of living (for example on 8 May 1949 in Istanbul). Other protests mobilized nationalists against communism.

In the early 1950s, the Democrats in government enjoyed a high level of public support in a booming economy; but while the market economy worked well in the short term, the lack of longer-term plans for investment was reflected in economic decline by the second half of the decade. Inflation brought about the devaluation of the currency by 330 per cent in 1957, with particularly negative consequences for fixed salary earners. Fear of popular resentment was then reflected in illiberal measures such as increased fines for journalists as well as the amendment to the public demonstrations law (1956), 'which ruled out political party meetings except for electoral propaganda, submitted protest gatherings to governors' permission, and gave the police the right to indiscriminately fire shots if the demonstrating crowd did not disperse upon warning' (Atak 2012; also Demirel 2011, 251).

In April 1960, a parliamentary investigatory committee (*tahkikat komisyonu*) was established whose tasks included surveillance of the media and oppositional activities. Protests erupted on several occasions. On 28 and 29 April 1960, thousands of students protested against police repression as well as the very existence of that committee. In the ensuing clashes with police, who used gas bombs and firearms, two students were shot dead and another crushed by a military tank. Protests in Ankara were similarly repressed. Martial law was then promulgated in Istanbul and Ankara, public meetings were outlawed, publishing on the events was prohibited, and universities were closed down for one month (Feyizoğlu 1993, 21–2).

In May 1960, discontent with the government, fuelled by deteriorating economic conditions, spread especially among young officers, 'Coupled with the historical role they self-ascribed as not only guardians but also proprietors of the regime' (Atak 2012). On 21 May 1960, military school students marched on the streets in Ankara, and on 27 May Colonel Alparslan Türkeş proclaimed a takeover that aimed to 'extricate the parties from the irreconcilable situation into which they had fallen' (Zürcher 2004, 241). The officers then formed a Committee of National Union, which replaced the civilian government, suspended the activities of the Democratic Party, and appointed a supreme court to investigate party leaders. However, they also facilitated the establishment of a constituent assembly in December 1960.

Protest was very constrained in this period, although there were exceptions—such as the collective resignation by university rectors and faculty members to protest the expulsion of 147 professors for political reasons, which eventually led to the reappointment of the expelled professors in March 1962 (Zürcher 2004, 354), as well as marches by workers for the right to strike and improvements in salaries. As many as 100,000 marched in Istanbul in December 1961, under slogans such as 'Unions without strike is like soldiers without arms!', 'He who considers strike as crime is criminal himself!', 'Misery destroys the morality of the society!' (Anonymous 1996, 566–8). Students also mobilized against the low quotas allocated for new recruitments in the universities.

New liberalization allowed for the development of social movements, although with polarization and escalation. Differently than in 1960, the military memorandum of 1971 was a law-and-order response to what was perceived as 'anarchy, fratricidal fight, social and economic unrest' (*Milliyet* 13.03.1971). The constitutional regime starting in 1961 had in fact facilitated the development and politicization of growing social movements, with frequent confrontations with authorities especially concerning student protest. The 'Bloody Sunday' of February 1969, when two people died and hundreds were wounded in clashes between anti-NATO protestors and anti-communist groups, as well as the workers' protests on 15 and 16 June 1971, which mobilized hundreds of thousands (four protesters died in clashes with the police), testified of an ongoing escalation. After 1971, political polarization 'came to characterize not only the parties, but was insinuated into other important social sectors as well, including organized labor, the teaching profession, the civil bureaucracy, and even the police' (Tachau and Heper 1983, 24).

Polarization went along with radicalization. Political violence escalated as 'Political assassinations came to include members of the parliament, an ex-prime minister, prominent journalists, and university professors. Some of the victims were extremists of left or right but others (particularly among journalists and professors) were moderates. The latter type of assassination was clearly designed to undermine the political center and accelerate the process of polarization' (Tachau and Heper 1983, 24–5). In this situation, the military interrupted the escalation through mass incarcerations and even assassinations (Atak 2012).

On 12 September 1980, the military dissolved parliament once again, this time with a much more repressive attitude than in 1960. Differently from the one in 1960, the 1980 coup was led by the military leadership that formed the National Security Council (NSC) presided over by Kenan Evren: 'Leaders of political parties were kept under custody, all political activities were suspended, martial law prevailed, and tens of thousands unionists, students, activists were arrested as political suspects' (Atak 2012). The NSC even made it illegal 'to criticize the advocatory speeches of the head of the state concerning the new constitution on radio-television and during his travels in the country; and to make any written or oral declaration against them' (*Turkish Official Gazette* 17845, 21 October 1982).

A return to a democratic regime, under a new constitution, was facilitated in 1983 by external pressure from the US and EC, which also denounced human rights violations using the threat of suspension of the association agreement with the Community (Dagi 1996, 129), as well as the non-release of an increased economic aid package of 600 million ECU that had been planned for Turkey (Dagi 1996, 130). Democracy remained weak, however. In May 1984, a petition signed by around 1,400 people was sent to the office of the Presidency and to the chief office of the Grand National Assembly. Under the title 'Observations and Demands Concerning the Democratic Order in Turkey', it stated that

> In light of these considerations, we are aware of our responsibilities to our society, and sincerely believe, that modern democracy has a stable essence despite changes in practices in different countries and their specific conditions; that the institutions and principles as the makeup of this essence are already acknowledged by our nation; that legal regulations and practices in breach of these principles should be lifted through democratic methods; that we can thus overcome the depression in a healthy and secure way.[8]

---

[8] <http://bianet.org/biamag/bianet/19444-aydinlar-dilekcesi-tam-metni>.

Petitioners were tried, but then acquitted, for unlawfully circulating a petition.

Human rights organizations had developed from the activities of the families of political prisoners after the 1980s coups, the military having sent almost 200,000 activists to prison, often under inhuman conditions (Stork 2011). Women organized silent Saturday vigils: after the first was held on 27 May 1995, the protest continued for four years, gaining publicity thanks to international networks on human rights (Gulru Goker 2011).

After 1983 there was a succession of waves of liberalization and deliberalization, especially in addressing the Kurdish protests but also labour mobilization, while the constitution recognized the Turkish Armed Forces' high level of discretion in political intervention. After Turkey became an official candidate to enter the EC in 1999, the years between 2002 and 2005 witnessed a series of liberal reforms, fuelling the expectation that Turkey was 'going from a hybrid regime that blended elements of democracy, autocracy, and pluralism to one that is more liberal *and* democratic' (Diamond et al. 2003, xviii). However, authoritarian tendencies remained well alive: 'Students, journalists, Kurdish politicians have been imprisoned; the rule of law has been thwarted by courts with extraordinary competences; the opposition in the media has been pacified, and so forth. All this signaled an authoritarian backlash that is becoming increasingly effectual' (Atak 2012).

Liberalization (even if selective and with low levels of political freedom) clearly facilitated a resurgence of the civil society. But 'state repression on leftist and Kurdish activists, in the first place, continued variably through clandestine (e.g. murders), judicial (e.g. State Security Courts, and after 2002, courts with extraordinary competences) and street (e.g. protest policing) forms' (Atak 2012). In 1989 a wave of protest involved 600,000 workers in 'slowing down and late-starting work, collective medical visits, food and bus service boycott, beard boycott, quiet marches, stoppage, sit-in, obstruction of traffic, collective petitioning for divorce' (Çelik 1996, 103). These politicized protests were successful in obtaining salary increases. Intense protest activities on labour issues followed in 1994 and 1995, sometimes succeeding (through pressure on the RPP) even in pushing a whole cabinet out of office (see Figure 7.1).

The labour movement was a democratizing actor, even if with some ambivalent positions on ethno-nationalist and religious issues. Especially,

> when it comes to certain cleavage structures in the society, e.g. on the Kurdish issue, the status of Muslim and non-Muslim minorities, civilian-military relations and so on, the divided nature of the labor adduced to a lack of shared understanding for further democratization. Still, those like KESK and affiliated unions, who are contentiously more active and relatively independent from the political mainstream, mobilize frequently for the drafting of a pluralist constitution,

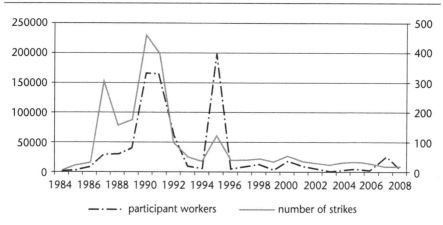

Figure 7.1 Official strike statistics in Turkey (1984–2008)
Source: ILO; Atak 2012

education in mother tongue (for Kurds in particular); and against state repression on unionists and tough police strategies on the street (Çelik 1996).

As for the Kurdish mobilization, while it was the target of the most severe repression, justified by the armed insurgency, it also contributed to non-violent domestic mobilizations for more democracy (Watts 2006, 125). In fact, 'the representation of the Kurdish movement in the parliament had a pivotal role both for the recognition of the Kurdish identity and for a chance to the pluralist practice of democracy' (Atak 2012). At the same time, especially in the south-east with the Kurdish movement, mass protests developed around symbolic occasions such as the celebrations for the New Year, *Newroz*, which often ended up in severe clashes with the security forces. A sort of Kurdish *intifada* (*serhildan* or uprising) involved large numbers of participants in often violent action. To the guerrilla attacks of the PKK the state responded with 'counter-guerilla tactics, mystery killings, torture, kidnapping activists, imprisoning politicians, setting villages in fire, banning Kurdish publications and so forth' (Atak 2012). After some hope for solution in the first half of the year 2000s, a new escalation followed. The Kurdish intellectuals developed a concept of 'democratic autonomy' (Democratic Society Congress, DTK), stressing local reinterpretations of self-government, autonomy, and federalism with 'less state' and 'more society', 'less restrictions' and 'more freedom' (Peace and Democracy Party 2011). Protest actions included mass sit-ins as well as the holding of Friday prayers outside the mosques' own space. Islamist groups benefitted from the junta's attempt to promote religion as a catalyst for the depoliticization of the society. On some occasions, some of the Muslim groups put forward general claims for freedom and against repression.

The Global Justice Movement (GJM), which in Turkey largely overlapped with the anti-war mobilization against the US occupation of Iraq and Afghanistan between 2002 and 2005, contributed greatly to the enrichment of the democratic practices. On the issue of democracy, moreover, ad hoc platforms brought together civil society organizations of various types (including labour unions, vocational associations, human rights groups, and other type of NGOs) on a common agenda for democratization and against military interventions in politics. One national example is the Labor and Democracy Platform in the 1990s (Koç 2010); but in the last ten years such platforms have also developed at the local level, using protest as a main means to express their claims. The recent protests in Gezi Park represent a continuation of this struggle for democracy (Atak 2013).

In sum, social movements accompanied the waves of democratization and de-democratization, sometimes succeeding in pushing elites towards liberalization policies.

Participated Pacts: A Summary

Social movements do not always promote democratization through disruptive regime breakdowns. In some cases, they instead play the resources they have accumulated in bargaining for change, finding reformist supporters among the incumbents, and strengthening this counterpart. However, even pacted democratizations are rich in episodes of contention, which often help the development of democratization processes.

In 1989, differently than Czechoslovakia and GDR, Hungary and Poland were cases of divided elites, with reformers inside the regime appropriating the emerging opportunities that opened up with reformist policies in the Soviet Union, as well as the perceived need for political and economic changes. While the dominance of hardliners in Czechoslovakia and GDR brought about capitulation through mass protests, the larger presence of reformists in Hungary and Poland allowed for the establishment of participated pacts (Goodwin 2001).

Economic decline played a role in this environment as the elites, already in the 1970s, started to struggle over the reforms, with increased trade outside the bloc, nationalist and more independent foreign policies, expansion of consumption, or—as in the cases I have analysed in this chapter—through a slow liberalization of domestic politics. Reforms notwithstanding, socialism was unsuccessful in recovering economic growth, and by the 1980s it appeared in economic and political crisis.

The different degrees of repression in Eastern Europe—with relatively more liberal regimes, for example, in Hungary and liberalization in Poland—have influenced the emergence of early risers, which functioned as examples to emulate for those who followed. So, in Hungary and Poland, which shared not only economic crisis but also party internal divisions, 'leaders of weak party-states at the outset of the transition period attempted to increase their capacity for economic change by reforming but not entirely dismantling the political institutions of the old regime' (Stark and Bruszt 1998, 9). The availability of allies inside the party explains why the transition in Central Eastern Europe took different paths: capitulation in GDR and Czechoslovakia, and compromise in Poland and Hungary.

No participated pact developed in the MENA regions, where oil-rich countries as well as monarchies tried instead to co-opt the opposition through some moderate liberalization and spoil distributions. In countries such as Morocco or Yemen, however, protests did produce some political liberalization and economic concessions: these achievements could prove important in building up new waves of protests. The troubled history of Turkish democratization can also tell us something about the potential for liberalization from above in this area, and its complex dynamics as allowed for and then pushed by the protest. In Turkey, in fact, in the alternation of liberalization and deliberalization, we saw the frequent shift of allegiances by military and non-military elites. If after World War II liberalization was driven from above, it did improve the contextual conditions for the development of social movement organizations that later acted as democracy promoters, but also as challengers, which were often repressed through coups d'état and other forms of military intervention.

In these cases, protests did not jeopardize, but rather accompanied democratization, a point also made by Nancy Bermeo in addressing various democratic waves. As she observed, the Portuguese transition, which began in April 1974, 'violated most of the cautionary parameters set out by the literature on democratization. The laboring classes were far from docile. Capitalist property rights were challenged successfully on a very broad scale. The country's position in international alliances was the subject of strenuous debate, and decolonization shattered the territorial integrity of the state. The vertical command structure of the armed forces was completely transformed. Nevertheless, democracy muddled through' (Bermeo 1997, 307).

The moderation argument is not even uncontested for the most celebrated cases such as the Spanish one, where elites did pact, but in a situation in which radical conflicts developed. According to Bermeo, together with Portugal, Spain is 'particularly instructive in understanding the limits of the moderation argument because it is so often held up as the model of peaceful and "pacted" transition. Elite pacts were certainly key to the democratization of Spain, but these pacts were forged in a situation in which extremism and moderation existed simultaneously'. Similarly, the transition in Peru in 1977–8 is seen as 'compelling evidence that formal democracies can be constructed amid violence and high levels of popular mobilization' (Bermeo 1997, 312). And the transition from dictatorship in the Philippines is seen as proof that 'electoral democracy can be constructed in a state with an even larger guerrilla presence', given the increasing relevance of the New People's Army (NPA), which aimed at an armed mobilization of the rural poor.

In our cases of participated pacts, as well, we saw a mix of moderation and radicalization, compromise and contestation, as protest pushed elites towards changes. Bermeo explains the accommodation of even radical forms of action as related to the changes in elites' expectations. As elites calculate the costs of tolerance and repression, what is important is their perceptions of these costs. In fact, as she noted (Bermeo 1997, 315), the cost of suppression increases together with the level of popular mobilization. So, 'If antiregime forces of any sort succeed in elevating the sense of struggle and raising the costs of suppression, they affect half the decision calculus and win half the battle'. The other half of the calculus addresses, in fact, the costs of toleration: 'For the costs of toleration to seem bearable, pivotal elites must believe that they will not be ruined by reform. Dictatorial regimes will pay extremely high suppression costs if the costs of toleration leave them no other choice'. In this sense, 'Neither the presence nor the scope of extremist activities is as important an element in elite calculations as their estimates of what the effects of extremism will be' (Bermeo 1997).

This was also the case for the countries we have analysed here, confirming that moderation alone is not the condition for democratization. Indeed, while literature on the third wave praised moderation, slow processes, bargaining, and compromise among elites because of stalemate, this was not true for the fourth wave, where one found, instead, negotiation only rarely, and confrontation more often (McFaul 2010b, 11). In fact, 'bridging' emerged as a most successful strategy in the South, but 'breaking' appeared more successful in the East (Bunce 2000)—or, at least, these were the two diverging narratives.

Our cases indicated, in fact, that a neat classification of pact as opposed to rupture is indeed unconvincing. Even in participated pacts, moments of disruption were necessary to push timorous elites, by convincing them of the need to compromise. Indeed, elite moderation was often produced by perceptions of threats as well as opportunities. In a sort of virtuous circle, the perceived costs of toleration lowered with oppositional integration into bargaining processes, which moderated resistance and then further pushed towards negotiation.

8

Violent Uprisings, Troubled Democratization

Introduction

> *The long experience of repression of dissent did not allow intellectuals to play the role they had in Central Europe: nothing like tolerated dissident groups could be found in Albania. In addition, the isolation of the country was such that the European dissident debates could not include the local cultural elite in any form. For instance, in the years before the regime collapsed, the debates were not even framed in the language of civil society used by central European intellectuals. Right up until its final days, the regime's apparatus of repression had been very successful in preventing the emergence of open criticism, and not even the few people who, under the severe control of the secret services, could travel abroad did dare to openly challenge even the language of the system* (Chiodi 2012).

In Albania, as in the other cases we will address in this chapter, episodes of democratization turned violent. Jeff Goodwin (2001) distinguished the peculiarities of the Eastern European cases—in contrast to the Third World revolutions—in the spontaneous and peaceful nature of the process, its urban character, and the absence of counter-revolutionary violence. Spontaneity and non-violence had developed, he suggested, from the absence of other options, given the despotic nature of the regimes and negative past examples such as the repression of the Hungarian rebellion in 1956.

Regime capacity and willingness to repress indeed emerged as relevant issues in explaining eventful democratization (Chapter 5). However, violence was also present in the mobilization for democracy in 1989 and, even more so, in 2011–12. Looking at these cases, we shall focus particular attention on two dimensions that apparently interacted in explaining violence. The first is indeed the capacity of the regime to repress, through the control of coercive forces. The second is the strength of civil society organizations in driving the protest towards peaceful forms. If a strong civil society does not explain per se eventful transition, as existing resources can be oriented to negotiations when the opponents are available, a weak civil society seems to characterize violent uprisings and troubled democratizations. Once again, protests—even very disruptive ones—might occasionally emerge, but they are unlikely to produce an easy democratization process. In a situation with a weak civil society, costs of repression are seen as low, while repression in turn keeps civil society weak. Eventually, however, repression itself can become a catalyst for rebellion, that might then produce dealignment among the elites.

Disruption from below in fact seemed very relevant in some episodes of democratization in both Eastern Europe and, especially, the MENA region. In these cases, violence erupted, in various forms and degrees, prompted by brutal state repression. The characteristics and behaviour of the military played an extremely salient role. In particular, splits within the military as well as external military intervention influenced the evolution of violent insurgencies. As we shall see, democratization does require collective actors that push for it, but this is a necessary but insufficient condition, as it is the outcome of complex processes in which many (domestic and international, from above and from below) actors play a role.

While research on transition has in fact recognized a pivotal role for the army—especially, but not only in military regimes—it has mainly seen the prevalence of a democratic orientation in the military as a precondition for democratization. In this chapter, I suggest instead that we look, within a more dynamic perspective, at how strategies change in action through the interaction of various actors and their shifting views on the process.

If protest is therefore relevant in both non-violent and violent transition, a debate is also open about which type of protest tends to be successful in what circumstances. If and how much non-violence is a key to democratization is in fact a much discussed issue. While literature on revolutions often considered violence as necessary for change, non-violence studies stressed non-violence as a successful repertoire. And as the wave of democratization in Eastern Europe is often cited as a successful example of non-violent strategies achieving their aims, further reflections raised some doubts on the ability to generalize those lessons, identifying the conditions for, instead, a sort of insurgent democratization (Wood 2000).

Social movement studies have provided several explanations for the choice of a peaceful versus violent repertoire, pointing first and foremost at the political opportunities available for social movements. Looking at the exogenous determinants of protest repertoire, social movement scholars have stressed the roles of both stable institutions and contingent developments (see Chapters 1 and 6). Regarding the former, more centralized political power is seen as making political institutions less accessible 'from below' and, thus, fuelling more violent protest. Additionally, radicalization has been considered more likely when historically rooted cultural elements about the proper ways to deal with opponents orient authorities towards exclusive strategies. Less durable political contingencies such as the lack of availability and influence of political allies have also been mentioned as closing windows of opportunity for protestors, often producing escalation (see della Porta and Diani 2006, ch. 8 for a review).

Low levels of freedom and democracy have been linked to violence at the national level, even in Western Europe (Engene 2004), and less proportional electoral systems to ethnic violence (in Crenshaw 2011). The weakness of democracy, civil liberties, human rights, rule of law, and so on are often considered as root causes for radicalization. When normal channels of access to the political system are blocked, violence might be perceived as necessary, as there is 'no other way out' (Goodwin 2001). As we are going to see, radicalization happens indeed after the failure of non-violent mobilization.

Another political precondition identified in explaining high levels of political violence is the weakness of the state in terms of repressive capacity and even territorial control. The related power vacuum can be occupied by violent groups that find safe havens for training and socialization into violence. As Huntington (1968) suggested long ago, the corruption of those in government might justify violence by reducing not only their legitimacy, but also the hope that change can be achieved through non-violent channels. This is all the more true if powerful foreign actors are seen as supporting corrupt regimes. On the other hand, also democracies have been targets of clandestine violence that has been defined as attacking and at the same time exploiting the very liberty that democracies provide to their citizens. Here, the interruption of incomplete democratization processes have often been said to produce political violence (della Porta 1990; Zwerman, della Porta, and Steinhof 2000).

In addition, blockages in international relations have been mentioned as pushing superpowers to fuel violence as surrogate wars. During the Cold War, for example, clandestine attacks as well as civil wars have been defined as 'proxy wars' between the two superpowers, which they fuelled but also controlled. However, the end of the Cold War has also seen an increase in civil wars, as new groups and interests have mobilized in systems not yet endowed with democratic structures. Conditions of occupation by foreign powers have also been said to trigger the temptation to use clandestine violence as a cheap form of opposition, when it is impossible to address and mobilize large groups of the population.

As mentioned, the policing of protest is a central factor in radicalization. Social science research has linked the style of police intervention to some characteristics of the external environment (see also Chapter 5). First, police have been seen as sensitive to the perceived threat but also to the expected demands from authorities and public opinion. Research on the police has stressed that the organizational imperative is keeping control over situations, rather than enforcing the law (Bittner 1967; Rubinstein 1980; Skolnick 1966). If police officers enjoy a certain degree of discretion in their encounters with citizens, they must also maintain (to varying degrees) the support of authorities and the public. Research on the policing of social movements has identified a tendency to use harsher styles of protest policing against social and political groups that are perceived as larger threats to political elites, given that they are more ideologically driven or more radical in their aims (Davenport 2000, 1995; della Porta and Fillieule 2004; Earl 2003). Additionally, police repression is more likely to be directed against groups that are poorer in material resources as well as in political connections (della Porta 1998; Earl, Soule, and McCarthy 2003).

In addition, the forms state power takes have a clear impact on the policing of protest. If repression is always much more brutal in authoritarian than in democratic regimes (e.g. Uysal 2005 on Turkey), even authoritarian regimes vary in the amount, forms, and actors of protest they are willing to tolerate, as well as in the forms in which they police the opposition (Boudreau 2004). The police's strategies in addressing the demonstrations reflect some more general characteristics of law enforcement, including its organizational resources and professional culture. The degree of militarization of the structure and equipment, legal competences, and level of professionalization all influence their strategic choices. In addition, police tactics in the control of protest follow some general conceptions of the role of the police (Noakes and Gillham 2006).

Conversely, protest has an impact on police forces and strategies. The policing of protest is a key feature for the development and self-definition of the police as an institution and as a profession. Its gradual affirmation as the main agency specializing in this task was of fundamental importance to the process of modernization and professionalization of the European police forces in the nineteenth and twentieth centuries. Moreover, waves of protest have had important effects on both police strategies and the organization of the police force (Morgan 1987).

In contemporary democratic societies, the way in which the police address protest is a significant aspect of its self-image (Winter 1998). In authoritarian regimes, such as the ones we will analyse in this chapter, the military also plays an important role in the dynamics of the uprising. Not only does the military de-alignment from the dictator weaken him, but when parts of the military join the opposition, this changes the nature of the democratization movement, usually towards violent spirals.

This chapter will discuss cases of violent uprisings for democracy, looking at escalation in the relations between regime and challengers in Romania and Albania in Eastern Europe, and in Libya and Syria in the MENA region. The role of the military seems very relevant in these cases; but another common feature is the weakness of the civil society. In contrast to the previous two paths, very authoritarian regimes thwarted the development of social movements by mobilizing supporters from above. Experiences of protests were limited here and, in particular, their promoters remained fragmented. When protest erupted, as a consequence of diffusion to states in which preconditions for democratization were weak, it did not build upon a pluralist basis. In different ways in the two areas, initial eruptions of peaceful protest were unsuccessful in bringing about democratization, instead developing into either coups d'état or armed conflicts.

Violent Transitions in Eastern Europe

Clearly very weak, social movement organizations in Romania and Albania made limited contributions to episodes of democratization, which involved contentious moments of protest. While transition was achieved quickly in the four cases in Eastern Europe we have already addressed, Romania and Albania lagged behind, with violence erupting in both countries.[1]

Romania

Romania was involved in the 1989 wave as a latecomer. Protest in fact erupted at the end of 1989 from outrage at the forced expulsion from his parish of an ethnic Hungarian priest, and the harsh repression of the mobilization that followed. Romania was an exception in Central Eastern Europe in its evolution as a most personalized regime (significantly defined as 'socialism in one family', or socialist patrimonialism), which was overthrown when the army abandoned the dictator Nicolae Ceaușescu (who had privileged the *securitate*) and party members expressed dissatisfaction with his personalist and familist management.

Romania's events in 1989 have been in fact defined variously as an elite coup against Nicolae Ceaușescu by a faction of the Romanian Communist Party, RCP (Chilton 1994; Haerpfer 2009; Roper 2000), a coup accompanied by a popular uprising (Verdery and Kligman 1992), or a revolution (Hall 1999; Siani-Davies 2005). The wave of protests that started in Timișoara on 17 December resulted in the end of a sultanistic regime, but the emerging

---

[1] In Bulgaria, some regime transformation followed those in other countries, with limited protest but also limited change.

241

civil-led coalition with the army was still dominated by part of the old elites (even if the communist party was dissolved).

The catalyst for the rebellion was the jailing on 15 December 1989 of dissident pastor Lázló Tőkés of the Hungarian Reform Church in Timișoara, in the Transylvania region, which comprises a large part of the Hungarian ethnic minority. On that day demonstrators gathered in front of the pastor's house to prevent his arrest, also joined by football club members—sport associations being among the very few allowed organizations. On 16 December, protests became politicized as 'earlier calls for bread and meat were now replaced with "down with Ceaucescu," "down with tyranny," and an all pervasive "freedom"' (Siani-Davies 2005, 60), while the protestors were presented by the regime as infiltrated agents from the Soviet Union and US. After three days of mobilization, the military charged the protestors on the night of 17 December 1989, killing about sixty of them (Siani-Davies 2005, 68).

Notwithstanding this heavy repression, demonstrations continued. Mobilization spread then to factories, as 'The communist penchant for constructing factories in large industrial complexes allowed for a concentration of sentiment and facilitated the free flow of information between the many workers' (Siani-Davies 2005, 70). With a wave of moral shocks similar to the ones we saw in cases of eventful democratization, even if people were scared, 'hatred turned into rage' (Siani-Davies 2005, 225). So, Timișoara's workers initiated a strike, in protest against repression—until all factories shut down on 19 and 20 December (Siani-Davies 2005, ch. 2). The strike was followed by withdrawal of the army. As between 15 and 22 December (when Ceaușescu was executed), protests spread from Timișoara to the rest of the country.

After 20 December, protest reached other cities such as Cluj, Sibiu, and finally Bucharest, while calls for freedom and human rights became louder. For the 21 December demonstration, comprising actors, poets, and film directors, the regime staged a large display of Securitate, with the outcome of forty-nine demonstrators dead, 463 wounded, and 698 arrested. Attempts to mobilize the 5,000 members of the patriotic guards failed, as only 300 of them responded (Siani-Davies 2005, 93).

Riots in Bucharest's centre lasted until 22 December, when people stormed the Ceaușescu headquarters (Stokes 1993). Returning to Romania on 20 December after a visit abroad, Nicolae Ceaușescu had criticized the dissidents as well as the elites in Timișoara, accusing the latter of having disobeyed the order to repress protestors. He then called for a pro-government demonstration, where, however, slogans were shouted against the dictator. On the same day, the Minister of the Interior died, amidst rumours that he had been killed by Ceaușescu's supporters for his refusal to repress protests (Siani-Davies 2005).

Events then escalated quickly. When Ceaușescu tried to speak from the RCP headquarters on 22 December, dissidents threw shoes and potatoes at him. As the military refused to intervene, the protestors eventually entered the RCP headquarters, while the dictator and his wife escaped by helicopter from the roof of the building. Violence then spread in Bucharest, with riots, lootings, cross-shootings, and tank attacks; many lost their lives in only three days (Verdery and Kligman 1992; Siani-Davies 2005). The official death toll of the upheaval was 1,104 (492 of them taking place in Bucharest), with 162 killed between 17 and 22 December (Siani-Davies 2005).

After that, between 23 and 25 December, violent clashes involved the Securitate (secret police), the military, and protestors, until the formation of the Provisional Council of National Unity on 9 February 1990. While the regime broke down, the National Salvation Front (NSF) was founded, gathering anti-Ceaușescu RCP elites, among them Ion Iliescu. Captured while on the run, Nicolae and Elena Ceaușescu were tried, sentenced (in a two-hour long trial), and then executed on 24 December.

The NSF then called for elections, in which it participated as a party, while some anti-NSF protests were organized on 28 and 29 January 1990 by pre-communist parties and students (Siani-Davies 2005, ch. 5). On 9 February 1990, the NSF founded the Provisional Council of National Unity, a coordination of anti-Ceaușescu organizations formed to govern in the transitional period until elections. The endpoint of the revolutionary process, according to Siani-Davies (2005), was 22 April, when a few hundred students mobilized in a sit-in at the University of Bucharest in support of the pro-democratic Timișoara Proclamation (Tismaneanu 1997). The first free elections, on 20 May, were then won by Iliescu's NSF, with eighty-five per cent of the votes.

The totalitarian patrimonialism of the regime, mixed with its weak control of the security forces, contribute to explain the characteristics of the short, violent uprisings. Romania under Ceaușescu was variously defined as a personalized, sultanistic, neo-patrimonial, totalitarian neo-Stalinist regime (Carey and Eisterhold 2004; Siani-Davies 2005, 16; Tismaneanu, 1997, 410–11). Rejecting de-Stalinization in 1953 (Roper 2000, 30), RCP leaders had played a nationalist card, refusing to enter the Warsaw Pact or the COMECON and instead developing their relations with China as well as their economic ties with the West. After a strong effort at industrialization during the 1970s, austerity measures following economic decline resulted in a lack of products to consume (Kaser 2010). As Siani-Davies (2005, 32) summarized,

> The spark of the crisis of the early 1980s largely came from adverse developments in the global economy. Building on Romania's traditional interests in the oil industry, a great deal of investment had been poured into facilities for the processing of secondary petroleum products as well as other energy intensive sectors,

such as steel manufacturing and aluminium refining.... The Romanians intended to cover the cost of these new investments by exporting the goods produced to the West, but not only was this fateful decision made at a time when reliance on oil imports was decreasing because of decline in domestic production—this fell by 20 per cent between 1982 and 1988—but also the new plant began to come on stream just as the price of oil tripled during the second OPEC crisis. This was largely caused by the revolution in Iran, a country that had traditionally been an oil supplier to the Romanians.... The result was that in 1980 the spectacular growth of the 1970s was brought to a shuddering halt. Ceaucescu's reaction to the crisis was belated but, when it came, it displayed the same single-mindedness which had earlier driven his quest for industrialization. A massive campaign of export promotion and import substitution was launched in which the most marketable products, especially foodstuffs, were shipped abroad, leaving only 'patriots' such as pig's feet at home (2005, 32–3).

Ceaușescu's decision to repay all foreign debts further depressed the economy (Siani-Davies 2005, 33).

Notwithstanding economic and political tensions, only very sporadic protests had preceded the 1989–90 events, as the highly repressive nature of the regime had thwarted the development of social movement organizations. According to Chilton (1994, 170), 'Romania is the purest example of an extremely strong and repressive state apparatus and a very weak civil society' (cf. also Pralong 2004). Civil society was not only extremely weak, but also internationally isolated, with the only existing transnational links being those of the Hungarian minority with Hungarian human rights groups. In fact, 'Until the '70s, the Communist Party lived up to its commitment made to the workers, while the workers accepted the leading position and the self-assumed objectives of the Party'.

Some protest did emerge, however, on economic issues, politicizing slowly. Since the 1970s there had been resistance against assimilationist policies towards the Hungarian minority. The economic deterioration in the 1980s led to discontent especially among workers. The first signs of emerging dissatisfaction had appeared in 1977, when 35,000 miners in the Jiu Valley went on a strike that continued even when Ceaușescu promised concessions, but arrested the strike leaders. Miners and metalworkers also went on strike in Cluj in 1983. Dissatisfaction was also produced by a strong anti-intellectual orientation, resulting in low pay for intellectuals. More in general, 'The homogenized structure of the state, which was characterized by an absence of differentials and an ideological stress on egalitarianism and centralized decision making, produced a commonality of experience, which during the 1980s became a commonality of grievance' (Siani-Davies 2005, 42).

In the second half of the 1980s, the scarcity of fuel and heating in the winter of 1984–5 increased disaffection, while the Hungarian Reformed Church started to offer some free spaces to the opposition (Siani-Davies 2005, 43). Even more dramatic was the revolt of the workers in Brașov on 15 November 1987: while workers protested wage cuts, singing patriotic songs from 1948, the Hungarian Reformed Church and its local networks mobilized for the first time against the regime (Siani-Davies 2005, 35). As it was factory workers who mobilized, 'with some irony, it can be said that Ceaușescu was toppled by mass protests that stemmed from an organizational form, the factory, that communism had elevated to be both the actual and also the mythical heart of the state' (Siani-Davies 2005, 44). Radicalized football supporters also contributed to violent protests (Sampson 1984–6).

Societal organizations remained extremely weak, however. As it has been summarized, in fact,

> Unlike in Poland, the Czech Republic or Hungary, there was no dissident movement and no organized civil society to speak of in Romania prior to 1989. No independent 'civil life' was claimed by the few who dared oppose...society was atomized and the people were traumatized. Terrorized by the prevailing surveillance of the secret police, the Romanian people were fearful of getting together and speaking up. With the exception of a handful of state-run associations (Communist Youth, Writers' Union...) and a state-run labor union (Pralong 2004, 231).

While trade unions did sometimes protest, strikes were rare events. The only attempt to create an independent union in 1979 failed, due to strong repression (Siani-Davies 2005, 35). The students mobilized only after the fall of the regime, with the Students' League and the Students' Union organizing protests for democracy on 29 January and 9 February 1990 (Siani-Davies 2005, 234–5).

Moreover, Romanian civil society organizations were isolated from the main transnational coalitions for human rights (no Romanian group signed the Helsinki Memorandum of 1986). So, 'The complete absence of any liberalization movement in the country meant that Romania, unlike some other countries of the region, had no human rights groups, independent unions, environmental groups, or other entities that Western organizations could support' (Carothers 1996, 19). Opposition groups to Ceaușescu were limited to a pro-Soviet Union, RCP old guard, well-educated anti-Stalinist technocrats, and intellectuals open to the West (Siani-Davies 2005, 195–9).

Very oppressive conditions plus patrimonialistic power and nationalist appeals had thwarted the development of a democratic opposition. Besides his use of strong repression, Ceaușescu had won a reputation as a nationalist when he refused to participate in the invasion of Czechoslovakia in 1968. While he initially appeared as a reformer, after a trip in North Korea, he then developed a belief in a strong state with total control over society, a planned economy, and the building of socialism in one country. In a freezing patrimonialist regime, he then built his personal power, as fifty members of his family controlled key positions (Saxonberg 2012, 127).

The end of the regime was indeed linked to the disalignment of the security apparatuses for the dictator. The non-professional and non-privileged military (heavy cuts were made in 1986) was little oriented to repress, while the militia and the Securitate, even if under the personal control of Ceauşescu, were not particularly loyal to him (Siani-Davies 2005). The attempt by the regime to divide and control the coercive apparatus did not work, and when the dictator ordered violence to break up protests, the army did not obey.

Albania

Also a latecomer to the 1989 wave of democratization in Eastern Europe, Albania too had one of the most authoritarian regimes, with a nevertheless weak state that collapsed together with the regime. In Chiodi's (2012) words,

> The turbulent Albanian transition was not a velvet revolution but after the long Stalinist regime no one expected a smooth regime change. The communist elite endeavoured to use power to limit the breadth of the political transformation but it only managed to postpone the regime collapse for a few months. However, when it realized the impossibility to control changes from above, it renounced to state violence. Thus, the Albanian transition was not characterized by bloodbaths but rather by a dripping of violence provoked by the economic and institutional breakdown.

Together with protest, mass flights abroad, looting, and other forms of violence to state property developed during the transition. After limited liberalization between December 1989 and November 1990, two short waves of street protests, lasting until March 1991, debouched in the formation of non-communist political parties and the organization of the first pluralist elections. Between April 1991 and February 1992 there was a period of widespread protests and state disintegration, followed by the election of the first non-communist government, democratization, and economic liberalization.

As in Romania, civil society was extremely weak, thwarted by a very high degree of repression. Albania has been considered, in fact, as a Stalinist and/or sultanistic regime, using the local traditional clan culture and customary repertoires (including the punishment of entire families for the anti-communist behaviour of one of their members) in order to impose its control. Repression was brutal: '34,135 people were imprisoned for political reasons during the four decades of communist rule, and 59,009 internally exiled. 5,487 people were executed after bogus trials' (Abrahams forthcoming). Collectivization of the economy meant that people could not privately own even an animal or

246

a car. Enver Hoxha, Secretary General of the Albanian Party of Labour (PLA), dominated the country from 1945 until his death in 1985. The Albanian communist regime imposed in 1956 a ban on all independent organizations: 'the only organisation that survived was the Red Cross that existed until 1964. From 1964 to 1990 the only non-governmental organisation working in Albania was the association of Hunters' (Baruti 1996).

The political and economic closure was reflected in extremely negative and quickly deteriorating economic conditions, which then constituted the basis for a politicization of claims, up to the breakdown of the regime. In 1990, at the ninth Communist Party Plenum, the dramatic economic situation was acknowledged and some very early attempts at liberalization followed. Premier Ramiz Alia attempted some moderate reforms. In the spring of 1990, political prisoners who had spent more than twenty-five years in prison were released and, in April, six Albanian citizens—members of the Popaj family who had been political refugees in the Italian embassy of Tirana since 1985—were allowed to leave the country. In May, internment and the death penalty for anti-socialist propaganda were abolished and the illegal crossing of the state border was no longer considered a counter-revolutionary act. The Ministry of Justice, closed since 1968, was reopened, while a private legal practice was reintroduced and the offence of religious propaganda was cancelled from the criminal law. Churches and mosques were also gradually allowed to work again.

In the first half of 1990, however, hundreds of arrests followed some first attempts at mobilization. On 2 July 1990, 5,000 Albanians sought refuge in foreign embassies while the government declared a partial state of emergency. Urgent material needs were at the basis of the protest: 'just like in the failed protests and riots early in 1990 in Shkodër, Kavaje and Tirana, the protagonists of the embassy crisis were young men deeply dissatisfied, often unemployed, that saw no life perspectives in Albania but were moved by strong myths of the West. They did not have a clear political orientation if not the dissatisfaction towards the regime. Yet, their mass migration was a fundamental chapter of the struggle against the regime' (Chiodi 2012). During the year, disorder intensified as material conditions became more difficult, with food and power shortages (Vickers 1997, 33).

On 6 December a wave of protests started with a focus on material conditions but moved quickly to requests for political pluralism (Vickers 1997), which were granted a few days later. The students joined the workers in their mobilizations for better living conditions and political liberalization. The emergence of a student movement in December 1990 became 'a catalyst for other civil society initiatives: the birth of the first independent trade union organization, the journalist struggles for editorial freedom, the establishment of the first human rights group etc. These experiences were nevertheless short-lived and many of the leaders soon joined the political parties that were re-emerging in the political arena in the same period of time. As an alternative, many of the participants of the mobilization emigrated abroad with the hundreds of thousands of people that left the country during the following years' (Chiodi 2012). Student protests started after a power cut in the Student City. On 10 December 1990, meeting in an open space on campus they named Democracy Square, protestors drafted a list of nine claims that included the acceleration of democratic reforms, political pluralism, punishment of the police officers involved in the repression of student protests, and legalization of the Organisation of Students and Young Intellectuals, born during the protest and soon to become the first opposition party (Chiodi 2012). On the fourth day of the protest, 80,000 people gathered in the square as the students were joined by professors, while delegates from the various faculties, democratically elected, met with the President of the Republic Alia. The students remained mobilized in the months to follow, pushing for rapid democratization.

Protest at the university moved in fact from material concerns to political ones, including a petition, signed by 8,000 of 11,000 students and professors, to change the name (Enver Hoxha) of the university (Mustafaj 1993, 124). On 18 February, 723 students and professors announced a hunger strike, which went on for three days, attracting workers and ordinary citizens as well. As the students continued their protest, on 20 February thousands of protestors moved from the university campus to the main city plaza, the Skanderbeg Square. Hoxha's statue was pulled down, while members of the security forces were said to sympathize with the protestors (Abrahams forthcoming). The government then resigned, and an eight-member Presidential Council was formed. On 20 February, the Partia Demokratike e Shqipërisë (PDsh) or Democratic Party of Albania was founded, including some participants from the student movement and former members of the Communist party.

The days following the student protests were characterized by riots in cities like Shkodër, Kavaja, Durres, and Elbasan, where especially young men destroyed signs of the regime (such as busts and books of Hoxha), looted shops, and clashed with police (Chiodi 2012). As part of the opposition had an anarchic character, '[an] attack on a public building at night by a few people who would then rapidly disappear into the darkness was much more typical expression of the public mood than the kind of large-scale organized meetings and street demonstration that had developed elsewhere in Eastern Europe' (Vickers 1997, 34).

On 22 February, rumours spread that the army was conspiring to bring Hoxha's monument back to its place in Tirana. Around the Military Academy barricades were built and bullets shot into the air. During the confrontation with the special police forces sent to disperse the protest, four people were killed, including one member of the police (Abrahams forthcoming). After the first elections, protests by workers and students continued, while a few demonstrators were killed and several injured (Champseix and Champ 1992; Lawrence 2011). Violent protests in April were repressed (four people died).

Workers also continued their struggle for democracy, especially after the foundation of free unions in 1991. On 16 May, 250,000 workers went on strike, especially in the industry and transportation sectors (Champseix and Champ 1992, 186). The Union of Independent Trade Unions (BSPSH) called for a fifty per cent wage increase for all workers, better working conditions, and prosecutions for the 2 April killings. Two hundred miners began a hunger strike deep in the mine, with ensuing solidarity protests (Mustafaj 1993, 109) that paralysed the country, bringing about the resignation of the communist-led government. A Stability Government was formed on 4 June including the Party of Labour and opposition members. Foreign aid was insufficient to stop the wave of people fleeing the country in their thousands (Vickers and Pettifer 1997, 70).

Strikes continued in the autumn. In October, protest rallies took place in Tirana, while strikes against worsening living conditions included teachers, miners, and transport workers (Keesing 1991a). In November, shortages of food and energy produced a breakdown in public order in the Tropojë and Shkodër districts (Keesing 1991b). In December, 20,000 people gathered in Tirana to protest against food and fuel shortages as well as to celebrate the first anniversary of the democratic movement. By the end of the winter, dozens had been killed in food riots (Vickers and Pettifer 1997, 72). The unions organized another major strike in January 1992, which gathered 20,000 participants (Keesing 1992). As Chiodi (2012) summarized, 'The country collapsed into a spiral of lawlessness and dozens of people died during street riots in the following months as also private violence spread. During the dramatic winter 1991–92, to placate food riots and lawlessness, the first foreign military intervention—the so-called *Operazione Pellicano*—constituted by 1,000 disarmed Italian soldiers distributed humanitarian aid in various parts of the country, especially in the remote mountain areas where people risked famine'.

Human rights issues, however, were late to emerge—among others, thanks to the work of the Association of Former Political Prisoners, set up in 1991, which also organized a hunger strike in Tirana, asking for rehabilitation, restitution of confiscated properties, economic support and housing assistance, identification of the graves of prisoners who died in detention, and return of the bodies to their families.

On 22 March 1992 the Albanian Democratic Party (DP), with US support, won the elections. Nevertheless, the new democratic institutions 'failed to achieve either a degree of stability or a sufficient level of legitimacy' in the years to come (Elbasani 2008, 5). While former president Ramiz Alia was arrested for alleged misappropriation of state funds, no investigation addressed the secret police, the Sigurimi (HRW 1992). In March, 25,000 Albanians left for Italy, while others crossed the Albanian–Greek mountain borders. The first pluralist elections saw the victory of the Party of Labour of Albania (PLA).

Strikes were to continue also in 1992. Notwithstanding the deteriorating economic conditions, 'From April 1992 the resumption of widespread strike activities saw the BSPSH under pressure to continue to represent the radical demands coming from workers while the new government expected it to stabilize the political and economic situation' (Chiodi 2012). In order to stop the strikers, the government used paramilitary forces as well as its control over the media (Vickers and Pettifer 1997, 90).

Violence continued even under the non-communist government. On 26 August the workers of a munitions factory surrounded the town of Berat, took two public officers hostage, and set fire to the office building, pushing the government to some concessions (Chiodi 2012). According to Vickers (1997, 86), the conflict showed 'the unpredictability of outbreaks of violence in urban centres, and the fact that trade unions were still an independent force'. In December, during the hunger strike and occupation in the Bulquize chrome mine, paramilitary units intimidated workers by placing dynamite around the top of the mineshaft. A few weeks later, workers asking for the land compensations that had been promised to them were also met by paramilitary troops (Vickers 1997, 86). As Chiodi (2012, see also Vickers 1997, 132) noted: 'The problems with public order were not only due to violent strikes, looting and food riots connected with the economic collapse: the break down in state authority also resulted in a crime wave between 1991 and 1992. A few protests were organized to denounce the mounting of violence. The government reacted by channelling resources to improve policing and by frequently applying death penalty. In 1993 there were 15 executions in Tirana alone'.

An economic collapse of much higher proportions than in the other East European cases characterized the transition period. In fact,

the risk of famine during the winter of 1991–1992 in mountain areas of the North of the country distinguished the Albanian transition from any other regime change in the region. In the last few years of communist rule, the shortage of spare parts and fuel, as well as the absenteeism at work, had reduced the production to half of its capacity but once factories and mines had been abandoned, the entire economy was barely functioning. While the regime procrastinated the needed economic reforms, by late 1990 people started spontaneously to de-collectivize the land, abandoned factories and destroyed state properties. When the anti-communist mobilization increased from early 1991 onward, the economy was basically paralysed. On the one hand the economic crisis during the transition was so severe that almost everything came to be seen as a possible source of income, pieces of public buildings included. Literately anything was seized for this purpose: windows, chairs, tables from the buildings, manhole covers from the streets. Everything that could be taken away from public properties was dismantled and taken home. On the other hand, the political meaning of such acts should not be underestimated: the looting and the attacks to state properties also expressed the rage against the regime (Chiodi 2012).

Albania's transition started by contagion from Eastern Europe, but there were learning processes as well. The Albanian elites feared a Romanian evolution, and this pushed them to initiate some limited reforms. The events in neighbouring Yugoslavia also taught them lessons about what to avoid. The fear of a civil war could explain the reduced level of violence, as 'the communist elite initially endeavoured to limit the breadth of the political transformation but when it realized the impossibility to control changes from above it renounced to state violence. As for the opposition, during the first few months after the introduction of the multiparty system, the uncertain political context and the fear of losing the achievements made DP leaders cautious' (Chiodi 2012). Even though the army was under the complete control of the party, the military did not intervene in the conflict.

The lack of a civil society was, however, felt in the chaotic evolution of the post-transition phase. So, 'The peculiarity and the paradox of the Albanian transition is that such late-coming protest waves occurred in a situation of state disintegration. The totalitarian state that for 45 years had profoundly transformed the Albanian society fell down under large-scale exoduses, spontaneous de-collectivization of the land, the abandonment of factories and widespread destruction of public property. Such situation of state collapse, unprecedented for a European state, constituted a considerable encumbrance for the re-emerging Albanian civil society' (Chiodi 2012).

Violent Transition in The MENA Region

In the MENA region as well, violent mobilizations happened where civil society was weaker and the regime more repressive. This is, in particular, the case for Libya and Syria where, together with brutal and indiscriminate repression, defection from the military and international interventions fuelled civil war dynamics.

Libya

In Libya in 2011 and 2012, a popular uprising against long-term authoritarianism evolved into a civil conflict that was ultimately ended through the direct military involvement of a coalition of foreign states. Given the extremely repressive nature of the patrimonialistic regime, social movement organizations were nonexistent.

Although it has a small population, Libya holds the fifth largest oil reserves in the world (OPEC 2012). As Poljarevic (2012) put it, 'With a traditionally weak state administration, a tribal-based civil society and a cult-based political system, Libya is a state unlike any of its regional neighbors'. A weak post-colonial regime, Libya remained politically and administratively fragmented: 'Libyan society has been fractured, and every national institution, including the military, is divided by the cleavages of kinship and region. As opposed to Tunisia and Egypt, Libya has no system of political alliances, network of economic associations, or national organizations of any kind. Thus, what seemed to begin as nonviolent protests similar to those staged in Tunisia and Egypt soon became an all-out secession—or multiple separate secessions—from a failed state' (Anderson 2011, 6).

On 1 September 1969, Colonel Qaddafi, together with seventy officers, took over the government by a coup d'état, transforming the monarchy into a republic. Power then shifted to members of relatively disadvantaged (small) Libyan tribes and urban middle class professionals, emulating the 1952 Free Officers' 'revolution' in Egypt. Qaddafi's political project then moved towards a totalitarian-style state in which popular rhetoric combined with brutal repression in the control of all elements of civil and political life. State institutions remained underdeveloped, viewed as potential hotspots of opposition, and were left to deteriorate as Qaddafi disbanded the (tribally based) National Congressional Council. Tribal belonging and traditional values persisted in playing a role and were utilized by the regime in order to divide and control. Qaddafi in fact played the tribes against each other, but also tried to accommodate some of their requests for power resource sharing, privileging some over others. Together with patron–client networks, inter-tribal distrust therefore contributed to the dictator's power.

Within a very personalized form of patrimonialism, 'Direct interpersonal dealings came to dominate domestic administrative procedures, allowing a great amount of corruption and personal favoritism to dominate governmental practices. At the higher levels of government, Qaddafi would personally communicate with a limited number of representatives who would oversee and follow up all political decisions and their implementation' (Poljarevic 2012, see also Obeidi 2001).

In 1977, Qaddafi elaborated a political system he called *Jamahiriyyah* ('self-rule of the masses'), with local popular councils (Popular Social Committees) to deal with issues such as arbitration between individuals or land distribution, at the same time representing communal interests at the regional and national levels. De facto, 'the system of local councils was based on the personal interests of a selected few (usually local representatives sympathetic to the regime) who were supported by the Qaddafi regime and who could protect the regime's interests in return for various kinds of benefits (e.g. housing, building permits, employment etc.)' (Poljarevic 2012).

Additionally, in the distribution of arms and equipment to the army, the dictator privileged the regions inhabited by loyal tribes and, mistrusting the army, financed his own militia (Khosrokhavar 2012). The regime so developed an apparently loyal security system: 'The most important characteristic of these security organizations is that they are neither subject to institutional political control nor to control by the public but have been controlled exclusively by the Revolutionary Leadership led by Colonel Qadhafi' (Cerone 2011, 790). By the end of the 1990s a special elite-military 'People's Guard', composed of select loyalists, was formed with the task of protecting Qaddafi's family and the regime infrastructure, especially from 'internal enemies' (Mattes 2004). Libya so became a militarized state under the personalistic control of Qaddafi and his family. In fact, 'the regime did not operate only through sheer force, but also through creating a lasting sense of fear and suspicion among the general public' (Poljarevic 2012).

These characteristics of the regime jeopardized the development of a civil society. During the period of Qaddafi's rule, all independent forms of civil society organizations were prohibited (Clark 2011), while less than ten per cent of the people attended direct democratic institutions promoted by the regime. There were, however, latent tribal conflicts, involving especially Berbers, Warfalla, and Cyrenaica groups, and there was violent Islamism. Repressed Islamism escalated in fact into violence, as Libyan mujahideen returning from the Afghan–Soviet war formed the Libyan Islamic Fighting Group (LIFG) which, between 1995 and 1998, acted underground against the Qaddafi regime, plotting several attempts on his life (Ashour 2012). In the same period, the largest tribe, Warfalla, rebelled against a biased distribution of power. The government tended to respond to both sources of opposition with carrots and sticks. It repressed the leaders of the rebellions, but it also began a campaign of social and educational Islamization, increasing funding for mosque-run social programs and religious education, while co-opting some members of the Warfalla tribe.

Since the late 1990s, Qaddafi's attempt to normalize relations with the US and the EU brought about some, very limited, liberalization, but also the dismissal of more than a third of those employed in the public administration. This period was marked by a few manifestations of dissent. When some pressure for internal reform became visible, it was in the form of protests for compensation to the family of the killed prisoners. In the summer of 2000, anti-Qaddafi (family) slogans were shouted during disorders at a football match. Public grievances were expressed at a commemoration of the regime's massacre of 1,200 prisoners at Tripoli's Abu Salim prison in 1996. In 2006, ten protestors were killed during demonstrations against Italian minister Roberto Calderoli's appearance in public while wearing a T-shirt with Danish anti-Islam cartoons (*BBC News* 2006).

Notwithstanding this weakness of the civil society and the repressiveness of the regime, the Arab Spring contagion did reach Libya. On 13 January 2011, demonstrations against political corruption took place in several eastern and western cities (Abdel-Bak 2011). On 12 February, a small group of relatives and activists protested the arrest of a lawyer for human rights who had defended the families of the disappeared Abu Salim prisoners. On 13 and 14 February, a limited number of protests took place in several coastal cities, including Benghazi and the desert city Bani Walid.

Concerns initially addressed material needs. Protesting the delayed completion of housing projects in these coastal regions, people squatted in several hundred uninhabited, half-finished buildings. There were also local demonstrations against inefficient distribution of government services. The regime initially tolerated these protests, even allocating a US$24 billion investment fund to address the housing crisis (*Reuters* 2011). The protest politicized nevertheless, with demonstrations organized by the families of prisoners killed in the mentioned Abu Salim prison massacre (HRW 2003; *Reuters* 2009; Dziadosz 2011) as well as against the growing repression of those very protests, primarily but not only in Benghazi.

Protest then intensified from 15 February onwards. A day of rage was called on 17 February, with the mobilization spreading also to Benghazi where seven people were killed on 25 February. The initial slogan read 'Libya free, nation united' (Quesnay 2013, 114). Uprisings started then in eastern Libya, spreading after a few days to Tripoli. Benghazi was the eastern base of the anti-regime protests, which grew also in Zawiya, Misrata, and even in the capital, Tripoli. Two days later, protest and repression started to spiral into violent confrontations. As Poljarevic (2012) summarized,

> initially, disorganized groups, usually made up of a couple of hundred demonstrators, managed to incite larger crowds of people to join the violent clashes with the regime forces in the eastern urban centers. The protesters started to raid local security forces' headquarters, thereby accumulating weapons and ammunition. The regime quickly blocked all social network sites, Al-Jazeera, youtube, and other Internet-based media outlets. At this point, the revolutionaries resorted to wireless communication technology. GSM mobile and satellite phones became by far the most important devices in coordinating the revolutionaries' actions throughout the country.

About 300–400 people were killed in the first half of February (FIDH 2011; Schemm 2011), while violent clashes spread quickly to the capital, Misrata (the third largest city), Ajdabiya, and other cities. At the same time, there was however also a quick development of NGOs to support and protect the communities. In March a Coalition of Libyan NGOs was created, grouping 240 NGOs (Quesnay 2013, 124).

The development of the events was clearly influenced by the Egyptian and Tunisian rebellions. Lessons were learned by people emulating protest, but also by the dictator attempting to avoid the fate of his counterparts in those countries. As Poljarevic (2012) noted,

> The Libyan popular uprising in February 2011 can be attributed first of all to a turning point in the growth of the regime-critical section of the population, and, second, to the precipitous falls of the two neighboring countries' long-term authoritarian regimes. These two status quo disrupting processes contributed to initiate the first period of the transition during which popular demands for improved public services evolved into political claims-making events. These increasingly more demanding events climaxed on February 16 when about 500 people gathered in the central square of Benghazi to demonstrate against the regime. The seemingly well-prepared protesters seemed to have a particular demand, the release of several human rights advocates, including the lawyer Fathi Terbil arrested just days before. The protesters used gasoline-filled bottles as home-made bombs and on this particular occasion the security forces cracked down on the protest first with water cannons and then with rubber bullets, and then resorted to live ammunition.

Following the example of Tahrir, Benghazi protestors set up a camp in the middle of the city (Jacinto 2011), in Liberation Square, voicing numerous criticisms against the regime—which used brutal force to repress this protest as well, but also released over a hundred imprisoned Islamists. On 17 February 2011, on the anniversary of Benghazi's anti-regime soccer rally, activists called for a Day of Rage, starting what was to be known as the 17 February Revolution. Violence escalated in various parts of the country, while the regime sent a text message warning citizens that the state security would use force to disperse any collective actions perceived as promoting public sedition (Reporters Without Borders 2011).

Even though the regime successfully preempted demonstrations in the western regions, protest grew in size and frequency, partly thanks to some coordination. After the first defections from the regime, the opposition's coordinating body, the National Transitional Council (NTC), was founded on 27 February (Abbas and Blair 2011). As for the oppositional diaspora, protestors included exiled Libyans (Ahmida 2012), who helped spread abroad information on the resistance as well as facilitating communication inside—even if, 'given the very different trajectory of the Libyan uprising—namely, its rapid metamorphosis from unarmed protests to armed rebellion to international war—the importance of social media as a catalyzing force for revolution took a back seat. Twitter's influence paled in comparison to NATO bombs' (Fahim et al. 2011, A1). In a country with seventy per cent unemployment among young people, unemployed young men constituted the largest part of the protestors on the streets. Women, especially the relatives of the victims of the Abu Salim massacre in 1996, also played an important role in initiating the protest, as well as in the provision of logistical support during the conflicts.

As in Tunisia and Egypt, calls for dignity, freedom, and justice were frequent, sometimes accompanied by claims for more job opportunities, improved economic conditions, and better education (Michael 2011). The Abu Salim massacre, the frequent disappearances of well-known public intellectuals, everyday police brutality, and corruption were often mentioned during the uprisings. Increased internet access enabled reports of police repression to spread. The killing of protestors fuelled the mobilization. Even though clans and tribes were more influent than ideological groups in organizing collective action, an analysis of tribes' issued statements revealed a common call for national unity or national salvation rather than reflecting tribal interests (Bamyeh 2011).

In contrast to Egypt and Tunisia, however, were the level and style of the regime's repression as well as the deployment of the army and foreign mercenaries against the protestors. In March, the conflict moved in fact into a civil war phase, with external military intervention. As the brutality of the fights increased, on 17 March the UN Security Council approved a resolution imposing a no-fly zone over Libya; soon thereafter, US and French warships in the Mediterranean started bombing Qaddafi's security forces on the outskirts of Benghazi, allowing the rebels to advance towards the west (United Nations 2011). The opposition then received aid in terms of communication equipment, training, and above all military support from a substantial number of countries and NATO. NATO's aerial forces helped the rebels advance to the east, culminating in the fall of Tripoli on 20 August and the killing of Mu'ammar Qaddafi and one of his sons in Sirte on 20 October.

Even if with a very low level of organizational structuration, protests weakened a regime that had seemed stable before mobilization started. Elites' disalignment developed quickly, in fact, as early as February. Among the most important government officials who resigned from their posts and joined the opposition were Qaddafi's Justice Minister, Mustafa Abdul Jaleel (who resigned on 21 February), and Interior Minister Abdul-Fattah Yunis (22 February), who was also an army general and went on to head a large part of the opposition forces. Defecting government officials later included high-profile figures such as Mahmoud Jibril (former head of National Planning Council of Libya, an intergovernmental body set up by Saif al-Qaddafi to introduce a neo-liberal economic system in Libya), Ali Essawi (former deputy foreign minister), and Qaddafi's close aide Abdel-Salam Jalloud. During the revolt, representatives of economic interests—such as the Arabian Gulf Oil Company, the second-largest state-owned oil company in Libya—also defected to the rebels, as did Islamic leaders and clerics, among them the Network of Free Ulema and some key tribes such as Warfalla, Tuareg, and Magarha. As Poljarevic (2012) summarized,

> Initial high-level defectors from the regime contributed much needed political and military leadership, which in turn facilitated much needed logistical knowledge in creating an opposition structure within the increasingly violent conflict. Moreover, it seems that the availability of Internet connections and other information technology devices (e.g. mobile and satellite phones, radio etc.) further met the need for inexpensive modes of information dissemination and the coordination of political and military activities among the relatively fragmented sections of the political opposition (i.e. the NTC's various branches, its armed wing and the numerous local militias). This is relevant as the main bulk of opposition organizers, if not the outright leaders, were based abroad. The increased availability of Internet services and relatively underdeveloped state mechanisms for controlling information flows allowed opposition groups to communicate, exchange information, discuss and coordinate activities to some extent.

The collapse of the regime was triggered by the lost support of the key Libyan tribes as well as of key individuals within the government and the army. A quick loss of territorial control by the regime security forces has been linked to Libya's geographic structure, with population concentrated in Tripoli and Benghazi and a desert in between. The military conflict ended on 23 October 2011 (Saleh and Rohan 2011) with the regime's breakdown. Parliamentary elections took place on 7 July 2012 and the official power transfer from the NTC to the Libyan parliament on 8 August. However, tensions between tribal elites from east and west (Cyrenaica and Tripolitania), with respective militias, continued to fuel insecurity, under still strained economic conditions.

Syria

Still in the wake of Tunisian and Egyptian events, in Syria, as well, the dynamics of the protests dramatically changed during the upheavals evolution. Mobilization started in March 2011 in the southern city of Dara', moving

> From largely peaceful protests (that were immediately repressed using live ammunition by police) to a full out civil war in which an increasing amount of heavily armed and well trained cadre of army defectors, regular Syrian and foreign fighters are staging an armed insurrection against the regime of Bashar al-Assad. Blaming salafis and armed gangs, supported by the US and Israeli for the disorders, the

regime promised however also reform (while however help after the shocks to the international food supply chain had been promised but not implemented) (Gelvin 2011, 108–9).

The opposition was heterogeneous, being composed of human rights groups, but also spontaneous crowds, as well as more traditional oppositional actors such as Kurds, MBs, tribal leaders, and oppositional politicians, who were then joined by army deserters (Gelvin 2011). Also artists mobilized; cineastes signed a petition, issued on 20 May, for reform against repression, calling for 'the end of the control of the security forces on the citizens, the end of their impunity to kill, put in prison and provoke peaceful demonstrators' (Boex 2013, 94).

In fact, lacking the capacity to effectively repress the dissent, the regime resorted to most brutal means, such as random bombings of civilian quarters by fighter jets. After peaceful protests from March to June, violence then increased on both sides of the conflict, with actual civil war developing from July on and increasing internationalization of the conflict.

As in Libya, civil society was weak. Before 2011, sporadic mobilizations had included the so-called 'Damascus Spring' in 2001, the Kurdish uprising of 2004, and the Sadnaya prison riots in 2008. With mobilization at the beginning of Bashar al-Assad's presidency, some opposition developed among intellectuals, especially in Damascus, with public discussion forums and published declarations. When they started calling for democratic reforms, however, arrests blocked them from public protest, although some networks remained active. Public critical declarations demanding political liberalizations also emerged after the assassination of former Lebanese President Rafiq Hariri in February 2005, with the aim of bridging different actors in the mobilization (Landis and Pace 2007). Repression followed this time as well.

After the fall of Saddam Hussein, Kurds in Syria also hoped for more freedoms, only to be disillusioned by the repression that followed riots during a football match in the (majority Kurdish) town of Qamishli in March 2004, with police firing at the Kurdish crowd. In a quick escalation, hundreds of thousands protested against repression and for more freedom (Landis and Pace 2007, 53–4), but encountered a harsh reaction: thirty-six people died, 200 were wounded, about 2,000 arrested, many tortured (Amnesty International 2005). In the same period, some religious freedom fuelled *dawa'* related (educational) activities, which were then themselves repressed. Between 2003 and 2009, Salafist Jihadi groups were also active, in some cases getting involved in anti-American activities in Iraq. In July 2008, Islamist prisoners took over the Sadnaya prison in protest against poor living standards.

Even this weak civil society mobilized, however, in the wake of the Tunisian and Egyptian upheavals. While the day of rage called on 1 February 2011 had little resonance, a turning point was, instead, the protests on 6 March in

Dara'. There, young people (none older than fifteen) were arrested and tortured for writing '*As-sha'ab yurid isqat an-nizam*' (the people want the fall of the regime) on a wall. Reportedly, the local governor responded to requests for their release by telling family members and friends that if they missed their children so much, they should give him their wives, and he would make some new children. On 11 March, relatives of the arrested youths marched to the governor's house, where they were shot at with bullets. Nevertheless, mobilization continued, on 15, and again on 18 March, after Friday prayers. About 3,000 people joined the protest, and four were killed. Their funerals on the following day were the occasion for large protests, during which local Ba'ath party offices were attacked and burned.

Using (new) social media and old social and religious networks, protest spread into a Friday of Dignity. Fridays of Rage were also organized in Damascus, Homs, Idlib, and Banyas. Initially small, the number of protestors increased quickly, so on the following two Fridays (on 25 March and 1 April), protests happened in Homs, Dara', and Banyas, mobilizing from hundreds to a few thousand people. As Friday prayers were the occasion for people to gather, protests often started there even if the claims were explicitly non-religious, targeting the (power of) the security services and corruption and calling for political liberalization. Repression intensified, then: on 25 March, nineteen were killed, and twenty-nine on the next Friday, funerals then providing new occasions to mobilize.

After they met at rallies, protestors built councils, which tended to institutionalize into Local Coordination Committees (LCCs) with the task of organizing protests, gathering information and disseminating it. Even if Kurds, Sunnis, or other minority groups often dominated in terms of numbers, committees aimed at being inclusive. Demands for reform dominated in the beginning. Trans-sectarian appeals were also spread by the movement: 'we Syrian are one people', declared the singer and activist, Fadwa Soliman (Khosrokhavar 2012, 218), and a song read 'Come on, Bashar, leave.... You, the US agent! The Syrian people will not accept humiliation anymore' (Khosrokhavar 2012, 241).

Retreating from areas such as Homs and Hama, the regime focused repression on the two main cities of Aleppo and Damascus, while at the same time making some concessions. This only fuelled protest, as on 8 April 2011, hundreds of thousands mobilized in various Syrian cities on the 'Friday of Patience' (*sumud*); seventy-three protestors were killed. A week later, tens of thousands again mobilized in a 'Friday of Insistence', with the coercive regime apparatuses killing yet another eleven protestors.

Notwithstanding heavy repression, efforts at mobilizing brought about the creation of an umbrella organization for the local committees: the Local Coordinating Committees of Syria (LCCS). Claims had at this point escalated into requests for the fall of the regime, while forms of action, which followed the Tunisian and Egyptian examples, usually remained non-violent. Protestors learned to make use of posters and songs, Facebook pages and youtube videos and, in some localities, as in Hama, they tried to build camps on central squares.

As the regime continued to use live ammunition, although still unable to suppress opposition, the situation escalated, notwithstanding LCCS calls for peaceful protest. At the start of Ramadan of 2011, after about five months of mobilization, 2,000 had been killed, with another thousand slain by the end of the month. Violence then increased on the part of the protestors as well, initially mainly in little-organized attacks against regime officials, security services, army personnel, and the Ba'ath party buildings. The violence then became more organized, as Syrian soldiers started to defect and violent uprisings succeeded in pulling down the dictator in Libya. Defecting soldiers brought to the opposition army and military expertise, together with some trust in armed mobilization.

While repression increased defections from the army, the Libyan example showed the effectiveness of violent rebellion. In addition, repression was taken as proof of the ineffectiveness of the alternative, non-violent option—this especially after the killing of 138 during the first day of Ramadan, and the shelling and takeover of Hama and Deir ez-Zor as well as Idlib and Latakya in August. Successful assassinations of members of the Syrian security elites on 19 July 2012 in Damascus confirmed the vulnerability of the regime to armed attacks. Support from Saudi Arabia and Qatar strengthened the Islamist wing of the opposition over the secular one.

In June, militias also began to spring up in various parts of the country, initially with defensive aims. Militias were formed on the basis of friendships, clan allegiances, and neighbourhood solidarity. Despite the initial understanding that violence by the protestors was to be avoided as it would fuel violence by the regime, violent defensive reactions to violent regime repression started to spread. On 6 June 2011 at Jisr as-Shourough there was, apparently, one of the first liberations of a town through local residents' ambush of the army and government buildings. Notwithstanding heavy army intervention, which allowed the regime to retake control, the example was followed.

In a macabre dance, rebels freed cities, which the regime would then re-occupy while 'residents became increasingly well armed, trained and organized in resisting violent Syrian repression. Increasingly non-violent protests followed the dynamic of the violent conflict (for instance the "Friday of the Free Army" on 14 October 2011) instead of the other way around' (Donker 2012a). The most active regions were those around Idlib, Homs, and Hama—a conservative Sunni majority region, with mobilized shaykhs such as Adnan al-Arour—as well as the Kurdish areas.

Soldiers' defections also increased in numbers and level of organization; although involving only a small number of Sunni rank-and-file soldiers (while the Alawi in power remained loyal), they kept providing the opposition with armies and military expertise. A turning point in the spiral of escalation was in fact, on 29 July 2011, the foundation of the Free Syrian Army (FSA), which aimed at promoting desertions and protecting civilians from repression.

If the FSA and popular militias proclaimed their task as protecting the people, they more and more often acted proactively. Initially gathering around small cliques of relatives, clan members, or followers of shaykhs, they later tended to become increasingly structured and well trained. Jihadists, including Arabs from other countries in the region, also joined militias; al-Qaeda Salafists are said to have formed their own group, autonomous from the FSA or the National Coalition.

Religious and ethnic enmities were in fact mobilized, fuelling radicalization. With time passing, 'The uprising has taken an increasing sectarian tone, pitting the Sunni majority against the Alawi minority, and has shown the lengths to which the regime and its supporters will go to defend their own survival' (Donker 2012a).

External interventions helped militarization. On 18 July 2012, the FSA and the Jihadi group Liwa al-Islam (Brigade of Islam) claimed responsibility for the killing of Asef Shawkat (the minister of defense) and three other elite security leaders. Rebels then attacked both Damascus and Aleppo, the attacks showing increasing inter-militia coordination and often support from Gulf countries. By 18 July 2012, around 20,000 had died during the uprisings. With a civil war in action, and as the coordinator committees left ground to the militias, many people also started to flee from their homes and the risk of violence. With the conflict ever escalating, the death toll in November 2012 was around 40,000.

With the escalation, internationalization also increased. Based on a Syrian diaspora that had mobilized since the very beginning, the so-called Syrian National Council (SNC) was founded on 23 August 2011. After claims of corruption and domination by the MB spread, in November 2012 it was superseded by the National Coalition for Syrian Revolutionary and Opposition Forces, or National Coalition (NC). Built around Syrians in exile, these groups tried to find international allies, but had weak ties at home. Inside the country, Palestinian refugees also took positions, and Kurds contacted foreign Kurdish parties (mainly the PKK and Iraqi Kurdistan Democratic Party, KDP). Turkey and Iraq became more involved, as international allies of the regime took sides; but those countries were also often internally divided, with ethnic and religious groups supporting the Syrian opposition. In general, in fact, as Donker (2012a) summarized,

international attempts at finding a resolution have been marked by the lack of consensus within the United Nations Security Council (UNSC) where Russia vetoed any (US, French and British) attempts at formulating a binding resolution against the Syrian regime. The furthest these attempts came was a temporary truce in April 2012 that UN observers would help implement. Though in the first weeks a decrease in hostilities could be observed, the cease-fire did not hold and the conflict eventually escalated further. Other UN based peace-plans have not been successful in getting any kind of project or road map on the ground (a recent 'Eid ceasefire' did not materialize for instance). As result international engagement has mostly taken place outside a UN framework: either bilaterally or through regional organizations.

At the same time, as single countries provided arms to the regime (see Russia and Iran), international support (from countries such as Saudi Arabia, Qatar, and Turkey) went to the rebels. Some Ulama (religious scholars) and Shaykhs (religious leaders) sided either with the regime (especially those of Sufi inclination) or the opposition (including some Salafists). As Donker (2012a) recalled, the oppositional Shaykhs 'have often taken a very active role in the uprising, with the Rifai' brothers apparently using their extensive contacts in the Gulf for financing and organizing secret arms purchases and smuggling them into the country'.

The uprising mobilized long-lasting opponents of the regime. Some came from the 'Damascus declaration', signed in October 2005, which had asked for the 'establishment of a democratic national regime' through a process that was imagined as 'peaceful, gradual, founded on accord, and based on dialogue'. Kurdish parties, the Committees for the Revival of Civil Society (emerged from 2001 'Damascus Spring'), as well as elite oppositional leaders had signed the mentioned petition as well as mobilizing later on. MBs in exile also mobilized, in the mid-2000s attempting, without success, to create a government in exile. In contrast, LCCs involved young people without previous political socialization. Unions, which had been co-opted by the regime, were instead absent from the uprisings (Hinnebusch 1993) as were student organizations, even if workers and students mobilized as individual citizens.

The characteristics of the Syrian regime surely provided constraints and opportunities for the opposition. Syria is an ethnically heterogeneous country, with ethnic minorities including Kurds, Palestinians, and Armenians, as well as religious minorities such as Christians, Druze, Sunnis, Shiites, Alawis and Ismaelis (as specific Shiite denominations), and small communities of Jews. As President Hafez al-Assad took power in 1970, he built the power of the Alawi tribe in the army (Perthes 1992). The regime addressed the various groups through patronage, as 'The army, intelligence services and Ba'ath party organizations became an instrument for institutionalized corruption in which powerful patrons secured support from lower ranking members, via a highly developed clientalist system' (Donker 2012a). Party connections were

fundamental for business, and the military became a main political and economic actor (Mora and Wiktorowicz 2003, 109). In the late 1970s, corruption
apparently also involved the protection of drug cartels, whose militias were
tolerated (Salih 2012). However, the economic recession of the mid-1970s and
related economic liberalization and privatization of state companies affected
the state capacity for patronage, increasing the power and revenues of a few
protected individuals (Perthes 1992, 124) while social inequalities increased.

The Syrian MB profited from related dissatisfaction, framing the problems
as related to the Alawi minority's dominance. In February 1982 in the city
of Hama there were fights between Islamists and the army, after the former
had proclaimed the city as 'liberated', and regime troops started shelling the
city. Between 5,000 and 40,000 civilians died, as well as thousands of regime
soldiers and about 500 mujahideen (Lobmayer 1995, 325–7). The uprising
having remained isolated to Sunni Muslims, it was then defeated, and with
it the potential for Islamic political organizations, which were now strongly
repressed.

Bashar al-Assad followed his father as Syrian President in June 2000, promising political liberalization; however, after the US invasion of Iraq, Syria
became internationally isolated. The president and his close family were at
the core of the regime, occupying leading positions in the army (al-Assad's
brother), military intelligence (his brother-in-law and one cousin), and the
economy. In general, clan loyalty also played a role, as Alawi elites continued
support for the regime, while defectors were Sunnis.

These contextual conditions influenced the dynamics of the uprising in
several ways. As Donker (2012a) summarized:

> First, the core pillars of the regime have remained stable throughout the uprising.
> The close connection between regime, security services and army—one can state
> that the army and intelligence services *are* the regime—renders that many within
> these organizations have a direct interest in regime maintenance. Stronger still,
> as many within the top echelons of power are Alawi, they fear the return of Sunni
> dominance as was the situation before the 1960s. Many feel they are fighting for
> their own survival—and will go to any extent to defend their group. As repression
> mounted—and Sunni feelings of vengeance towards Alawis increased—this effect
> exacerbated. Some regime supporters, by and large from (Alawi) minorities, have
> been given weapons to 'defend' their towns. Pro-regime militias were the result,
> soon named after regime related militias long forgotten: the Shabiha—Ghosts—
> of the 1970s. Now not involved in drug trade, they became a crucial tool in the
> application of repressive measures across the nation.

There were, moreover, internal tensions between different army divisions
and intelligence services, as state institutions being influenced by informal
allocation of power, intelligence services, and army divisions became sort of

states-within-states, some mobilizing larger resources than the army (Donker 2012a). As Alawi dominated militias emerged, differences increased, with these groups being accused of having perpetrated the most brutal attacks (Donker 2012a). An additional effect was the strong repression of protests that had thwarted political organizations, leaving religious, tribal, clan, and family ties as the main bases of identification and networking. So,

> pre-existing tribal and clan ties structured early dynamics of the uprising, with families and clan members going out in the first week in Dara'. We also see that protests emerge after (Friday) prayers, as this is the only occasion on which a large group of people could be gathered without being immediately arrested. Also religious leaders were forced to take sides in the uprising, due to the importance of religious institutions as mobilization structures. At the same time, the uprising itself was explicitly non-religious: protesters were not making any 'Islamic' demands as the previous (1979–82) uprising had shown the dangers of an uprising falling into the 'sectarian trap' (Donker 2012a).

In sum, brutal repression had thwarted the development of a civil society, but repressed cleavages re-emerged during the uprising. While the cross-national diffusion of the ideas of the Arab Spring brought about some mobilization on demands for freedom and non-violent repertoires dominated in the beginning, repression fuelled radicalization into civil war.

Violent Uprisings: A Summary

Violent uprisings do not require strong civil society organizational structures. Rather, they seem to develop when very repressive regimes have long thwarted any development of an autonomous associational life—let alone, of social movements. In all the cases we analysed, a weak civil society struggled against with internationally isolated regimes, facing increasing economic as well as political challenges.

In these situations, a brutal regime reaction to protests fuelled escalation. Research on democracies has already pointed at the relevance of encounters with unjust authorities in processes of radicalization. Empirical research has indicated that the policing of protest not only functions as an indicator of the willingness of the political authority to listen to the voices of protestors, but also affects the evolution of protest. Increasing the costs of protesting, repression might reduce the individual's availability to participate. However, the sense of injustice as well as the creation of intense feelings of identification and solidarity can strengthen the motivation to oppose an unjust and brutal regime (Davenport 2005a, 2005b; della Porta and Piazza 2008; Francisco 2005). So, especially when the protest is widespread and well supported, repression can backfire due to outrage about police disrespect for citizens' rights at the national as well as the transnational level (Davenport 2005b; Francisco 2005). Protest policing might also influence the organizational forms social movements use, for instance by spreading a sense of mutual mistrust through the use of infiltration (e.g. Fernandez 2008). Repression has also been said to play a major role in social movements in authoritarian regimes, as 'violence is only one of myriad possibilities in repertoires of contention and becomes most likely where regimes attempt to crush Islamic activism through broad repressive measures that leave few alternatives' (Hafez and Wiktorowicz 2004, 62). Authoritarian regimes have been said to fuel humiliation and, then, violence. This clearly happened in our cases.

Police control tends to impact the repertoires of protest through a reciprocal adaptation (or sometimes, escalation) of police and demonstrators' tactics (della Porta 1995). In fact, protest and its policing 'is a dance between those who challenge authority, speak true to power, and hope for a more just world and those who wish to extend their privilege and power' (Fernandez 2008, 171). Cross-nationally and transnationally, social movement and police strategies interact with each other in a process of double diffusion (della Porta and Tarrow 2012).

Also in our cases, we have seen moments of escalations in eventful democratization and even in participated pacts. They were, however, much more radical in Romania and Albania as well as (in different forms and greater degrees) in Libya and Syria. Involved in the respective waves of protest for democracy of 1989 and 2011, weak and fragmented civil society organizations started protests, which emulated those in neighbouring countries. To them, the regimes reacted brutally. As violence generated violence, armed forces split between regime loyals and regime opponents. Those who abandoned the regime, however, brought with them arms and military skills, which heavily affected the development of the conflicts, although with varying outcomes. More limited escalation in Romania and Albania brought about regimes that presented continuities with previous ones. Civil wars in Libya and Syria interacted with military involvement of superpowers against the dictators, but also (in Syria) with international alliances of the regime with Russia, Iran, and China. As guns became audible, civil society was silenced. While in both Romania and Albania the prospect and requirements of joining the EU smoothed escalation through promises of integration, in Libya and Syria foreign military intervention challenged the dictators, but also cost many lives among the civil population, with still open outcomes.

The repressive capacity of the regime emerged as central in the cases analysed here. According to comparative analyses (e.g. Nepstad 2011), in several cases civil resistance was spurred by blatant acts of repression, in others by

265

opening opportunities. Religious institutions, in particular, offered important free spaces. Economic crises and divided elites were also important, especially when they involved the loss of sanctioning power. Defection was facilitated in these cases by non-violent strategies, the sharing of a collective identity with the protestors, plus emulation. Boycotts and strikes have often been important in reducing the sanctioning power of the regime.

In this account, internal class and ethnic divisions can weaken the opponents, while the position of the military emerges as pivotal in the violent evolution of the confrontations, especially so in Libya and Syria. As Nepstad (2011) noted, while non-violent revolutions that win the support of the military tend to succeed, when the military is composed of different ethnic groups, endowed with different power, it is difficult for the army as a whole to side with the opposition. Rather, there will be defectors, and this will cause violent developments (as in Syria, where the army officers are Alawis, and rank-and-file mainly Sunnis).

Beyond the position of the military, violence might be produced by other characteristics of the regime, linked to the dominant political economy. In this direction, Elisabeth Wood (2000) pointed in fact at the intertwining of political and economic power in the repression and exploitation of the masses. In these cases, democratization often involved (at least partially) violent insurgencies. Past and present brutal repression impacted heavily on the activists' choices, reducing faith in a peaceful surrender of incumbents.

This was the case, for instance, in El Salvador, where the memory of *la matanza*, with 17,000 protestors killed during a 1932 insurrection that mobilized communists and indios, remained alive, influencing the new waves of protest that followed some political liberalization (Wood 2000). Violence and non-violent forms interacted during the long struggle. In the 1970s, unrest persisted notwithstanding repression, supported by members of the Catholic Church, who organized bible reading groups in the countryside. From there, a Christian federation of Salvadoran peasants developed, asking for land and better working conditions. But, in the early 1970s, from splits in the communist party, the Popular Revolutionary Army and the Popular Liberation Forces also started to organize underground, although with close ties with mass organizations. Students, workers, and peasants joined forces in the struggle for democratization, and all faced heavy and indiscriminate repression. In the 1980s, while the brutality of the regime raised domestic and international criticism, repression increased support for the guerrillas, especially after the assassination in 1980 of the archbishop Oscar Romero, who became a martyr of the movement. Especially indiscriminate repression against the peasants ended up fuelling support for the guerrillas. Also in our cases, strong repression thwarted, but did not destroyed, opposition. While for a long time, state brutality kept open contestation at bay, at a certain moment, police intervention started to enrage citizens more than scaring them.

If repression was a cost, resistance became a reward in itself. As a peasant told Elisabeth Wood, 'We were despised by the rich. We were seen as animals, working from 4:00 and without even enough to put the kids in school. This is the origin of the war: there was no alternative. The only alternative was the madness of desperation' (Wood 2000, 48). In our violent uprisings as well, participation then produced its own incentives, 'because participating in the organizations also meant participating in a greater movement, the experience of collective agency against the landlords and the state appealed to many activists: it undermined any self-perception that the disdain of the landlords had a basis in fact' (Wood 2000, 50). Similarly in our cases, memories of regime brutality worked as a constraint to mobilization in some moments, but in others fuelled protest as the only way to express a call for dignity. The costs of compliance with the regime became, that is, unbearable.

9

In The Name of The Nation: Nationalism as Opportunity and Risk

Introduction

> *Yugoslavia had neither a velvet revolution nor a velvet divorce. Midway through 1991 two of its six constituent republics, Slovenia and Croatia, declared their independence, provoking a vicious civil war that spread in 1992 to Bosnia and Herzegovina. Ethnic emotions run deep throughout Eastern Europe, but nowhere did they reach the level of bestiality as they did in Yugoslavia.... What happened? How did Yugoslavia, the first Communist state to break with the Soviet Union and the most open Communist state in the world in the 1960s, come to this depressing impasse?* (Stokes 1993, 218).

Nationalist mobilizations in the Yugoslavia federation, which reached the extreme brutality of civil war, in fact worked as a challenge to peaceful democratization. We have seen that democratization struggles often developed an appeal to the nation: as they needed to speak in the name of the people, references to shared patriotism were frequent. However, nationalism has also been considered as a potential risk for democratization processes. As a strong identity provider, ethnicity (defined as a familiar group of people sharing a culture, origins of language) does not necessarily have a relationship to the nation. It might, however, be mobilized in ethno-nationalist movements, often steered by mass media, political office holders, and the political rhetoric of charismatic leaders (Bozik 1999). But there are very different framing strategies and content related to ethno-nationalist identities, which could in some cases thwart and in others facilitate democratization processes.

A main distinction has been made between inclusive and exclusive nationalism. Classical works on the creation of the nation-state stressed the role of the nation (and nationalism) in its evolution. As Rokkan and Urwin (1983) noted, while intellectuals create the imagined (national) community, minority groups can mobilize against the centre, especially when the presence of a minority language or religion works as glue, while political and economic inequalities produce dissatisfaction among those minorities. Concentration in a certain territory, geostrategic importance, traditions of autonomous government, and possession of various types of resources often converge in the mobilization of ethno-nationalist movements. While the first wave of protests of the peripheries in Europe, during industrial and democratic revolutions, often developed an exclusive definition of the ethnic identity as race-based, the ethno-nationalist movements of the 1970s and 80s were usually more inclusive, defining their identity in cultural terms. Particular attention was paid here to the defence of linguistic and cultural traditions, often mixed with requests for social justice and political autonomy (Melucci and Diani 1992; Biorcio 1997). The evolution of Basque nationalism—from the appeal to the genetic purity of the race, considered as jeopardized by increasing immigration during the nineteenth century, to the opposition to colonial capitalism in the name of a culture and in alliance with the working class since the 1960s—is an often cited example of this evolution.

In fact, the 1970s saw not only the rise of new social movements, but also the revival of initiatives taken by 'old' collective actors such as the working class and ethno-linguistic minorities. The latter's capacity for mobilization has been reproduced in a variety of forms in recent years (Smith 1981; Melucci and Diani 1992; Breuilly 1993; Connor 1994).

Inclusive framings within nations have been said to have developed within multi-level attachments. Research on social movements thus identified a shift from nationalist identities with a strong ethnic component to identities that combine references to the nation with greater attention to multicultural-ism and the cohabitation of diverse cultural groups (Johnston 1991; Melucci 1996). While national and sub-national identities did not fade, the impact of values from other cultures and the growth of interactions between cultures increased the number of identifications that interwove into and competed with those anchored in the territory. In fact,

Western ethno-national movements of the 1960s and 1970s were often successful in linking traditional themes of peripheral nationalism, such as territory or language, which were previously perceived to be predominantly a conservative issue, with radical, anti-establishment perspectives typical of movements of that period. The defence of local culture thus came to be associated with youth counterculture, in a common reaction to mass culture. At the same time, the defence of territory took on new meanings in the light of the anti-militarist and anti-nuclear struggles of the period, to which was added the aspiration to reduce the control which the politico-military elites of centralized states had of peripheral territories. The critique of the distortion of capitalist development provided a common base for challenges to the economic subordination of 'internal colonies' and for solidarity with third world anti-colonialist movements (della Porta and Diani 2006, 83).

In these cases, ethno-nationalist appeals were often bridged with ones for democratization.

Social movement studies also pointed, however, at the emergence of exclusive, xenophobic reactions to the intensification of transnational contacts. As globalization in fact transforms everyday life, it is said to lead to local resistance oriented to defending cultural traditions against the intrusion of foreign ideas and global issues (Giddens 1990). The resurgence of forms of exclusive nationalism, ethnic movements, religious mobilizations, and Islamic (and other) fundamentalism have been read as in part a reaction to this type of intrusion. In addition, during democratization processes, ethno-nationalism was often bridged within a conservative religious tradition. So, 'The celebrations of the orthodox church provided the context for the production and spread of nationalist interpretative frames in the Baltic republics at the time of their involuntary association with the Soviet Union. The Catalan and Basque churches played a similar role during the Francoist period in Spain' (della Porta and Diani 2006, 110).

In sum, ethno-nationalist movements have contributed either to democratization, or to its opposite, and this has often being related to the very definition of the nation. Snyder (2000) has distinguished, in particular, different types of nationalism, linking them to democratic projects. In what he calls civic nationalism, there is an inclusive definition of the nation, which is strong, with political institutions and elites adaptable to democracy, as they do not fear it; in ethnic (exclusive) nationalism, the nation is weak and the elites are not adaptable to democracy. Lacking effective democratic institutions, political leaders try to create loyalty though cultural attachments (the other two types he calls revolutionary or counter-revolutionary).

These different framings have been linked to different conditions. As Laitin (2007) noted, violence is not intrinsically related with nationalism—on the contrary, inter-ethnic cooperation is much more frequent than radicalized conflicts. Comparing violence fuelled by ethnic nationalism during transitions to democracy in Eastern Europe, Snyder (2000) suggested that nationalism grows with intermediate levels of economic development, a quick and powerful rise of threats to elites through demands for participation, and ethno-federalist institutions. It has spread in particular in imperial centres that inherited military power from former empires. Patronage politics has also supported this development (Snyder 2000). According to Laitin (2007), it is in particular the weakness of the state which allows for escalation.

Even if no one-to-one relation exists between the definition of ethnic identity and the forms of action nationalism adopts, exclusive definitions are more likely to produce action radicalization. Identity politics, such as in ethnic conflicts, often led to religious war and racial violence (Eder 2003). Urban riots staged by excluded ethnic minorities as well as exclusionary riots against ethnic minorities (della Porta and Gbikpi 2012), and terrorist attacks by groups who believed in their own racial superiority against people belonging to other ethnic groups have been used in order to achieve ethnic cleansing.

In this chapter, I will address the issue of the relations between ethno-nationalism and democratization, looking at the different experiences represented by the Baltic republics, as a case of democratization through nationalist uprisings, and—vice-versa—to the Balkans as a case in which nationalism not only jeopardized the democratization process, but also resulted in brutal civil wars. While I will not directly analyse the inclusiveness versus exclusiveness of the ethnic framing, I will look at its bridging with issues of human rights and democracy. In particular, I will stress that (different) ethno-nationalist discourses and practices developed in action, through the activation of nationalist entrepreneurs in government and/or the opposition.

A prophetic-style leader who used emotional appeals to ethno-nationalist roots, the Serbian leader Milošević claimed victories such as an anti-bureaucratic revolution, the protection of Serbs in Kosovo, the unification of all Serbs in a single state (Malešević 2002). Differently, in the Baltic case, nationalism tended to be bridged with calls for democracy, with the three republics coordinating rather than competing against the common Russian enemy.

Nationalism and Democratization in The Baltic Republics

The independence movements in the Baltic countries were early risers in a broader wave of nationalist protests within the Soviet Union, which was triggered by political and economic liberalization under Gorbachev. Democratization was not the central frame but could develop within an ethno-nationalist discourse that claimed independence from a dictatorship. The three Baltic republics had in fact lost their independence after their forceful incorporation into the Soviet Union, following the much-contested Molotov–Ribbentrop Pact on 29 August 1939. Nationalist mobilizations sporadically emerged, beginning in the 1950s and increasing in the 1960s, initially claiming some autonomy. As Beissinger (2002, 54) observed:

> Out of 185 mass demonstrations identified with 100 participants or more that took place in the USSR between 1965 and 1986, only 20 raised the issue of secession, and all of these were located in the Baltics. The largest occurred in Vilnius on October 10, 1977, in the aftermath of a soccer game and included from ten to fifteen thousand participants.... Before August 1987 only four other secessionist demonstrations mobilized more than a thousand participants: on May 18, 1972, in Kaunas; on November 1, 1975, in Vilnius; on October 1, 1980, in Tallinn; and on October 26, 1980, in Trakai, Lithuania.

Approved at the Soviet Union's nineteenth Communist Party Conference in June 1988, glasnost was perceived in the Baltic countries as an opportunity to make the claim for more autonomy louder (Beissinger 2002). If 1988 can therefore be considered as the starting year of the democratization process in the Baltic countries, the Declarations of Independence of 1990 and the elections to the transitional State Councils in 1992 were main milestones in the process.

Historical roots then made the ethno-nationalist frames resonant, pushing their use in the definition of various types of conflicts. First of all, economic concerns were perceived through ethno-nationalist lenses. As Eglitis (2008, 236) noted,

> In terms of economic life, the Baltics were considered among the most 'prosperous' republics of the USSR: they had better access to consumer goods and a generally higher standard of living. While, on the face of it, this was a positive development for the Baltic republics, it made them a magnet for more migration from other republics, further shifting the demographics and driving the titular population, particularly in Latvia, closer to minority status. One prominent consequence of this was linguistic: while most Balts learned and spoke fluent Russian, few Russians learned republic languages. The 1970 census in the Latvian SSR, for instance, showed that over half of Latvians (and a higher proportion in younger generations) spoke Russian; however, less than a fifth of ethnic Russians in the republic could speak Latvian.

Notwithstanding relative economic success, the Soviet occupation was moreover considered as thwarting the potential for development. This was especially the case since,

> beginning in the 1970s and continuing into the 1980s, the rate of growth began to slow and shortages of goods in the shops became a regular feature of life. Food shortages were blamed on exports of food to other parts of the Soviet Union, raising charges of colonial exploitation by the centre. Housing was also in short supply. The relative lack of consumer goods meant that there was too little to buy and no alternative but to save....This situation caused frustration rather than happiness, showing that the Soviet economy was incapable of achieving a steadily improving standard of living for all its inhabitants (Lane 2001, 94–5).

In addition, especially after the Chernobyl disaster in April 1986, protests in the Baltic area also began to address environmental issues. They targeted the building of large infrastructures—such as, in 1987, the threat of expanded phosphate mining in northern Estonia or in Latvia and, in 1986, the plan to construct a hydroelectric complex on the Daugava River (Pabriks and Purs 2001, 52; Raun 1997, 345)—and with them the potential of immigration to build and operate them (Beissinger 2002, 168; Pabriks and Purs 2001, 50-51). Claims against environmental pollution spread, also embedded in a nationalist discourse, resonant in the Baltic population. In fact, 'the elevation of issues of nature and culture were profoundly symbolic: it can be argued that Soviet destruction of the natural and cultural environments was perceived as symbolic of the destruction the Latvian, Lithuanian, and Estonian nations themselves' (Eglitis 2008, 237). Environmental concerns for new economic plans were mixed with fear that they would bring new waves of Russian migrants (in the Baltics, the autochthonous population had already declined from about ninety-four per cent in 1945 to fifty-three per cent in 1985).

Especially with the Helsinki process, nationalist frames were also bridged with claims for human rights and freedom. In Lithuania, the Catholic Church denounced human rights violations in the country, especially through the publication, beginning in 1972, of *The Chronicle of the Catholic Church in Lithuania* (Krickus 1997), supported, among others, by the Vatican under the papacy of John Paul II. As early as 1960, a riot took place in Kaunas during the celebration of the twentieth anniversary of Lithuania's sovietization, with several protestors killed by the militia. Disorders also developed on 18 May 1972, after the self-immolation of a young student in the name of freedom for Lithuania, and in October 1977, after a football match between a local and a Russian team. Especially after the Helsinki Agreement, the struggle for independence began to be framed in the language of human rights: in 1979 the Lithuanian Helsinki Group was founded, and in 1980 emerged the Committee for the Defence of the Rights of Catholics, which later collected 46,905 signatures against the trial and exile of its two leaders (Shtromas 1994, 103–4).

Similarly in Estonia, already in the 1970s, the Estonian Democratic Movement, the Estonian National Front, the Estonian Patriots, the Association of Concerned Estonians, and the White Key Brotherhood were created—all of which would become founding members of the Estonian Popular Front in 1987 (Shtromas 1994, 104–5). The privileged relations with Finland, and free travel between the two countries, contributed to some access to uncensored information (Raun 1997, 342). The 1980s appeals for independence and protection of the language were bridged with calls for freedom and against the repression of Estonian students (Vardys 1981; Raun 1997, 341). Protest took place over cultural and sporting events, while 'the most significant Estonian youth demonstrations took place in Tallinn, Tartu, and some other places in October 1980 over the issue of increased time allocation to Russian lessons in Estonian schools. Subsequently, a letter from 40 prominent Estonian intellectuals expressed their full solidarity with and support for the demonstrators, who were extremely brutally dealt with by militia and army troops' (Shtromas 1994, 115-16, n. 40).

Nationalism in Latvia had been less contentious, discouraged by the strong Soviet military presence as well as by the large immigration of

Russians, which made up almost half of the population (Plakans 1997, 254–5). Some nationalist organizations were nevertheless created in the 1970s (Latvian Independence Movement, Latvia's Democratic Youth Committee, Latvia's Christian Democratic Organization), and 'by 1976 they started to co-ordinate their activities and issued joint statements' (Shtromas 1994, 104). Protest actions, including petitions, were also organized in the 1970s by the Organization for Latvia's Independence. Here as well, the Helsinki Agreement produced symbolic support for a human right discourse.

Cross-national diffusion developed inside and outside the Baltics. Long-lasting links among the three republics, with a tradition of cooperation against Soviet occupation, helped with cross-national diffusion. In fact, in the late 1970s, ethno-nationalist movements in the three countries started to coordinate their activities. On 29 August 1979, the fortieth anniversary of the Molotov–Ribbentrop Pact, a joint petition by the three Baltic republics asked for its abolition. Throughout the 1980s, cross-Baltic contacts intensified, contributing to transform the nationalist awakening into a pro-independence movement (Shtromas 1994, 105–6).

Prompted by the protests of the Crimean Tartars exiled in Uzbekistan in 1987 (Beissinger 2002, 61–2), a nationalist wave then grew quickly, its potential consequences having been underestimated by Gorbachev (Pabriks and Purs 2001, 46–7; Smith 1994, 139), who instead considered the Baltic States as ideal candidates to experiment with market-oriented reforms (Lane 2001, 98). So,

> The Baltic republics represented a paradox for Moscow throughout this transitional period. On the one hand, of all the Soviet republics it was Estonia, Latvia and Lithuania that were envisaged as likely to be most receptive to perestroika. Indeed Gorbachev gave his blessing to the setting up of grassroots-based movements in the region precisely because the Baltic was considered as the most likely flagship which the other republics would follow. Consequently, for the first time in half a century Baltic civil society was invited to participate in an experiment in socio-economic and political reform. On the other hand, it quickly became apparent to Moscow that the Baltic peoples wanted to go much further down the path to national self-determination than the centre's reformers had envisaged or were prepared to allow. So underpinning this paradox was Moscow's miscalculation both of the scale of national feeling in the least Sovietised of the republics and the effectiveness of a programme of reform that assumed that embarking upon economic and social restructuring would somehow automatically resolve the question of Baltic national self-determination (Smith 1994, 139).

Frames developed, in fact, towards a call for national independence. Initially,

> oppositional politics was usually of the single-issue type, in which organized opposition was mobilized against particular developmental projects which

carried, in particular, environmental ramifications. This included opposition to the proposed expansion of the Ignalina nuclear power station in Lithuania, plans to construct a hydroelectric power station on Latvia's Daugava river, proposals to develop a phosphate plant in northern Estonia, and plans to construct a subway in Riga. Even where oppositional politics seized upon other issues, such as those linked to human rights or religious freedoms, their reference points were national in content. However, despite their national frame of reference, overall the politics and political actions in which civil society engaged were issue-specific with only limited inter-group co-ordination and organizational capability. This in effect was a product of a society experimenting with the politics of the possible in which particular issues, actions and agendas were judged as less likely to result in retribution by either Moscow or the local party-state machine (Smith 1994, 129).

In the second half of the 1980s, the development of protest was facilitated by some liberalization. Between November 1986 and February 1987, several political prisoners were released, and 'in the second half of 1987 and early 1988, these activists organized a series of demonstrations (known as "calendar demonstrations") on the anniversaries of independence and occupation' (Beissinger 2002, 169). Gorbachev's visit to Latvia and Estonia in 1987, during which he called for democratization together with tolerance for dissent, created a perception of opening opportunities (Beissinger 2002, 63). As a result, the authorities barely intervened when Latvian dissidents protested at the Freedom Monument in Riga on 14 June 1987 (the anniversary of Stalin's 1941 deportations), or at the protests in Tallinn and Vilnius on 23 August 1987, on the anniversary of the Molotov–Ribbentrop Pact (Pabriks and Purs 2001; Beissinger 2002, 63). Protests here tended to bridge claims of further regime liberalization with (dominant) ethno-nationalist themes (Beissinger 2002, 76–8).

Local communist elites were split on the issue, with conservatives opposing the nationalist wave, but reformists supporting it, within a moderate discourse of autonomy within a Soviet Federation. The organizational coordination of the upheaval developed, in fact, around newly created Popular Fronts, the first founded in April 1988 in Estonia in support of perestroika, counting as many as 40,000 members six weeks after its creation (Beissinger 2002, 171). Popular Fronts then formed in Lithuania (in June) and Latvia. Supported by local communist leaders, they were built upon nationalist organizations (Shtromas 1994), initially calling for a Soviet confederation with sovereign states, as complete independence lacked majoritarian support among the population. As Rossi (2012b) summarized, 'The Popular Fronts were coalitions of environmental and cultural social movement organizations, religious groups, the Catholic Church, neo-communist elites and dissident groups organized by local intelligentsia profiting from glasnost' to revitalize their reform agendas'.

The ethno-nationalist mobilization then found tolerance both in national governments, and in Gorbachev. In fact, 'In Estonia, half of the 106 members of the leadership of the Estonian Popular Front were Communist Party members. In Latvia, thirty percent of the participants in the founding congress of the Latvian Popular Front were communists, whereas over half of the delegates to the founding conference of Interfront, the movement organized in 1989 to protect the rights of non-Latvians in Latvia, were Communist Party members' (Beissinger 2002, 98).

Under the coordination of these fronts, nationalist mobilizations grew and changed, however, embracing increasingly radical aims. In Estonia, a protest was called in February 1988 in Tartu to commemorate the anniversary of the 1920 peace treaty that had initiated the Estonian annexation to the Soviet Union. Three weeks later, 10,000 people converged in Tallinn to celebrate the seventieth anniversary of Estonian independence (Smith 2001, 46). The prohibited Estonian flag was then publically displayed, in particular at the Tallinn song festival (Smith 2001, 45–6). In response, on 17 June, the Soviet government removed the old guard leader Karl Vaino and his successor, Vaino Väljas, and expressed support for larger autonomy, initiating some reforms in that direction (Smith 2001, 47). In September 1988, Estonian was declared the national language, and on 16 November the Estonian Supreme Council declared the Estonian SSR's independence.

In Lithuania, a demonstration on 14 June 1988 to commemorate the Lithuanian victims of Stalinism started a wave of protest against the Soviet authorities, followed by a major mobilization on 24 June. As in Estonia, the old guard Communist First Secretary Ringaidas Songaila was replaced by a pro-Popular Front candidate, Algirdas Brazauskas. In Latvia, as well, demonstrations started in June 1988, organized by Helsinki 86. On 14 June 1987, 5,000 participants protested in the capital city (Pabriks and Purs 2001, 53). Protest spread with the creation of the Latvian National Independence Movement in November (Plakans 1997, 256).

The secessionist mood then grew, in the face of an uncertain Soviet response. While the first semi-competitive elections for the Congress of People's Deputies of the Soviet Union in March brought pro-independence Baltic groups into parliament, demonstrators were massacred in Tbilisi on 9 April 1988 (Beissinger 2002, 85–7). In Lithuania, a more radical organization, the Lithuanian Freedom League (LFL) was created after a protest on 16 February. Violent repression of a protest on 28 September pushed the LFL and the Popular Front to converge in a pro-independence struggle through non-violent means (Lane 2001, 102). Similarly in Latvia, the Latvian National Independence Movement (LNIM) was founded to push for more radical aims, then converging with the Latvian Popular Front; the same happened in Lithuania (Pabriks and Purs 2001, 54). In Estonia, the struggle for independence radicalized as, in February 1989, 'the Estonian Citizens' Committees, appeared on the scene, backed by the Estonian National Independence Party, the Estonian Heritage Society (founded in December 1987 for the purpose of reconnecting Estonians with a history they had been increasingly cut off from under Soviet rule), and the Estonian Christian Union. The Citizens' Committees, representing the right wing of the emerging Estonian political spectrum, feared that the Popular Front would make too many concessions to Moscow and the existing authorities' (Raun 1997, 346).

On 18 May 1989, the Lithuanian Supreme Council declared the sovereignty of the country, on 31 May the Latvian Popular Front called for complete independence, and on 27 July the Supreme Soviet accepted Baltic economic self-management (Smith 2001). On 26 August, a two-million-strong (the total population of the three countries was around five million) human chain, organized by the three Popular Fronts, connected the capital cities of the three Baltic countries in protest against the Molotov–Ribbentrop Pact, accused of having assigned the Baltic states to the Soviet Union. Immediately thereafter, the Supreme Soviets of the three republics declared their incorporation into the Soviet Union as illegal. According to Smith (1994, 133), 'Theirs was "a lawful struggle" against "occupation" by a "foreign power." In short, the nationalist cause could appeal to rectificatory justice further legitimized by an international community, including the United States, who had never officially acknowledged their de jure incorporation into the Soviet Union. Once Moscow had acknowledged this fact, emphasis shifted from the struggle for autonomy within the Soviet federation to demands for the restoration of independent statehood'.

Declarations of independence followed: on 11 March 1990 in Lithuania, on 30 March in Estonia, and on 4 May in Latvia (Krickus 1997; Plakans 1997; Raun 1997). Notwithstanding some military attacks by pro-Soviet troops (killing fifteen people in Vilnius on 13 January 1991 and some civilians in Riga on 20 January) and the counter-mobilization of hundreds of thousands of armed civilians for two weeks (Lane 2001; Plakans 1997, 257; Pabriks and Purs 2001, 62–4), 1991 ended with the proclamation of independence sanctioned by referenda.

The Balts were the early risers in a broader tide of nationalism, as protest emboldened a latent nationalism and built upon the historical experience of statehood and continuous resistance to Soviet domination by continuously testing the limits of what was possible (Beissinger 2002, 166). Developing upon a wave of environmental protest in 1986, initially framed in support of perestroika, secessionist frames then grew stronger and stronger, with a dynamic certainly embedded in the breakdown of the Soviet Union. In the Baltic republics, separatist master frames developed, in fact, in action, centred around a discourse of anti-imperialist secessionism: 'Secessionist mobilization emerged in the Soviet Union as a transnational tidal force, not as an isolated collection of movements, developing in the Baltic in the summer and fall of 1988 and then spreading in a massive way to Georgia, Armenia, Azerbaijan, Moldova, Ukraine, and eventually to Russia itself. The diffusion of this anti-imperial secessionist frame beyond the Baltic was in part an attempt to capitalize on the prior successes of others' (Beissinger 2002, 160). The call then arose in support of self-determination for all: no sovereign Estonia, without sovereignty of the other republics. In action, moreover, the secessionist frames came to dominate: while marginal until May 1988, and emboldening of a few nationalities between June 1988 and February 1989, between then and February 1990 secessionism became the dominant political issue (with a six-fold increase in the number of protests, see Beissinger 2002).

During the mobilization, in a short time, nationalist identities moved to the forefront (Beissinger 2002, 176), then quickly evolving from autonomy to sovereignty and then to secession. So, 'activists at first pressed within-system demands for autonomy, environmental protection and reform of language policy, gradually coming to realize the possibilities for a more radical secessionist politics' (Beissinger 2002, 166). The mentioned Tallinn song festival was a turning point, becoming an occasion for the showing of nationalist symbols that later motivated 300,000 people (one-third of the population) to mobilize in the street, after a repressive party first secretary was removed and replaced with a supporter of a confederation of sovereign states. Events developed similarly in the other two Baltic Republics, only slightly delayed in Latvia by the strength of a dissident, rather than nationalist, discourse.

Having prompted the ethno-nationalist tide in the Soviet Union, the Baltic republics then faced a much transformed (and weakened) imperial power. The travelling of the Baltic examples to other Soviet republics (Georgia, Armenia, Ukraine, and so on) ended up weakening the government, which entered into crisis early in 1990, thus favouring the independence of the Baltic republics. As Beissinger (2002, 191) noted, 'The spread of nationalist contention throughout the USSR was a prime cause of this crisis. But the crisis of the Soviet state in the last years also had its own independent effects on collective understanding of nationhood...alienation from the center bred identification with the position of the nationalist movement'.

The weakening of the Soviet Union also explains the success of non-violent protest (and the lack of escalation). Relevant for the choice of non-violence by protestors were the examples of the peace movement, as well as the memory of earlier failure of violent resistance to the Soviet Union, spreading the belief that violence would lead to failure while non-violence embodied moral pressure by large masses. The existence of strong collective identities also supported non-violent choices, as 'Successful non-violent resistance requires intense and widely shared commitment....These movements rely on the ability to mobilize large numbers of people to generate moral pressure on rulers, disrupt the normal operations of an ongoing order, and foster defections from the ruling elite' (Beissinger 2002, 242). At the same time, the Baltic migrant communities mobilized international support, which risked being jeopardized by violent actions.

Most important, however, was the position of the Soviet Union. In his analysis, Beissinger identified 'six conditions that help to render civil resistance a potent choice for ethnically defined nationalist movements: (l) appropriate goals of liberation; (2) political opening; (3) extreme imbalance in the means of coercion; (4) strong and broadly shared identities; (5) weak counter-movements; and (6) significant support from external allies' (Beissinger 2011, 231). A constrained strategy of repression is in fact cited to explain why violence remained limited for the Baltic countries. Notwithstanding experiences with violence in the past and vibrant nationalist culture, relatively few protesters were killed in the Baltic (mostly in 1991).

After Stalin, within the Soviet Union, brutal repression lay 'outside of the boundaries of acceptable force on the part of the officials themselves—in part because the elites had internalized a certain sense of how order should be created' (Beissinger 2002, 328). In particular, 'in the Brezhnev era the police developed tactics aimed at eliminating public acts of challenge without the use of severe force against crowds. Mass repressions against demonstrators were rare; rather, before or after demonstrations, the organizers were regularly targeted. They would typically be fired from their jobs, expelled from school, arrested (in some cases subsequently released, and less often sentenced to prison terms), or on rare occasions placed in prison psychiatric hospitals' (Beissinger 2002, 332). Under Gorbachev tolerance especially of pro-glasnost demonstrations increased. The massacres in Tbilisi in April 1989, when nineteen demonstrators were killed, were then perceived as a mistake to be avoided in the future. The reaction to that crackdown, as well as to the deaths of about fourteen people in Latvia, testified to the backlash effects.

Finally, despite some polarization, with counter-demonstrations in 1989, counter-movements remained weak. Some emerged in late 1988 in defence of Russian speakers. In particular, during the founding congress of the Estonian counter-movement, Interdvizheine, held in March 1989, delegates complained about the 'Estonianization of Soviet Estonia' and in particular of language and citizenship laws which threatened their social marginalization. Similar fears of 'nativization' were voiced by counter-movements in Latvia (Interfront) and in Lithuania (Yedinstvo), where the republics' large Polish minorities were also active. There was in fact a short-lived counter-movement by ethnic Russians as Estonian became the official national language. On 14 March, around 50,000 assembled in Tallinn (Smith 2001, 48–9). On 15 May 1989, while about 5,000 pro-Soviet Union activists tried to restore the

Soviet Estonian flag on the Supreme Council building, 15,000 nationalists mobilized against them (Smith 2001, 57). This counter-mobilization was short-lived, however. Unlike for the popular fronts, in fact, the support for the counter-movements was more limited, 'both to particular places (especially strong in the large industrial cities and in northeast Estonia, where Russians comprised over four-fifths of the population) and to particular social strata (blue-collar workers, army officers, economic managers, party apparatchiks)' (Smith 1994, 135–6).[1]

In sum, historically rooted, ethno-nationalist claims were revived in action, with economic, human rights, and environmental issues bridged with nationalist ones. Allied against the centre, the Baltic republics developed an anti-imperialistic frame: calls for cultural recognition escalated during the mobilization towards demands of autonomy, first, and secession, later on. The success of the ethno-nationalist mobilization, as well as the maintenance of mainly non-violent repertoires, were facilitated by the elites' accommodating position as well as the weakening of the repressive capacity of the centre, once the Balts had prompted a broad tide of nationalist protests in many other Soviet republics.

Nationalism and The Breakdown of Yugoslavia

Yugoslavia is the country that, on paper, enjoyed the best conditions for a peaceful and straightforward democratization process, such as high degrees of liberalization, which were reflected in a relatively high number of civil society organizations. Additionally, given its experimentations with alternative economic formula, on 'the eve of the 1989 revolutions in eastern and central Europe, Yugoslavia was better poised than any other socialist country to make a successful transition to a market economy and the west' (Woodward 1995, 1).

This was not the case, however. In 1989, in fact, as the nationalist appeals within the federated republics grew stronger, it became clear that the political and economic crises were having effects on the survival of Yugoslavia itself. The weak power of the federation, with domination of the republics over the centre (Bunce 1999, 111), then facilitated fragmentation into multiple states. Additionally, the historical enmities between the Catholic Croats and the

---

[1] Even though Estonians in Estonia accounted for only 61.5 per cent of the population in 1989 (Raun 1997, 335) and Latvians in Latvia for 52 per cent in the same year (while in contrast Lithuanians represented 81.4 per cent of the population in their country), a large Russian immigrant community existed only in Latvia (34 per cent in 1989) (Plakans 1997, 249; Krickus 1997, 320).

Orthodox Serbs—in particular between the Croatian fascists, the Utasha, and the Serbian Chetniks—were then revived.

Not only did the democratization process in most of the republics take longer than in other East European countries, but some also went through the brutality of a civil war. In sum, a rich civil society did not help democratization here—or, if this happened, it was selectively, where more inclusive nationalist frames prevailed, as was the case in Slovenia. In fact, 'the relatively advantageous position of civil society in Yugoslavia failed to generate a pro-democracy challenge against the state—at both the federal and republican levels—and was quickly marginalized by workers and nationalists. This does not mean that other civil society groups were unimportant, they were not, but their relative weakness contributed to steering Yugoslavia in the direction of ethnic strife rather than democratization' (Ritter 2012c).

Some characteristics of the Yugoslavian state building, and its position during the Cold War, provided the preconditions for inter-ethnic conflicts, even though the initial history of the country fuelled some optimism. After World War II, the mass armed struggle led by the Communist Party of Yugoslavia (CPY) against regional fascist forces during the war ended in the foundation of the Socialist Federal Republic of Yugoslavia (SFRY), composed of six republics (Croatia, Slovenia, Serbia, Bosnia and Herzegovina, Macedonia, and Montenegro) and two autonomous provinces (Vojvodina and Kosovo, both belonging to Serbia) (Bunce 1999, 111; Gibianiski 2006, 18). When relations with the Soviet Union had deteriorated in 1948, the particular status agreed upon in Yalta—foreseeing that 'Yugoslavia should be half within the Western sphere of influence and half within the Eastern sphere' (Licht 2000, 118)—saved the country from a Soviet invasion. Moreover, compensations came from the West, with economic aid in the late 1940s: after the breaking of relations with the Soviet Union in 1948, the US government 'released frozen Yugoslav assets, including million in gold, and later provided Tito's regime with loans, grants, and military aid in concert with aid from the World Bank and U.S. allies in Western Europe' (Schaeffer 2000, 49). Military and economic assistance from the US continued in the 1950s, even after Khrushchev had renormalized the relations between the two states in 1955, with ensuing rapid economic growth in the 1950s and 60s (Schaeffer 2000, 49). Moreover, a specific version of a socialist economy—with tolerance for small private business and a 'self management' system that gave workers control of their factories and workplaces by electing their management—initially seemed to benefit the country development.

The situation started to deteriorate, however, in the 1970s, as the oil crisis put an abrupt end to the so-called Yugoslav miracle (Stokes 1993, 229), forcing the country to adopt structural adjustment policies within various austerity programs in order to repay the large accumulated foreign debt (Schaeffer

2000, 51; Stokes 1993, 229–30). Increases in unemployment and prices fuelled discontent among the population (Stokes 1993, 238–41).

Territorial inequalities also became increasingly dramatic between rich Slovenia and Croatia, on the one hand, and poor Kosovo and Macedonia, on the other. These economic differences among the republics interacted with cultural differences. In particular, close to Italy and Austria, the Slovenes had long considered themselves as detached from Balkan politics (Stokes 1993, 236). They had enjoyed some freedom, with the flourishing of a student press, the emergence of new social movements on women's rights, gay rights, peace, and the environment, as well as of a group of intellectuals surrounding the avant-garde journal *Nova revija* (New Review) (Stokes 1993, 236). This was not the case for the other republics. There, historical conflicts between Serbs and Croats, as well as—in part overlapping—between Catholic, Protestant, and Muslim groups represented historical memories, sleeping but still there to be revived.

The effects of economic and cultural inequalities became all the more dramatic given another characteristic of Tito's Yugoslavia. As he had linked socialism and the nation, this 'contained a critical weakness that Tito and his colleagues could never have imagined. As long as the Communist movement remained strong, Yugoslavism was not in danger. If nationalism reared its head the party could and did push it back under the surface. If the League of Communists of Yugoslavia should disintegrate, however, then the Yugoslavism it championed would disintegrate too' (Stokes 1993, 223). So, by the mid-1980s, at stake were 'the political and economic foundations of the Yugoslav system—a system commonly called "Titoism"' (Vasilevski 2007, 5).

The crisis further spiralled with Tito's death, and the ensuing struggle on succession that brought a new generation of party leaders in the various republics. This change involved a pragmatic softening of repression (Vladisavljević 2008, 47), especially in Serbia and Slovenia, where the new leaders 'tolerated both cultural and political dissent and engaged in informal alliances with protest groups and dissident intellectuals in the second half of the 1980s' (Vladisavljević 2008, 48). However, it also increased internal competition among the republics. So, 'By 1988 the great majority of Tito's chosen coterie of republics' leaders had been replaced with leaders who had no common loyalties', and 'both the Yugoslav federation and the Yugoslav Communist party—the League of Communists—which nominally ruled the country had lost much of their legitimacy' (Pavković 2000, 76). So, during the 1980s:

Socioeconomic and cultural inequalities fuelled then internal conflicts, as

when the economic crisis began to affect politics in the republics in a very real way in the mid-1980s, each republic's leadership blamed the other republics for their nation's economic misfortunes in an attempt to maintain power and legitimacy.

Not only was this convenient for warding off economic criticism, it also resonated well with the burgeoning nationalist movements that were emerging throughout Yugoslavia, especially among Kosovo Serbs and Slovenes. Consequently, the economic crisis forced communist politicians to become nationalists, a move which could potentially save their positions of power but spelled disaster for the country at large (Ritter 2012c).

In this situation, political elites at the level of the republics started playing on nationalism as a way of maintaining their own power (Licht 2000, 113). In fact, this happened through the activation of multiple cleavages:

Old and new divisions in the political class came to the fore, such as between promoters of greater control of Serbia's central government over its autonomous provinces and their foes; between advocates of a stronger federal centre and protectors of the status quo; between proponents of change in the party's Kosovo policy and their opponents; between conservative and liberally minded politicians; between members of various political generations; and between high- and low-ranking officials. Since the divisions often cut across one another and high officials engaged in complex political maneuvering, relations within the political class became rather complicated (Vladisavljević 2008, 126).

Civil society organizations had developed in various contentious moments. In the early 1970s, repression and purges had followed Croatian communists' calls for reforms, strongly stigmatized by Serbian communists. In the mid-1970s, dissidents started to ask for pluralism and respect for human rights (Licht 2000, 120). In 1976 and 1977, in Belgrade, people signed petitions 'on political issues, such as the death penalty or asking about the fact that the police had the discretion to deny citizens their passports and their right to travel abroad' (Licht 2000, 120). Later on, in 1988, in Slovenia, the Committee for the Defense of Human Rights, together with the Slovene communists and the Catholic Church, campaigned in support of the 'Ljubljana Four', a group of journalists that had denounced the sale of arms to Ethiopia.

Especially in Slovenia, new social movement claims spread on issues of reproductive rights, gay and lesbian rights, and nuclear energy (Licht 2000, 120). There, a civil society developed out of a culturally driven alternative scene born with the 1970s punk movement (Figa 1997, 164). Their claims 'were rooted in postmodern concerns and included opposition to using violence in any form of human interaction, peace, minority rights, environmental issues, alternative forms of psychotherapy, and gay rights' (Figa 1997, 168–9). In the liberal climate of the late 1980s, feminists, environmentalists, and pacifists coordinated their protests (Figa 1997, 169), consisting of peaceful, direct actions (Figa 1997, 169).

Women's movement organizations were also quite developed in the other republics. The origin of women's groups active against the war is located in a long history of Yugoslav feminism, which had peaked in 1978 at the conference entitled 'Comrade Woman. The Women's Question. A New Approach' (Bilic 2012, 198). In 1980, a collective called Women and Society had been founded in Zagreb and Belgrade, contributing to intense interactions between Serbian and Croatian feminists (Bilic 2012, 91). In sum,

> Yugoslav feminism began in the late 1970s in Belgrade and Zagreb as a critique of Yugoslav socialism's failure to liberate women, a critique expressed mainly through scholarly publications and the media. The feminist pen provoked a fierce backlash in the academy, the media, and the organs of the Yugoslav state, including the official communist women's conference. By the mid-1980s, feminists in Zagreb, Belgrade, and Ljubljana launched a small but radical new social movement. This feminist activism centered around two new types of activity: public forums and protests and provision of independent self-help services for women, plus continuation of the academic and media work (Benderly 1997, 186).

Mainly composed of intellectuals, these groups developed a strong anti-nationalist stance (Bilic 2012, 94). The women's movement proved important later on, as well, when, during the civil wars in the 1990s,

> feminists in the Yugoslav successor states organized across national lines to protest the war's impact on women, and provided small-scale but significant opposition to the war. They also provided social services for its women survivors. However, a rift developed between those feminists who opposed nationalism and those who became more patriotic as they drew parallels between the victimization of women and the victimization of their nation. The new states marginalized the non-nationalist feminists and attempted to coopt the patriotic ones (Benderly 1997, 184).

One such organization, Women in Black, mobilized weekly silent vigils against the war in Belgrade's city centre.

Environmental organizations were active in the whole country, enjoying some level of tepid tolerance by the regime. In Zagreb, the group Svarun (named for the Slavonic god of the sun, fire, and the sky) was founded in 1986 as a Working Group for Environmental, Pacific, Feminist, and Spiritual Initiative. Claiming support for self-management, it found sympathizers in the youth organization of the communist party. Anti-nuclear mobilization also proliferated at the local level, blocking the construction of but one nuclear power station. Environmental campaigns, particularly in Slovenia and Serbia, succeeding there in overturning a decision to build a nuclear power plant (Licht 2000, 120–1). Petitions also demanded recognition of conscientious objection as a human right (Bilic 2012, 123).

The labour movement did mobilize mainly in Slovenia and Croatia, even though the working class had remained quiescent in the early 1980s despite deteriorating living standards (Vladisavljević 2008, 111). The number of strikes in the country increased, however, in the mid-1980s: in 1987 there were 1,685 registered strikes with roughly 4.3 per cent of all employees in the large state-controlled sector of the economy taking part, as opposed to less than 1 per cent in previous years. The workers' protests lasted more than one day on average and, significantly, the number of strikes in large state enterprises, with more than 500 workers, also rose sharply in the second half of the decade. Roughly half of the strikers came from heavy industries and mining, but strikes became increasingly frequent in other sectors of the economy, as well as in health services and education. In 1988, the number of strikes and strikers further increased, especially in large enterprises, and strikes became longer on average (Vladisavljević 2008, 111).

The nationalist agenda was then pushed from above, on a heterogeneous range of social movements that had developed thanks to relative liberalization. As Ritter (2012c) summarized,

> unlike elsewhere in the region, civil society was fairly strong in Yugoslavia. This state of affairs was a consequence of Yugoslavia's maintaining good economic and political relations with the West, and thus being affected by its liberalism, and by the fact that federal decentralization resulted in a less repressive republican context, as noted especially in Serbia and Slovenia. Furthermore, Yugoslavia's more participatory political arrangements and its tradition of labor organizing created a social context in which civic associations were perceived to be less threatening than within the Soviet sphere.

However, during the late 1980s, 'the groups that were able to mobilize the largest number of protesters were nationalist and workers' groups, and, to a lesser extent, students' (Ritter 2012c). The mentioned variety of autonomous civil society organizations notwithstanding, sponsored from above, nationalist groups came to dominate the public sphere by the end of the 1980s. This was the case especially in Serbia, where an aggressive framing about the 'big Serbia' developed, activating past memories.

Using nationalist propaganda that stressed the past and present victimization of the Serbs, Serbian leader Slobodan Milošević was able to exploit the support for the Serb minority in Kosovo that had been protesting since 1985 against the perceived discrimination by the Kosovo's Albanian majority. Initially, Serbian nationalism pushed for defensive frames. It has been suggested, in fact, that 'the road to civil war began in March 1981 when Albanian students took their demands for better conditions at the University of Prishtinë to the streets in the time-honored tradition of students everywhere. Their demonstration touched a nerve of Albanian patriotic feeling, and over the next month anti-Serbian demonstrations demanding that Kosovo become a Yugoslav republic became so massive that the federal government sent in troops' (Stokes 1993, 230). A few years later, in 1985, Kosovo Serbs protested outside the headquarters of the Kosovo Communist Party, the following year addressing to the presidency of the Serbian Communist Party a petition calling for a stop to the harassment of non-Albanians (Pavković 2000, 83). The relations between Kosovo Albanians and Kosovo Serbs then degenerated, as Kosovo Serbs staged rallies in Belgrade: 'The organisers of these protests were Serb and Montenegrin farmers, skilled workers, teachers and low-ranking communist officials. This gave the movement the look of an anti-elite, grassroots movement of harassed Serb and Montenegrin minorities in Kosovo' (Pavković 2000, 83).

A turning point happened in the night and early morning of 24 and 25 April 1987, as Milošević addressed a gathering of 15,000 Kosovo Serbs and Montenegrins with the following words:

> The first thing that I wish to tell you, comrades, is that you must remain here. This is your land, your houses are here, your fields and gardens, your memories.... It was never characteristic of the spirit of the Serb and Montenegrin people to knuckle under to difficulties, to demobilize itself when it must fight, to become demoralized when the going is tough. You must remain here on account of your ancestors and descendants. Otherwise, we would be shaming the ancestors and disillusioning the descendants (cit. in Banac 1992, 176–7).

Criticism of Tito would later address his identity as a Croat and a federalist.

Although in a different way, the Slovenian socialists also espoused the nationalist agenda, transforming themselves into the Party of Democratic Renewal, which with its slogan 'Europe now', initially called for a national party of all Slovenes in a sovereign state, part of a new confederal Yugoslavia (Pavković 2000, 110–11). Similarly, in Croatia, former party members came to lead the nationalist movement. Feeling threatened by Milošević's nationalist rhetoric, they tried to increase popular support by linking up with nationalist dissidents (Pavković 2000, 112).

As other republican leaders started to fear Milošević as a proponent of a Greater Serbia, they reacted in fact by mobilizing for their own sovereignty. As Pavković (2000, 97) summarized,

> One of the primary aims of each of the dissident national ideologies was to reaffirm the sovereignty of 'its' nation over the territory that was claimed for it. The Croat and Slovene national ideologues saw the reaffirmation of sovereignty necessitating the creation of national armed forces within a new Yugoslav confederation or outside Yugoslavia.... Albanian sovereignty was to be achieved first in a separate Yugoslav republic and then, possibly, in unification with Albania. Serb sovereignty was to be reaffirmed in the unification of all Serbs in a reorganized 'democratic integrative' Yugoslav federation; if this proved to be impossible, in a Serb state without other Yugoslav nations.

In this way, 'nationalism became a dominant political force largely as an unintended outcome of high levels of mobilization and spiralling social, economic and political conflicts in a complex, authoritarian multi-national state which experienced a severe economic crisis' (Vladisavljević 2008, 6).

Even though human rights associations had grown in the 1970s and 80s, the leaders of the six republics failed to find an agreement for a peaceful partition. This steered especially the reaction of Slobodan Milošević, leader of the Serbian League of Communists, who would rule Serbia for fourteen years, rewriting and manipulating the constitution. Milošević had been the leader of the Communist as well as the Socialist party; president of the Yugoslavia federation; and then president of Serbia. Under Milošević's leadership, there were high levels of mobilization between September 1988 and March 1989, including public meetings, strikes, marches, a few hunger strikes, and, eventually, some violence (Vladisavljević 2008, 145). In September 1988, 'high officials of Serbia now effectively certified specific protest groups and their demands and claims as fully legitimate. They openly embraced popular participation in politics, albeit on populist terms' (Vladisavljević 2008, 150). So-called rallies of solidarity in support of the Kosovo Serbs multiplied in Vojvodina, Serbia, and Montenegro, mobilizing tens of thousands—up to 700,000 in Belgrade on 19 October 1988. While the protests were initially mainly non-violent and moderate in their discourse, they radicalized later on: 'Unlike their earlier focus on protection for the Serbs by the courts and law enforcement agencies and the politics of inequality in Kosovo, they now principally demanded constitutional change in Serbia and a temporary shutting down of Kosovo's party and state organs. Instead of targeting Kosovo's high officials, they demanded the resignations of high officials of Vojvodina and their other opponents in the party Presidency and the Central Committee of the LCY, and denounced the leadership of Montenegro' (Vladisavljević 2008, 139).

So, while in other countries nationalism was framed in inclusive terms by social movements developing from below, steered from above, Serbian exclusive ethno-nationalism was a top-down mass movement, mobilized by the old Serbian leadership. As Stokes (1993, 235) has pointed out:

> In the rest of Eastern Europe people power, as it was called after huge popular demonstrations brought Corazon Aquino to power in the Philippines in 1986, was a force for democracy and pluralism. In Serbia, however, Milošević mobilized people power to destroy Yugoslavia and to create the conditions for civil war. In September and October 1988 thirty thousand, fifty thousand, one hundred thousand, even one million people gathered in Serbian cities to shout their approval of Milošević's effort to subdue Kosovo. When Albanians tried rallies of their own or conducted strikes in the important mining industry, as they did in November 1988, Milošević sent in the riot police and arrested their leaders....In the rest of Eastern Europe people power toppled the old Communist regimes in the name of democracy. In Serbia, Milošević manipulated the same force by racist appeals in

order to legitimate his transformation of the League of Communists of Serbia into a nationalist party organized on neo-Stalinist principles.

Initially justifying intervention as defence of oppressed (Serbian) minorities, during the mobilization the aims broadened to bringing both Vojvodina and Kosovo under Serbian control. The regional elites in Vojvodina and Montenegro, who feared the loss of their status as autonomous provinces, were indeed forced to resign after protestors were supported by Serbia, and replaced by Milošević's protégés. While Macedonia's leaders supported the Kosovo Serbs' nationalist claims, those of Croatia, Bosnia-Herzegovina, and Slovenia opposed them (Vladisavljević 2008, 180). On 20 February 1989, in Stari Trg, 1,300 Kosovo miners went on strike, several hundred meters below the earth's surface, asking for the resignation of the new pro-Milošević Kosovo leadership. A week later, they resurfaced, after those leaders had indeed resigned, but they were soon arrested for counter-revolutionary activities (Stokes 1993, 235), while the politicians' resignations were rejected (Vladisavljević 2008, 184–5). Then,

> The Serbian Assembly, along with the assemblies of Kosova and Vojvodina that Milošević now dominated, approved the new constitutional arrangements, putting the autonomous regions firmly under the control of the Serbian central government in March 1989. Acceptance of the constitutional provisions produced six days of rioting in Kosova, which Milošević subdued with substantial loss of life (estimates ranged from 20 to 140), but many Serbs rejoiced over the restoration of Serbian unity, as they thought of it. 'Sovereignty returned to Serbia', crowed the headline in *Politika*. 'What was more natural, more humane, more democratic, for the Serbian people', said Borisav Jović, Serbian representative to the federal presidency, 'than, in accordance with their peace-loving traditions, to again enter upon the stage of history and make a demand in the form of the simplest, the most noble formula of justice and equality.... [Serbs are] the people who in the modern history of the Balkans made the greatest sacrifices and demonstrated the greatest scope and evidence of its love for freedom and democracy.... Serbia is equal now' (Stokes 1993, 235).

After 1989 followed the years of dramatic events, such as the wars in Croatia (with about 25,000 people killed) and in Bosnia-Herzegovina (with about 200,000 deaths and a million people displaced), plus the seventy-eight days of the NATO bombing campaign, allegedly against violations of human rights in Kosovo, with rampant economic crisis and mounting corruption. The situation precipitated after the 1990 elections brought Milošević into power as president of Serbia, and the army sided with him in his attempt to conquer part of Croatia and Bosnia. Although no war was declared, a military draft was initiated in May 1991. When violence erupted in the Serbian-inhabited areas of Croatia, the Yugoslav people's army intervened in order, the Serbian government declared, to protect them. In the years to come, in the face of brutal escalation, Milošević continued to present himself as a reformist communist and a nationalist: he was described, in fact, as 'the proverbial example (though rare in actual fact in the region) of the communist who, recognizing the threats imposed by the dissolution of the communist order, opted nearly overnight (and helped along by audience reactions lo a speech given in Kosovo) to redefine himself as a nationalist' (Stokes 1993, 92).

With its monopoly of the media and educational system, the regime promoted a victimistic idea of Serbs as in need of protection from new suffering. Serbs were praised as the brave soldiers who had protected Austria from the Turks, heroes (even the Chetnik, who had collaborated with Nazis, were seen in a positive light, as freedom lovers). In contrast, the Croats were the murderers, traitors, and Serb-haters, as were (even if less central) the Turks and the Austro-Hungarians (Malešević 2002).

The increased power of the Serbian republic then spurred a declaration of independence by the others, all of which had become independent by 1993, while Montenegro achieved independence in 2006, and Vojvodina and Kosovo are still parts of what is now Serbia (Vasilevski 2007). The former communist elites played a most important role in all the new countries, even though, with the exception of Slovenia, democratization was delayed by the internal wars.

In Serbia, the democratization process was particularly long and troublesome. There, a quite vibrant civil society initially collapsed in the face of aggressive nationalism; however, it was from the revival of that civil society that a movement for democracy developed. Notwithstanding the dominance of nationalism, there was certainly some opposition as well. Already in early 1991, thousands of people had marched in Belgrade, demanding Milošević's retirement; the students did the same, some days later. In response, Milošević, in agreement with the president of the federation, deployed tanks against his citizens. Even during the most dramatic periods, many civil society organizations were founded: among them, the Center for Anti-war action, Women in Black, and the independent trade union Independence. Intellectuals also organized a 'preparliament' to find ways to avoid war. Peace activists and peace caravans traversed Serbia; Serbian citizens protested the shelling of Dubrovnik by the army, and a petition circulated against the siege on Croatian Vukovar. Tanks were used to curb the anti-war revolt in 1991. As many as 50,000 participated in April 1992 at a concert titled 'Don't count on us' (Vejvoda 2011, 299). A circle of independent intellectuals organized weekly gatherings under the label of 'another Serbia'.

However, the movement for democracy needed many more years to develop. Initially weakened by the nationalist tide, the Other-Serbia grew in the three months of mass protest of 1996–7, culminating in the mobilization against

Milošević's falsification of electoral results, with mobilizations in each of the cities in which the opposition had won. Major demonstrations against the government took place in 1991, 1992, 1996–7, and 1999, organized by students, oppositional parties, and reservists (Belgrade Circle, Center for Anti-war Action, Women in Black). However, the opposition had been ideologically divided, polemic, and exclusive: 'Opposition leaders were much more interested in keeping people out, rather than bringing people in' (Vejvoda 2011, 95). Divisions presented the opposition in a negative light. Only in 1996–7, a coalition (Together) was formed, and students and oppositional parties demonstrated together. The evidence of electoral fraud was perceived as so arrogant that it 'abruptly released the frustrations the middle classes had been accumulating for years' (Vejvoda 2011, 91).

Until 1997, the regime was characterized by soft authoritarianism, with limited power of parliament, increased power of the presidency, limits to pluralism, and ties with the police and the army as well as the Serbian mafia (Nepstad 2011). However, there were also competitive (even increasingly competitive) elections, with a visible role of the opposition (including in parliament), some independent media, and a vibrant civil society. It was when the regime turned more repressive that civil society mobilization eventually produced its breakdown. Non-violent resistance was led by old oppositional intellectuals and a new generation of students. After Serbia had lost three wars, the Alternative Academic Educational Network, funded by international donors, was founded when academics started to be dismissed because of their political activities. Founded in 1998, by 1999 Otpor had '60,000 members, and 100 offices located throughout Serbia. Although heavily repressed, Otpor was able to mobilize independent media as well as support in the broader population. International support developed as well, with contacts with, e.g., Slovakia activists. It had a flat, rather than hierarchical, organizational structure that protected the organization as a whole from attacks on individual offices and leaders launched by the authorities' (Nepstad 2011, 100–101). The movement was then able to use some international support, such as that offered through contacts with Slovakian activists, but also US$20 million provided by foreign donors to support civic organizations.

Concluding, while a relatively rich civil society did exist in Yugoslavia, promoting civil and human rights, the regime breakdown was heavily influenced by the emergence of exclusive nationalist frames, mobilized by nationalist entrepreneurs coming from within the incumbent elites. Civil war dynamics emerged when the Serbian leader, in control of the army, used force against the secession of other republics as well as against ethnic minorities.

In The Name of The Nation: A Summary

Democratization movements require integrative frames in which actions are taken in the name of not just the majority, but the entire community with a stake in the process. Indeed, they represent foundational moments in which, even when borders are not contested, the nation is advocated as the main point of reference. While many democratization processes do not address issues of territorial sovereignty, the 1989 wave did involve cases of border restructuring, especially in the federative systems. If Czechoslovakia faced national issues after the transition to democracy, in the Soviet Union and Yugoslavia the national borders became contested during the democratization process, with heavy consequences.

While what we saw in the cases addressed in the previous chapters were movements active on social and civil rights that also used nationalist appeals, in this chapter we have addressed two geopolitical areas in which the main movements to mobilize were nationalist ones. In both cases, we saw nationalism emerging in action, confirming that 'The idea that identities could be defined in the context of agency or that nationalism is both a structured and a structuring phenomenon has not received sufficient attention' (Beissinger 2002, 9). The action itself appeared, therefore, as constitutive of conceptions of nationhood that evolved over time (see Beissinger 2002, 11). In fact, these were heightened moments in which conceptions of nationalism developed in action—as 'Not all historical eras are alike. There are times when change occurs so slowly that time seems almost frozen, though beneath the surface considerable turbulence and evolution may be silently at work. There are other times when change is so compressed, blaring, and fundamental that it is almost impossible to take its measure' (Beissinger 2002, 47). The eventful perspective on nationness and nationalism that Brubaker (1996, 19) called for would see nationalism as something that sometimes crystallizes suddenly rather than developing gradually. Following Beissinger, we indeed saw nationalism 'not only as a cause of action, but also as the product of action. This recursive quality of human action—the fact that action can function as both cause and effect—and the significance of this for the study of nationalism are the central theoretical issues' (Beissinger 2002, 11).

As in the other cases we analysed, during contentious moments some actors might ask for democratization, others resist it. In many cases, calls for freedom and human rights are bridged with others on social issues or—as in the case mentioned here—nationalist ones, in others claims for democracy are contrasted in the name of the nation. Exclusive definition of the nation as well as its competitive use by the centre against the peripheries tend to jeopardize democratization efforts. This evolution is however affected by long and intense processes. In both the Baltics and the Balkans, emotionally intense events contributed to preference formation and transformation: processes of identification developed through conversion (Beissinger 2002, 155). Fear, revenge, rage were intense emotions produced in the course of the events, which forged nationalist discourses and identities.

The framing and structures of mobilizations were, however, deeply different in the two geopolitical areas. In the Balkans, the exclusive ethno-nationalism mobilized by the Serbian leadership brought about internal wars as well as external military interventions. In the Baltic republics, instead, claims for the protection of the local culture evolved into anti-imperialistic themes, which were bridged with calls for human rights, allowing for cross-national cooperation. While some legacy of the mobilization of ethno-nationalist frames was visible in the institutional outcome of all involved democratization processes in a restrictive definition of citizenship, the speed and disruptiveness of the territorial restructuring changed dramatically.

Interactions during the mobilization influenced the nationalist frames that emerged from the protest events as, in Beissinger's words, 'Thickened history had provided the context for a fundamental transformation of identities which, in "quieter" times, were once believed to be fixed and immutable' (2002, 148). While in quiet times nationalist entrepreneurs indeed aim at building some structural advantages, these advantages are then put to work in noisy times, when 'the constraining parameters of politics undergo fundamental challenges, leading to rapidly shifting assumptions about the limits of the possible' (Beissinger 2002, 151). Protest events did in fact bring about preference changes—both in positive and negative directions—converting the uncommitted, as well as emboldening or demoting supporters.

Violence has been located within cycles of protest that include different claims, pushed forward through different forms of action. As Beissinger observed about ethnic violence during the collapse of the Soviet State,

> Usually, at the beginning of waves of mobilized nationalist violence, specific chains of events crystallized widely shared moods of fear, revenge, outrage, and self-assertion which, when combined with a sense of license gained from supportive cues sent by state authority, erupted into violence. In other cases, the state itself directly initially mobilized violence in ethnic groups or ethnicized segments of the Soviet state as part of attempts to control challenges to its territoriality. Thus, within the context of 'thickened' history social norms proscribing nonstate violence between segments of a single state were set aside, and violent action came to be considered permissible and even moral by large numbers of people (2002, 318).

Often, protest tends to remain peaceful, escalating defensively, especially in the declining phase of mobilization and when repression peaks. Thus, it is not so much culture or social status that produces violence, but rather the dynamics of conflicts—as Beissinger (2002, 283) wrote, 'nationalist violence unfolds out of conflict and is contingent and dependent on what takes place within conflictual situations'. In the Balkans as well, violence moved from less to more organized forms, with violent entrepreneurs acquiring power (della Porta 2013b), tending to jump in scale when paramilitary groups were formed and acquired arms. In particular, violence was fuelled when the centre mobilized the army against the rebellious peripheries.

Our cases confirmed, in fact, that the characteristics nationalism assumes in quiet times influence, but do not determine those that develop in heightened times. As other research has indicated, past conflicts are not so easily and automatically reproduced. This explains why episodes of inter-ethnic violence appear so unexpected.[2] In intense moments, in fact, violent performances produced new identity (e.g. Feldman 1991). The past conflicts were indeed mobilized in both areas—but they pointed at rather different experiences: the illegitimacy of the Molotov–Ribbentrop pact that allowed the Soviet Union to annex the Baltic republics on the one hand, the Croat versus Serb history of reciprocal violence and revenge, in particular under Nazi occupation during World War II, on the other.

If 'what was once understood as normal it is no longer recognizable', this is also because 'once initiated, violence exercised its own independent effect on subsequent events, altering cultural identities' (Beissinger 2002, 273). In fact, violent nationalism is even more difficult to predict than non-violent, as 'nationalist violence unfolds out of conflict and is contingent and dependent on what takes place within conflictual situations' (Beissinger 2002, 281). So, 'Within a compressed period of time, the world of social norms was inverted and violent actions came to be considered as "normal"' (Beissinger 2002, 294). During the breakdown of the Soviet Union, mass violence was most widespread among Georgians, Armenians, Azerbaijanis, Abkhaz, Armenians, and Moldovans, who, with the exception of Moldovans, did not have much tradition of violent conflicts. Similarly, in the breakdown of former Yugoslavia, 'violence took a dynamics of its own, feeding on the victimization it created' (Beissinger 2002, 305).

Cultural processes clearly impacted the definition of the imagined communities (and their enemies). However, it was especially the Serbian control of

---

[2] As a survivor of the Sungait pogroms in 1988 stated, 'it was all so farfetched, so unheard of in our lives, that it was just impossible to take it seriously' (Beissinger 2002, 274). So, as pogroms spread, 'it is not unusual for the victims to be aware of rumors about impending violence against them, often refusing to believe their veracity' (Beissinger 2002, 274).

the Yugoslavian army, and the willingness of Serbian leaders to use it aggres-sively—as opposed to the lack of control of instruments of force in the Baltic republics—that made the difference. In sum, in the face of economic and political challenges, elites adopted competitive nationalistic frames, activat-ing historical memories of brutal inter-ethnic conflicts. While different types of movements were present in the different republics, ethno-nationalist ones became dominant, fuelled by ethnic entrepreneurs who were endowed with military resources.

10

Mobilizing for Democracy: Some Conclusions

Democratization from below has been a little studied process. On the one hand, considering democracy as a sort of precondition for protest, social movement studies have not paid much attention to non-democratic regimes. On the other, democratization studies have focused on either structural conditions or elites' predispositions, only recently developing some interest to contentious politics. In this volume, I tried to show the potential theoretical and empirical gains from attempts at bridging concepts and hypotheses coming from the two fields of study, in a comparison of two waves of democratization in different historical times and geographical areas.

Building also upon emerging research on border-fields—such as civil society and (nonviolent) revolutions—I aimed at understanding some different paths of democracy from below. Considering the role of disruptive action as separate from the role of social movements in the democratization process, I have identified three paths of democratization from below, in which either protest or social movements, or both, are important. I have categorized as *eventful democratizations* those processes in which the role of protest by social movements is most important; as *participatory pacts* those processes in which social movements achieve democratic reforms through (mainly) bargaining; and as *participated coups d'état* those processes in which elites manipulate mass protest in order to win over conservative groups. While focusing most attention to the first path, I have also developed some comparisons with the other two.

Attribution of political opportunities and resource mobilization emerged as fundamental processes in all three paths. These are not static variables, however, but rather processes (composed of mechanisms) that develop in action. During emotionally intense and relationally dense waves of protest, opportunities and resources were used, but also produced. That is, the events changed the contexts in which they developed. While both agency and structures clearly influenced each other, democratization from below was an emergent moment, whose evolution was influenced by the (intensified) interactions among different actors and their construction of a (quickly changing) reality. These moments were not only—as literature on regime transitions has suggested—structurally underdetermined, but also quite complex to address strategically, given the rapid evolution of chances and stakes, with little time and information available to solve difficult dilemmas.

While most research in the field has focused either on case studies or on intra-area, small-N comparisons, I adopted in my case selection a mixed strategy, including most similar and most different research designs, with intra-area and well as cross-area comparisons. In this sense I went beyond the deeply rooted tradition in the political and social sciences—as well as historical studies—of comparing like with like, venturing into the comparison of quite different cases. This mixed strategy allowed me, I believe, to single out the presence not of common causes but of similar mechanisms whose robust capacity to explain democratization is indicated exactly from their re-emergence in different times and spaces. Analysing various episodes of democratization—not necessarily involving a change of regime—within Eastern Europe in 1989–90 and the MENA region in 2011–12, I also looked at specific intra-area commonalities and cross-area differences. These comparisons included the type of regime in terms of political institutions but also the social relations that developed: post-Stalinist regimes versus liberal patrimonial autocracies had peculiar forms of elite building and societal control, and the geopolitics of the two areas also varied. Differences emerged, however, within areas as well—especially in the relative strength of civil society and relative capacity of the regime to repress.

These multiple lines of comparison allowed me to single out similarities and differences within and across waves of democratization, and therefore to address several debates in both social movement studies and democratization studies.

Going back to the model presented in the Introduction, we can single out some fundamental differences among the three paths of democratization episodes I have examined. In eventful democratization (see Figure 10.1), a vivacious civil society—which has already undergone some coordination processes and embraced broadly democratic frames—encounters closed political opportunities. As attempts at repression fail, however, the elites split on demands for democracy. The difference with participated pacts is mainly in the attitudes of the elites, which are in this second path already deeply split before the spread of protest (see Figure 10.2). Finally, in the most troubled path (see Figure 10.3), a weak civil society has to face high levels of repression, with violence spreading especially as a result of splits in the military.

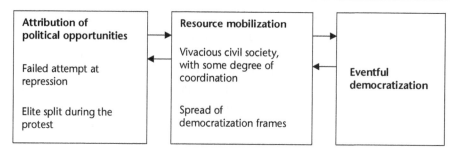

Figure 10.1 Eventful democratization

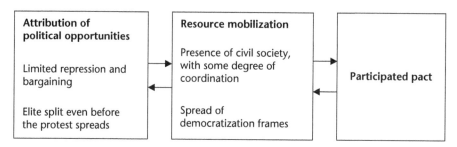

Figure 10.2 Participated pacts

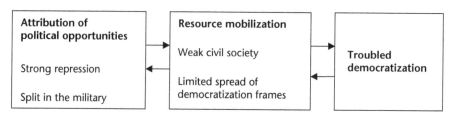

Figure 10.3 Disruptive coups

In this chapter, I will revisit some of these observations, summarizing the results of the empirical analysis of the different paths of democracy from below.

Repertoires of Protest and Democratization: The Eventfulness of Protest

Social movement studies do not expect protest to develop in authoritarian regimes. However, recent research has identified some forms of resistance to dictators. Charities help citizens in overcoming various types of hardship, labour unions call for strikes, and peace, women's, human rights and/or environmental groups launch protest, but also educational campaigns. Resistance also has an everyday, symbolic dimension: discontent is expressed in oppositional talk which, under authoritarian regimes, is often 'marked by double entendre, symbolism, monitoring of participants, specific rules of speech, that is, what it is appropriated to say, how to say it, and to whom' (Johnston 2011, 115).

In the cases I studied, protests did emerge under authoritarian regimes, in fact, even if their characteristics differed from the ones widespread under democratic systems. Also these protests involved sort of hit-and-run forms, such as the writing of graffiti, the clandestine placement of flowered flags or crosses in symbolic places, or the seizure of official events (for example, prohibited songs at concerts or sporting events, or diversions of funerals) (Johnston 2011). As in other cases, underground humour works as an escape valve for anxiety (Johnston 2011, 116).

All of these forms did indeed emerge before and during the transition periods. In most of the cases in Eastern Europe, non-violent actions dominated the repertoire of protest, which was built upon the tradition of pre-existing movements at the national level (from labour to religious issues), but also through learning and imitation of what happened abroad. In these cases, as predicted by other researchers, oppositional methods of dispersion (based on loose networks, broad coalitions, decentralization) did reduce the risks of repression, and methods of concentration in public spaces helped to build solidarity and show support (Schock 2005, 51). Variable mixes of old and new social movements brought their own experiences within cross-class, cross-ethnic or cross-ideological coalitions.

The repertoire of action was rather different in the Arab Spring, building upon intellectuals and workers (the latter being even more present than in Eastern Europe) but also upon the practices of resistance by what Bayat refers to as 'nonmovements'. Collective actions of non-collective actors, these are not ideologically driven but rather aimed at redistribution and autonomy through the use of dissimulation, sabotage, and false compliance. So, 'the story of nonmovements is the story of agency in the times of constraints' (Bayat 2010, 26). Everyday strategies of survival by the poor and the emarginated showed a capacity for resistance through a quiet encroachment of the ordinary: 'a silent, patient, protracted and pervasive advancement of ordinary people on the propertied and powerful in order to survive hardships and better their lives' (Bayat 1997, 7). Threats to survival brought about an activation of those networks for collective mobilization. Like *basismo* in Latin America, these forms of mobilization put an emphasis on local democracy. They are not interested in ideology, but in practice, even getting involved in pragmatic alliances with patrons, as well as ideological ones (which bring about resources but also the potential for repression). In this sense, localized struggles appear as more meaningful and feasible than do revolutions (Bayat 1997).

These actions politicized in the face of a repression that comprised everyday harassment and extraordinary brutality. Also in Tunisia and Egypt, research confirmed that 'The repressive policy of the state renders individual, quiet, and hidden mobilization a more viable strategy than open, collective protest.... However, where some degree of political openness prevails, competition between political parties provides a breathing ground for the collective action of ordinary people' (Bayat 2010, 21). As Bayat recalled, in the cases he studied, 'vendors resisted the eviction policy in different ways. They organized street demonstrations, withstood the eviction agents on the spot, took legal actions, and publicized their plight in the press. The most enduring method was the everyday guerrilla-type tactic of "sell and run"' (Bayat 2010, 149). These tactics spread street politics, defined as 'a set of conflicts and the attendant implications between a collective populace and the authorities, shaped and expressed episodically in the physical and social space of the streets' (Bayat 2010, 15). A street vendor, and his self-immolation, were in fact at the root of the Tunisian upheaval and in Egypt the protest spread when it involved the poor peripheries.

In all the cases, if traditions were visible in the waves of protest for democracy, these waves were also powerful producers of new forms of action that often merged the disruption of everyday life with the construction of prohibited free spaces. As Fillieule (2013) has suggested looking at the Arab Spring, a logic of the situation emerged, inscripted in norms. Oppositional roundtables in Eastern Europe, like the camps in main squares during the Arab Spring, had acquired an important role in the reconstruction of that public space that the authority coerced and denied. They constituted powerful symbols, but also safe havens where fear was kept at bay and solidarity developed.

What is more, the short but intense waves of protests were punctuated by transformative events, often related to moments of brutal repression and/or innovative resistance to it. Intense emotions of rage and indignation then allowed protestors to overcome the fear that usually keeps squares (and streets) empty in authoritarian regimes. Claims became politicized, as growing participation created a sense of empowerment and relations became increasingly dense, with formal and informal networks connecting recently mobilized individuals into broad oppositional webs.

While social movement studies mainly assume political opportunities and organizational resources to be preconditions for action, the eventful nature of the protests we analysed emerged during the mobilization. These processes of intensification and densification help to explain a paradox from which several analyses of democratization waves begin: the unexpected surprise of a change that nobody (among scholars and observers, but also often opposi-tional activists and repressive apparatuses) had predicted or expected. Going beyond the individual changes in calculations of risks and advantages that the increase in the number of protestors brings about (e.g. Kuran 1991), I have also pointed at collective processes that developed in action. In this sense the protests did produce more resources and opportunities than they, so to speak, consumed, showing that social movements and protests waves can also develop when few resources and opportunities are available, or when these are declining rather than expanding.

The eventfulness of the protests was all the more evident in the path that I called, indeed, 'eventful democratization', in which a chain of disruptive events, in part led by social movement organizations of various types, struc-tured the transition. This we saw in particular in the GDR and Czechoslovakia in Eastern Europe, and in Tunisia and Egypt in the MENA region, where transitions were relatively peaceful. Intense moments of protest for democ-racy did, however, sometimes develop into violent forms, especially where civil society groups were weaker and repressive apparatuses (or the regime's willingness to use them) stronger. This was indeed the case in Romania and Albania, or—even more so—in Libya and Syria. In yet other cases, those I called participated pacts, eventful protests were more occasional, as civil society organizations invested their reputations for action, rather than collec-tive action itself, in the bargaining with elites. Poland and Hungary emerged as particular examples of this path.

Differently from what the transition studies have suggested, we saw that some forms of mobilization from below were therefore present in different paths, and that they were not only occasional or episodic. Protest was used during different phases of the transition: it produced liberalization, pushed for breakdown, influenced negotiations.

Even when social movement organizations were present in the streets, however, they had limited control over protest. While social movement stud-ies tend to assume some overlap between collective actions and (somewhat) organized actors, we saw instead different constellations, not only in differ-ent cases but also in different moments within each case. As the wave of protest drew large masses of first-comers into the streets, the capacity of their promoters to control (or lead) participants tended to drop.

Mobilizing Resources: Between Disruptive Movements and Civil Society

If resources and opportunities developed in action through emerging pro-cesses, previously existing resources and opportunities—themselves built in (previous) action—cannot be overlooked. As mentioned, refuting a structuralist for a dynamic explanation does not mean to deny that agency and structures do influence each other. So while we saw during the protest important moments of coordination in action, with a flourishing of new organizational forms (especially but not only coordinating committees), pre-existing social movement organizations and experiences were important as well.

Given the repressive nature of the regimes, these social movement organizations—often defined under the label of civil society—often had specific characteristics vis-à-vis those in democratic countries. First of all, they were smaller in members, even if occasionally capable of mobilizing hundreds or thousands in petitions, vigils, or demonstrations. Second, the more openly oppositional they were, the more they were forced to live a semi-clandestine life, alternating public statements in moments of liberalization with low-profile activities in moments of higher repression. Third, oppositional groups were sometimes connected to official institutions, occasionally carving out free spaces in churches, firms, schools, and universities. Officially recognized unions or professional associations also sometimes left some spaces for autonomous initiatives at the margins.

With social movement organizations in democracy, however, they shared their preference for loosely networked horizontal structures. Giving a positive value to direct participation, they also often took the form of affinity groups, building upon family or friendship ties. Sometimes, political solidarities grew out of previous contentious moments, remaining alive in little-visible forms. But new oppositional groups also emerged, mobilizing new generations of activists.

If horizontality granted the flexibility that was all the more necessary given strong repressive apparatuses, loose networks still needed some coordination, especially when the number of protests and protestors increased. New social movement umbrella organizations then emerged, often with these specific tasks; but their coordination was also helped considerably by previous experiences. Coalition building in fact happened during the protest waves, but the process was facilitated by previous experiences of coordination. Exactly these efforts at coordination were challenged by the authoritarian regimes, which used hidden intelligence and visible selective incentives oriented to divide the oppositional forces. In Eastern Europe, the regimes attempted to split the opposition by playing the workers against the intellectuals. In the MENA region, the divisions between secular and Islamist groups have often been fuelled by the authoritarian regimes, which co-opted sometimes the ones, sometimes the others. Reciprocal accusations of collaboration with the dictator in the brutal repression of the other have in fact long jeopardized alliances between religious and secular groups.

Transnational networks increased the organizational resources of those mobilizing for democracy, giving international visibility to the oppositional claims, as well as some protection from repression to the activists. The capacity to build up ties was unequally distributed, however, as it presupposed some liberalization. Moreover, the protective umbrella of transnational organizations required, in order to be effective, some sensitivity by the authoritarian regimes to potential pressures by external actors.

In particular, as the protest intensified, an arduous task for small and tendentially scattered—or loosely structured—networks was the development of a discourse capable of resonating with a broad range of political and social groups. The stigmatization of opponents as corrupt often emerged as an effective framing strategy. This approach targeted, in a more literal sense, the enrichment of the political elites as well as the political influence of the business elites—but also, in a more symbolic way, elites' betrayal of their original promises, and thus the social pacts upon which the state was built.

In parallel, the framing of the self needed a broader appeal, which was often found in reference to the nation. As protest expanded, demands became more politicized but also more radical, converging on the call for the fall of the authoritarian regime. Patriotic appeals were visible in the use of national anthems and flags, as well as in the organization of protest on important national anniversaries. This allowed activists to propose an alternative vision of the nation to the one presented by the authoritarian state, at the same time exploiting the possibility of occupying public spaces, transforming the meaning of permitted public demonstrations into acts of defiance.

Beyond the definition of the 'us' and the 'them', an important part in the claiming and framing referred to the visions and practices of democracy. Waves of protest for democracy often debouched in institutional reforms that provided some institutions of representative democracy—first of all, basic civic freedoms and free elections. Often, however, activists were less than satisfied with these reforms, which also, paradoxically, did not seem to favour those very actors from below that had succeeded in putting the dictators down. This can be explained in part by the misfit between the participatory appeals of those who protested and the delegated nature of the democratic institutions they achieved, but also by the tensions between the majoritarian logic of elections and the consensus-building, deliberative visions of the activists.

Pre-existing organizations offered organizational skills and a patrimony of relations and memories, but new groups also emerged to coordinate informal nets of activists. As mentioned, if domestic and transnational organizational resources are important in the logistics of the mobilization, during eventful protests we also saw the limited (and oscillating) capacity of these loosely structured networks to actually control the moods and claims of the large mobilized masses.

If these aspects emerged, more or less clearly, in all the cases we analysed, there were infra-area and inter-area differences in the mobilization of protest as well. First, eventful democratizations happened when and where social movement organizations were somewhat rooted, while violent eruptions were connected with the weakness of the civil society. As the Polish case indicates so well, however, the strength of social movement organizations can at times be used on the negotiation table rather than on the streets. In fact, SMOs even fear—as did Solidarity—the emergence of protests they cannot control, and prefer to bargain with the authorities before losing ground.

Another difference—to a certain extent cross-area—is related to the types of social movements and civil society organizations that dominated the action. Human rights organizations, student organizations, peace groups, environmental associations, women's organizations, religious actors were present in almost all of our cases, finding some space in part by adapting to the discourse of the regime, in part by seeking protection in international norms. The balance of old and new social movements varied, however, with the labour movements being more present in the Middle East (but also in Poland) and human rights groups (and frames) more present in Eastern Europe. Moreover, even if religious figures were present in all cases, secular versus religious cleavages were more relevant in the Middle East than in Eastern Europe. And while nationalism appeals spread in all the analysed protest waves, inclusive nationalism and ethnical homogeneity facilitated democratization in some cases, while exclusive nationalism and intra-ethnic (linguistic, religious, tribal) conflicts instead delayed it (as, for example, the Yugoslavian case, but also Syria indicated).

The Social Background

Organizational coalitions also reflected the social groups which mobilized for democracy. Some research on authoritarian regimes has looked at the role of various institutions as (involuntary) carriers of oppositional spaces. This is first of all the case of *cultural institutions*. Dictators need to provide education, even if often of low or unequal quality. Sometimes, they have even invested in higher education in order to promote economic modernization or military projects. Especially as demands for educational equality have expanded and the quality of the offer declined, or expectations of future social mobility were blocked, students have tended to become main actors in political transformations. As Parsa summarized: 'Students in developing countries have been at the forefront of revolutionary struggles and have revealed an intense interest in fundamentally transforming the social structures' (Parsa 2000, 94). In fact,

> They have enjoyed immense prestige and have often played a very significant role in the revolutionary process. Highly concentrated in colleges and universities, students possess extensive communication networks, which facilitate their collective action. Students in higher education often benefit from universities' relative autonomy—where it exists—and academic freedom, which provide them, at least theoretically, with immunity and insulation from state repression (Parsa 2000).

According to Parsa, lacking direct involvement in production, they do not so much articulate economic claims, but rather 'develop greater interest in theoretical and ideological issues, especially as they are immersed in the production and reproduction of knowledge and ideas' (Parsa 2000, 95).

Moreover, student protests have often been linked to those of intellectuals, who can also sometimes count on the construction of free spaces through cultural events, literary circles, and so on. For instance, in China in 1989, protest developed especially inside the universities, more specifically in Beijing, but expanded as forty-two intellectuals signed a petition asking for democratization, freedom of speech and the press, release of political prisoners, more funds for education and research, and higher salaries for intellectuals. After presenting a petition to the authorities, they also called for recognition of an autonomous student movement. The university and the intellectuals also tended to dominate the mobilization later on.[1]

In our cases, students and intellectuals were in fact mobilized with central relevance in Czechoslovakia and Poland as well as in Tunisia and Egypt. If students are often the first social group to engage in collective action, and those who do it more often, in our cases students were involved to different extents—for example, more in Czechoslovakia than in the GDR, more in Poland than in Hungary, more in Albania than in Romania, probably more in Tunisia than in Egypt.[2] Moreover, their degree of ideologization varied: even if usually more radical in their demands than other mobilized groups (for example, in Poland in 1980–1 or Czechoslovakia in 1989), their protest often started with some specific grievance on cultural freedom (especially in the Eastern European cases), or bridging the calls for freedom with a call for (fair) employment (especially in

---

[1] On 23 April, 10,000 converged in protest on the field of Beijing University. The movement spread quickly after that. On 27 April, 100,000 to half a million marched, notwithstanding fear of tough repression (Calhoun 1994, 54). As a federation of autonomous student unions was formed and students asked for its recognition, some calls for dialogue emerged in the party, and a minor figure was sent by the government.

[2] In fact, 'Everywhere students were the majority of those arrested, imprisoned, tortured, killed or disappeared' (Parsa 2000, 129). This was possible thanks to some degree of tolerance in the respective institutions and expanding higher education.

the MENA region). In this sense, we found, in particular in the MENA region, a similar path to the one observed in the Sub-Saharan countries, where, on the campuses, 'The protests usually began with corporate demands by interest groups seeking to improve material conditions within their own sector of the urban economy. Typically, unrest originated among students demonstrating against a government decision to impose austerity measures which affected them directly.'[3] Unemployed, educated youth had particular importance in the MENA region, where the Arab Spring has been defined as a revolution of the young. This was less the case in other countries where, for example in the GDR or Syria, access to the university had been controlled by the regime, which had selected out potentially critical students.

Oppositional intellectuals played an important role everywhere, keeping alive the oppositional ideas in moments of latency, as well as prompting the beginning of the rebellious moments. Dissidence also developed in fact among writers, musicians, intellectual circles, and so on. Writers and journalists played a role in Hungary in 1956 and Czechoslovakia in the 1960s. Musicians such as the Plastic People of the Universe and the Prague Jazz Days were important in Czechoslovakia, as was the rock band Azra in Yugoslavia. Intellectuals played a role in Poland and Hungary (with flying universities in both countries), as well as in Czechoslovakia, the Soviet Union, and Serbia. Singers, actors, and writers also supported the protests in the MENA region.

Similarly to the students and intellectuals, the clergy—even if often considered as conservative—is also sometimes politicized; struggles for change are sometimes catalysed by the end of alliances between church and state. According to Parsa's research, 'The clergy's relative immunity and control of a social space safe from government interference enable them to play an important part in political mobilization' (Parsa 2000, 131).[4] As mentioned, in

---

[3] 'In Gabon in January 1990, for example, students took strike action over teaching shortages and poor study facilities; in Cote d'Ivoire in February 1990 several inopportune electricity cuts before mid-term exams sparked the first significant protests. Not all student demands, however, were confined to parochial and material concerns. In Zimbabwe in October 1989 campus troubles broke out over the issue of elite corruption and quickly escalated into a critique of the government's use of state of emergency powers to quell dissent. In Kenya in February 1990, where students had long complained about overcrowded educational facilities and soaring unemployment rates, protesters decried the alleged implication of government security forces in the murder of Foreign Minister Robert Ouko. Civil unrest gathered momentum when it became an outlet for a coalition of diverse corporate interests. Students were joined by faculty and civil servants complaining about their own conditions, e.g. in Cote d'Ivoire, Benin, Zambia and Kenya' (Bratton and van de Walle 1992, 422).

[4] Clerics were involved in all three cases Parsa studied. Some oppositional activities were in fact directly embedded in these types of religious milieus. In Iran, clerics opened the mosques to mourn the victims of the shah's repression; if some supported Khomeini, most asked for social justice and freedom. In Nicaragua, where the clergy was active already in the late sixties (Parsa 2000, 146), their criticism of the regime increased after the poor management of the post-earthquake intervention in 1972, including denunciation of repression in the late 1970s. Some priests even allied with Sandinistas in the 1970s. In the Philippines, where the church initially played a more moderate role, some clergy in fact left in protest at the hierarchy's silence on the regime's violation

all our cases religious organizations were—more or less centrally—involved, providing protection, inspiration, and free spaces for protest, even though the dominant church hierarchy was usually fearful of exacerbating already tense relations with the dictators. The importance of religion was especially clear in the case of Poland, where, although secular, Solidarity often referred to the Catholic origin of the nation, also enjoying a sort of special protection by the Catholic Church and its Polish Pope. Also in the GDR, however, some part of the Protestant Church, even if with internal tensions, provided free spaces and logistic resources, as well as some institutional protection to the activists. In some cases, it was minority churches that supported the opposition; in others (as in Syria), inter-religious fights were reflected in the composition of incumbents and opponents, with some religious leaders playing important roles especially in the second phase of the revolt. As mentioned, the cleavage between secular and religious forces was especially strong in the MENA region.

Workers have often been a vital actor in struggles for democratization. As mentioned in the introduction, Ruth Collier has distinguished three meanings of the term 'from below', related respectively to the position vis-à-vis the regime (challengers rather than incumbents), the arena of action (protest rather than negotiation), and the class basis (labour versus elites). Beyond a once widespread stereotype that related democratic values to the middle class, historical comparisons have pointed at the centrality of labour in most historical cases of democratization. As we saw, our cases, like others, also varied in terms of the presence of workers as an organized force in the oppositional coalitions.

Some of the main works in historical sociology have linked democratization to class relations, stressing the importance of the working class as promoter of democracy. Although recognizing a path of democratization from below, these studies still tended to explain it mainly based on structural conditions. In fact, class accounts that recognized a role for workers tended to adopt a structural perspective (Collier 1999), predicting democratization when democracy-demanding classes (especially the working class) are stronger than democracy-resisting ones (Foweraker and Landman 1997).

Much research has stressed the importance of workers' organizations in waves of democratization in Latin America and southern Europe, as well as in 'first democratizations' in western Europe. The Spanish case provides a clear illustration of the development of opposition within free spaces conquered inside economic institutions. As Maravall (1982) noted, 'popular pressure "from below", especially that coming from the workers' movement, played

---

of human rights, while radical clergy formed Christian base communities, until in the late 1970s, the high hierarchy level also took a differentiated position.

a crucial part in the transition. It was a causal factor in the Francoist crisis, in the non-viability of any mere "liberalization" policy, in the willingness on the part of the "democratic right" to negotiate the transition and carry through reform up to the point of breaking with Francoism, and in the initiative displayed by the Left up to the 1977 elections'.[5] Labour continued to exercise pressure later on, during the transition: 'Labor protest destabilized the authoritarian regime, made impossible a reform that stopped short of democratization, and thus forced incumbents to undertake a rather speedy extrication' (Collier and Mahoney 1997, 294).

A similar capacity of mobilization to spread from factory issues to political issues has also been noted in several transitions in Latin America. Collier and Mahoney (1997) thus concluded their comparative analysis:

> In sum, our analysis has supplemented the focus on elites with one on collective action by paying particular attention to the labor movement. In initial stages of democratization, labor mobilization in the pattern of destabilization/extrication contributed to divisions among authoritarian incumbents, who previously had no transitional project. During relatively early stages in the transitions game labor protest for democracy helped to derail the legitimation projects of incumbents. In later stages of the transition labor mobilization had two effects. First, depending on the pattern, protest provoked or quickened the transition and kept it on track. These effects were the consequence of pressure exerted to the very end. Our case evidence thus calls into question the perspective that labor restraint during the final transition phase contributes to democracy by convincing elites that democracy can lead to social and political order, thereby facilitating elite negotiations.... Second, mobilization and protest won labor-based parties a place among the negotiators and also in the successor regimes.... The collective action of labor movements thus played a key democratic role not only in propelling a transition, but also in expanding political space and the scope of contestation in the new democratic regime (Collier and Mahoney 1997, 299–300).

High levels of labour mobilization in Peru, Brazil, Uruguay, and Argentina not only contributed to the breakdown of the regimes but also won the workers' representatives a place in the elites' negotiations towards the establishment of a new regime.

---

[5] Notwithstanding repression, there were important waves of strikes in the 1960s (Fishman 1990) and labour protest was extremely frequent in the 1970s, with peaks in 1974 and 1976: 'Labor protest thus undermined the strategy of limited liberalization pursued by Arias.... By the time Suarez became prime minister, then, the labour movement had done much both to destabilize the authoritarian regime and to reject government attempts to respond in ways that fell short of democracy. It seemed clear that the government had to find some means of effecting a speedy transition' (Collier and Mahoney 1997, 293). The number of workers on strike grew from about 500,000 in 1975 (with ten million hours of strikes) to more than three and a half million (with 110 million hours) in 1976. There were similar strike rates in 1977 and 1978, even increasing to 5.8 million (and 170 million hours) in 1979, to decline in 1980 to below the 1976 level (Fishman 1990).

Workers also played an important role in all three cases analysed by Parsa (2000). Less ideological in Iran, where they were weakened by high levels of repression, they organized nevertheless wildcat strikes. Well organized and, even by the 1970s, also very politicized, in Nicaragua workers allied in a coalition against Somoza, and then tended to join the Sandinistas. In the Philippines, the workers, initially moderate, radicalized during the struggle.

Popular protests on socio-economic problems have also been considered as relevant in the case of Sub-Saharan Africa. As Michael Bratton and Nicolas van de Walle (1992) noted,

> In and around 1990, citizens took to the streets of capital cities in some sixteen sub-Saharan African countries to express discontent with economic hardship and political repression and to demand civic reforms. Governments in the region faced pressures for political change on a scale unprecedented since the dissolution of colonial rule thirty years earlier. In response, between November 1989 and May 1991, at least twenty-one governments adopted significant reform measures to permit greater pluralism and competition within the polity. Multiparty elections were actually held for the first time in a generation in five African countries (Bratton and van de Walle 1992, 419).[6]

Workers were present among the protestors in most of the cases I have analysed, but their role as organized actors varied widely. With the exception of Poland, workers did mobilize in Eastern Europe, but not within their organizations. Regime controls on the union, as well as the offer of services and reduced inequalities, converged to discourage such participation. Free unions did not exist, and the ideology of a 'workers' dictatorship' contributed, at the same time, to thwart protests (for instance, the strike was considered as a relevant instrument in capitalist society, but dismissed as unnecessary in 'real socialism'), and to pushing toward compromise when they occurred. Workers contributed however specific forms and episodes of contention: the general strike represented a tipping point in Czechoslovakia, and workers mobilized in labour conflicts in Kosovo as well as Romania. In addition, as in Albania, waves of strikes and labour protests followed the pace of the waves of protest for democracy. Nevertheless, with the mentioned exception of Poland, there was no free space within the official unions that could contribute to the development of autonomous struggles by the workers.

---

[6] Based on newspaper sources on protest, they suggested that the 'African governments introduce political reforms primarily in response to active demands, spontaneous and organized, from a loose, multi-class assemblage of indigenous protest groups. Explanation of reform outcomes requires reference to the resources, skills, and styles of leaders and their oppositions. Protest and reform occur in a dynamic, reiterative process of action and counteraction in which strategic actors take their cues from the behavior of adversaries. Indeed, these two sets of events are difficult to separate analytically' (Bratton and van de Walle 1992).

Very different was the case of the MENA region (although with the exception of Libya and Syria). Here, economic complaints increased during various waves of economic liberalization, with privatizations and cuts in services and subsidies producing riots and strikes. Even if the respective regimes controlled the trade unions, some autonomous spaces were carved out at the periphery. Waves of strikes were in fact particularly intense, not only during the struggles that led to the fall of the dictators but especially afterwards—in Egypt and, even more so, in Tunisia. Particularly the latter case points at the importance of past historical experiences: although later fully co-opted by the regime, the Tunisian unions had played a fundamental role in the anti-colonial struggle, thus gaining prestige and specific concessions. Not only the labour unions, but also the unions of lawyers (in Tunisia), judges (in Egypt), journalists, and other professionals were important actors during the protests for democracy.

Especially in the MENA region, we saw also the mobilization of the poor. The Arab Spring in fact mobilized groups like the ones Bayat had studied in Iran. There, the squatters of the shantytowns who had mobilized to ask for basic services sometimes acquired them through illicit or do-it-yourself practices, tapping water and electricity, constructing roads, clinics, mosques, and libraries, forming their own associations and consumer cooperatives (Bayat 2010, 2). Similar was the resistance of the unemployed, often young, who protested, but also engaged in street vending and street services, putting up kiosks or stalls, as 'their collective operation converted the street sidewalks into vibrant and colorful shopping places' (Bayat 2010, 3). As Bayat stated, 'contrary to the prevailing stereotypes that portray them as "passive poor", "fatalistic Muslim masses", or "disoriented marginal", the disenfranchised do not sit around to wait for their fate but are actively engaged, within their constraints, in shaping their own destiny' (1997, 158).[7]

Concluding, to different extents and in different constellations, free spaces were created in authoritarian regimes, in part through the appropriation of institutional spaces such as schools, universities, factories, or religious places. Forms of resistance developed there, directly linked to the characteristics of the mobilized actors. Especially in the MENA region, in line with Rueschemeyer, Stephens, and Stephens' analysis, the counter-hegemonic growth of working classes has emerged as critical for the promotion of democracy as 'a dense civil society establishes a counterweight to the state, so favouring democracy' (1992, 50). It was, however, not their 'objective' interest, but rather their cognitive activation that pushed the mobilization—as 'classes may indeed have objective interests, but in historical reality class interests are inevitably subject to social construction' (Rueschemeyer et al. 1992, 53). The definition

---

[7] For example, in Cairo there were over a hundred spontaneous communities, hosting seven million people (Bayat 2010).

309

and redefinition of the (broadly underdetermined) interests of the working class are especially reliant upon the development of autonomous leaders. Also in our cases, 'the relative size and density of organization of the working class—of employed manual workers outside agriculture—are of critical importance for the advance of democracy' (Rueschemeyer et al. 1992, 59), as 'the many acquire power essentially through organization' (Rueschemeyer et al. 1992, 66).

Violent, Non-Violent and Beyond

Theorization, especially on the Orange Revolutions, has pointed at the role of non-violent resistance in the development of democratization processes. Some research within the non-violence perspective has also addressed the ways in which authoritarian regimes do indeed affect the organizational strategies of social movements through repression. As Kurt Schock observed, 'In nondemocratic contexts, the forging of oppositional networks is vital to successfully challenging the state and developing civil society and democratic relations' (2005, 29). According to non-violence theorists, these networks should use a mix of non-violent strategies to forge new autonomous relations (Schock 2005, 40). They involve methods of protest, persuasion, and non-cooperation, with non-violent interventions as acts of interposition oriented to disrupt order or develop alternatives (Schock 2005, 39). Strategically, they aim at a political jujitsu: non-violence in the face of state repression should reduce support for the regime, as it produces doubts about state legitimacy, divisions in the elites, sympathy for the opposition by other (also international) actors. The dynamics of mobilization are therefore influenced by the availability of allies, which however do not necessarily precede the emergence of protest. First, liberalization supports further mobilization, as 'When concessions are made by the authorities, mobilization is usually encouraged. Recognizing that even larger concessions might be wrought with larger numbers of participants in collective action, more people are mobilized, and with each new concession mobilization increases' (Schock 2005, 31).

Many of the recent democratization campaigns from below adopted a strategy of unarmed or civil resistance (Nepstad 2011), usually defined as non-violence, which was justified either morally or pragmatically. Timothy Garton Ash (2011) called non-violent action a distinctive form of power: people power against force. Non-violence relies on a relational conception of power, which is linked to the idea that rulers need to rely on support from the subordinated, that is, they have no intrinsic power, and can be weakened if citizens devise strategies of non-cooperation by refusing to acknowledge the rulers as legitimate, contesting the mentality and ideology of obedience, refusing to obey laws and cooperate with the regime (Nepstad 2011). Withdrawal of material resources is extremely important, as is the refusal to use one's own skills to support the regime's activities. Non-violence can also undermine the state's sanctioning power, in particular, by persuading soldiers and police to side with the citizens; protests for democratization are in fact said to be forty-six times more likely to succeed if security forces defect (Nepstad 2011). In general, 'Civil resistance often creates a situation in which a major power is shamed into acting—even into using military force' (Roberts 2011, 16). Central to the non-violence relational approach to power are in fact the concepts of resilience, as the capacity of the opposition to maintain mobilization in the face of constraining activities; and leverage, as the capacity to affect resources that are relevant for the regime (Schock 2005, 142–3). Non-violence is said to facilitate convergence (Garton Ash 2011),[8] as well as capable of diffusing power and maximizing the segments of the population that can take part (Schock 2005, 22).

Linking non-violence to regime transformation, Kurt Schock (2005) talked of unarmed insurrections, which he defined as 'organized challenges to government authorities that depend primarily on methods of nonviolent action' (xvi). As he observed in his research on successful unarmed insurrections in South Africa, Philippines, Nepal, and Thailand, and on unsuccessful ones in Burma and China, non-violent resistance is neither just passivity nor a simple compromise or necessarily oriented towards moderate aims, but it is non-institutionalized, involving risks. In general, he observed that, in developing countries, there is less and less use of violent means (such as guerrilla) and more and more non-violent campaigns. This is favoured by new communication means, global civil society, and transnational advocacy networks, which document violations and promote non-violence.

In the cases covered in this volume, as mentioned, the repertoires of action were always complex and multifaceted. While the dominant narratives tended to hide moments of violence, those were quite present in many, if not all cases. While what I defined as eventful democratization remained mainly peaceful, violence erupted in Tunisia and Egypt, as escalations of long-term tensions between the police and the people as well as by regime attempts at brutal repression. These traditions were to a certain extent important in providing protestors with tactical knowledge about how to protect themselves from repression. Violence was less present in participated pacts, even if—also there—there was repression and resistance to it, but particularly brutal events

---

[8] Turning points in reflections on nonviolence include Mahatma Gandhi's campaigns in South Africa in 1906–14 and in India in 1919–48 (Carter 2011). Defined as *satyagraha*, 'the true force', Gandhi's principle implies a determination to resist injustice without violence. In a strategic dramaturgy, 'The history of civil resistance is also art history. The logos, flags, symbols, improvised posters, street performances, music, slogans and graffiti' (Garton Ash 2011, 382).

punctuated the route to democratization in Romania and Albania in 1989 and 1990, while democratization struggles were intertwined with civil wars in the former Yugoslavia as well as in the Syrian and Libyan cases. A main cause for escalation in these cases was, together with brutal repression, divisions in the repressive apparatuses that, through defections from armies and police, also provided the opposition with arms and military skills. Often, foreign actors contributed to this armament and related radicalization.

The Appropriation of Opportunities: Between The State and The Market

The impact of type of regime, as a mix of political institutions and state-market arrangements, has been addressed in the democratization literature within two main streams of research. One, as mentioned, focused on political institutions, building typologies that usually combined the degree of repressiveness and the main actors in the elites. So totalitarian regimes have been contrasted with authoritarian ones and—more recently—hybrids, sometimes defined as liberalized autocracies, where elections take place (even if the autocrats always win by large margins) and some fluctuating amount of civil rights are (formally or informally) recognized. Moreover, militaristic versus non-militaristic regimes have been singled out, according to the importance attributed to the army; monarchies have been contrasted to non-monarchies; one-party regimes distinguished from others; patronage opposed to non-patronage based regimes; and religious autocracies recently identified as a specific category. Of course, all these being ideal-types, empirical cases have been singled out as mixing different characteristics, as well as evolving in time. Social movement studies have looked especially at political institutions, (strangely) leaving economic relations out of the picture (Goodwin and Hetlan 2009).

Our case studies confirmed that regime reactions were extremely important in influencing which type of paths democratization would take. In particular, some liberalization seemed crucial for the emergence of social movements of different types and their networking, as well as in constraining the repressive capacity of the dictators. So, inclusive elites were noted in participated pacts, while brutal repressions produced violent evolutions and eventful democratizations went along with the presence of exclusive elites—which had however been constrained in their use of violence, often by changing international conditions.

Linked to capacity and willingness to repress, the role of the army and other coercive apparatuses during the upheaval was, as mentioned, often very important. Authoritarian regimes of different types showed attempts at mobilizing various actors of coercion: military and non-military, public and private (as militias). While peaceful evolutions were usually linked to refusal by these actors to obey dictators' orders, splits in and defections among these forces brought about the availability of military skills and logistics for the opposition, with violent evolution (as in Romania or in Libya and Syria). Not only elites' use of coercion, but also co-optation and/or nationalist mobilizations clearly interacted with the democratization paths that influenced social movements and protest intensity and forms. Moreover, during mobilizations, cleavages emerged within the elites—for example, between party leaders and the elites in government.

Looking at the dynamics of democratization from below does not therefore imply overlooking the role of the elites, but rather locating it in a web of interactions. However, institutional elites, their interests and their predispositions, were not the only determinants of more-repressive versus less-repressive attitudes. The types of elites' coalitions that reacted to protest were in fact more complex, including non-institutional actors, among them those of an economic type.

While the abundant literature on transitional studies focused especially on institutional characteristics, another approach looked more carefully at the relationships between political and economic elites—with special consideration for the role of specific classes. In particular, the relationship between class and democratization can be, and has been, approached within various perspectives. In the tradition of Barrington Moore and historical sociology, scholars have debated the issue of class structure as a root cause of democracy. Similarly, although with different focuses, research on social stratification has associated democratization with the growth of the middle class, while only more recently has research stressed, as mentioned, the role of the working class. Economic characteristics—not only the amount of resources but also the degree of economic inequality and international market integration—have been examined in a search for the preconditions of democracy. In a different approach—the so-called second wave of research on democratization—researchers have focused on the strategies and predispositions of elites and masses rather than on classes as an aggregate.

This also brought attention to the specific economic grievances that emerged in capitalist versus non-capitalist authoritarian regimes as frequent bases for politicization. Together with the contrasts between stucturalist and contingent explanations or domestic versus international ones, Bratton and van de Walle (1997) located a main cleavage in democratization studies between those based on economic factors and those based on political explanations. Economic explanations often cite rapid economic growth as destabilizing, but also consider economic crises as producing either democratization or authoritarian turns (for example, third wave democratization have been seen as fuelled by weak economic performance of Latin American elites). Effects are filtered, however, through visions of democracy—so that political democratization is often seen as linked to reduction of economic inequalities but also to tensions, as protests accompanied austerity policies imposed by the donor countries and increased inequalities that require authoritarian repressive regimes to be implemented (Bratton and van de Walle 1997, 35). If economic success can give authoritarian leaders enough confidence to support liberalization, in reverse, it can also give them more leverage to remain in power. Economic crises can undermine democracy, but also autocracies.

Indeed, my comparisons tended to indicate economic difficulties as fundamental bases for dissatisfaction and complaints, which eventually resulted in politicization and collective protest. Economic strains were in fact at the origins of waves of protest that took place even in the most repressive regimes, which often used a mix of coercion and concessions when addressing them. Cuts in subsidies for basic goods produced contentious reactions in countries as different as Poland and Tunisia, in the forms of strikes but also of riots. In addition, policies of economic liberalization increased inequalities and dissatisfaction in 'real socialist' Eastern Europe as well as in the MENA region. These not only produced growth in poverty and especially feelings of injustice, but also meant a break in the promises of modernization dictators had made to their citizens. Dramatic economic difficulties, up to state bankruptcy, under some conditions pushed moderates in the regime to negotiate with moderates in the opposition, in their search for reforms that could allow redressing those difficulties.

The corruption of elites through the contamination of politics and business has been seen as a main negative evolution in both geopolitical areas, where the founders of the nations were considered as sometimes more brutal, but at least more idealist, and their followers instead as increasingly interested in personal material gains. Patrimonialism as a way to selectively secure consensus to the regime at both elite and mass levels was stigmatized in Eastern Europe as in the MENA region, dictators in both areas being accused of accumulating not only power but also wealth for themselves and restricted cliques of relatives. The more personalized these circles, the more exclusive the regimes tended to be—suffice it to think about Romania or Libya.

However, these similarities should not obfuscate some differences, which are also reflected in the different compositions of elites and opposition in Eastern Europe versus the MENA region. In real socialism, the potential for personal enrichment of the members of the regime apparatuses had been an important reason for the alienation of the masses from the regime, but also for the availability to negotiate among the elites. In the capitalist MENA countries, each neo-liberal turn in economic and social policies brought about an increase in social inequalities, with the growth of politically protected business elites, and of kleptocratic political elites. Limited inequalities meant that class issues were

less explicitly addressed in Eastern Europe than in the MENA region—as mentioned, human rights discourses dominated in the former, while in the latter
social justice was a central frame. Also, while in Eastern Europe socialism had
produced a sort of petite bourgeoisie (with secure jobs and welfare protection,
even when dreams of consumption were frustrated), in the MENA region the
middle classes felt themselves victims of privatization and cuts in services.

The International Dimension of Democratization
from Below

An additional issue related to the attribution of opportunities is the degree
and form of international opportunities for democratization movements.
While both social movement studies and democratization studies have traditionally focused on domestic conditions and processes, more recently the
relevance of international and transnational levels of action has come to the
fore. In this volume, I have discussed two main supranational dimensions.
One was related to international opportunities and constraints, addressing
the impact of other countries—mainly superpowers—as well as international
organizations on struggles for democratization; the other to diffusion.

The role of European countries, through the signing of the Helsinki
Charter, and especially of shifts in Soviet politics and policies, emerged as
most relevant in setting political opportunities for the 1989 democratization
processes. Cross-national diffusion of social movements' ideas (on organizational structures, forms of action, framing) was then relevant in determining
the timing and characteristics of each wave of protest for democracy. These
processes were also facilitated by a sort of 'détente from below', with development of transnational ties among movements in Eastern Europe (especially
Central Eastern Europe) and with Western groups.

The international and transnational dimensions have been mentioned for
the Arab Spring as well. Here, however, the international arena mainly constrained the movements, as it meant Western (US and EU) support for dictators. Instead, aspects of cross-national diffusion had a greater impact, even if
their effects—constrained by domestic opportunities—varied broadly.

Cross-national diffusion has been studied in literature on democratization
in particular when looking at electoral transitions, in particular in so-called
colour revolutions. From Romania in 1996 and Bulgaria in 1996–7 a repertoire of protest linked to election spread, thanks to support by domestic
NGOs or NGOs active in other countries in the region (often sponsored by
USAID), to Slovakia in 1998 and Croatia in 2000. Here, activists stressed the
importance of previous meetings with Romanian and Bulgarian activists, as
they 'showed us the way, the light appeared at the end of the tunnel' (Bunce and

Wolchik 2011, 77) indicating that 'it can be done' (Bunce and Wolchik 2011, 78). As Bunce and Wolchik observed, 'In the Croatian case, we see the network of "graduates" of civic movements that succeeded in defeating undemocratic or semiautocratic leaders thicken. Just as Bulgarian and Romanian activists proved to be very important as inspirations and practical advisors in Slovakia, so Slovak "graduates" of OK '98 played a key role in bringing new electoral strategies and techniques to Croatia—a process encouraged in part by geographical proximity and commonalities in language' (Bunce and Wolchik 2011, 83). Similar transnational mechanisms were also at work in the protests around the Yugoslav elections of September 2000, when non-violent resistance was led by old oppositional intellectuals and new generation organized in the student group Otpor.

While much theorization developed on the colour revolutions, some specific aspects of transnationalization could be peculiar to them. In particular, the possibility and willingness of Western powers (especially the US) to promote democracy was related to a context of liberalized autocracies, with dictators that did not gravitate in the Western geopolitical spheres of influence. Distributing funds to actors aiming at democratization from below was not possible in Eastern Europe, still under the control of the Soviet Union. Additionally, while funds went to civil society in the MENA region, they were selectively oriented to the groups considered as loyal (or loyal enough) by the regime. Also, while in Eastern Europe the Helsinki treaty had provided normative resources, in the MENA region, civil society organizations were materially sponsored by international funds, which had been, as mentioned, selectively oriented towards some types of organizations rather than others, the former often enjoying some degree of regime recognition. As in the colour revolutions, in the MENA region international funds also spread a particular type of conception of civil society—as surrogating declining public services and gathering consensus for the states, rather than promoting contentious action and public criticism.[9]

If support from Western powers was limited in both waves I studied, there was instead cross-national diffusion of frames of resistance. So the interactions of opposition and incumbents, institutions, and movements were

[9] The example of these countries was followed: unsuccessfully in Armenia, Azerbaijan and Belarus; (temporarily) successfully in Ukraine, Georgia, and Kyrgyzstan. In Georgia, following the example of Otpor (Serbian activists offered two films to share their experiences), young activists founded Kmara ('enough', a slogan of Otpor's campaign). While NGOs and media monitored the elections, Western-funded NGOs having received training in the US, in the fall of 2002, activists from Otpor visited Tbilisi. Autochthonous NGOs benefited from information and training offered by a transnational advocacy network. Support from the west had 'led to the creation of a network of "professional revolutionaries" (or "consultants" if they were paid), supported by Western states, transnational organizations and international NGOs' (Jones 2011, 325). International support was strong: the US government invested in contributions to civil society $700 million between 1995 and 2000, and 350 million euros came from the EU. Shevardnadze tolerated it. With 9,000 NGOs in 2005, this was the largest third sector in the Caucasus (Jones 2011, 330).

influenced not only by the position of (properly defined) international actors, but also by the (changing) interactions among different actors in neighbouring countries. Successful non-violent strategies of early risers' movements were imitated and learned by latecomers, while, however, elites also learned from the failures of their counterparts. Elites and movements alike feared violent solutions—such as in Albania, after the Romanian revolution—but movements and institutions also copied successful violent strategies (as in the Syrian opposition after the apparent success of violent rebellion in Libya).

These phenomena of cross-national diffusion point at a methodological challenge, as the countries as units of analysis for comparative studies can no longer be considered as independent (Schmitter 2009). As Beissinger recalled, 'cross-case influence has played an important role in fostering democratization...yet, much of the comparative politics literature continues to treat cases as if they were totally independent of one another' (2007, 260). Waves of protest for democracy challenge instead the implicit teleology of the structural determination, based on the assumption that history contains an inherent logic, beyond control. While 'teleological explanation celebrates the determination of structure over action' (Beissinger 2002, 7), these processes show instead the interaction between structure and agency—which is a main lesson from this research.

Bibliographical References

Abbas, Mohammed, and Blair, Edmund (2011) 'Anti-Gaddafi Figures Say Form National Council', *Reuters*, 27 Feb., www.reuters.com/article/2011/02/27/ libya-council-revolution-idUSWEB194120110227 (accessed 5 May 2013).

Abdel-Baky, Mohamed (2011) 'Libya Protest over Housing Enters Its Third Day', *Ahraam Online*, 16 Jan., http://english.ahram.org.eg/NewsContent/2/8/4032/World/Region/ Libya-protest-over-housing-enters-its-third-day.aspx (accessed 5 May 2013).

Abdelrahman, Maha (2011) 'The Transnational and the Local: Egyptian Activists and Transnational Protest Networks', *British Journal of Middle Eastern Studies*, 38: 407–24.

Abdul-Magd, Zeinab (2011) 'The Army and the Economy in Egypt', *Jadaliyya*, http:// www.jadaliyya.com/pages/index/3732/the-army-and-the-economy-in-egypt (accessed 14 April 2013).

Abrahams, Fred (forthcoming) *Martyrs Boulevard: Albania's Wild Road to Freedom.* New York: New York University Press.

Abu-Lughod, Lila (2012) 'Living the "Revolution" in an Egyptian Village: Moral Action in a National Space', *American Ethnologist*, 39(1): 21–5.

Ahmida, Ali Abdullatif (2012) 'Libya, Social Origins of Dictatorship, and the Challenge for Democracy', *The Journal of the Middle East and Africa*, 3: 1.

Akar, Rıdvan (2009) *Aşkale Yolcuları. Varlık Vergisi Ve Çalışma Kampları.* Istanbul: Doğan Kitap.

Alexander, Christopher (1997) 'Back from the Democratic Brink: Authoritarianism and Civil Society in Tunisia', *Middle East Report*, 205 (1 Oct.): 34–8. doi: 10.2307/3013093.

Alexander, Christopher (2010) *Tunisia: Stability and Reform in the Modern Maghreb.* London: Routledge.

Alexander, Jeffrey C. (1998) 'Introduction. Civil Society I, II, III: Constructing an Empirical Concept from Normative Controversies and Historical Transformations', in Jeffrey C. Alexander, *Real Civil Societies: Dilemmas of Institutionalization.* London: Sage, 1–20.

Alexander, Jeffrey C. (2011) *Performative Revolution in Egypt: An Essay in Cultural Power.* London: Bloomsbury Academic.

Allal, Amin (2012) 'Trajectoires "révolutionnaires" en Tunisie. Processus de radicalizations politiques 2007–2011', *Revue francaise de science politique*, 62: 821–41.

Allal, Amin, and Geisser, Vincent (2011) 'Tunisie: "Révolution de Jasmin" ou Intifada', *Mouvements*, 2(66): 62–8.

Allani, Alaya (2009) 'The Islamists in Tunisia between Confrontation and Participation: 1980–2008', *The Journal of North African Studies*, 14: 257–72.

Amin, Samir (2012) 'The Arab Revolutions: A Year After', *Interface: a journal for and about social movements*, 4(1): 33–42.

Amnesty International (2005) 'Syria: Kurds in the Syrian Arab Republic One Year after the March 2004 Events', http://www.amnesty.org/en/library/info/MDE24/002/2005 (accessed 5 May 2013).

Amnesty International (2012) *Year of Rebellion: The State of Human Rights in the Middle East and North Africa*. London: Amnesty International.

Anderson, Lisa (2011) 'Demystifying the Arab Spring: Parsing the Differences between Tunisia, Egypt, and Libya', *Foreign Affairs*, May/June.

Anonymous (1996) 'Saraçhane Mitingi, 31.12.1961', in *Türkiye Sendikacılık Ansiklopedisi*. Istanbul: Türkiye Ekonomik ve Toplumsal Tarih Vakfı.

Aouragh, Miriyam, and Alexander, Anne (2011) 'The Egyptian Experience: Sense and Nonsense of the Internet Revolution', *International Journal of Communication*, 5: 1344–58.

Arendt, Hannah (1963) *On Violence*. New York: Harcourt Brace and Company.

Ashour, Omar (2012) 'Libyan Islamists Unpacked: Rise, Transformation, and Future', Brookings Institute, Policy Brief, Brookings Doha Institute, May.

Ayeb, Habib (2011) 'Social and Political Geography of the Tunisian Revolution: The Alfa Grass Revolution', *Review of African Political Economy*, 38(129): 467–79.

Ayubi, Nazih (2001) *Overstating the Arab State: Politics and Society in the Middle East*. London: I.B. Tauris.

Badie, Bertrand (2011) 'Printemps arabe: un commencement', *Études*, 415(7–8): 7–18.

Baker, Gideon (1999) 'The Taming Idea of Civil Society', *Democratization*, 6/3: 1–29.

Baker, Raymond W. (1990) *Sadat and After: Struggles for Egypt's Political Soul*. London: I.B. Tauris.

Baker, Raymond William (2012) 'Understanding Egypt's Worldly Miracles', *The Middle East Journal*, 66(1): 163–70.

Bamaare, Layla (2013). 'Quand les protestataires s'autolimitent. Le cas de mobilization étudiante de 2011 en Algerie', in Amin Allal and Thomas Pierret (eds), *Au coer des révolte arabes. Devenir revolutionaries*. Paris: Armand Colin, 137–59.

Bamyeh, Mohammed (2011) 'Is the 2011 Libyan Revolution an Exception', *Jadaliyya*, http://www.jadaliyya.com/pages/index/1001/is-the-2011-libyan-revolution-an-exception (accessed 25 March 2013).

Banac, Ivo (1992) 'Post-Communism as Post-Yugoslavism: The Yugoslav Non-Revolutions of 1989–1990', in Ivo Banac (ed.) *Eastern Europe in Revolution*. Ithaca, NY: Cornell University Press, 168–87.

Barany, Zoltan (2011) 'Comparing the Arab Revolts: The Role of the Military', *Journal of Democracy*, 22(4).

Barker, Collin (2001) 'Fear, Laughter and Collective Power: The Making of Solidarity at the Lenin Shipyard in Gdansk, Poland, August 1980', in James Goodwin, James M. Jasper, and Francesca Polletta (eds), *Passionate Politics: Emotions and Social Movements*. Chicago: The University of Chicago Press, 175–94.

Baruti, Fasfi (1996) 'A General Outlook on Albanian NGOs '96', *NGO Bulletin*, no. 12 (Dec.): Special Issue.

Bayat, Asef (1997) *Street Politics*. New York: Columbia University Press.

Bayat, Asef (2010) *Life as Politics*. Stanford, CA: Stanford University Press.

Bayat, Asef (2012) 'The "Arab Street"', in Jeannie Sowers and Chris Toensing (eds), *The Journey to Tahrir: Revolution, Protest, and Social Change in Egypt*. London: Verso, 73–84.

BBC News (2006) 'Ten Die in Libya Cartoon Clash', 18 Feb., http://news.bbc.co.uk/2/hi/africa/4726204.stm (accessed 5 May 2013).

Beattie, Kirk J. (2000) *Egypt during the Sadat Years*. Houndsmills and Hampshire: Palgrave.

Beinin, Joel (2011) 'A Workers' Social Movement on the Margin of the Global Neoliberal Order, Egypt 2004–2009', in Joel Benin and Frédéric Vairel (eds), *Social Movements, Mobilization and Contestation in the Middle East and North Africa*. Stanford, CA: Stanford University Press, 181–201.

Beinin, Joel (2012) 'The Working Class and the Popular Movement in Egypt', in Jeannie Sowers and Chris Toensing (eds), *The Journey to Tahrir: Revolution, Protest, and Social Change in Egypt*. London: Verso, 92–106.

Beinin, Joel, and Vairel, Frédéric (2011a) 'Afterword: Popular Uprising in Tunisia and Egypt', in Joel Benin and Frédéric Vairel (eds), *Social Movements, Mobilization and Contestation in the Middle East and North Africa*. Stanford, CA: Stanford University Press, 237–54.

Beinin, Joel, and Vairel, Frédéric (2011b) 'Introduction: The Middle East and North Africa. Beyond Classical Social Movement Theory', in Joel Benin and Frédéric Vairel (eds), *Social Movements, Mobilization and Contestation in the Middle East and North Africa*. Stanford, CA: Stanford University Press, 1–23.

Beinin, Joel, and Vairel, Frédéric (eds) (2011c) *Social Movements, Mobilization and Contestation in the Middle East and North Africa*. Stanford, CA: Stanford University Press.

Begir Ayari, Michael (2013) 'La "révolution tunisienne," une émeute politique qui a réussi?', in Amin Allal and Thomas Pierret (eds), *Au coer des révolte arabes. Devenir revolutionaries*. Paris: Armand Colin, 241–60.

Beissinger, Mark R. (2002) *Nationalist Mobilization and the Collapse of the Soviet State*. Cambridge: Cambridge University Press.

Beissinger, Mark R. (2007) 'Structure and Example in Modular Political Phenomena: The Diffusion of Bulldozer/Rose/Orange/Tulip Revolutions', *Perspectives on Politics*, 5: 259–76.

Beissinger, Mark R. (2011) 'The Intersection of Ethnic Nationalism and People Power Tactics in the Baltic States, 1987–91', in Adam Roberts and Timothy Garton Ash (eds), *Civil Resistance and Power Politics, The Experience of Non-violent Action from Gandhi to the Present*. Oxford: Oxford University Press, 231–46.

Belakhdar, Naoual (2011) 'Wir hatte im Oktober 1988 unsere Revolution'. Eine Analyse der gescheiterten Protestbewegug in Algerien 2011, Hardersm Cilja. Arbeitsstella Politik des Vorderen Orients (ed.), *Proteste, Revolutionen, Transformationen—die Arabische Weld im Umbruch*. Berlin: Freie Universitates, WP 1/2011, 82–91.

Bellin, Eva (2004) 'Why Have the Middle East and North Africa Remained So Singularly Resistant to Democratization', *Comparative Politics*, 36(2), 139–58.

Benderly, Jill (1997) 'Feminist Movements in Yugoslavia, 1978–1992', in Melissa K. Bokovoy, Jill A. Irvine, and Carol S. Lilly, *State-Society Relations in Yugoslavia, 1945–1992*. New York: St. Martin's, 183–210.

Bendix, Reinhard (1964) *Nation Building and Citizenship*. New York: Wiley & Sons.

Bennani-Chaibri, Mounia, and Jeghllaly, Mohamed (2012) 'La dynamique protestataire di mouvements du 20 Février à Casablanca', *Revue francaise de science politique*, 62(5): 867–94.

Bennani-Chraibi, Mounia, and Fillieule, Olivier (2012) 'Pour une sociologie des situations révolutionnaires', *Revue francaise de science politique*, 62(5): 767–96.

Bennet, Lance and Segenber, Alexandra (2013) *The Logics of Connective Action*. Cambridge: Cambridge University Press.

Berlin, Isaiah (1954) *Historical Inevitability*. Oxford: Oxford University Press.

Bermeo, Nancy (1990) 'Rethinking Regime Change' (review article): 'Transitions from Authoritarian Rule: Southern Europe' by Guillermo O'Donnell, Philippe C. Schmitter, and Laurence Whitehead; 'Transitions from Authoritarian Rule: Latin America' by Guillermo O'Donnell, Philippe C. Schmitter, and Laurence Whitehead; 'Transitions from Authoritarian Rule: Comparative Perspectives' by Guillermo O'Donnell, Philippe C. Schmitter, and Laurence Whitehead; 'Transitions from Authoritarian Rule: Tentative Conclusions about Uncertain Democracies' by Guillermo O'Donnell and Philippe C. Schmitter, *Comparative Politics*, 22(3): 359–77.

Bermeo, Nancy (1997) 'Myths of Moderation: Confrontation and Conflict during Democratic Transition', *Comparative Politics*, 29(2): 205–322.

Bettaieb, Viviane, and Bettaieb, Mohamed-Salah (2011) *Dégage. La révolution tunisienne*. Paris: Editions Layeur.

Bilic, Bojan (2012) *We Were Gasping for Air*. Baden-Baden: Nomos.

Biorcio, Roberto (1997) *La Padania Promessa*. Milano: Il Saggiatore.

Bittner, Egon (1967) 'The Police Skid-Row', *American Sociological Review*, 32: 699–715.

Blades, Lisa (2008) 'Authoritarian Elections and Elite Management, The Case of Egypt'. Paper prepared for delivery at the Princeton University Conference on Dictatorships, April.

Boex, Cécile (2013) 'Mobilisations d'artistes dans le mouvenebt de révolte en Syrie: Modes d'action et limites de l'engagement', in Amin Allal and Thomas Pierret (eds), *Au coer des révolte arabes. Devenir revolutionaries*. Paris: Armand Colin, 87–108.

Bollen, Kenneth A. (1979) 'Political Democracy and the Timing of Development', *American Sociological Review*, 44: 572–87.

Bonnefoy, Laurent, and Poirier, Marine (2012) 'La structuration de la revolution Yéménite', *Revue francaise de science politique*, 62(5): 895–913.

Boudreau, Vincent (2004) *Resisting Dictatorship: Repression and Protest in Southeast Asia*. Cambridge: Cambridge University Press.

Bouziane, Malika, and Lenner, Katharina (2011) 'Protests in Jordan: Rumblings in the Kingdom of Dialogue', in Hardersm Cilja, *Arbeitsstella Politik des Vorderen Orients (ed.), Proteste, Revolutionen, Transformationen—die Arabische Weld im Umbruch*. Berlin: Freie Universitates, WP 1/2011, 148–65.

Bozik, Agneza (1999) 'Democratization and Ethnopolitics in Yougoslavia', in Karl Cordell (ed.), *Ethnicity and Democratisation in the New Europe*. London, New York: Routledge, 117–30.

Bozoki, Andras (2010) '?A magyar demokratikus ellenzék: önreflexió, identitás és politikai diskurzus?' [The Hungarian Democratic Opposition: Self-Reflection, Identity and Political Discourse], *Politikatudományi Szemle*, 19(2): 7–45.

Branford, Sue, and Rocha, Jan (2002) *Cutting the Wire: The Story of the Landless Movement in Brazil*. London: Latin American Bureau.

Bratton, Michael, and van de Walle, Nicolas (1992) 'Popular Protest and Political Reform in Africa', *Comparative Politics*, 24(4): 419–42.

Bratton, Michael, and van de Walle, Nicolas (1994) 'Neopatrimonial Regimes and Political Transitions in Africa', *World Politics*, 46(4): 453–89.

Bratton, Michael, and van de Walle, Nicolas (1997) *Democratic Experiments in Africa: Regime Transition in Comparative Perspective*. Cambridge: Cambridge University Press.

Breines, Wini (1989) *Community and Organization in the New Left, 1962–1968: The Great Refusal*. New Brunswick, N.J.: Rutgers University Press.

Breuilly, John (1993) *Nationalism and the State*. Chicago: University of Chicago Press.

Brito, Alexandra Barahona de (1997) *Human Rights and Democratization in Latin America: Uruguay and Chile*. Oxford: Oxford University Press.

Brockett, Charles D. (2005) *Political Movements and Violence in Central America*. Cambridge: Cambridge University Press.

Brubaker, Roger (1996) *Nationalism Reframed: Nationhood and the National Question in the New Europe*. Cambridge: Cambridge University Press.

Bruszt, László (1989) 'The Negotiated Revolution in Hungary', *Social Research*, 57(2): 365–87.

Bruszt, László, and Stark, David (1991) 'Remaking the Political Field in Hungary: From the Politics of Confrontation to the Politics of Competition', *Journal of International Affairs*, 45(1): 201–45.

Brysk, Alison (1993) 'From Above and Below: Social Movements, the International System, and Human Rights in Argentina', *Comparative Political Studies*, 26(3): 259–85.

Bunce, Valerie (1999) *Subversive Institutions. The Design and the Destruction of Socialism and the State*. Cambridge: Cambridge University Press.

Bunce, Valerie (2000) 'Comparative Democratization: Big and Bounded Generalizations', *Comparative Political Studies*, 33: 703–34.

Bunce, Valerie (2011) 'The Diffusion of Popular Mobilization against Authoritarian Rule', paper presented at Cornell University, 3–4 June.

Bunce, Valerie, and Wolchik, Sharon (2010a) 'A Regional Tradition', in Valerie Bunce, Michael McFaul, and Stoner Weiss (eds), *Democracy and Authoritarianism in the Postcommunist World*. Cambridge: Cambridge University Press, 30–58.

Bunce, Valerie, and Wolchik, Sharon (2010b) 'Transnational Networks, Diffusion Dynamics and Electoral Change in Post-Communist World', in Rebecca Kolins Givan, Kenneth M. Roberts, and Sarah A. Soule (eds), *The Diffusion of Social Movements*. Cambridge: Cambridge University Press, 140–62.

Bunce, Valerie, and Wolchik, Sharon (2011) *Defeating Authoritarian leaders*. Cambridge: Cambridge University Press.

Burawoy, Michael (2005) 'Provincializing the Social Sciences', in George Steinmetz (ed.), *The Politics of Methods in the Social Sciences*. Durham: Duke University Press, 508–25.

Burdick, John (1992) 'Rethinking the Study of Social Movements: The Case of Christian Base Communities in Urban Brazil', in Arturo Escobar and Sonia Álvarez (eds), *The*

Making of Social Movements in Latin America: Identity, Strategy and Democracy. Boulder, Co.: Westview, 171–84.

Burdick, John (2004) *Legacies of Liberation: The Progressive Catholic Church in Brazil at the Start of a New Millennium*. Aldershot: Ashgate.

Burris, Greg (2011) 'Lawrence of E-rabia. Facebook and the New Arab Revolt', *Jadaliyya*, http://www.jadaliyya.com/pages/index/2884/lawrence-ofe-rabia_facebook-and-the-new-arab-revo (accessed 28 April 2013).

Calhoun, Craig (1994) *Neither Gods, nor Emperors*. Berkeley: University of California Press.

Camau, Michel (2011) 'La disgrâce du chef. Mobilisations populaires arabes et crise du leadership', *Mouvements*, 66: 22–9.

Carapico, Sheila (1998) *Civil Society in Yemen: The Political Economy of Activism in Modern Arabia*. Cambridge: Cambridge University Press.

Carey, Henry, and Eisterhold, Christopher (2004) 'Introduction', in Henry Carey, *Romania Since 1989: Politics, Economics, and Society*. Lanham, Md: Lexington Books.

Carothers, Thomas (1996) *Assessing Democracy Assistance: The Case of Romania*. Washington, DC: Carnegie Endowment.

Carter, April (2011) 'People Power and Protest', in Adam Roberts and Timothy Garton Ash (eds), *Civil Resistance and Power Politics, The Experience of Non-violent Action from Gandhi to the Present*. Oxford: Oxford University Press, 25–42.

Casper, Gretchen, and Taylor, Michelle M. (1996) *Negotiating Democracy: Transitions from Authoritarian Rule*. Pittsburgh: University of Pittsburgh Press.

Cavatorta, Francesco (2006) 'Civil Society, Islamism and Democratisation: The Case of Morocco', *The Journal of Modern African Studies*, 44(2): 203–22.

Cavatorta, Francesco (2007) 'More than Repression: The Significance of Divide et Impera in the Middle East and North Africa—The case of Morocco', *Journal of Contemporary African Studies*, 25(2): 187–203.

Çelik, Aziz (1996) 'Bahar Eylemleri', in *Türkiye Sendikacılık Ansiklopedisi*. Istanbul: Türkiye Ekonomik ve Toplumsal Tarih Vakfı.

Çelik, Aziz (2010) *Vesayetten Siyasete Türkiye'de Sendikacılık (1946–1967)*. Istanbul: İletişim.

Cerone, John (2011) 'Documents on Libya, Introductory Note', *International Legal Materials*, 50(5).

Challand, Benoît (2008) *Palestinian Civil Society: Foreign Donors and the Power to Promote and Exclude*. London: Routledge.

Champseix, Elisabeth, and Champ, Jean-Paul (1992) *L'Albanie out la logique du désespoir*. Paris: Édition la Découvert.

Chandhoke, Neera (2003) *The Conceits of Civil Society*. New Delhi: Oxford University Press.

Chessa, Cecilia (2004) 'State Subsidies, International Diffusion, and Transnational Civil Society: The Case of Frankfurt-Oder and Slubice', *East European Politics and Societies*, 18: 70.

Chilton, Patricia (1994) 'Mechanics of Change: Social Movements, Transnational Coalitions, and the Transformation Processes in Eastern Europe', *Democratization*, 1: 151–81.

Chilton, Patricia (1995) 'Mechanics of Change: Social Movements, Transnational Coalitions, and the Transformation Processes in Eastern Europe', in Thomas Risse-Kappen (ed.), *Bringing Transnational Relations Back In: Non-State Actors, Domestic Structures and International Institutions*. Cambridge, UK: Cambridge University Press, 189–226.

Chiodi, Luisa (2007a) *Transnational Policies of Emancipation or Colonization? Civil Society Promotion in Post-communist Albania*. PhD thesis, European University Institute.

Chiodi, Luisa (2007b) 'The Profession of Civil Society in Post-Communist Albania', *Albanian Journal of Politics*, IV(I).

Clark, Howard (2011) 'The Limits of Prudence: Civil Resistance in Kosovo, 1990–98', in Adam Roberts and Timothy Garton Ash (eds), *Civil Resistance and Power Politics, The Experience of Non-violent Action from Gandhi to the Present*. Oxford: Oxford University Press, 277–94.

Clark, Janine A. (2004) *Islam, Charity, and Activism: Middle-class Networks and Social Welfare in Egypt, Jordan, and Yemen*. Bloomington: Indiana University Press.

Clemens, Elisabeth S. (1993) 'Women's Groups and the Transformation of U.S. Politics, 1892–1920', *American Journal of Sociology*, 98: 755–98.

Cohen, Jean L., and Arato, Andrew (1992) *Civil Society and Political Theory*. Cambridge, Mass.: MIT Press.

Cohen, Joshua (1989) 'Deliberation and Democratic Legitimacy', in Alan Hamlin and Philip Pettit (eds), *The Good Polity*. Oxford: Blackwell, 17–34.

Cohen, Lenard J. (2011) *Embracing Democracy in the Western Balkans: From Postconflict Struggles toward European Integration*. Baltimore: Johns Hopkins University Press.

Collier, Ruth Berins (1999) *Paths toward Democracy: The Working Class and Elites in Western Europe and South America*. New York: Cambridge University Press.

Collier, Ruth Berins, and Collier, David (2002) *Shaping the Political Arena. Critical Junctures, the Labour Movement and Regime Dynamics in Latin America*. Notre Dame, IN: University of Notre Dame Press.

Collier, Ruth Berins, and Mahoney, James (1997) 'Adding Collective Actors to Collective Outcomes: Labor and Recent Democratization in South America and Southern Europe', *Comparative Politics*, 29(3): 285–303.

Collombier, Virginie (2007) 'The Internal Stakes of the 2005 Elections: The Struggle for Influence in Egypt's National Democratic Party', *Middle East Journal*, 61(1).

Connor, Walker (1994) *Ethnonationalism: The Quest for Understanding*. Princeton, NJ: Princeton University Press.

Corm, Georges (2011) 'Première approche d'une contextualisation des révoltes populaires arabes', *Confluences Méditerranée*, 79: 93–111.

Corradi, Juan E., Weiss Fagen, Patricia, and Garretón, Manuel Antonio (eds) (1992) *Fear at the Edge: State Terror and Resistance in Latin America*. Berkeley: University of California Press.

Crenshaw, Martha (2011) *Explaining Terrorism: Causes, Processes and Consequences*. London: Routledge.

Cutright, Phillips (1963) 'National Political Development: Measurement and Analysis', *American Sociological Review*, 28: 253–64.

Cutright, Phillips, and Wiley, James A. (1969) 'Modernization and Political Representation', *Studies in Comparative International Development*, 5: 3–44.

Dagi, Ihsan D. (1996) 'Democratic Transition in Turkey, 1980–83: The Impact of European Diplomacy', *Middle Eastern Studies*, 32(2): 124–41.

Daguzan, Jean-François (2011) 'De la crise économique à la révolution arabe', *Maghreb-Machrek*, 206: 9–15.

Dahl, Robert A. (1971) *Poliarchies*. New Haven, Conn.: Yale University Press.

Dahl, Robert A. (1998) *On Democracy*. New Haven, Conn.: Yale University Press.

Dale, Gareth (2005) *Popular Protest in East Germany, 1945–1989*. London: Routledge.

Davenport, Christian (1995) 'Multi-dimensional Threat Perception and State Repression: An Inquiry into Why States Apply Negative Sanctions', *American Journal of Political Science*, 39: 683–713.

Davenport, Christian (2005a) 'Repression and Mobilization: Insights from Political Science and Sociology', in Christian Davenport, Hank Johnston, and Carol Mueller (eds), *Repression and Mobilization: Social Movements, Protest, and Contention*. Minneapolis: The University of Minnesota Press.

Davenport, Christian (2005b) 'Introduction: Repression and Mobilization: Insights from Political Science and Sociology', in Christian Davenport, Hank Johnston, and Carol Mueller (eds), *Repression and Mobilization*. Minneapolis: The University of Minnesota Press, vii–xli.

Davenport, Christian (ed.) (2000) *Paths to State Repression: Human Rights Violations and Contentious Politics*. Boulder, Co.: Rowman and Littlefield.

De Angelis, Enrico (2011) 'The State of Disarray of a Networked Revolution: The Syrian Uprising's Information Environment', *Sociologica*, 3: 1–24.

Della Porta, Donatella (1990) *Il terrorismo di sinistra*. Bologna: Il Mulino.

Della Porta, Donatella (1995) *Social Movements, Political Violence and the State*. Cambridge: Cambridge University Press.

Della Porta, Donatella (1998) 'The Political Discourse on Protest Policing', in Mario Giugni, Doug McAdam, and Charles Tilly (eds), *How Movements Matter*. Minneapolis: The University of Minnesota Press.

Della Porta, Donatella (2005a) 'Deliberation in Movement: Why and How to Study Deliberative Democracy and Social Movements', *Acta Politica*, 40: 336–50.

Della Porta, Donatella (2005b) 'Globalization and Democracy', *Democratization*, 5(12): 668–85.

Della Porta, Donatella (2007) *The Global Justice Movement in Cross-National and Transnational Perspective*. Boulder, Co.: Paradigm.

Della Porta, Donatella (2008) 'Eventful Protests, Global Conflicts', *Distinktion: Scandinavian Journal of Social Theory*, 17: 27–56.

Della Porta, Donatella (2011) 'Movimenti sociali e Stato democratico', in A. Pizzorno (ed.), *La democrazia di fronte allo stato*. Milano: Feltrinelli, 193–232.

Della Porta, Donatella (2013a) *Can Democracy Be Saved?* Oxford: Polity.

Della Porta, Donatella (2013b) *Clandestine Political Violence*. Cambridge: Cambridge University Press.

Della Porta, Donatella (ed.) (2009b) *Democracy in Social Movements*. Houndsmill: Palgrave.

Della Porta, Donatella (ed.) (2009a) *Another Europe*. London: Routledge.

Della Porta, Donatella, and Diani, Mario (2006) *Social Movements: An Introduction*. Oxford: Blackwell.

Della Porta, Donatella, and Fillieule, Olivier (2004) 'Policing Social Movements', in David A. Snow, Sarah A. Soule, and Hanspeter Kriesi (eds), *The Blackwell Companion to Social Movements*. Oxford: Blackwell, 217–41.

Della Porta, Donatella, and Gbikpi, Bernard (2012) 'The Riots: A Dynamic View', in Seraphim Seferiades and Hank Johnston (eds), *Violent Protest, Contentious Politics and the Neo-liberal State*. Farnham: Ashgate, 87–102.

Della Porta, Donatella and Keating, Michael (eds.) (2008) *Approaches and Methodologies in the Social Sciences: A Pluralist Perspective*. Cambridge: Cambridge University Press.

Della Porta, Donatella, and Mattina, Liborio (1986) 'Ciclos políticos y movilización étnica. El caso Vasco', *Revista Española de Investigaciones Sociológicas*, 35: 123–48.

Della Porta, Donatella, and Piazza, Gianni (2008) *Voices of the Valley. Voices of the Straits: How Protest Creates Community*. New York and Oxford: Berghahn.

Della Porta, Donatella, and Reiter, Herbert (eds) (1998) *Policing Protest: The Control of Mass Demonstrations in Western Democracies*. Minneapolis: The University of Minnesota Press.

Della Porta, Donatella, and Rucht, Dieter (1995) 'Left-Libertarian Movements in Context: Comparing Italy and West Germany, 1965-1990', in Craig L. Jenkins and Bert Klandermans (eds), *The Politics of Social Protest*. Minneapolis/London: The University of Minnesota Press, 299–372.

Della Porta, Donatella, and Rucht, Dieter (eds) (2013) *Meeting Democracy*. Cambridge: Cambridge University Press.

Della Porta, Donatella, and Tarrow, Sidney (2012) 'Interactive Diffusion: The Coevolution of Police and Protest Behavior with an Application to Transnational Contention', *Comparative Political Studies*, xx: 1–4.

Della Porta, Donatella, Andretta, Massimiliano, Mosca, Lorenzo, and Reiter, Herbert (2006) *Globalization from Below. Global Movement and Transnational Protest*. Minneapolis: The University of Minnesota Press.

Della Porta, Donatella, Valiente, Celia, and Kousis, Maria (forthcoming) 'Sisters of the South. The Women's Movement and Democratization', in Richard Gunther, P. Nikiforos Diamandouros, and Hans-Jürgen Puhle (eds), *Democratic Consolidation in Southern Europe: The Cultural Dimension*. Baltimore: The Johns Hopkins University Press.

Demirel, Tanel (2011) *Türkiye'nin Uzun On Yılı. Demokrat Parti İktidarı Ve 27 Mayıs Darbesi*. Istanbul: Bilgi Üniversitesi Yayınları.

Denoeux, Guilain (1993) *Urban Unrest in the Middle East: A Comparative Study of Informal Networks in Egypt, Iran, and Lebanon*. Albany: State University of New York Press.

Di Palma, Giuseppe (1991) 'Legitimation from the Top to Civil Society: Politico-Cultural Change in Eastern Europe', *World Politics*, 44(1): 49–80.

Diamond, Larry J., Plattner, Marc F., and Brumberg, Daniel (2003) *Islam and Democracy in the Middle East*. Baltimore: Johns Hopkins University Press.

Donnelly, Jack (1983) 'Human Rights, Humanitarian Interventions and American Foreign Policy', *Journal of International Affairs*, 37: 311–28.

Dorronsoro, Gilles (ed.) (2005) *La Turquie conteste. Mobilisations sociales et régime sécuritaire*. Paris: CNRS Editions.

Dryzek, John S. (2000) *Deliberative Democracy and Beyond*. New York: Oxford University Press.

Duboc, Marie (2011) 'Egyptian Leftwing Intellectuals' Activism from the Margins', in Joel Benin and Frédéric Vairel (eds), *Social Movements, Mobilization and Contestation in the Middle East and North Africa*. Stanford, CA: Stanford University Press, 61–79.

Duman, Doğan (1999) *Demokrasi Sürecinde Türkiye'de İslamcılık*. İzmir: Dokuz Eylül Yayınları.

Dunn, Alix (2011) 'How the Internet Kill Switch Didn't Kill Egypt's Protests', Meta-Activism project, http://www.meta-activism.org/2011/02/how-the-internet-kill-switch-didnt-kill-egypts-protests/ (accessed 28 April 2013).

Dutton, Michael (2005) 'The Trick of Words: Asian Studies, Translation, and the Problem of Knowledge', in George Steinmetz (ed.), *The Politics of Methods in the Social Sciences*. Durham: Duke University Press, 89–125.

Dziadosz, Alexander (2011) 'Benghazi, Cradle of Revolt, Condemns Gaddafi', *Reuters*, 23 Feb., http://www.reuters.com/article/2011/02/23/us-libya-protests-east-idUSTRE71M3J920110223?pageNumber=1 (accessed 5 May 2013).

Earl, Jennifer (2003) 'Tanks, Tear Gas and Taxes', *Sociological Theory*, 21: 44–68.

Earl, Jennifer, Soule, Sarah A., and McCarthy, John (2003) 'Protest Under Fire? Explaining Protest Policing', *American Sociological Review*, 69: 581–606.

East, Roger (1992) *Revolutions in Eastern Europe*. London: Pinter.

Eckert, Rainer (2011) 'Organizations geschichte ost deutscher Parteien und Bewegungen', in Martin Gutzeit, Helge Heidemeyer, and Bettina Tueffers (eds), *Opposition un SED in der Friedlichen Revolution*. Duesseldorf: Droste verlag, 117–29.

Eckstein, Susan (ed.) (2001) *Power and Popular Protest: Latin American Social Movements* (2nd ed.). Berkeley: University of California Press.

Eckstein, Susan, and Wickham-Crowley, Timothy (2003) *What Justice? Whose Justice? Fighting for Fairness in Latin America*. Berkeley: University of California Press.

Eder, Klaus (2003) 'Identity Mobilization and Democracy: An Ambivalent Relation', in Pedro Ibarra (ed.), *Social Movements and Democracy*. New York: Palgrave, 61–80.

Eglitis, Daina Stukuls (2008) 'The Baltic States: Remembering the Past, Building the Future', in Sharon Wolchik and Jane Curry (eds), *Central and East European Politics: From Communism to Democracy*. Lanham, Md.: Rowman and Littlefield, 233–52.

Eisenstadt, Shmuel N. (1973) *Traditional Patrimonialism and Modern Neopatrimonialism*. Beverly Hills, CA: Sage Publications.

Eisinger, Peter K. (1973) 'The Conditions of Protest Behavior in American Cities', *American Journal of Political Science*, 67: 11–28.

Ekiert, Grzegorz (1996) *The State Against Society: Political Crises and Their Aftermath in East Central Europe*. Princeton, NJ: Princeton University Press.

el-Chazli, Youssef (2012) 'Sur les sentiers de la revolution', *Revue francaise de science politique*, 62(5): 843–65.

el-Chazli, Youssef, and Hassabo, Chaymaa (2013) 'Sociohistoire d'un processus révolutionnaire', in Amin Allal and Thomas Pierret (eds), *Au coer des révolte arabes. Devenir revolutionaries*. Paris: Armand Colin, 185–212.

Elbasani, Arolda (2008) 'Political Transformation and Implementation of the EU's Democratic Requirements in Albania', in Arolda Elbasani, Anuela Ristani, and Gjergji Vurmo, *Integration Perspectives and Synergic Effects of European Transformation*. Budapest: Centre for EU Enlargement Studies.

el-Ghobashy, Mona (2011) 'The Praxis of the Egyptian Revolution', *Middle East Report*, 258: 2–13.

el-Ghobashy, Mona (2012a) 'The Praxis of the Egyptian Revolution', in Jeannie Sowers and Chris Toensing (eds), *The Journey to Tahrir: Revolution, Protest, and Social Change in Egypt*. London: Verso, 21–40.

el-Ghobashy, Mona (2012b) 'Unsettling the Authorities: Constitutional Reform in Egypt', in Jeannie Sowers and Chris Toensing (eds), *The Journey to Tahrir: Revolution, Protest, and Social Change in Egypt*. London: Verso, 121–31.

el-Ghobashy, Mona (2012c) 'The Dynamics of Elections under Mubarak', in Jeannie Sowers and Chris Toensing (eds), *The Journey to Tahrir: Revolution, Protest, and Social Change in Egypt*. London: Verso, 132–48.

Eliasoph, Nina (1998) *Avoiding Politics: How Americans Produce Apathy in Everyday Life*. Cambridge and New York: Cambridge University Press.

el-Nawawy, Mohammed, and Khamis, Sahar (2012) 'Political Activism 2.0: Comparing the Role of Social Media in Egypt's Facebook Revolution and Iran's Twitter Uprising', *CyberOrient*, 6(1).

el-Sherif, Ashraf (2012) 'The Ultras' Politics of Fun Confront Tyranny', *Jadaliyya*, http://www.jadaliyya.com/pages/index/4243/the-ultras-politics-of-fun-confront-tyranny (accessed 28 April 2013).

Elster, Jon (1998) 'Deliberation and Constitution Making', in Jon Elster (ed.), *Deliberative Democracy*. Cambridge: Cambridge University Press, 97–122.

Eltantawy, Nahed, and Wiest, Julie B. (2011) 'Social Media in the Egyptian Revolution: Reconsidering Resource Mobilization Theory', *International Journal of Communication*, 5: 1207–24.

Emperador Badimon, Monserrat (2011) 'Unemployed Moroccan University Graduates and Strategies for "Apolitical" Mobilization', in Joel Benin and Frédéric Vairel (eds), *Social Movements, Mobilization and Contestation in the Middle East and North Africa*. Stanford, CA: Stanford University Press, 217–36.

Engene, Jan Oscar (2004) *Terrorism in Western Europe*. Cheltenham, Edward Elgar.

Escobar, Arturo, and Álvarez, Sonia (1992) (eds), *The Making of Social Movements in Latin America: Identity, Strategy and Democracy*. Boulder, CO: Westview.

Esposito, John L. (2002) *Unholy War: Terror in the Name of Islam*. New York: Oxford University Press.

Esposito, John L., and Voll, John (2001) *Makers of Contemporary Islam*. Oxford: Oxford University Press.

Eyal, Gil (2003) *The Origins of Postcommunist Elites: From Prague Spring to the Breakup of Czechoslovakia*. Minneapolis: The University of Minnesota Press.

Fahim, Kareem, et al. (2011) 'Violent End to an Era as Qaddafi Dies in Libya', *The New York Times*, 20 Oct.: A1.

Falk, Barbara J. (2003) *The Dilemmas of Dissidence in East-Central Europe: Citizen Intellectuals and Philosopher Kings*. Budapest: Central European University Press.

Fantasia, Rick (1988) *Cultures of Solidarity. Consciousness, Action, and Contemporary American Workers*. Berkeley, Los Angeles: University of California Press.

Fehr, Helmut (1995) 'Von der Dissidenz zum Gegen-Elite. Ein Vergleich der politische Opposition in Polen, der Tschechoslowakei, Ungarn und der DDR (1976 bis 1989)', in Ulrike Poppe, Rainer Eckert, and Ilko-Sascha Kowlczuk (eds), *Zwischen Selbstbehauptung und Anpassung. Formen des Widerstandes und der Opposition in der DDR*. Berlin: Ch. Links Verlag, 301–34.

Feldman, Allen (1991) *Formations of Violence*. Chicago: University of Chicago Press.

Felkay, Andrew (1989) *Hungary and the USSR 1956–1988: Kadar's Political Leadership*. New York: Greenwood Press.

Fernandez, Luis A. (2008) *Policing Dissent: Social Control and the Anti-Globalization Movement*. New Brunswick, NJ: Rutgers University Press.

Feyizoğlu, Turan (1993) *Türkiye'de Devrimci Gençlik Hareketleri Tarihi (1960–68)*. Istanbul: Belge Yayınları.

FIDH (2011) 'Massacres in Libya: The International Community Must Respond Urgently', *International Federation for Human Rights (FIDH)*, 21 Feb., http://www.fidh.org/Massacres-in-Libya-The (accessed 5 May 2013).

Figa, Jozef (1997) 'Socializing the State: Civil Society and Democratization from Below in Slovenia', in Melissa K. Bokovoy, Jill A. Irvine, and Carol S. Lilly, *State-Society Relations in Yugoslavia, 1945–1992*. New York: St. Martin's, 163–82.

Fillieule, Olivier (2013) 'Postface. Des marées aux inundations', in Amin Allal and Thomas Pierret (eds), *Au coer des révolte arabes. Devenir revolutionaries*. Paris: Armand Colin, 287–308.

Findlay, Cassie (2012) 'Witness and Trace: January 25 Graffiti and Public Art as Archive', *Interface: a journal for and about social movements*, 4(1): 178–82.

Fishman, Robert (1990) *Working Class Organizations and the Return of Democracy in Spain*. Ithaca N.Y.: Cornell University Press.

Flam, Helena (2001) *Pink, Purple, Green: Women's, Religious, Environmental and Gay/Lesbian Movements in Central Europe Today*. New York: Columbia University Press.

Flam, Helena (2005) 'Emotions' Map: A Research Agenda', in Helena Flam and Debra King (eds), *Emotions and Social Movements*. London: Routledge, 19–41.

Foran, John (2005) *Taking Power. On the Origins of Third World Revolutions*. Cambridge: Cambridge University Press.

Foweraker, Joe (1989) *Making Democracy in Spain: Grassroots Struggle in the South, 1955–1975*. Cambridge: Cambridge University Press.

Foweraker, Joe (1995) *Theorizing Social Movements*. London: Pluto Press.

Foweraker, Joe, and Landman, Todd (1997) *Citizenship Rights and Social Movements: A Comparative and Statistical Analysis*. Oxford: Oxford University Press.

Francisco, Ronald A. (2005) 'The Dictator's Dilemma', in Christian Davenport, Hank Johnston, and Carol Mueller (eds), *Repression and Mobilization*. Minneapolis: The University of Minnesota Press.

Gamson, William A. (1988) 'Political Discourse and Collective Action', in Bert Klandermans, Hanspeter Kriesi, and Sidney Tarrow (eds), *From Structure to Action*. Greenwich, CT: JAI Press, 219–46.

Gamson, William A. (2011) 'Arab Spring, Israeli Summer and the Process of Cognitive Liberation' *Swiss Political Science Journal*, 17: 463–8.

Gandhi, Jennifer (2008) *Political Institutions under Dictatorship*. Cambridge, New York: Cambridge University Press.

Garton Ash, Timothy (2011) 'A Century of Civil Resistance: Some Lessons and Questions', in Adam Roberts and Timothy Garton Ash (eds), *Civil Resistance and Power Politics, The Experience of Non-violent Action from Gandhi to the Present*. Oxford: Oxford University Press.

Gause III, F. Gregory (2011) 'Why Middle East Studies Missed the Arab Spring?...', art. cité, 86.

Geddes, Barbara (1999) 'What Do We Know about Democratization after Twenty Years?', *Annual Review of Political Science*, 2: 115–44.

Gelvin, James L. (2011) *Divided Loyalties: Nationalism and Mass Politics in Syria at the Close of Empire* (3rd ed.). Berkeley: University of California Press.

Gelvin, James L. (2012) *The Arab Uprisings: What Everyone Needs to Know*. Oxford: Oxford University Press.

Gerbaudo, Paolo (2012) *Tweets and the Streets*. London: Verso.

Gerring, John (2007) 'The Mechanismic Worldview: Thinking inside the Box', *British Journal of Political Science*, 38: 161–79.

Ghonim, Wael (2012) *Revolution 2.0: The Power of the People is Greater than the People in Power: A Memoir*. Boston: Houghton Mifflin Harcourt.

Gibianski, Leonid (2006) 'The Soviet–Yugoslav Split', in Kevin McDermott and Matthew Stibbe (eds), *Revolution and Resistance in Eastern Europe: Challenges to Communist Rule*. Oxford: Berg, 17–36.

Giddens, Anthony (1979) *Central Problems in Social Theory*. London: Macmillan.

Giddens, Anthony (1990) *The Consequences of Modernity*. Cambridge/Stanford, CA: Polity Press/Stanford University Press.

Giner, Salvador (1986) 'Political Economy, Legitimation, and the State in Southern Europe', in Guillermo A. O'Donnell, Philippe C. Schmitter, and Laurence Whitehead (eds), *Transitions from Authoritarian Rule: Prospects for Democracy*. Baltimore: Johns Hopkins University Press, 11–44.

Glenn, John K. (2003) 'Contentious Politics and Democratization: Comparing the Impact of Social Movements on the Fall of Communism in Eastern Europe', *Political Studies*, 51: 103–20.

Glenn, John K., III (2001) *Framing Democracy: Civil Society and Civic Movements in Eastern Europe*. Stanford, CA: Stanford University Press.

Gliński, Piotr, and Palska, Hanna (1996) 'Cztery wymiary społecznej aktywności obywatelskiej', in Henryk Domański and Andrzej Rychard (eds), *Elementy nowego ładu*. Warsaw: IFiS PAN.

Goldstone, Jack (2011) 'Cross-class Coalition and The Making of the Arab Revolt of 2011', *Swiss Political Science Review*, 17: 457–62.

Goodwin, James, Jasper, James M., and Polletta, Francesca (eds) (2001) *Passionate Politics: Emotions and Social Movements*. Chicago: University of Chicago Press.

Goodwin, Jeff (2001) *No Other Way Out*. Cambridge: Cambridge University Press.

Goodwin, Jeff, and Hetland, Gabriel (2009) 'The Strange Disappearance of Capitalism from Social Movement Studies', http://www2.asanet.org/sectionchs/09conf/goodwin.pdf (accessed 22 March 2013).

Gould, Deborah B. (2004) 'Passionate Political Processes: Bringing Emotions Back into the Study of Social Movements', in Jeff Goodwin and James J. Jasper (eds), *Rethinking Social Movements*. Lanham, Md: Rowman and Littlefield, 155–75.

Grieder, Peter (2006) '"To learn from the Soviet Union is to learn How to Win": The East German Revolution 1989–90', in Kevin McDermott and Matthew Stibbe (eds), *Revolution and Resistance in Eastern Europe: Challenges to Communist Rule*. Oxford: Berg, 157–74.

Guibal, Claude, and Tangi, Salaun (2011) *L'Egypt de Tahrir: anatomie d'une revolution*. Paris: Seuil.

Gulru Goker, Zeynep (2011) 'Presence in Silence. Feminists and Democratic Implications of the Saturday Vigils in Turkey', in Joel Benin and Frédéric Vairel (eds), *Social Movements, Mobilization and Contestation in the Middle East and North Africa*. Stanford, CA: Stanford University Press, 107–24.

Gunning, Jeroen (2009) 'Social Movement Theory and the Study of Terrorism', in Richard Jackson, Marie Breen Smyth, and Jeroen Gunning (eds), *Critical Terrorism Studies: A New Research Agenda*. London: Routledge, 156–77.

Güzel, M. Şehmus (1993) *Türkiye'de İşçi Hareketi (Yazılar-Belgeler)*. İstanbul: Sosyalist Yayınlar.

Habermas, Jürgen (1996) *Between Facts and Norms: Contribution to a Discursive Theory of Law and Democracy*. Cambridge, Mass.: MIT Press.

Haddad, Bassam (2012) 'Syria, the Arab Uprisings, and the Political Economy of Authoritarian Resilience', *Interface: a journal for and about social movements*, 4(1): 113–30.

Hadenius, Axel, and Teorell, Jan (2007) 'Pathways from Authoritarianism', *Journal of Democracy*, 18(1): 143–57.

Haerpfer, Christian (2009) 'Post-Communist Europe and Post-Soviet Russia', in Christian Haerpfer et al., *Democratization*. Oxford: Oxford University Press.

Hafez, Mohammed M. (2003) *Why Muslims Rebel*. Boulder: Lynne Rienner.

Hafez, Mohammed M., and Wiktorowicz, Quintan (2004) 'Violence as Contention in the Egyptian Islamic Movement', in Quintan Wiktorowicz (ed.), *Islamic Activism: A Social Movement Theory Approach*. Bloomington: Indiana University Press, 61–88.

Hall, Peter A. (2003) 'Aligning Ontology and Methodology in Comparative Research', in James Mahoney and Dietrich Rueschemeyer (eds), *Comparative Historical Research*. Cambridge: Cambridge University Press, 373–404.

Hall, Richard (1999) 'The Uses of Absurdity: The Staged War Theory and the Romanian Revolution of December 1989', *East European Politics and Societies*, 13: 501–42.

Hankiss, Elemér (1990) 'What the Hungarians Saw First', in Gwyn Prins (eds), *Spring in Winter: The 1989 Revolutions*. Manchester, UK: Manchester University Press, 13–36.

Harris, Erika (2002) *Nationalism and democratization: Politics of Slovakia and Slovenia*. Aldershot: Ashgate.

Hassabo, Chaymaa (2005) 'Gamal Moubarak au centre du pouvoir: une succession achevée?', Centre d'Études et de Documentation Économiques, Juridiques et Sociales, http://www.cedej.org.eg/article.php3?id_article= 258&var_recherche=hassabo.

Haynes, Jeff (1997) *Democracy and Civil Society in the Third World. Politics and New Political Movements.* Cambridge: Polity.

Hedstrom, Peter, and Bearman, Peter (2009) 'What is Analytic Sociology All About? An Introductory Essay', in Peter Hedstrom and Peter Bearman, *The Oxford Handbook of Analytic Sociology.* Oxford: Oxford University Press, 3–15.

Heibach, Jens (2011) 'Er Anfang vor Ende? Der Jamen. Hardersm Cilja 2011. Arbeitsstella Politik des Vorderen Orients (ed.), *Proteste, Revolutionen, Transformationen—die Arabische Weld im Umbruch.* Berlin: Freie Universitates, WP 1/2011, 130–47.

Heimann, Mary (2009) *Czechoslovakia: The State that Failed.* New Haven, CT: Yale University Press.

Henderson, Sarah L. (2002) 'Selling Civil Society: Western Aids and the Nongovernmental Organization Sector in Russia', *Comparative Political Studies*, 35: 139–67.

Hess, David, and Martin, Brian (2006) 'Repression, Backfire, and the Theory of Transformative Events', *Mobilization*, 11: 249–67.

Hibou, Béatrice (2011) *The Force of Obedience: The Political Economy of Repression in Tunisia.* Oxford: Polity Press.

Higley, John, and Gunther, Richard (1992) *Elites and Democratic Consolidation in Latin America and Southern Europe.* New York: Cambridge University Press.

Hinnebusch, Raymond A. (1993) 'State and Civil Society in Syria', *Middle East Journal*, 47(2): 243–57. doi: 10.2307/4328570.

Hinnebusch, Raymond A. (2006) 'Authoritarian Persistence, and the Middle East', *Democratization*, 13.

Hipsher, Patricia L. (1998a) 'Democratic Transitions as Protest Cycles: Social Movements Dynamics in Democratizing Latin America', in David Meyer and Sidney Tarrow (eds), *The Social Movement Society: Contentious Politics for a New Century.* Lanham, Md: Rowman & Littlefield, 153–72.

Hipsher, Patricia L. (1998b) 'Democratic Transitions and Social Movements Outcomes: The Chilean Shantytown Dwellers' Movement in Comparative Perspective', in Mario Giugni, Doug McAdam, and Charles Tilly (eds), *From Contention to Democracy.* Lanham, Md: Rowman & Littlefield, 149–67.

Hmed, Choukri (2012) 'Réseaux dormants, contingence et structures. Genèse de la revolution tunisienne', *Revue francaise de science politique*, 62(5): 797–820.

Hoffmann, Anja (2011) Wem gehoert der marokkanische Wandel? Eine Analyse des umkaemoften politischen Felds in Marokko, Hardersm Cilja (2011. Arbeitsstella Politik des Vorderen Orients (ed.), *Proteste, Revolutionen, Transformationen—die Arabische Weld im Umbruch.* Berlin: Freie Universitates, WP 1/2011, 92–109.

Howard, Philip N. (2010) *The Digital Origins of Dictatorship and Democracy: Information Technology and Political Islam.* Oxford: Oxford University Press.

Howard, Philip N., and Hussain, Muzammil M. (2013) *Democracy's Fourth Wave? Digital Media and the Arab Spring.* Oxford: Oxford University Press.

HRW (1992) *Human Rights Watch World Report 1992—Albania*, 1 Jan., http://www.unhcr.org/refworld/docid/467fca541e.html (accessed 5 May 2013).

HRW (2003) 'Libya: June 1996 Killings at Abu Salim Prison', New York: Human Rights Watch.

Huebner, Peter (1995) 'Arbeitskonflikte in Industriebetrieben der DDR nach 1953. Annaerung und eine Historische Struktur- und Prozessanalyse', in Ulrike Poppe, Rainer Eckert, and Ilko-Sascha Kowlczuk (eds). *Zwischen Selbstbehauptung und Anpassung. Formen des Widerstandes und der Opposition in der DDR*. Berlin: Ch. Links Verlag, 178–91.

Humphrey, Sarah (1990) 'A Comparative Chronology of Revolution, 1988–1990'. Appendix without page numbers in Gwyn Prins (ed.), *Spring in Winter: The 1989 Revolutions*. Manchester, UK: Manchester University Press.

Huntington, Samuel (1965) *Political Order in Changing Societies*. New Haven, Conn.: Yale University Press.

Huntington, Samuel (1968) *Political Order in Changing Society*. New Haven, Conn.: Yale University Press.

Huntington, Samuel (1991) 'How Countries Democratize', *Political Science Quarterly*, 106(4): 579–616.

Idle, Nadia, and Nunns, Alex (eds) (2011) *Tweets from Tahrir*. New York: OR Books.

Innes, Abby (2001) *Czechoslovakia: The Long Goodbye*. New Haven, CT: Yale University Press.

Jacinto, Leela (2011) 'Benghazi's Tahrir Square: Times Square Style Meets Revolutionary Zeal', 25 Apr., http://www.france24.com/en/20110425-libya-benghazi-tahrir-square-times-reporters-notebook-leela-jacinto (accessed 5 May 2013).

Jamal, Manal A. (2012) 'Democracy Promotion, Civil Society Building, and the Primacy of Politics', *Comparative Political Studies*, 45: 3–31.

Javial, Angela (2011) 'The Egyptian Revolution', *Review of African Political Economy*, 38: 367–86.

Jehlicka, Petr (2001) 'The New Subversives: Czech Environmentalists after 1989', in Helena Flam (ed.), *Pink, Purple and Green. Women's, religious, environmental and Gay/lesbian Movements in Central Europe Today*. New York: Columbia University Press.

Jelin, Elizabeth (1987) (ed.) *Movimientos Sociales y Democracia Emergente*, 2 vols. Buenos Aires: Centro Editor de América Latina.

Jessen, Ralph (2009) 'Massenprotest und zivilgesellschaftliche Selbstorganisation in the Buergerbewegung von 1989/90', in Kalis-Dietmar Henke (ed.), *Revolution und Vereinigung 1989/90*. Also in Deutschland dir Realitatet die Phantasie Ueberholte, Deutscher Taschenbuch Verlag, 163–77.

Joffé, George (2011) 'The Arab Spring in North Africa. Origins and Prospects', *The Journal of North African Studies*, 16(4): 507–32.

Johnston, Hank (1991) *Tales of Nationalism: Catalonia, 1939–1979*. New Brunswick, NJ: Rutgers University Press.

Johnston, Hank (2011) *States and Social Movements*. London, Oxford: Polity Press.

Johnston, Hank, and Noakes, John (eds) (2005) *Frames of Protest: Social Movements and the Framing Perspective*. Lanham, Md.: Rowman and Littlefield.

Jones, Stephen (2011) 'Georgia's "Rose Revolution" of 2003: Enforcing Peaceful Change', in Adam Roberts and Timothy Garton Ash (eds), *Civil Resistance and Power Politics, The Experience of Non-violent Action from Gandhi to the Present*. Oxford: Oxford University Press, 317–35.

Joppke, Christian (1995) *East German Dissidents and the Revolution of 1989: Social Movement in a Leninist Regime*. New York: New York University Press.

Jorgensen, Knud Erik (1992) 'The End of Anti-politics in Central Europe', in Paul G. Lewis (ed.), *Democracy and Civil Society in Eastern Europe*. New York: St. Martin's Press, 32–60.

Judt, Tony R. (1992) 'Metamorphosis: The Democratic Revolution in Czechoslovakia', in Ivo Banac (ed.), *Eastern Europe in Revolution*. Ithaca, NY: Cornell University Press, 96–116.

Juris, Jeffrey S. (2012) 'Reflections on #Occupy Everywhere: Social Media, Public Spaces, and Emerging Logics of Aggregation', *American Ethnologist*, 39(2): 259–79.

Kaldor, Mary (2003) *Global Civil Society. An Answer to War*. Cambridge: Polity Press.

Karatnycky, Adrian, and Ackerman, Peter (2005) *How Freedom is Won: From Civic Resistance to Durable Democracy*. New York: Freedom House.

Karl, Terry Lynn (1990) 'Dilemmas of Democratization in Latin America', *Comparative Politics*, 23(1): 1–21.

Karpat, Kemal (1964) 'Society, Economics, and Politics in Contemporary Turkey', *World Politics*, 17(1): 50–74.

Kaser, Karl (2010) 'Economic Reforms and the Illusion of Transition', in Sabrina Ramet (ed.), *Central and Southeast European Politics since 1989*. New York: Cambridge University Press.

Keane, John (2003) *Global Civil Society?* Cambridge: Cambridge University Press.

Keck, Margaret, and Sikkink, Kathryn (1998) *Activists beyond Borders: Advocacy Networks in International Politics*. Ithaca, NY: Cornell University Press.

Keesing's Record of World Events (1991a) *Wave of Strikes and Protests Economy*, 37 (Oct.).

Keesing's Record of World Events (1991b) *Economy—Continuing strikes*, 37 (Nov.).

Keesing's Record of World Events (1992) *Public Order bill-Postponement of Elections*, 38 (Feb.).

Kemper, Theodore (2001) 'A Structural Approach to Social Movement Emotions', in Jeffrey Goodwin, James J. Jasper, and Francesca Polletta (eds), *Passionate Politics. Emotions and Social Movements*. Chicago: The University of Chicago Press, 58–73.

Kende, Pierre (1982) 'The Post-1956 Hungarian Normalization', in Włodzimierz Brus, Pierre Kende, and Zdeněk Mlynar, '*"Normalization" Processes in Soviet-dominated Central Europe: Hungary, Czechoslovakia, Poland'*. Cologne: Index, 5–13.

Kenney, Padraic (2002) *A Carnival of Revolution: Central Europe 1989*. Princeton, NJ: Princeton University Press.

Khader, Bichara (2012) 'Le "printemps arabe": un premier bilan', *Alternatives Sud*, 19: 7–39.

Khalidi, Rashid (2011) *Preliminary Historical Observations on the Arab Revolutions of 2011*, Jadaliyya, http://www.jadaliyya.com/pages/index/970/preliminary-historicalobservations-on-the-arab-re (accessed 22 May 2013).

Khamis, Sahar, and Vaughn, Katherine (2011) 'Cyberactivism in the Egyptian Revolution: How Civic Engagement and Citizen Journalism Tilted the Balance', *Arab Media and Society*, 14, http://www.arabmediasociety.com/index.php?article=769&printarticle (accessed 22 May 2013).

Khamis, Sahar, Gold, Paul B., and Vaughn, Katherine (2012) 'Beyond Egypt's "Facebook Revolution" and Syria's "YouTube Uprising"', *Arab Media & Society*, 15, http://www.arabmediasociety.com/?article=791 (accessed 28 April 2013).

Khosrokhavar, Farhad (2012) *The New Arab Revolutions that Shook the World*. Boulder, Colo.: Paradigm Publishers.

Kienle, Eberhard (ed.) (2003) *Politics from Above, Politics from Below: The Middle East in the Age of Economic Reform*. London: Saqi.

Killingsworth, Matt (2012) *Civil Society in Communist Eastern Europe: Opposition and Dissent in Totalitarian Regimes*. Essex: ECPr press.

Kis, János (1995) 'Between Reform and Revolution: Three Hypotheses About the Nature of the Regime Change', in Béla K. Király, *Lawful Revolution in Hungary 1989–94*. Highland Lakes, NJ: Atlantic Research and Publications, 33–59.

Kitschelt, Herbert (1986) 'Political Opportunity Structures and Political Protest: Anti-Nuclear Movements in Four Democracies', *British Journal of Political Science*, 16: 57–85.

Kitschelt, Herbert (1990) 'New Social Movements and the Decline of Party Organization', in Russell J. Dalton and Manfred Kuechler (eds), *Challenging the Political Order*. Cambridge: Polity Press, 179–208.

Kitschelt, Herbert (1993a) 'Comparative Historical Research and Rational Choice Theory: The Case of Transitions to Democracy', *Theory and Society*, 22(3): 413–42.

Kitschelt, Herbert (1993b) 'Social Movements, Political Parties, and Democratic Theory', *The Annals of the AAPSS*, 528: 13–29.

Klein, Thomas (1995) 'Die Vielfalt widertawendigen Verhaltens in der DDR', in Ulrike Poppe, Rainer Eckert, and Ilko-Sascha Kowlczuk (eds), *Zwischen Selbstbehauptung und Anpassung. Formen des Widerstandes und der Opposition in der DDR*. Berlin: Ch. Links Verlag, 125–41.

Koç, Yıldırım (2010) *Türkiye İşçi Sınıf Tarihi: Osmanlı'dan 2010'a*. Ankara: Epos.

Kontler, László (2002) *A History of Hungary: Millennium in Central Europe*. Houndmills, UK: Palgrave Macmillan.

Kramer, Mark (2011) 'The Dialectic of Empire: Soviet Leaders and the Challenge of Civil Resistance in East-Central Europe, 1968–91', in Adam Roberts and Timothy Garton Ash (eds), *Civil Resistance and Power Politics, The Experience of Non-violent Action from Gandhi to the Present*. Oxford: Oxford University Press, 91–109.

Kranz, Susanne (2010) 'Women's Role in the German Democratic Republic and the State's Policy toward Women', *Journal of International Women's Studies*, 7(1).

Krickus, Richard (1997) 'Democratization in Lithuania', in Karen Dawisha and Bruce Parrott (eds), *The Consolidation of Democracy in East-Central Europe*. Cambridge: Cambridge University Press, 290–333.

Kriesi, Hanspeter (1991) 'The Political Opportunity Structure of New Social Movements: Its Impact on their Mobilization', Paper FS III, Wissenschaftszentrum, Berlin: 91–103.

Kriesi, Hanspeter (1996) 'The Organizational Structure of New Social Movements in a Political Context', in Doug McAdam, John McCarthy, and Mayer N. Zald (eds), *Comparative Perspectives on Social Movements: Political Opportunities, Mobilizing Structures, and Cultural Framing*. Cambridge/New York: Cambridge University Press, 152–84.

Kriesi, Hanspeter, Koopmans, Ruud, Duyvendak, Jan Willem, and Giugni, Marco G. (1995) *New Social Movements in Western Europe*. Minneapolis: The University of Minnesota Press.

Kukutz, Irene (1995) ' "Nicht Raedchen, sondern Sand in Getriebe, den Kreis der Gewalt zu durchbrechen." Frauenwiederstand in der DDr in den achtziger Jahren', in Ulrike Poppe, Rainer Eckert, and Ilko-Sascha Kowlczuk (eds), *Zwischen Selbstbehauptung und Anpassung. Formen des Widerstandes und der Opposition in der DDR*. Berlin: Ch. Links Verlag, 273–83.

Kuran, Timur (1991) 'Now Out of Never: The Element of Surprise in the East European Revolution of 1989', *World Politics*, 44(1): 7–48.

Kurzman, Charles (1996) 'Structural Opportunities and Perceived Opportunities in Social Movement Theory. The Iranian Revolution of 1979.' *American Sociological Review* 61: 153-170.

Kurzman, Charles (2004) *The Unthinkable Revolution in Iran*. Cambridge: Harvard University Press.

Kurzman, Charles (2012) 'The Arab Spring Uncoiled,' *Mobilization* 17: 377–90.

Kusin, Vladimir V. (1978) *From Dubček to Charter 77: A Study of 'Normalization' in Czechoslovakia 1968–78*. New York: St. Martin's.

Laitin, David D. (2007) *Nations, States and Violence*. Oxford: Oxford University Press.

Landis, Joshua, and Pace, Joe (2007) 'The Syrian Opposition', *The Washington Quarterly*, 30(1): 45–68.

Lane, Thomas (2001) *Lithuania: Stepping Westward*. London: Routledge.

Langohr, Vickie (2004) 'Too Much Civil Society, Too Little Politics: Egypt and Liberalizing Arab Regimes', *Comparative Politics*, 36(2): 181–204.

Lawrence, William (2011) 'Albanians Force Out Communist Government, 1991', *Global Non Violent Action Database*, http://nvdatabase.swarthmore.edu/content/albanians-force-out-communist-government-1991 (accessed 5 May 2013).

Lelandais, Gülçin Erdi (2008) 'Du printemps ouvrier à l'altermondialisme…le champ militant et le champ politique en Turquie', *Cultures & conflits*, 70(2).

Levine, Daniel H., and Mainwaring, Scott (2001) 'Religion and Popular Protest in Latin America: Contrasting Experiences', in Susan Eckstein (ed.), *Power and Popular Protest*, 203–40.

Licht, Sonja (2000) 'Civil Society, Democracy, and the Yugoslav Wars', in Metta Spencer (ed.), *The Lesson of Yugoslavia*. New York: Elsevier, 111–24.

Lieven, Anatol (1993) *The Baltic Revolution: Estonia, Latvia, Lithuania and the Path to Independence*. New Haven, Conn.: Yale University Press.

Lindner, Bernd (2010) *Die demokratische Revolution in der DDR 1989/1990*. Bonn: Bundeszentrale fuer politische Bildung.

Linz, Juan, and Stepan, Alfred (1996) *Problems of Democratic Transition and Consolidation: Southern Europe, South America, and post-Communist Europe*. Baltimore: The Johns Hopkins University Press.

Lipset, Martin S. (1959) 'Some Social Requisites to Democracy: Economic Development and Political Legitimacy', *American Political Science Review*, 55: 69–105.

Lobmayer, Hans Gunter (1995) *Opposition Und Widerstand in Syrien*. Deutschen Orient-Instituts.

Lomax, Bill (1982) 'Hungary: The Rise of the Democratic Opposition', *Labour Focus on Eastern Europe*, 5(3–4): 2–7.

Long, Michael (1996) *Making History. Czech voices of Dissent and the Revolution of 1989*. Lanham, Md.: Rowman and Littlefield.

Long, Michael (2005) *Making History: Czech Voices of Dissent and the Revolution of 1989*. Lanham, Md: Rowman & Littlefield.

Lotan, Gilad, Graeff, Ehrhardt, Ananny, Mike, Gaffney, Devin, Pearce, Ian, and Boyd, Danah (2011) 'Information Flows during the 2011 Tunisian and Egyptian Revolutions', *International Journal of Communication*, 5: 1375–405.

Louer, Laurance (2013) 'D'une intifada à l'autre. La dynamique des soulèvements au Bahrein', in Amin Allal and Thomas Pierret (eds), *Au coer des révolte arabes. Devenir revolutionaries*. Paris: Armand Colin, 263–85.

Lovenduski, Joni, and Woodall, Jean (1987) *Politics and Society in Eastern Europe*. Bloomington: Indiana University Press.

Lowden, Pamela Susan (1996) *Moral Opposition to Authoritarian Rule in Chile, 1973–1990*. London: Macmillan.

Lust-Okar, Ellen (2004) 'Divided They Rule: The Management and Manipulation of Political Opposition', *Comparative Politics*, 36: 159–79.

Lust-Okar, Ellen (2005) *Structuring Conflict in the Arab World: Incumbents. Opponents, and Institutions*. Cambridge, UK: Cambridge University Press.

Mabrouk, Mehdi (2012) 'A Revolution for Dignity and Freedom: Preliminary Observations on the Social and Cultural Background to the Tunisian Devolution', *The Journal of North African Studies*, 17.

McAdam, Doug, Tarrow, Sidney, and Tilly, Charles (2001) *Dynamics of Contention*. New York: Cambridge University Press.

Mackell, Austin (2012) 'Weaving Revolution', *Interface: a journal for and about social movements*, 4(1): 17–32.

McFaul, Michael (2010a) 'Importing Revolutions', in Valerie Bunce, Michael McFaul, and Stoner Weiss (eds), *Democracy and Authoritarianism in the Postcommunist World*. Cambridge: Cambridge University Press, 189–229.

McFaul, Michael (2010b) 'The Missing Variable', in Valerie Bunce, Michael McFaul, and Stoner Weiss (eds), *Democracy and Authoritarianism in the Postcommunist World*, Cambridge: Cambridge University Press, 3–28.

Mahoney, James (2003) *Tentative Answers to Questions about Causal Mechanisms*, APSA, Philadelphia.

Maier, Charles S. (1997) *Dissolution: The Crisis of Communism and the End of East Germany*. Princeton, NJ: Princeton University Press.

Maier, Charles S. (2011) 'Civil Resistance and Civil Society: Lessons from the Collapse of the German Democratic Republic in 1989', in Adam Roberts and Timothy Garton Ash (eds), *Civil Resistance and Power Politics, The Experience of Non-violent Action from Gandhi to the Present*. Oxford: Oxford University Press, 260–76.

Mainwaring, Scott (1987) 'Urban Popular Movements, Identity, and Democratization in Brazil', *Comparative Political Studies*, 20(2): 131–59.

Malešević, Siniša (2002) *Ideology, Legitimacy and the New State: Yugoslavia, Serbia and Croatia*. London: Frank Cass.

Malthaner, Stefan (2011) *Mobilizing the Faithful*. Frankfurt am Main: Campus Verlag.

Mansbridge, Jane (1996) 'Using Power/Fighting Power: The Polity', in S. Benhabib (ed.) *Democracy and Difference: Contesting the Boundaries of the Political*. Princeton, NJ: Princeton University Press, 46–66.

Maravall, Jose M. (1978) *Dictatorship and Political Dissent: Workers and Students in Franco's Spain*. New York: St. Martin's Press.

Maravall, Jose M. (1982) *The Transition to Democracy in Spain*. London: Croom Helm.

Markoff, John (1996) *Waves of Democracy: Social Movements and Political Change*. Thousand Oaks, CA: Pine Forge Press.

Marks, Gary, Mbaye, Heather A.D., and Kim, Hyung Min (2009) 'Radicalism or Reformism? Socialist Parties before World War I', *American Sociological Review*, 74: 615–35.

Marshall, T. H. (1992; original 1950) 'Citizenship and Social Class', in T. H. Marshall and T. Bottomore (eds), *Citizenship and Social Class*. London: Pluto Press, 3–51.

Martinez, Luis (2011) 'Le printemps arabe, une surprise pour l'Europe', *Projet*, 322: 5–12.

Mattes, Hanspeter (2004) 'Challenges to Security Sector Governance in the Middle East: The Libyan Case', Conference Paper presented at Geneva Center for the Democratic Control of Armed Forces (DCAF) as a part of Security Governance in the Mediterranean Project, 12–13 July.

Mayntz, Renate (2003). *Mechanisms in the Analysis of Macro-Social Phenomena*, MPIfG Discussion Paper 03/3, Max Planck Institute for the Study of Societies, Cologne.

Meijer, Roel (2011) 'The Egyptian Jama'a al-Islamiyya as a Social Movement', in Joel Benin and Frédéric Vairel (eds), *Social Movements, Mobilization and Contestation in the Middle east and North Africa*. Stanford, CA: Stanford University Press,143–62.

Melucci, Alberto (1996) *Challenging Codes*. Cambridge/New York: Cambridge University Press.

Melucci, Alberto, and Diani, Mario (1992) *Nazioni Senza Stato. I Movimenti Etnico-Nazionali in Occidente* (2nd ed.). Milano: Feltrinelli.

Mersal, Iman (2011) 'Revolutionary Humor', *Globalizations*, 8(5): 669–74.

Michael, Maggie (2011) 'Protesters in Libya Demand Gaddafi Ouster and Reforms', *The Washington Post*, 17 Feb., http://www.washingtonpost.com/wp-dyn/content/article/2011/02/16/AR2011021607292.html (accessed 5 May 2013).

Miete, Ingrid, and Hampele, Hanne Ulrich (2001) 'Preference for Informal Democracy: The Astern-German Case', in Helena Flam (ed.), *Pink, Purple and Green. Women's, religious, enviromental and Gay/lesbian Movements in Central Europe Today*. New York: Columbia University Press, 23–32.

Moore, Barrington (1966) *Social Origins of Dictatorship and Democracy: Lord and Peasant in the Making of the Modern World*. Boston, Mass.: Beacon Press.

Mora, Frank O., and Wiktorowicz, Quintan (2003) 'Economic Reform and the Military: China, Cuba, and Syria in Comparative Perspective', *International Journal of Comparative Sociology*, 44(2): 87–128. doi: 10.1177/002071520304400201.

Morgan, Jane (1987) *Conflict and Order: The Police and Labour Disputes in England and Wales, 1900–1939*. Oxford: Clarendon Press.

Morlino, Leonardo (2009) 'Are There Hybrid Regimes? Or Are They Just an Optical Illusion?', *European Political Science Review*, 1: 273–96.

Morris, Aldon (2000) 'Charting Futures for Sociology. Social Organization. Reflections on Social Movement Theory. Criticisms and Proposals', *Contemporary Sociology*, 29: 445–54.

Mouhoud, El Mouhoub (2011–12) 'Economie politique des révolutions arabes: analyse et perspectives', *Maghreb-Machrek*, 210: 35–47.

Muehlen, von zur, Patrik (1995) 'Widerstand in einer thueringischen Kleinstadt 1953 bis 1958. Der "Eisenberger Kreis" ', in Ulrike Poppe, Rainer Eckert, and Ilko-Sascha Kowlczuk (eds), *Zwischen Selbstbehauptung und Anpassung. Formen des Widerstandes und der Opposition in der DDR*. Berlin: Ch. Links Verlag, 162–77.

Mueller, Carol (1999) 'Claim "Radicalization"? The 1989 Protest Cycle in the GDR', *Social Problems*, 46: 528–547.

Mungiu-Pippiddi, Alina (2010) 'When Europeanization Meets Transformation', in Valerie Bunce, Michael McFaul, and Stoner Weiss (eds), *Democracy and Authoritarianism in the Postcommunist World*. Cambridge: Cambridge University Press, 59–81.

Munson, Ziad (2001) 'Islamic Mobilization: Social Movement Theory and the Egyptian 1m Brotherhood', *Sociological Quarterly*, 42: 487–510.

Mustafaj, Besnik (1993) *Albania: Tra crimini e miraggi*. Milano: Garzanti.

Naimark, Norman M. (1992) ' "Ich will hier raus": Emigration and the Collapse of the German Democratic Republic', in Ivo Banac (ed.), *Eastern Europe in Revolution*. Ithaca, NY: Cornell University Press, 72–95.

Nanabhay, Mohamed, and Farmanfarmaian, Roxane (2011) 'From Spectacle to Spectacular: How Physical Space, Social Media and Mainstream Broadcast Amplified the Public Sphere in Egypt's "Revolution" ', *The Journal of North African Studies*, 16(4): 573–603.

Nepstad, Sharon Erickson (2011) *Nonviolent Revolutions: Civil Resistance in the Late 20th Century*. New York: Oxford University Press.

Neubert, Ehrhart (1997) *Geschichte der Opposition in der DDR 1949–1989*. Bonn: Bundeszentrale fuer politische Bildung.

Nigam, Aditya (2012) 'The Arab Upsurge and the 'Viral' Revolutions of Our Times', *Interface: a journal for and about social movements*, 4(1): 165–77.

Noakes, John, and Gillham, Patrick F. (2006) 'Aspects of the "New Penology" in the Police Response to Major Political Protests in the United States, 1999–2000', in Donatella della Porta, Abby Peterson, and Herbert Reiter (eds), *Policing Transnational Protest: In the Aftermath of the 'Battle of Seattle'*. Aldershot: Ashgate.

O'Donnell, Guillermo A. (1973) *Modernization and Bureaucratic–Authoritarianism: Studies in South American Politics*. Berkeley: University of California Press.

O'Donnell, Guillermo A. (1993) 'On the State, Democratization and some Conceptual Problems (A Latin American View with Glances at some post-Communist Countries)'. Working Paper Series No. 92 (Notre Dame: The Helen Kellogg Institute for International Studies, University of Notre Dame).

O'Donnell, Guillermo A. (1994) 'Delegative Democracy?', *Journal of Democracy*, 5: 56–69.

O'Donnell, Guillermo A., and Schmitter, Philippe C. (1986) *Transitions from Authoritarian Rule. Tentative Conclusions about Uncertain Democracies*. Baltimore: The Johns Hopkins University Press.

O'Donnell, Guillermo, and Schmitter, Philippe (1986) 'Tentative Conclusions about Uncertain Democracies', in Guillermo O'Donnell, Philippe Schmitter, and Laurence Whitehead (eds), *Transitions from Authoritarian Rule*. Baltimore: The Johns Hopkins University Press.

Obeidi, Amal (2001) *Political Culture in Libya*. Richmond: Curzon Press.

Oberschall, Anthony (2000) 'Social Movements and the Transitions to Democracy', *Democratization*, 7(3): 25–45.

Oberschall, Anthony (2007) 'Social Movements and the Transition to Democracy', *Democratization*, 7: 25–45.

Offe, Claus, and Wiesenthal, Helmut (1980) 'The Two Logics of Collective Action', *Social Theory*, 1: 67–115.

Okutan, M. Çağatay (2009) *Tek Parti Döneminde Azınlık Politikaları*. Istanbul: Bilgi Üniversitesi Yayınları.

Olivo, Christiane (2001) *Creating a Democratic Civil Society in Eastern Germany, The Case of the Citizen Movements and Alliance 90*. London: Palgrave.

Onondera, Henri (2011) ' "Raise Your Head High, You're An Egyptian!": Youth, Politics, and Citizen Journalism in Egypt', *Sociologica*, 3.

OPEC (2012) 'Annual Statistical Bulletin', Organization of the Petroleum Exporting Countries, Vienna: Organization of the Petroleum Exporting Countries (OPEC), http://www.opec.org/opec_web/static_files_project/media/downloads/publications/ASB2012.pdf (accessed 5 May 2013).

Opp, Karl-Dieter, Voss, Peter, and Gern, Christiane (1995) *Origins of a Spontaneous Revolution: East Germany, 1989*. Ann Arbor, MI: University of Michigan Press.

Ortoleva, Peppino (1988) *Saggio sui Movimenti del 68 in Europa e in America*. Rome: Editori Riuniti.

Osa, Maryjane (2003a) 'Networks in Opposition: Linking Organizations Through Activists in the Polish People's Republic', in Mario Diani and Doug McAdam (eds), *Social Movements and Networks: Relational Approaches to Collective Action*. Oxford: Oxford University Press, 77–104.

Osa, Maryjane (2003b) *Solidarity and Contention: Networks of Polish Opposition*. Minneapolis: The University of Minnesota Press.

Osa, Maryjane, and Cordunenanu-Huci, Cristina (2003) 'Running Uphill: Political Opportunity in Non-Democracies', *Comparative Sociology*, 2: 606–629.

Öztürk, Osman (1996) '1946 Sendikacılığı'. *Türkiye Sendikacılık Ansiklopedisi*. Istanbul: Türkiye Ekonomik ve Toplumsal Tarih Vakfı.

Pabriks, Artis, and Purs, Aldis (2001) *Latvia: The Challenges of Change*. London: Routledge.

Pagnucco, Ron (1995) 'The Comparative Study of Social Movements and Democratization: Political Interaction and Political Process Approaches', in Michael N. Dobkowski, Isidor Wallimann, and Christo Stojanov (eds), *Research in Social Movements, Conflict and Change*. London: JAI Press, 18: 145–83.

Parkin, Frank (1968) *Middle Class Radicalism*. Manchester: Manchester University Press.

Parsa, Misagh (2000) *States, Ideologies and Social Revolutions: A Comparative Analysis of Iran, Nicaragua and the Philippines*. Cambridge: Cambridge University Press.

Pateman, Carole (1970) *Participation and Democratic Theory*. Cambridge: Cambridge University Press.

Pavković, Aleksandar (2000) *The Fragmentation of Yugoslavia: Nationalism and War in the Balkans* (2nd ed.). Houndmills, UK: Macmillan.

Perkins, Kenneth (2004) *A History of Modern Tunisia.* Cambridge University Press.

Perthes, Volker (1992) 'The Syrian Private Industrial and Commercial Sectors and the State', *International Journal of Middle East Studies,* 24(2): 207–30.

Perthes, Volker (2004) *Syria Under Bashar al-Asad: Modernisation and the Limits of Change.* Abingdon, UK: Routledge.

Pfaff, Steven (2006) *Exit-Voice Dynamics and the Collapse of East Germany: The Crisis of Leninism and the Revolution of 1989.* Durham, NC: Duke University Press.

Pickvance, Katy and Luca Gabor (2001) 'Green Future—in Hungary?', in Helena Flam (ed.), *Pink, Purple and Green: Women's, Religious, Environmental and Gay/lesbian Movements in Central Europe Today.* New York: Columbia University Press, 104–11.

Pizzorno, Alessandro (ed.) (1993) *Le Radici della Politica Assoluta e Altri Saggi.* Milan: Feltrinelli.

Plakans, Andrejs (1997) 'Democratization and Political Participation in Postcommunist Societies: The Case of Latvia', in Karen Dawisha and Bruce Parrott (eds), *The Consolidation of Democracy in East-Central Europe.* Cambridge: Cambridge University Press, 245–88.

Poirer, Marine (2013) 'De la place de la Libération (al-Tahrir) à la place du Changement (al-Taghyir): transformations des espaces et expression du politique au Yémen', in Amin Allal and Thomas Pierret (eds), *Au coer des révolte arabes. Devenir revolutionaries.* Paris: Armand Colin, 31–51.

Pollack, Detlef (2009) ' "Wir sind das Volk!." Sozialstrukturelle und ereign geschichtliche Bedingungen des friedlichen Massenproteste', in Kalis-Dietmar Henke (ed.), *Revolution und Vereinigung 1989/90. Als in Deutschland dir Realitatet die Phantasie Ueberholte.* Deutscher Taschenbuch Verlag, 178–205.

Polletta, Francesca (2002) *Freedom is an Endless Meeting: Democracy in American Social Movements.* Chicago: Chicago University Press.

Poppe, Ulrike (1995) "Der Weg is das Ziel." Zum Selbstversaendnis und der politischen Rolle oppositioneller Gruppen der achtziger Jahre, in Ulrike Poppe, Rainer Eckert, and Ilko-Sascha Kowlczuk (eds), *Zwischen Selbstbehauptung und Anpassung. Formen des Widerstandes und der Opposition in der DDR.* Berlin: Ch. Links Verlag, 244–72.

Poppe, Ulrike, Eckert, Rainer, and Kowlczuk, Ilko-Sascha (1995) 'Einfuehrung', in Ulrike Poppe, Rainer Eckert, and Ilko-Sascha Kowlczuk (eds), *Zwischen Selbstbehauptung und Anpassung. Formen des Widerstandes und der Opposition in der DDR.* Berlin: Ch. Links Verlag, 9–26.

Port, Andrew I. (2007) *Conflict and Stability in the German Democratic Republic.* Cambridge: Cambridge University Press.

Postill, John (2012) 'New Protest Movements and Viral Media', *Media/Anthropology,* 26 Mar.

Powell, Charles (1996) 'International Aspects of Democratization: The Case of Spain', in Laurence Whitehead (ed.), *The International Dimensions of Democratization: Europe and the Americas.* Oxford: Oxford University Press.

Pralong, Sandra (2004) 'NGOs and the Development of Civil Society', in Henry Carey (ed.), *Romania Since 1989: Politics, Economics, and Society*. Lanham, Md.: Lexington Books.

Prashad, Vijay (2012) 'Dream History of the Global South', *Interface: a journal for and about social movements*, 4(1): 43–53.

Preuss, Ulrich (1995) *Constitutional Revolution*. Atlantic Highlands, N.J.: Humanities Press.

Przeworski, Adam (1991) *Democracy and the Market: Political and Economic Reforms in Eastern Europe and Latin America*. Cambridge: Cambridge University Press.

Pugliese, Joseph (2013) 'Permanent Revolution: Mohamed Bouazizi's Incendiary Ethics of Revolt', *Law, Culture and the Humanities*' (12 June): 1–13.

Quesnay, Arthur (2013) 'L'insurrection libyenne, un movement révolutionnaire decentralize', in Amin Allal and Thomas Pierret (eds), *Au coer des révolte arabes. Devenir revolutionaries*. Paris: Armand Colin, 113–32.

Rasler, Karen (1996) 'Concessions, Repression, and Political Protest in the Iranian Revolution.' *American Sociological Review* 61(1): 132–53.

Raun, Tovio (1997) 'Democratization and Political Development in Estonia, 1987–96', in Karen Dawisha and Bruce Parrott (eds), *The Consolidation of Democracy in East-Central Europe*. Cambridge: Cambridge University Press, 334–74.

Reich, Jens (1990) 'Reflections on Becoming an East German dissident, on losing the Wall and a Country', in Gwyn Prins (ed.), *Spring in Winter: The 1989 Revolutions*. Manchester: Manchester University Press, 65–98.

Reinares, Fernando (1987) 'The Dynamics of Terrorism during the Transition to Democracy in Spain', in Paul Wilkinson and Alasdair Stewart (eds), *Contemporary Research on Terrorism*. Aberdeen: Aberdeen University Press.

Reporters Without Borders (2011) 'The Birth of "Free Media" in Eastern Libya'. Paris: International Secretariat—Reporters Without Borders, http://en.rsf.org/IMG/pdf/libye_2011_gb.pdf (accessed 5 May 2013).

Reuters (2009) 'Libya "to Probe Police Massacre of Islamists in Prison"', *Islamweb*, 9 July, http://islamweb.net/emainpage/index.php?page=articles&id=154092 (accessed 5 May 2013).

Reuters (2011) 'Libya sets up $24 bln Fund for Housing', 27 Jan., www.reuters.com/article/2011/01/27/libya-fund-investment-idUSLDE70Q1ZM20110127 (accessed 5 May 2013).

Rink, Dieter (2001) 'Institutionalization instead of Mobilization—The Environmental Movement in Eastern Germany', in Helena Flam (ed.), *Pink, Purple and Green: Women's, Religious, Environmental and Gay/lesbian Movements in Central Europe Today*. New York: Columbia University Press.

Roberts, Adam (2011) 'Introduction', in Adam Roberts and Timothy Garton Ash (eds), *Civil Resistance and Power Politics, The Experience of Non-violent Action from Gandhi to the Present*. Oxford: Oxford University Press, 1–24.

Rochon, Thomas R. (1998) *Culture Moves. Ideas, Activism, and Changing Values*. Princeton, NJ: Princeton University Press.

Rokkan, Stein (1970) *Citizens, Elections, and Parties*. Oslo: Oslo University Press.

Rokkan, Stein, and Urwin, Derek W. (1983) *Economy, Territory, Identity: Politics of West European Peripheries*. London: Sage.

Ronsin, Caroline (2013) 'La remise en question "contrat social" jordanien', in Amin Allal and Thomas Pierret (eds), *Au coer des révolte arabes. Devenir revolutionaries*. Paris: Armand Colin, 219–38.

Roper, Steven (2000) *Romania: the Unfinished Revolution*. London: Routledge.

Rosanvallon, Pierre (2006) *La contre-démocratie: La politique a l'age de la defiance*. Paris: Seuil.

Rossi, Federico, and della Porta, Donatella (2009) 'Social Movement, Trade Unions and Advocacy Networks', in Christian W. Haerpfer, Patrick Bernhagen, Ronald F. Inglehart, and Christian Welzel (eds), *Democratization*, 172–85.

Rubinstein, Jonathan (1980) 'Cops' Rules', in R.J. Landman (ed.), *Police Behavior*. New York: Oxford University Press.

Rucht, Dieter (1996) 'The Impact of National Contexts on Social Movement Structures', in Doug McAdam, John McCarthy, and Mayer N. Zald (eds), *Comparative Perspectives on Social Movements: Political Opportunities, Mobilizing Structures, and Cultural Framing*. Cambridge/New York: Cambridge University Press, 185–204.

Rueschemeyer, Dietrich, Stephens, Evlyne Huber, and Stephens, John D. (1992) *Capitalist Development and Democracy*. Chicago: University of Chicago Press.

Rupp, Leila, and Taylor, Verta (1987) *Survival in the Doldrums: The American Women's Rights Movement, 1945 to the 1960s*. New York: Oxford University Press.

Saad, Reem (2012) 'The Egyptian Revolution: A Triumph of Poetry', *American Ethnologist*, 39(1): 63–6.

Sajó, András (1996) 'The Roundtable Talks in Hungary', in Jon Elster (ed.), *The Roundtable Talks and the Breakdown of Communism*. Chicago: University of Chicago Press, 69–98.

Salaita, Steven (2012) 'Corporate American Media Coverage of Arab Revolutions: The Contradictory Messages of Modernity', *Interface: a journal for and about social movements*, 4(1): 131–45.

Salem, Paul, and Kadlec, Amanda (2012) 'Libya's Troubled Transition', Carnegie Paper, June, http://carnegieendowment.org/2012/06/14/libya-s-troubled-transition/bzw4 (accessed 5 May 2013).

Salih, By Yassin al-Haj (2012) 'The Syrian Shabiha and Their State—Statehood & Participation—Heinrich Böll Foundation', www.lb.boell.org, http://www.lb.boell.org/web/52-801.html (accessed 5 May 2013).

Salt, Jeremy (2012) 'Containing the "Arab Spring"', *Interface: a journal for and about social movements*, 4(1): 54–66.

Salvatore, Armando (2011) 'New Media and Collective Action in the Middle East: Can Sociological Research Help Avoiding Orientalist Traps?', *Sociologica*, 3.

Sampson, Steven (1984-6), 'Regime and Society in Rumania', *International Journal of Rumanian Studies*, 4(1), 41-51).

Sánchez-Cuenca, Ignacio, and Aguilar, Paloma (2009) 'Terrorist Violence and Popular Mobilization: The Case of the Spanish Transition to Democracy', *Politics & Society*, 37(3): 428–53.

Santos, Boaventura de Sousa (2005) (ed.) *Democratizing Democracy: Beyond the Liberal Democratic Canon*. London: Verso.

Saxonberg, Steven (2001) *The Fall: A Comparative Study of the End of Communism in Czechoslovakia, East Germany, Hungary and Poland*. Amsterdam: Harwood Academic Publishers.

Saxonberg, Steven (2012) *Transitions and Non-transitions from Communism: Regime Survival in China, Cuba, North Korea and Vietnam*. Cambridge: Cambridge University Press.

Schaeffer, Robert K. (2000) 'Democratization, Division and War in Yugoslavia: A Comparative Perspective', in Metta Spencer (ed.), *The Lesson of Yugoslavia*. New York: Elsevier, 47–63.

Schemm, Paul (2011) 'Battle at Army Base Broke Gadhafi Hold in Benghazi', *The Washington Post*, 25 Feb., http://www.washingtonpost.com/wp-dyn/content/article/2011/02/25/AR2011022505021.html (accessed 5 May 2013).

Schmitter, Philippe C. (2009) 'The Nature and Future of Comparative Politics', *European Political Science Review*, 1: 33–61.

Schneider, Cathy (1992) 'Radical Opposition Parties and Squatter Movements in Pinochet's Chile', in Arturo Escobar and Sonia Álvarez, *The Making of Social Movements in Latin America*, 60–75.

Schneider, Cathy (1995) *Shantytown Protests in Pinochet's Chile*. Philadelphia: Temple University Press.

Schock, Kurt (2005) *Unarmed Insurrections: People Power Movements in Nondemocracies*. Minneapolis: The University of Minnesota Press.

Schoene, Jenz (2011) 'Vorbedingunged der Revolution. Anmerkungen zur Opposition in der DDR bis zum Oktober 1989', in Martin Gutzeit, Helge Heidemeyer, and Bettina Tueffers (eds),*Opposition und SED in der Friedlichen Revolution*. Duesseldorf: Droste verlag, 42–52.

Sergi, Vittorio, and Vogiatzoglou, Markos (2013) 'Think globally, act locally? Symbolic memory and global repertoires in the Tunisian uprising and the Greek anti-austerity mobilization', in Laurence Cox and Cristina Flesher (eds.), *Understanding European Movements*. London: Routledge.

Sewell, William H. (1990) 'Collective Violence and Collective Loyalties in France: Why the French Revolution Made a Difference', *Politics and Society*, 18: 527–52.

Sewell, William H. (1996) 'Three Temporalities: Toward an Eventful Sociology', in Terence J. McDonald (ed.), *The Historic Turn in the Human Sciences*. Ann Arbor: University of Michigan Press, 245–80.

Shahshahani, Azadeh, and Mullin, Corinna (2012) 'The Legacy of US Intervention and the Tunisian Revolution: Promises and Challenges One Year On', *Interface: a journal for and about social movements*, 4(1): 67–101.

Shepherd, Robin H. E. (2000) *Czechoslovakia: The Velvet Revolution and Beyond*. Houndmills, UK: MacMillan.

Shokr, Ahmad (2012) 'The Eighteen Days of Tahrir', in Jeannie Sowers and Chris Toensing (eds), *The Journey to Tahrir: Revolution, Protest, and Social Change in Egypt*. London: Verso, 41.

Shorbagy, Manar (2007) 'Understanding Kefaya: The New Politics in Egypt', *Arab Studies Quarterly* 29(1).

Shtromas, Aleksandras (1994) 'The Baltic States as Soviet Republics: Tensions and Contradictions', in Graham Smith (ed.), *The Baltic States: The National*

Self-Determination of Estonia, Latvia, and Lithuania. New York: St. Martin's Press, 86–117.

Siani-Davies, Peter (2005) *The Romanian Revolution of December 1989.* Ithaca, NY: Cornell University Press.

Sikkink, Kathryn (1996) 'The Emergence, Evolution, and Effectiveness of the Latin American Human Rights Network', in Elizabeth Jelin and Eric Hershberg (eds), *Constructing Democracy: Human Rights, Citizenship, and Society in Latin America.* Boulder, CO: Westview Press, 59–84.

Silver, Beverly (2003) *Forces of Labour.* New York: Cambridge University Press.

Skilling, H. Gordon (1991) 'Introductory Essay', in H. Gordon Skilling and Paul Wilson (eds), *Civic Freedom in Central Europe: Voices from Czechoslovakia.* Houndmills, UK: Macmillan, 3–32.

Skolnick, Jerome H. (1966) *Justice Without Trial: Law Enforcement in Democratic Society.* New York: John Wiley and Sons.

Slater, Dan (1985) *New Social Movements and the State in Latin America.* Amsterdam: CEDLA.

Slater, Dan (2010) *Ordering Power. Contentious Politics and Authoritarian Leviathan in Southeast Asia.* Cambridge: Cambridge University Press.

Smaoui, Sélim, and Mohamed Wazif (2013) 'Etendard de lutte ou pavillon de complaisance? S'engager sous la bannière du "mouvement du 20 février" a Casablanca', in Amin Allal and Thomas Pierret (eds), *Au coer des révolte arabes. Devenir revolutionaries.* Paris: Armand Colin, 55–80.

Smith, Anthony D. (1981) *The Ethnic Revival.* Cambridge: Cambridge University Press.

Smith, Graham (1994) 'The Resurgence of Nationalism', in Graham Smith (ed.), *The Baltic States: The National Self-Determination of Estonia, Latvia, and Lithuania.* New York: St. Martin's Press, 121–43.

Smith, Graham (2001) *Estonia: Independence and European Integration.* London: Routledge.

Smolar, Aleksander (2011) 'Towards "Self-Limiting Revolution": Poland 1970–89', in Adam Roberts and Timothy Garton Ash (eds), *Civil Resistance and Power Politics, The Experience of Non-violent Action from Gandhi to the Present.* Oxford: Oxford University Press, 127–43.

Snajdr, Edward (2001) 'Grassroots and Global Visions: Slovakia's Post-socialist Environmental Movement', in Helena Flam (ed.), *Pink, Purple and Green: Women's, Religious, Environmental and Gay/Lesbian Movements in Central Europe Today.* New York: Columbia University Press, 95–104.

Snow, David A., and Benford, Robert D. (1988) 'Ideology, Frame Resonance, and Participant Mobilization', in Bert Klandermans, Hanspeter Kriesi, and Sidney Tarrow (eds), *From Structure to Action.* Greenwich, CT: JAI Press, 197–218.

Snow, David A., Rochford, E. Burke, Worden, Steven K. Jr., and Benford, Robert D. (1986) 'Frame Alignment Processes, Micromobilization, and Movement Participation', *American Sociological Review*, 51: 464–81.

Snyder, Jack (2000) *From Voting to Violence: Democratization and Nationalist Conflict.* New York: Norton.

Solidarity Center (2010) 'The Struggle for Worker Rights in Egypt'. Washington, DC: Solidarity Center.

Stacher, Joshua (2004) 'Parties Over: The Demise of Egypt's Opposition Parties', *The British Journal of Middle Eastern Studies*, 31: 215–34.

Stark, David, and Bruszt, Laszlo (1998) *Postsocialist Pathways: Transforming Politics and Property in East Central Europe*. Cambridge: Cambridge University Press.

Stokes, Gale (1993) *The Walls Came Tumbling Down: The Collapse of Communism in Eastern Europe*. Oxford: Oxford University Press.

Stork, Joe (2011) 'Three Decades of Human Rights Activism in the Middle East and North Africa', in Joel Benin and Frédéric Vairel (eds), *Social Movements, Mobilization and Contestation in the Middle East and North Africa*. Stanford, CA: Stanford University Press, 83–106.

Sunar, İlkay, and Sayarı, Sabri (1986) 'Democracy in Turkey: Problems and Prospects', in Guillermo A. O'Donnell, Philippe C. Schmitter, and Laurence Whitehead (eds), *Transitions from Authoritarian Rule: Prospects for Democracy*. Baltimore and London: Johns Hopkins University Press, 165–86.

Swain, Nigel (1992) *Hungary: The Rise and Fall of Feasible Socialism*. London: Verso.

Swain, Nigel (2006) 'Negotiated Revolution in Poland and Hungary, 1989', in Kevin McDermott and Matthew Stibbe (eds), *Revolution and Resistance in Eastern Europe: Challenges to Communist Rule*. Oxford: Berghahn, 139–55.

Tachau, Frank, and Heper, Metin (1983) 'The State, Politics, and the Military in Turkey', *Comparative Politics*, 16(1): 17–33.

Tarrow, Sidney (1989) *Democracy and Disorder: Protest and Politics in Italy, 1965–1975*. Oxford: Oxford University Press.

Tarrow, Sidney (1995) 'Mass Mobilization and Regime Change: Pacts, Reform and Popular Power in Italy (1918–1922) and Spain (1975–1978)', in Richard Gunther, Nikiforos Diamandouros, and Hans-Jürgen Puhle, *Democratic Consolidation in Southern Europe*. Baltimore: The Johns Hopkins University Press, 204–30.

Tarrow, Sidney (1996) 'The People's Two Rhythms: Charles Tilly and the Study of Contentious Politics', *Comparative Studies in society and History*, 38 (3): 586–600.

Taylor, Verta, and van Dyke, Nella (2004) ' "Get up, Stand up." Tactical Repertoires of Social Movements', in David A. Snow, Sarah H. Soule, and Hanspeter Kriesi (eds), *The Blackwell Companion to Social Movements*. Oxford: Blackwell.

Teti, Andrea, and Gervasio, Gennaro (2012) 'After Mubarak, Before Transition: The Challenges for Egypt's Democratic Opposition', *Interface: a journal for and about social movements*, 4(1): 102–12.

Theborn, Goran (1995) *European Modernity and Beyond*. London: Sage.

Tilly, Charles (1978) *From Mobilization to Revolution*. Reading, MA: Addison Wesley.

Tilly, Charles (2001) 'Mechanisms in Political Science', *Annual Review of Political Science*, 4: 1–41.

Tilly, Charles (2004) *Social Movements, 1768–2004*. Boulder, CO: Paradigm.

Tilly, Charles (2006) *Regimes and Repertoires*. Chicago: University of Chicago Press.

Tismaneanu, Vladimir (1997). 'Romanian Exceptionalism? Democracy, Ethnocracy, and Uncertain Pluralism in Post-Ceausescu Romania', in Karen Dawisha and Bruce Parrott (eds), *Politics, Power and the Struggle for Democracy in South-East Europe*. Cambridge: Cambridge University Press.

Tocqueville, Alexis de (1955) (original 1856) *The Old Regime and The Revolution.* New York: Anchor Books.

Tőkés, Rudolf L. (1996) *Hungary's Negotiated Revolution: Economic Reform, Social Change, and Political Succession, 1957–1990.* Cambridge, UK: Cambridge University Press.

Toprak, Binnaz (1981) *Islam and Political Development in Turkey.* Leiden: Brill Academic Pub.

Toprak, Zafer (1996) '1946 Sendikacılığı, Sendika Gazetesi, İşçi Sendikaları Birlikleri Ve İşçi Kulüpleri.' *Toplumsal Tarih,* 6(31): 19–29.

Touraine, Alain, Dubet, Francois, Wieviorka, Michel, and Strzelecki, Jan. (1982) *Solidarité. Analyse d'un movement social. Pologne 1980–1981.* Paris: Fayard.

Tucker, Aviezer (2000) *The Philosophy and Politics of Czech Dissidence from Patočka to Havel.* Pittsburgh: University of Pittsburgh Press.

Tufekci, Zeynep, and Wilson, Christopher (2012) 'Social Media and the Decision to Participate in Political Protest: Observations from Tahrir Square', *Journal of Communication,* 62(2): 363–79.

Tyszka, Juliusz (1998) 'The Orange Alternative: Street Happenings as Social Performance in Poland under Martial Law', *New Theatre Quarterly,* 14(56): 311–23.

Ulfelder, Jay (2005) 'Contentious Collective Action and the Breakdown of Authoritarian Regimes', *International Political Science Review,* 26(3): 311–34.

United Nations (2011) United Nations Security Council Resolution 1973 (17 Mar.), http://www.un.org/News/Press/docs/2011/sc10200.doc.htm (accessed 5 May 2013).

Urban, Jan (1990) 'Czechoslovakia: The Power and Politics of Humiliation' in Gwyn Prins (ed.), *Spring in Winter.* Manchester: Manchester University Press, 99–138.

Uysal, Ayshen (2005) 'Organisation du maintien de l'ordre et répression policière en Turquie', in Donatella della Porta and Olivier Fillieule (eds), *Maintien de l'ordre et police des foules.* Paris: Presses de Science Po.

Vairel, Frédéric (2011) 'Protesting in Authoritarian Situation: Egypt and Morocco Compared', in Joel Benin and Frédéric Vairel (eds), *Social Movements, Mobilization and Contestation in the Middle East and North Africa.* Stanford, CA: Stanford University Press, 27–42.

Valeriani, Augusto (2011) 'Bridges of the Revolution. Linking People, Sharing Information, and Remixing Practices', *Sociologica,* 3.

VanderLippe, John M. (2005) *The Politics of Turkish Democracy: İsmet İnönü and the Formation of the Multi-party System, 1938-1950.* Albany: State University of New York Press.

Vardys, Stanley (1981) 'Human Rights Issues in Estonia, Latvia, and Lithuania', *Journal of Baltic Studies,* 12: 275–98.

Vasilevski, Steven (2007) 'Diverging Paths, Diverging Outcomes: A Comparative Analysis of Post- Communist Transition in the Successor States of Yugoslavia', *YCISS Post-Communist Studies Programme Research Paper Series.* Toronto: York Centre for International and Security Studies.

Verdery, Katherine, and Klingman, Gail (1992) 'Romania after Ceaușescu: Post-Communist Communism?', in Ivo Banac (ed.). *Eastern Europe in Revolution.* Ithaca, NY: Cornell University Press.

Vejvoda, Ivan, 2011. 'Civil Society Versus Slobodan Milosevis, 1991-2000', in Adam Roberts and Timothy Garton Ash (eds), *Civil Resistance and Power Politics, The Experience of Non-violent Action from Gandhi to the Present*. Oxford: Oxford University Press, 295–316.

Vickers, Miranda, and Pettifer, James (1997) *Albania: From Anarchy to a Balkan Identity*. London: Hurst & Company.

Vladisavljević, Nebojša (2008) *Serbia's Antibureaucratic Revolution: Milosevic, the Fall of Communism and Nationalist Mobilization*. Houndmills, UK: Palgrave Macmillan.

Wada, Takeshi (2006) 'Claim Network Analysis: How Are Social Protests Transformed into Political Protests in Mexico?', in Hank Johnston and Paul Almeida (eds), *Latin American Social Movements*. Lanham, Md: Rowman and Littlefield, 95–114.

Wall, Melissa, and El Zahed, Sahar (2011) ' "I'll Be Waiting for You Guys": A YouTube Call to Action in the Egyptian Revolution', *International Journal of Communication*, 5: 1333–43.

Wallerstein, Immanuel (2011) 'The Contradictions of the Arab Spring', 14 Nov., http://www.aljazeera.com/indepth/opinion/2011/11/20111111101711539134.html (accessed 7 March 2013).

Watts, Nicole F. (2006) 'Activists in Office: Pro-Kurdish Contentious Politics in Turkey', *Ethnopolitics*, 5(2): 125–44.

Waylen, Georgina (2007) *Engendering Transitions: Women's Mobilizations, Institutions, and Gender Outcomes*. Oxford: Oxford University Press.

Wheaton, Bernard, and Kavan, Zdenek (1992) *The Velvet Revolution: Czechoslovakia (1988–1991)*. Boulder, Co.: Westview Press.

Whitehead, Laurence (1996) *The International Dimensions of Democratization: Europe and the Americas*. Oxford: Oxford University Press.

Wiktorowicz, Quintan (2000) 'Civil Society as Social Control: State Power in Jordan', *Comparative Politics*, 33(1): 43–61.

Wiktorowicz, Quintan (ed.) (2004) *Islamic Activism: A Social Movement Perspective*. Bloomington: Indiana University Press.

Williams, Kieran (2011) 'Civil Resistance in Czechoslovakia: From Soviet Invasion to "Velvet revolution," 1968–89', in Adam Roberts and Timothy Garton Ash (eds), *Civil Resistance and Power Politics, The Experience of Non-violent Action from Gandhi to the Present*. Oxford: Oxford University Press, 110–26.

Winegard, Jessica (2012) 'Taking out the Trash: Youth Clean up Egypt after Mubarak', in Jeannie Sowers and Chris Toensing (eds), *The Journey to Tahrir: Revolution, Protest, and Social Change in Egypt*. London: Verso, 64–9.

Winter, Martin (1998) 'Police Philosophy and Protest Policing in the Federal Republic of Germany (1960–1990)', in Donatella della Porta and Herbert Reiter (eds), *Policing Protest: The Control of Mass Demonstrations in Western Democracies*. Minneapolis: The University of Minnesota Press, 188–212.

Wolle, Stefan (2008) *Der Traum von der Revolte Die DDR 1968*. Bonn: Bumdeszentrale fuer politische Bildung.

Wood, Elisabeth (2000) *Forging Democracy from Below. Insurgent Transitions in South Africa and El Salvador*. Cambridge: Cambridge University Press.

Woodward, Susan L. (1995) *Balkan Tragedy: Chaos and Dissolution after the Cold War*. Washington, D.C.: Brookings Institution.

Wright, Thomas C. (2007) *State Terrorism in Latin America: Chile, Argentina and International Human Rights*. Lanham, Md: Rowman & Littlefield.

Yashar, Deborah J. (2005) *Contesting Citizenship in Latin America: The Rise of Indigenous Movements and the Postliberal Challenge*. New York: Cambridge University Press.

Zuo, Jiping, and Benford, Robert D. (1995) 'Mobilization Processes and the 1989 Chinese Democracy Movement', *The Sociological Quarterly*, 36(1): 131–56.

Zürcher, Erik Jan (2004) *Turkey: A Modern History* (3rd ed., new ed.). New York: I.B. Tauris.

Zwerman, Gilda, Steinhoff, Patricia G., and della Porta, Donatella (2000) 'Disappearing Social Movements: Clandestinity in the Cycle of New Left Protest in the US, Japan, Germany and Italy', *Mobilization*, 5: 83–100.

Mobilizing for Democracy working papers (available at http://cosmos.eui.eu)

Atak, Kıvanç (2012) *Whose Democratization? Periods of Transition and Voices from Below in Turkey*http://cosmos.eui.eu/Documents/Publications/WorkingPapers/2012WP08COSMOS.pdf

Chiodi, Luisa (2012) *Mass Migration, Student Protests and the Intelligentsia Popullore in the Albanian Transition to Democracy*http://cosmos.eui.eu/Documents/Publications/WorkingPapers/2012WP02COSMOS.pdf

Della Porta, Donatella (2012) *Mobilizing for Democracy: A Research Project*http://cosmos.eui.eu/Documents/Publications/WorkingPapers/2012WP01COSMOS.pdf

Donker, Teije H. (2012a) *Mobilizing for Democracy in Syria*http://cosmos.eui.eu

Donker, Teije H. (2012b) *Tunisia amid Surprise, Change and Continuity*http://cosmos.eui.eu/Documents/Publications/WorkingPapers/2012WP12COSMOS.pdf

Piotrowski, Grzegorz (2012) *Grassroots Groups and Civil Society Actors in Pro-Democratic Transitions in Poland*http://cosmos.eui.eu/Documents/Publications/WorkingPapers/2012WP07COSMOS.pdf

Poljarevic, Emin (2012) *Libya's Violent Revolution* http://cosmos.eui.eu/Documents/Publications/WorkingPapers/2012WP05COSMOS.pdf

Ritter, Daniel P. (2012a) *Civil Society and the Paralyzed State: Mobilizing for Democracy in East Germany* http://cosmos.eui.eu/Documents/Publications/WorkingPapers/2012WP06COSMOS.pdf

Ritter, Daniel P. (2012b) *Civil Society and the Velvet Revolution: Mobilizing for Democracy in Czechoslovakia*http://cosmos.eui.eu/Documents/Publications/WorkingPapers/2012WP04COSMOS.pdf

Ritter, Daniel P. (2012c) *Nationalism and Transitions: Mobilizing for Democracy in Yugoslavia*http://cosmos.eui.eu/Documents/Publications/WorkingPapers/2012WP03COSMOS.pdf

Ritter, Daniel P. (2012d) *Reluctant Rulers and the Negotiated Transition: Mobilizing for Democracy in Hungary*http://cosmos.eui.eu/Documents/Publications/WorkingPapers/2012WP09COSMOS.pdf

Rossi, Federico M. (2012a) *The Elite Coup: The Transition to Democracy in Bulgaria* http://cosmos.eui.eu/Documents/Publications/WorkingPapers/2012WP10COSMOS.pdf

Rossi, Federico M. (2012b) *The Unintended Consequence of the Struggle for Independence: The Transition to Democracy in the Baltic Countries* http://cosmos.eui.eu/Documents/Publications/WorkingPapers/2012WP11COSMOS.pdf

Rossi, Federico M.(2012c) *From the Coup to the Escalation of Violence: The Transition to Democracy in Romania* http://cosmos.eui.eu/Documents/Publications/ WorkingPapers/2012WP13COSMOS.pdf

Warkotsch, Jana (2012) *Bread, Freedom, Human Dignity: Tales of an Unfinished Revolution in Egypt*http://cosmos.eui.eu/Documents/Publications/WorkingPapers/ 2012WP14COSMOS.pdf

Index

Index